Jewish Morocco

Jewish Morocco

A History from Pre-Islamic to Postcolonial Times

Emily Gottreich

I.B. TAURIS
LONDON • NEW YORK • OXFORD • NEW DELHI • SYDNEY

I.B. TAURIS
Bloomsbury Publishing Plc
50 Bedford Square, London, WC1B 3DP, UK
1385 Broadway, New York, NY 10018, USA
29 Earlsfort Terrace, Dublin 2, Ireland

BLOOMSBURY, I.B. TAURIS and the Diana logo are trademarks
of Bloomsbury Publishing Plc

First published in Great Britain 2020
Paperback edition published 2021

Copyright © Emily Benichou Gottreich 2020

Emily Benichou Gottreich has asserted her right under the Copyright, Designs
and Patents Act, 1988, to be identified as Author of this work.

For legal purposes the Acknowledgments on pp. vi-ix constitute an
extension of this copyright page.

Cover design by Alice Marwick
Cover image © *Jeunes Filles Juives D'Oudjda*, 1922, anonymous artist, postcard.

All rights reserved. No part of this publication may be reproduced or transmitted
in any form or by any means, electronic or mechanical, including photocopying,
recording, or any information storage or retrieval system, without
prior permission in writing from the publishers.

Bloomsbury Publishing Plc does not have any control over, or responsibility for,
any third-party websites referred to or in this book. All internet addresses given
in this book were correct at the time of going to press. The author and publisher
regret any inconvenience caused if addresses have changed or sites have ceased
to exist, but can accept no responsibility for any such changes.

A catalogue record for this book is available from the British Library.

A catalog record for this book is available from the Library of Congress.

ISBN:	HB:	978-1-7807-6849-6
	PB:	978-0-7556-4436-0
	eISBN:	978-1-8386-0362-5
	ePDF:	978-1-8386-0361-8

Typeset by Integra Software Services Pvt. Ltd.

To find out more about our authors and books visit www.bloomsbury.com
and sign up for our newsletters.

Contents

Acknowledgments	vi
List of Maps	xi
Introduction: Moroccan Themes, Jewish Variations	1
1 Malikism: The Jewish Encounter with Islam in the Far Maghrib (Seventh–Tenth Centuries)	19
2 Amazighity: "Berber" Morocco—A Jewish History (Eleventh–Fifteenth Centuries)	51
3 Sharifism: Religious Authority and the Rise of the Moroccan State (Sixteenth–Eighteenth Centuries)	77
4 Europeanization: Imperialism and the Transformation of Muslim-Jewish Relations (the Long Nineteenth Century)	102
5 Arabness: Nationalism in an Old-New Key (Twentieth Century)	130
Conclusion: Postmodern Jewish Morocco	171
Notes	184
Bibliography	229
Index	245

Acknowledgments

What made me consider writing a book like the current one—a synthetic history based mostly on secondary sources—was the observation that so much excellent scholarship has been produced on the topic of Moroccan Jewish history, society, and culture in recent years, and yet in no single place was it possible to find an overall narrative that incorporated its main findings. Moreover, when it comes to this topic, there is a serious language barrier facing English-language audiences, like those I encounter in the classroom. Of the publications in English, most take the form of monographs and journal articles, and as such are highly specialized; what general approaches to the subject do exist are written in French, Hebrew, or Arabic and tend to be outdated. Hence the perceived need for a book like *Jewish Morocco*, whose overarching goal is to increase access to the fine work of today's scholars of Moroccan history, Moroccan Jewry, and MENA Jews writ large, while at the same time contributing in some small way to this rapidly growing subregion of both Jewish and Middle Eastern studies. Once a bridge between fields, MENA Jewish studies is now a field in its own right.

Many of the individuals whose work I rely on here I am fortunate to count among my colleagues, friends, teachers, and students. My interactions with this cohort have helped me immeasurably in formulating and writing this book. One of the few places where the *grandes lignes* of Moroccan Jewish history are drawn is in the article by Samir Ben-Layashi and Bruce Maddy-Weitzman, "Myth, History, and Realpolitik: Morocco and Its Jewish Community" (2010). The avenues of inquiry its authors suggest provided early guideposts for the current work. At the same time, Susan Gilson Miller's *History of Modern Morocco* (2012) served as an important model for linking the Moroccan past with contemporary concerns, reinforcing the tried and true maxim that history really exists only in the present. Susan also gave generously of her time in reviewing the final manuscript. Jonathan Wyrtzen's *Making Morocco: Colonial Intervention and the Politics of Identity* (2015) includes a particularly insightful chapter on Moroccan Jewish identity in the modern era that helped me sharpen some of my own arguments. Daniel Schroeter's monumental oeuvre on the history of the maghrib and its Jews, along with his mentorship and unflagging collegiality, is a continuous source of inspiration. As anyone who knows him can attest,

Aomar Boum is one of the most generous and communal-minded colleagues with whom one could ask to share a calling. Much of the material presented here has been sifted through with his help, including during a Fulbright-Hayes Group Projects Abroad program we ran together in Marrakech, Ouirgane, and Essaouira in the summer of 2017 with the participation of a lively group of middle and high school teachers from the San Francisco Bay Area.

For the sake of Anglophone audiences, I have tried to keep references to works in languages other than English to a minimum, but it should be obvious to specialists just how much this work owes to the foundational body of scholarship on Morocco and its Jews in other languages. I am particularly indebted to my Moroccan colleagues who have provided me with source material, translation help, thoughtful analyses, warm friendships, and much couscous over the years. *Shukran bi-zaf* to Khalid Ben-Srhir, Mohammed Kenbib, Mohammed Hatimi, Hanan Sekkat Hatimi, Jamaâ Baïda, and Mina Mghari. Other friends in Morocco who provided support to this project at crucial junctures include André Azoulay, Jacky Kadoch, Vivian Cohen, Kati Roumani, and David Zaffran. Several institutions deserve special mention for the many kindnesses they showed me while I developed this project, beginning with the Tangier American Legation and Institute for Moroccan Studies (TALIM) and the Moroccan American Commission for Educational and Cultural Exchange (MACECE) in Rabat. At the former, Thor Kuniholm, John Davison, and Yhtimad Bouziane have always provided me with a warm reception, and Jim Miller and his supremely capable staff did the same at the latter. The Fulbright Program of the US Department of Education, administered in Morocco through MACECE, has supported my research from its earliest stages, including through a Fulbright Senior Scholars grant to Marrakech in 2010–2011, a crucial year to have been able to spend in the region. The American Institute for maghrib Studies (AIMS) has also supported my research at various junctures. I have also enjoyed the cooperation of Michael Fitzgerald and Hamza Weinman at the Center for Language and Culture in Marrakech. The incomparable Gita Sellmann of the Swedish *Academia Arabesca* has provided me with a second home in Marrakech on several occasions, often through the intermediary efforts of the Nordic Society for Middle Eastern Studies and my friend Marianne Laanatza of the University of Uppsala.

California, of all places, has emerged as a dynamic center for MENA Jewish studies. Jessica Marglin deserves special credit for corralling those of us who work on such topics into CALJEMM, the California Working Group on Jews of the Maghrib and the Middle East. Originally based at the University of Southern California and now divided between that institution and my home institution of UC Berkeley, CALJEMM meets twice a year to read and critique members' works in progress (including drafts of some of the chapters here). In addition to Jessica and colleagues mentioned above, other members of this group who have lent their time and expertise to improving different parts of this book include Sarah Abrevaya Stein, Alma Heckman, Mostafa Hussein, Susan Slyomovics, Marie-Pierre Ulloa, and Sarah Levin. I also wish to recognize those colleagues who were kind enough to include me on various panels and roundtables at the annual meetings of the Middle East Studies Association (MESA) which helped me think broadly and deeply about MENA Jewish history. In particular, a long ago panel on "Arabness and Otherness" organized with Lisa Pollard, Sarah Savant, and James McDougall allowed for the incubation of ideas on historicizing this question with regard to Jews in the Maghrib, while a 2016 panel entitled "Methodology and Margins: Studying Jewish Histories of the MENA" helped me work through some of the structural implications of our field, with inspiration provided by panelists Orit Bashkin, Susan Gilson Miller, Alma Heckman, Lior Sternfeld, and Rami Ginat. In addition, I have received valuable feedback on this project in response to lectures I gave at the Department of Near Eastern Studies at Cornell University; the Taube Center for Jewish Studies at Stanford University; the Center for Jewish Studies at the Graduate Theological Union; and the Department of Ethnology, Religion and Gender and the Department of Oriental Languages at Stockholm University.

My students at UC Berkeley are a continuous source of energy and inspiration. Those who participated in the University Research Apprentice Program (URAP) helped me complete crucial aspects of this project; I hope in return they got a taste of the rewards of conducting academic research. These students include Romain Julien, Ariel Ulansky, Madison Margolin Hannah Jewell, Rebecca Rosen, Sam Metz, Taqwa El-Hindi, Charles Culioli, Farah Oraby, and Nicholas Shafer. Summayah Bostan's fastidious attention to detail helped bring order to the manuscript in its latter stages. At the Center for Middle Eastern Studies, Amir Ebtehadj, Deellan Khanaka, and Jenail Mobaraki assisted me with preparing the timelines, while Lydia Kiesling lent her sharp eye to editing. Then graduate students now scholars in their own right David Moshfegh and Saima Akhtar read and commented on parts of the manuscript. For patiently answering my questions as I dipped my toe into the sea of Maliki jurisprudence for Chapter 1, I thank Lena Salaymeh, Etty Terem, and Asad Ahmed. David Stenner generously shared his expertise on the *istiqlal* and history of northern Morocco in the twentieth century and did a careful reading of Chapter 5. Finally, my thanks go to the librarians, without whom books would no longer beget more books:

special thanks to UC Berkeley Middle East/Islamica librarians Shayee Khanaka and Mohammed Hamed, and Judaica librarian Paul Hamburg. Francesco Spagnolo at UC Berkeley's Magnes Collection of Jewish Art and Life granted me access to its exquisite collection of Moroccan Judaica on several occasions.

My thanks to the patient staff at IB Tauris, and especially Azmina Siddique and Sophie Rudland. I am especially grateful to them for locating four such generous and hardworking anonymous readers for the manuscript. The maps that appear at the beginning of Chapters 2–4 were originally created by Omar Tounsi. An earlier, abbreviated version of Chapter 3 appeared in *Modern Jewish Studies* (2013). Part of the Introduction was given as a video lecture at the Tangier April Seminars of 2019, whose proceedings appear in special volume of *Journal of North Africa Studies* (2020). Paul Dahan has once again given me permission to use an image from his spectacular collection at the Centre de la Culture Judeo-Marocaine in Brussels for the cover of the book. Sadly, I have been unable to identify the two women from Oujda pictured in the photograph, but I hope their memories are honored by this book.

This book is dedicated to my beloved spouse, Albert. *Enfin bref.*

Maps

INTRODUCTION
Map I.1 Jewish communities of Morocco — xii

CHAPTER 1
Map 1.1 The Maghrib after the Berber Revolt — 18

CHAPTER 2
Map 2.1 Almoravid era Morocco — 48
Map 2.2 Almohad era Morocco — 49
Map 2.3 Marinid era Morocco — 49
Map 2.4 Central Atlas Tamazight — 50

CHAPTER 3
Map 3.1 Sa'di era Morocco — 75
Map 3.2 Alawi era Morocco — 76

CHAPTER 4
Map 4.1 French and Spanish Protectorates — 101

CHAPTER 5
Map 5.1 Modern Morocco — 129

CONCLUSION
Map C.1 Morocco in the world — 170

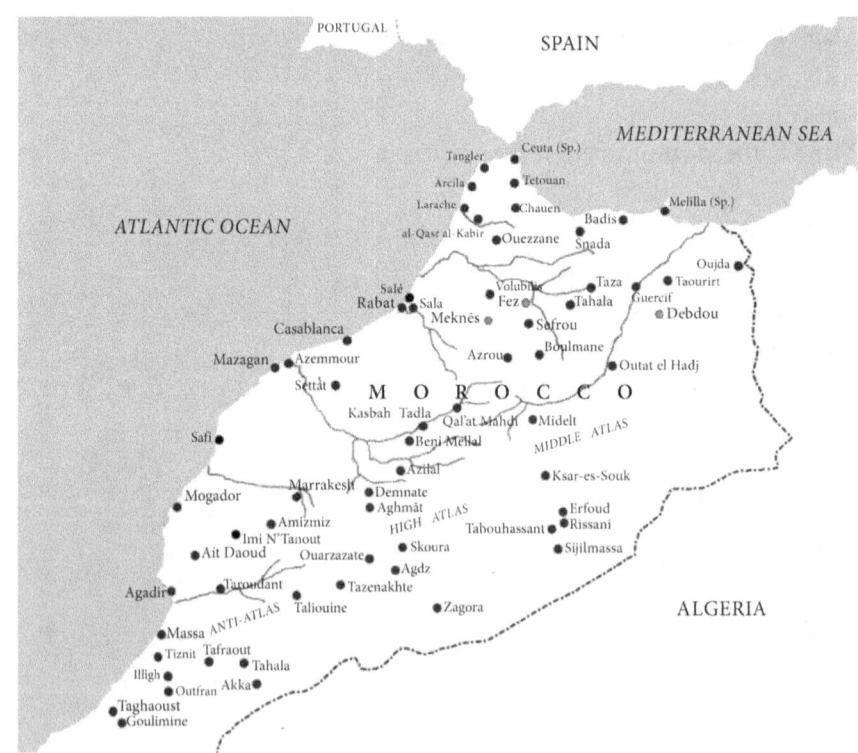

Map I.1 Jewish Communities of Morocco.
Encyclopaedia Judaica: Jews in Morocco, vol. 12.

Introduction
Moroccan Themes, Jewish Variations

On May 16, 2003, Morocco got a wake-up call. Despite the overpowering moral hegemony of the Moroccan monarch as commander of the faithful, despite the steps toward democratization undertaken by the then new king, Mohammed VI, and despite a longstanding tradition of toleration[1] for minorities, it turned out that Morocco was not, after all, immune to Islamist violence. In the half century since Morocco's independence from France in 1956, most of the significant threats to the political order had come from the left or the military. But on that day in the middle of May, a group linked with the *salafiya jihadiya* movement came to the forefront of the Moroccan political stage by coordinating a series of five simultaneous suicide attacks in Casablanca that resulted in the deaths of forty-five people. The targets were chosen carefully. Two were identifiably European: the *Casa de España*, a Spanish restaurant and cultural center, where a guard was stabbed and the perpetrators blew themselves and many bystanders up, and the Belgian consulate, in front of which a car bomb was detonated. The remaining three targets were all associated with Moroccan Jews. They included the *Cercle de l'Alliance* Jewish community center, a well-known Jewish-owned Italian restaurant, and even a Jewish cemetery—as if the dead could die twice. No Moroccan Jews actually perished in the attacks, probably because they occurred on a Friday night when Jews would be more likely to be at home celebrating the Sabbath than out on the town. But as Salvador Bentolila, a fifty-five-year-old Jewish printer in Casablanca, put it in an interview with the *New York Times*: "The goal wasn't to kill Jewish people, it was symbols of the Jews they wanted to strike."[2] What Jews may symbolize in contemporary Morocco, for whom, since when, and why, are just a few of the questions that will help launch our inquiry and provide a touchstone in the coming pages.

Immediately after the Casablanca attacks, King Mohammed VI (1999–) set about finding and punishing the perpetrators and comforting the victims.

However, stemming the tide of despair that underlay the violence would prove challenging; high unemployment and feelings of hopelessness had been breeding radicalism in the slums of big cities like Casablanca since the 1980s. By the twenty-first century, disaffected young people were increasingly turning toward transnational Islamist groups like *salafiya jihadiya*, al-Qaeda in the Islamic Maghrib (AQIM), and, in time, ISIS.[3] Recognizing the threat both to the country and to its own authority, the *makhzan* (Moroccan government and administration) responded with a multifaceted program to promote an alternative, emphatically *Moroccan* Islam to displace the Islam of the radicals. This Moroccan Islam would be Sunni, Maliki, moderate, inclusive, and outward looking. It would be inculcated through new institutions like the Muhammadiya Association of Scholars (*al-rabita al-muhammadiya li-l-'ulama*), a decidedly moderate body created by royal edict (*dahir*) in 2006. To house it, the government built a multimillion-dollar national institute in the suburbs of Rabat, the Mohammed VI Institute for the Training of Imams, where a state-sanctioned religious curriculum would be taught that emphasizes human rights and the contextualization of scriptural truths. The institute is noteworthy for training female (*murshidat*) as well as male imams. It has also been active in evaluating the textbooks used in public schools, with an eye toward emphasizing tolerance and diversity in Morocco's national history. The institute welcomes foreign imams from sub-Saharan Africa, France, and Russia, in addition to Moroccans. Its program to challenge the "fake" Islam of the extremists with the "real" Islam of the moderates has been so successful that the French government has contracted with the institute to create a similar body in France. Moroccan Islam would even have its own symbol: the hand of *fatima*, known as the *khamsa* for its five fingers, emblazoned with the slogan, in Moroccan dialect, "Don't touch my country."[4]

These efforts would culminate in the promulgation of the 2011 constitution, whose carefully worded preamble articulates Islam's role in Moroccan society: "the preeminence accorded to the Muslim religion in the national reference is consistent with the attachment of the Moroccan people to the values of openness, of moderation, of tolerance and of dialogue for mutual understanding between all the cultures and the civilizations of the world." Islam in Morocco would henceforth have no place for violence of the type visited on the country in 2003. The Salafis had struck against Jewish belonging. For them, Jews were symbols of the West who had no place in the Islamic world.[5] For their opponents, however, namely the Moroccan government and its supporters, Jewish belonging has become an important means of advancing their program and measuring its success.[6] Not only was Jewish belonging enshrined in the 2011 constitution, but its visible manifestation is seemingly everywhere. Ancient synagogues are being rebuilt and rededicated, Jewish cemeteries and saints' tombs are being restored, Jewish museums are being opened, street signs named for rabbis mark the intersections of the various *mellah*-s. These days, it is rare to open a newspaper or watch Moroccan television without seeing a "Jewish" story. Moreover, there is a consistent, intertwined narrative that tends to dominate the official discourse about Jews in Morocco: the long duration of Jewish life in Morocco, peaceful coexistence between Muslims and Jews, and the symbiotic relationship between Moroccan Judaism and Moroccan Islam.[7] All of this new attention to Moroccan Jewish civilization is surely welcome and signals a shift away from the Arab nationalism of years past that benefits all minorities, not just Jews. Yet care must also be taken so that the specificity of the past is not lost in the amalgamations of the present. Just as Moroccan Islam is being recast to suit the requirements and values of today's world—particularly the struggle between globalization and tribalism[8]—so, given the dialectical relationship between the two, is Moroccan Jewishness, which brings us to the current book and its aspirations.

Jewish Morocco is not a history of the Jews of Morocco; rather, it is a history of Morocco from the perspective of its Jews.[9] This distinction is of course subtle, and it may be difficult in the coming pages to tell where one ends and the other begins. Still, something more than mere semantics is at stake in this particular reading of the Moroccan past, one that is as much genealogical as it is strictly historical, as thematic in its approach as it is chronological. Specifically, I seek evidence for the Jewish historical experience in places where one doesn't ordinarily look; namely at the pivotal junctures in the development of Moroccan (Muslim) identity as well as within the characteristic elements of that identity itself. These pillars of Moroccanness, enumerated below, are a particularly underutilized and promising guide to Jewish Morocco. Taken sequentially, they allow us to outline both a rough chronology for Moroccan history that goes beyond the usual dynastic frameworks as well as a new *problematique* for fully integrating Jews into it. But first, a few demographic observations in order to justify the pursuit.

While Jews were a minority in Morocco, they were anything but marginal. Morocco is ethnically diverse, but not religiously—internal variety within Islam aside. Jews, in fact, are Morocco's only officially recognized non-Muslim minority. Historically, Jews comprised an average of 3–5 percent of Morocco's total population (with much higher percentages in cities), making them the single largest Jewish community in the Arab world,[10] a claim they can still make today despite greatly diminished numbers. At their height they numbered around 250,000; today the Jewish population of Morocco hovers around 3000. Jews are also among the oldest inhabitants of Morocco, having arrived in Northwest Africa centuries, possibly millennia, before the arrival of Arabs and Islam. The significance of Moroccan Jews is important by both quantitative and qualitative measures. Their deep roots are evident at every level of Moroccan society: political, economic, or social. Quite simply, the history of Morocco cannot be told without the story of its Jews.[11]

If Jews are essential to Moroccan history, the reverse is also true: Morocco is important to Jewish history. Morocco has produced some of the Jewish world's most outstanding rabbis, merchants, ambassadors, communities, and cultural figures. Yet Jewish microhistory—i.e., relating the history of Jews from one particular place—is tricky, historiographically speaking. What does Morocco count for in the lives of its Jews? And, in turn, in the lives of Jews in general? Jewish history, wherever it unfolds, requires the historian to strike a balance between internal and external frameworks, between Jewish life and the "outside," to ask whether Jews in a particular setting were more like each other, i.e., like Jews in other settings, or more like the non-Jews among whom they lived. Which sets of relationships and social frameworks were more significant for the individual and the collective? Which context (Jewish or general) was more important? These are not easy questions, and yet our understanding of Jewish history as a field (let alone of Jewishness itself) is completely dependent on how they have been answered over the years, both by scholars and by more casual observers. Over the last half century or so, contemporary (or "postmodern") scholarship has staked out an approach, sometimes called "diasporism," that retains an investment in the formative power of place by emphasizing the multicultural nature of Jewish society, implicitly in opposition to the coercive power of the nation and nation-state.[12] In each location where Jews live, it is argued, their history and identity are "constructed": that is, shaped in relation to a specific time and place meaningfully shared with non-Jews. From this perspective, religion as such may recede to the background, giving greater prominence to issues cutting across confessional boundaries, such as gender, class, and culture. Historians of the Ottoman Empire have been especially successful at writing Jews into local histories, highlighting such themes as patriotism and belonging without glossing over ruptures or eliding difference.[13] In non-Ottoman Morocco, select urban histories have broken similar ground,[14] while a newer generation of scholars has extended this approach to specific themes as well as places, integrating the Jewish experience into detailed studies of Moroccan legal history,[15] the function of memory and nostalgia in Morocco's rural south,[16] and constructions of the Moroccan nation.[17] This book will attempt to synthesize recent work on Moroccan and MENA Jewish history into a coherent narrative for the interested generalist and scholar alike.

Jews and the places they live

The question remains where exactly in the battle between text and context does the boundary between internal and external Jewish life lie? Which, if any, activities can be construed as purely Jewish, partly Jewish, or not at all Jewish? As a recent book title asks, "*How Jewish Is Jewish History?*"[18] As astute a question as that may be, it is also slightly misplaced in an Islamicate context.[19] That is, in the Islamic world, (as opposed to the European contexts in which modern Jewish historiography mostly developed), the dichotomy between Jews' inner and outer worlds was not so sharp as to justify this formulation in the first place. From the rise of Islam to the end of the medieval period, the vast majority of the world's Jews (perhaps up to 85 percent) lived in the Islamic world, spread out between Morocco in the west to Iran in the east, an area much larger than continental Europe. Deep integration, for better or worse (exclusion has its advantages, after all), was the norm for them throughout most of their history. In his response to the hackneyed question of whether Islam was ultimately "good for the Jews," Bernard Lewis has noted: "[Jewish life under Islamic rule was] never as bad as in Christendom at its worst, nor ever as good as in Christendom at its best." He continues, "There is nothing in Islamic history to parallel the Spanish expulsion and Inquisition, the Russian pogroms, or the Nazi Holocaust."[20] Nor was the relatively better treatment of Jews under Islamic rule arbitrary. As Lewis himself helped show in his earlier work, Muslim rulers' relatively benign attitude toward their Jewish minorities was the natural outgrowth of a shared social ethos based on centuries of lives lived closely together, a distance made even shorter by the theological proximity of the two religions themselves.[21] Indeed Judaism and Islam share much in common in theological terms, more than either does with Christianity. Beyond their shared foundation of strict monotheism, Islam and Judaism are both articulated through a sacred law, known as *shari'a* in Arabic and *halakha* in Hebrew. Studying this law and its sources is considered a religious obligation in both traditions. Special institutions were established exclusively for this purpose, namely the *madrasa* and the *yeshiva*, where Muslims and Jews studied remarkably similar texts and tenets, including the proper observance of dietary rules (*kashrut* and *halal*), fasting, holidays, ritual purity, and so on. These similarities are closely linked to the Islamic tradition of what in today's parlance would be termed the "tolerance" of Jews and Judaism as so-called Peoples of the Book, defined as pre-Islamic monotheists with their own holy scripture. Islam does not share the existential problem the Christian Church traditionally had with Jews *qua* Jews, insofar as their failure to disappear with the advent of Christianity was perceived as a challenge to the veracity of Jesus himself. In the unkind words of the British historian Arnold Toynbee, Jews, seen through a Christocentric lens, were "living fossils," a people who should not exist but somehow insisted on doing so. In contrast, the Islamic legal tradition mandates the protection of Jews (through the status known as *dhimma*) and allows them to practice their religious rites and rituals so long as they do not disturb the majority population.

How *dhimma* became manifest in the actual treatment of Jews differed greatly across the wide geographic and chronological expanse of Islamicate civilizations; thus it is difficult to generalize about the treatment of Jews under Muslim rule (although this has not stopped some commentators from doing so).[22] There were plentiful Jewish cultural variations in the Islamic world, but they were precisely that: variations, and for the most part not independent or isolated phenomena. Jews in the Islamic world neither lived in ghettos nor spoke an exclusively Jewish vernacular. Whatever evidence of a distinct Jewish quarter exists in the form of the Moroccan *mellah*, the Tunisian *hara*, or the more common *hay/derb al-yahud* found throughout the Middle East and North Africa, it is worth noting that these sites existed well within Islamicate spatial and architectural norms and rarely if ever functioned as exclusively Jewish spaces.[23] (The European ghetto had a very different trajectory and purpose, mostly to stigmatize and isolate Jews.[24]) In terms of language, Jews commonly used Judeo-Arabic, Judeo-Persian, and various forms of Judeo-Spanish (*Hakétia*, Ladino, etc.) in the Middle East and North Africa. In written form, these languages employed Hebrew script, which was not legible to non-Jews. In spoken form, however, which was the medium through which most communication took place, these languages were easily understood by non-Jews. Language did not generally function as a means for Islamicate Jews to forge a "psychic separation" from non-Jews, as Yiddish did in Europe.[25] In the case of Judeo-Arabic specifically—known simply as *"yahudiya"* ("Jewish")—the fact that Arabic and Hebrew are both Semitic languages with innumerable cognates, shared vocabularies, and similar grammar further augured for mutual intelligibility.

A similarly powerful and widespread manifestation of the shared cultural world of Jews and Muslims existed in the realm of music. In Iraq, the vast majority of the members of the national orchestra prior to the Baʻth era (1968–2003) were Jewish, while the music for the first Iraqi motion picture was made by the Jewish composer Salah al-Kuwaiti. Songs by Salah and his brother Daʻud can still be heard on the radio in their native Kuwait. In Egypt, Daʻud Hosni helped found modern Egyptian music, and performers like Leila Mourad and Nagwa Salem were among Egypt's most beloved celebrities. The man considered the greatest North African pianist of the first half of the twentieth century, who was the head of the beylical orchestra at the same time as he pursued a successful recording career, was the Tunisian Jew, Messaoud (Masʻud) Habib.[26] The number of famous Jewish musicians and performers in the Middle East and North Africa goes on and on, and yet, at the same time, other than the *piyyutim* of the synagogue, one finds no explicitly and exclusively Jewish musical form in the Islamicate world equivalent to Eastern Europe's Klezmer.

In all of these areas, Jewish cultural production was typically understood as a component of rather than an alternative to the cultural mainstream. Jewish culture was not inaccessible to Muslims. Nor, for that matter, was Muslim culture inaccessible to Jews. Language again plays a key role in this regard, as can be seen by comparing Moroccan Jewish culture to European Jewish culture: Jews never fully adopted Latin—the lingua franca of premodern European intellectual and cultural elites—due to its intrinsic connection to an overtly hostile Church. Despite its intrinsic connection to the Qur'an and Islam, Arabic posed no similar threat, and it is well known that Jews adopted Arabic letters with gusto. Some of the greatest compositions in Arabic were written by Jews, beginning with the pre-Islamic poetry of the Hijazi Jewish poet al-Sammawʼal extolling tribal life and warfare, through the medieval philosophy and medical texts of the great Andalusian thinker Moses Maimonides and eventually onto the plays, cartoons, and essays of Arabic renaissance (*al-nahda*) figures like the Egyptian satirist Yaʻqub Sannuʻ. Despite having left Iraq for Israel in 1951 at the age of 13, the Iraqi author Samir Naqqash wrote and published in Arabic until his death in 2004. In the Middle East and North Africa, whatever boundary may have existed between the inner and outer worlds of Jewish society was constantly crossed on all levels. Even confessional lines sometimes became blurred.[27] The joint veneration of "saints" (Heb. *tsaddik/im*, Ar. *wali/awliya*), for example, is both unique to North Africa and of vital cultural importance there. As a practice that permeates Moroccan Judaism and Moroccan Islam in particular, saint veneration is indicative of how even in the midst of the most "religious" of acts, Jews were deeply ingrained and served essential functions within Muslim societies. The reverse is also the case: the Moroccan Jewish holiday of Mimouna requires the participation of Muslims to be celebrated properly. Mimouna takes place at the end of Passover when Muslims bring Jews their first leavened foods after an eight-day period of abstinence. Only non-Jews would have the materials available at home to prepare the holiday dishes in time for the end of Passover.

Further underlining the specificity of the Maghrib is the fact that the line separating Muslims from non-Muslims was less clearly defined in North Africa than it was in the Middle East. The porous and shifting border between the two groups in Morocco will be evident throughout the coming pages. By contrast, the rise of pan-Islamic and pan-Arab ideologies during the late nineteenth and early twentieth century challenged the so-called cosmopolitanism associated with European colonialism in places like Egypt and Iraq, causing traditionally diverse societies to grow increasingly homogenous.[28] While Morocco was subject to many of the same ideological currents as its neighbors in the *mashriq*, [Middle East] the country's ethnic diversity and religious duality proved much harder to elide or erase. Even today, as much of the region looks to exclusivist Islamist parties to rule them, greater inclusiveness (of Imazighen in this case) is still high on the list of demands among the opposition groups that emerged in the uprisings of spring 2011 in the Maghrib. As noted above, the official position of the Moroccan government is that the country's ethnic, religious, and cultural diversity is a source of national pride. As enshrined by Morocco's 2011 constitution, "[the country's] unity, is forged by the convergence of its Arab-Islamic, Amazigh, and Saharan-Hassani components, nourished and enriched by its African, Andalusian, Hebraic, and Mediterranean influences."[29] Though it is certainly neither without ambivalence (particularly when it comes to the Amazigh question) nor without complicated economic and political motives (particularly when it comes to Jews), Moroccan officialdom's embrace of what in the West is called multiculturalism is still unique in the region and rests to a surprising degree on Jewish Morocco's long history.

Morocco offers the historian a profound example of Jewish integration in the Islamic world. While the level of this integration is inconsistent across eras and regions, most scholars recognize Muslim-Jewish relations in Morocco as having been intimate and successful in terms of intercommunal "symbiosis," to use the popular biological metaphor coined by S.D. Goitein.[30] This closeness includes elements both dramatic and mundane, symbolic and manifest, mythic and real. But its signs are easily recognized by most Moroccans, even today. Partly, it exists (and is constantly reinforced) on the level of official discourse. The daily government-sponsored newspaper *Le Matin du Sahara* includes the Hebrew date on its masthead along with *hijri*, Amazigh, and Gregorian dates; the Moroccan flag and Moroccan coinage at various junctures prominently featured what in Jewish tradition is known as the Star of David.[31] These symbols, moreover, are based on actual historical experience. In the palace, Jewish women were often the wives, wet nurses, and even mothers of sultans;[32] Jewish men served as counselors and diplomats, cabinet ministers, treasurers, and royal cooks. Moroccan Jews were not restricted to any particular professions, as in Europe: they worked as merchants, farmers, water carriers, jewelers, leather workers, spice sellers, winemakers, clairvoyants, doctors, prostitutes; correspondingly, they were also the friends, business partners, lovers, and enemies of Muslims. Sometimes even religious identities themselves merged; the ancient imbrication of Jews in rural areas has led many observers to recognize great mobility across religious lines in the pre-Islamic period; the question of whether Jews became Amazigh or Imazighen became Jews was once a topic of considerable debate (see Chapter 2).[33] Still today, among the elite families of Fez, it is not uncommon to meet Muslims with the last name of Cohen, who are likely to be descendants of Jews who converted to Islam.[34]

When it comes to Jewish Morocco, then, the historian has the uncommon privilege of not having to choose between text and context, between telling the story of "Jews" *or* "Moroccans." On this basis, a new generation of Moroccan Muslim scholars is emerging as a vanguard of Jewish studies in the Islamic world. Casablanca boasts the only Jewish museum in the Arab world, *le Musee du judaisme marocain*, and another such entity recently opened in Essaouira, the *bayt al-dhakra* (House of Memory). Mohammed V University is home to an active working group on Moroccan Judaism. Hebrew is taught in the major universities, and a relatively unbiased treatment of Judaism is part of the standard primary school curriculum. The Mimouna club, founded in 2007 by students at Al Akhawayn University in the mountains outside of Fez, works to preserve and promote Morocco's Jewish traditions, beginning with the intercommunal feast for which the club is named.[35] It now has chapters throughout the country. All this is to say that Jews are not exceptions to a rule in Morocco; they are an important and recognized part of the country's past. And yet, as it is impossible not to notice, in strictly numerical terms they are only barely part of its present.

Jews and the places they no longer live

A community that numbered over than a quarter of a million individuals in the mid-twentieth century has now all but disappeared. Ascertaining the causes of this phenomenon requires looking to the less convivial moments in the Jewish history of Morocco, as well as to the outside forces that acted upon it. On the one hand, Morocco was not a temporary "host society" for Jews. Jewish roots in Morocco reach far deeper than those of a mere "guest." To begin with, Jews were living in Morocco long before Muslims, today's majority population, arrived. Over the centuries, they developed an undeniable sense of "cultural athomeness".[36] Yet their history is not without its gray, or even black, areas. A minority can be well rooted in a given society but still *feel* alien, and/or be *treated* as alien, by others; alterity is not always measurable by conventional means. Nor does integration necessarily preclude persecution. Targeted anti-Jewish violence was exceptional in Moroccan history and could not easily be sanctioned by Islamic law, but by no means was it nonexistent. Almohad rule (1121–1269) is a case in point. The Almohads rejected the Sunni Maliki jurisprudence introduced by their predecessors, the Almoravids, and the lenience it afforded minorities. During their brutal reign, many Jews went into exile, including Moses Maimonides and his family, who fled the Almohad centers of Cordoba and then Fez for Fustat (Cairo). Morocco's indigenous Christian community disappeared altogether during this period. But one must jump forward many centuries to come to a low point of similar proportions, during the short but bloody rule of the Alawi sultan Mawlay Yazid in the eighteenth century. Yazid's reign was marked by the ruthless persecution of Jews who had sided with his adversaries. Two hundred years later, riots broke out in Oujda and Jerada in eastern Morocco as a response to the first Arab-Israeli war in 1948, leaving forty-four Jews dead, including women and children, and more than one hundred wounded. Soon thereafter in the uncertain period of Moroccan independence in the 1950s, Jews grew increasingly skittish as representatives of the emerging nation paid lip service to equality but offered little in the way of real assurances. In the following decades, the majority of Morocco's Jews left for what at the time seemed like safer shores of France and Israel, and later, francophone Canada and the United States. Nor has the violence ended, as the events of May 16, 2003, make clear. More recently, the Argana café in Marrakech's Jma' al-Fna square was bombed on April 28, 2011. Ostensibly aimed at the café's foreign clientele that frequented the second-floor balcony where the explosives were carefully placed, the bombing took the lives of a number of Jews, whether intentionally or not, as the attack occurred just after Passover, when many Jews of Moroccan descent are known to visit Marrakech.

Yet even the most horrific events (perhaps especially these) must be contextualized in order to be fully understood, taking into account both the contemporary political climate as well as the reactions of Moroccan people and government. For example, to dismiss Moroccan radio personality Ahmed Rami's anti-Semitic rants on *Radio Islam*[37] as mere hate-mongering would be to ignore the major role such discourse plays in the Islamists' larger challenge to the Moroccan king and government, who are popularly perceived as Moroccan Jews' major supporters, and whose efforts at peacemaking in the Middle East call their legitimacy into question for many Islamists. That is, if we focus only on the impact of these events on Morocco's Jews, and not on their larger political, social, and historical meanings, we risk missing the oasis for the palm trees, so to speak. This holds equally true in the context of historical inquiry, where gray areas are the rule. As Jessica Marglin has observed,

> On the one hand, seeing Jews only as victims obscures any agency that Jews had by reducing them to objects of oppression. On the other, asserting that Jews and Muslims generally "got along" ignores the real religious and social inequalities inherent in Islamic society and tends to shift the emphasis of historical analysis to the problems created by Western imperialism rather than the internal history of Islamic societies.[38]

The Jews who fled Morocco in the middle of the twentieth century left behind an enormous void whose scope and impact is only now being realized. As an editorial in the Moroccan news magazine *Tel Quel* put it during a sad week in December 2010 when both Edmond Amran El Maleh and Abraham Sarfaty, two pillars of modern Moroccan intellectual and political life, passed away: "Morocco already had too few Jews when it lost the most illustrious among them."[39] Indeed, the majority of young Moroccans today—which, given the country's demographics, means most Moroccans—have never met a Jew. They do not think of Jews as indigenous to their society, despite the millennia-long Jewish presence in Morocco, predating the arrival of both Islam and the Arabs. Instead, they associate them with Israeli settlers and soldiers and the oppression of Palestinians, figures omnipresent in the media. A backlash against Israel and Zionism, rather than traditional formulations of anti-Semitism, seems to be the primary drivers behind the troubling incidents of anti-Jewish violence that have taken place in Morocco in recent years and are out of step with Morocco's past. That Jews today are largely (though not entirely) an element of the Moroccan past makes their story that much more critical to tell but also risks veering toward clichés and generalizations. It is especially important to avoid the tendency toward a romantic Moroccan exceptionalism—that is, to hold Morocco up as host to a utopic "golden age." Integration, as alluded to above, is more slippery than that.

There is no quick and easy way to tell the complex history of Morocco and its Jews, though the book before you strives to be succinct without sacrificing too much in the way of nuance or detail. The period it covers stretches (somewhat elliptically) from just before the arrival of Islam in Northwest Africa in the seventh century to the present day. It proceeds chronologically, though there is necessarily some overlap as well as the inclusion of thematically relevant information in the treatment of periods where it may not strictly belong. It is important to note from the outset that Morocco as a state with defined borders and a distinct political culture did not exist during much of this time; the "Morocco" of the coming pages is more practical convention—the acceptance of a current borders and political identity as reasonably static—than historical reality. That said, Moroccans are perhaps able to lay a more convincing claim to proto-national coherence than most of their neighbors in North Africa or the Middle East, not to mention in Europe. Already in the sixteenth century, Morocco's political borders began taking the shape by which we know them today. They were dictated in large part by natural boundaries: the Mediterranean to the north, the Atlantic to the west, mountains to the east. Only the south was (and remains) an ill-defined limit. Morocco was also a periphery. Centers of authority, both Islamic and Jewish (Mecca, Medina, Baghdad, Damascus, Jerusalem, Hebron, Safed, etc.) were quite distant. As in America's western frontier, there was often greater leeway to improvise and to respond to immediate circumstances, which in turn allowed Moroccans to develop a strong sense of independence. Moroccans even managed, though not without difficulty, to remain outside the Ottoman political sphere, the only Arab country other than Yemen and the interior of the Arabian Peninsula to do so. In the modern period as well, Morocco staved off direct colonial control longer than its neighbors in North Africa. Algeria was conquered by the French in 1830 in a watershed event marking North Africa's previously unimagined vulnerability. Tunisia became a French Protectorate in 1881; Morocco followed suit only in 1912, but even then, some areas in the south and the Rif never fully bent to European control.

Morocco's relatively long independence and its geographic coherence allowed for the unfettered development of the country's defining institutions, including the *makhzan*, its personification in the monarch as *amir al-mu'minin* (commander of the faithful), and the means of disseminating its power through the *mahalla* (itinerant court).[40] Such institutions helped shape and sustain Moroccan society. They were in turn reinforced by the country's religious authorities, whether in the form of the scholarly elites (ulema) and/or mystics of the Sufi lodges (*zawiya*-s). No sultan could rule without their explicit consent (*bay'a*). Finally, the cultural context in which these institutions developed and operated remained strongly Amazigh despite the Arab and European overlay. From tattoos to couscous to silver jewelry, music, and dances, Amazigh traditions are profound and omnipresent in Morocco.

Who are Morocco's Jews?

Just as we might question the existence of something called "Morocco" in the premodern period, "Jews" as a category of analysis can also be called into question (though it rarely is).[41] What Moroccan Judaism consisted of, its textual and practical variations, and its ties to "normative" Judaism, are likewise inextricably bound to the changes and continuities over time in Northwest Africa.[42] For example, at the time that Jews are believed to have first arrived in the region, Judaism was not yet fully formed. The Talmud, which constitutes the basis of Jewish law and practice, was written and redacted between 200 and 500 CE, in the centuries after the destruction of the Temple and the dispersion of the Jews. Depending on which origin story for Moroccan Jewry one believes (see Chapter 1), this event was still several centuries after Jews had begun to settle in the Maghrib. As has been pondered in other settings, are Jews still Jews without Jewish law?[43] Or is it more accurate to consider Moroccan Jews of this early era a tribe of monotheists—a radically new idea at the time, but still not quite the same thing? In any event, we can assume little in the way of a direct line between the Judaism as practiced in North Africa in the pre-Islamic period and the Judaism of today.

Moroccan Jewry also developed strong regional characteristics, reflecting the country's geographic and cultural diversity. The north was heavily influenced by Spanish culture. In Tetuan, Tangier, and elsewhere in the north of the country, Jews spoke *Hakétia*, a Moroccan form of Judeo-Spanish, and organized their communities in *juntas*. In the inland capitals of Fez, Meknes, and Marrakech, the traditional Arab-Islamic culture of the *hadariya* (civilization) prevailed. These cities had the oldest *mellah*-s, located adjacent to the sultan's kasbah, and preserved a close vertical relationship between the Jews and the ruler. They were important centers of Jewish learning and the sites of great *yeshivot*. Fez in particular produced some of Judaism's finest scholars, including Ishaq al-Fassi, whose presence there was partly what attracted the aforementioned Maimonides to the city when his family fled Cordoba. On the Atlantic coasts, Jews were integral to the bustling markets of port cities, particularly as places like Agadir, Safi, and Essaouira were drawn into the world economy in the early modern era. The port cities were home to many of the *tujjar al-sultan*, the official merchants of the Moroccan sultan, men like Meir Macnin and Samuel Pallache, whose knowledge and expertise led successive sultans to appoint them as royal ambassadors to European courts and governments. Finally, the Rif and Atlas Mountains and the oases beyond were home to hundreds of small Jewish communities, living close to the land with their Amazigh, Arab, and Haratin (black African) neighbors.

In all these places, the history of the Jews developed within the broader outlines of Moroccan history and was deeply affected by trends in the larger society. We begin with the most formative event for the Maghrib as a whole: the arrival of Islam in Northwest Africa in the late seventh century. Eventually the majority of North Africans adopted the new religion, but it was a slow process, bringing about gradual shifts in daily life and spiritual orientations, as new systems of law and government were imported by the conquerors along with the new faith.

The Muslims were hardly the first invaders the region had known, yet the impact of their arrival was unprecedented. The Romanized and Amazigh populations they encountered, some of whom were Jews, dealt with the incursion in different ways. Along with their pagan neighbors, many Jews became Muslim, but others did not, choosing instead to remain Jews and live as a minority under Islamic rule. Many of those who remained Jews nonetheless became Arabized, either replacing their Tamazight tongue with Arabic or becoming bilingual.[44] Islamization and even more so Arabization were not only gradual processes but also highly incomplete ones.

The arrival of the exiles (Heb. *megorashim*) in the fifteenth century from the Iberian Peninsula once again shook Moroccan Jewish life. During the Spanish Inquisition and expulsion of Jews in 1492, Sephardim began landing on North African shores en masse. They brought with them yet another new cultural orientation, and sense of European superiority generally preferring to impose their rituals and religious practice rather than assimilate to local norms established by the autochthonous Jews (*toshavim*). It took many generations for these disparate strains of Jewish life in Morocco to harmonize.

While Muslim authorities throughout the Middle East and North Africa generally allowed Jews autonomy over civil matters (marriage, divorce, inheritance, intra-Jewish contracts), their legal status vis-à-vis the Muslim majority was dictated by Islamic law. As a juridical and theological concept, *dhimma* status has been well elaborated,[45] yet our knowledge of its application in specific historical contexts is patchy. Jews in the Arab, Turkic, and Persian worlds experienced *dhimma* in myriad different ways, which is hardly surprising considering that the Jewish communities in question were spread out over thousands of miles. Though their lives may have been structured by the same basic legal frameworks, both the external Islamic one and the internal Jewish one, they often shared little else in terms of cultural context. In Shi'i Iran, for example, the principle of *najas*, ritual uncleanness or impurity, was not only more exaggerated than in Sunni areas but at certain junctures was linked to the physical bodies of non-Muslims, causing them to be shunned;[46] this was never the case in Morocco. Even internally, within a specific country or region, there might be significant variation, particularly over time: the Qajars did not impose *najas* the same way as the Pahlavi shahs or the Ayatollahs. In Morocco as well, the application of *dhimma* was inconsistent. At times, *dhimma* was even rejected by the authorities altogether. Part of what made the experience of the Almohads so frightening for Moroccan Jews was precisely their abrogation of *dhimma*, which we might recall literally means "protection" (i.e., of the inferior non-Muslims by the stronger Muslim majority or ruler). The Almohads favored their founding theologian Ibn Tumart's own doctrine of *tawhid*, which was much less accepting of non-Muslim minorities. Under the Unitarianism of the Almohads, non-Muslims were removed from positions of power, stringent dress codes were enforced for Jews, and coerced conversions to Islam were frequent. Fortunately for Jews, the underlying vision of Islam in Morocco, based on the relatively "moderate" jurisprudential school of Malikism, survived the Almohad period. Its reassertion in the following centuries led to it becoming a basic characteristic of Moroccan identity. Jews' particular experience of Moroccan Islam, beginning with its arrival in the seventh century and continuing through the institutionalization of Malikism, will form the basis of Chapter 1, which will also include a discussion of Jewish origins in Morocco.

Along with their doctrinal revolution, the Almohads gave new form to an assertively autonomous Amazigh rule in Northwest Africa. To be sure, Imazighen had been prominent in the area since well before the eleventh century, having found in Islam a powerful vocabulary and related mechanisms for advancing their own agendas. The idea of an Amazigh "permanence," underlying the Roman, Muslim, Arab, Andalusian, and imperial accretions, is an important trope in Moroccan historiography, one which extends in a very particular way to Jewish Morocco. Both Imazighen and Jews endured each foreign invasion, creating a special bond—even a merging—between the two groups. What does their common autochthony count for in a Moroccan context? What is at stake in the construction of an Amazigh identity for Jews, and vice versa? How is it that Jews have come to play such a central role in the strategies of the Amazigh cultural movement of today, which include direct intervention in the Arab-Israeli conflict? In Chapter 2, the meaning of these contemporary reverberations of the Amazigh question on Jewish Morocco will be traced back in time to the period when Imazighen dynasties ruled much of North Africa and Amazighity as a pillar of Moroccan identity was first formulated, covering roughly the eleventh to fifteenth century.

Sharifism, connoting descent from Muhammad through his grandson Hasan b. 'Ali, is the third pillar of Moroccan identity we will examine from the perspective of Jewish Morocco.[47] As a litmus test for a ruling dynasty's legitimacy, Sharifism emerged in the sixteenth century as a bold assertion of the superior status of Arabness in a largely Amazigh world. Some of Morocco's most powerful dynastic families, including the Idrisids (788–934), the Sa'dis (1549–1659), and the Alawis (1631–), bolstered their rule with this claim. But during this seminal period of Moroccan history, Morocco's *sharif*-s could only ascend to the political stage once they had neutralized the competing force of Sufism, the strong mystical tradition centered around holy figures and their lodges [*zawiya*-s]. Although the two affiliations often overlapped in a single person, during the formative years of the Moroccan state Sharifism subsumed, coopted, or marginalized Sufism to become the primary path to power. As this process played itself out among various Muslim contenders, a parallel struggle took place on a microscale among Moroccan Jews as a wave of apocalyptic and messianic thought arrived in Morocco from the Ottoman Empire. Moroccan Jews, already divided between *toshavim* and *megorashim*, faced the prospect of an even deeper rift on the spiritual level. How the rabbinical authorities harnessed the power of the nascent Alawi *makhzan* to unify Moroccan Jews during the early modern period (sixteenth–eighteenth centuries) is the subject of Chapter 3, which examines the concurrent rise of the Moroccan state and the cohesion of Moroccan Judaism through authority claims and challenges to them made by charismatic mystics, rebellious Sufis, and false messiahs during the early modern period.

European imperial interest in Morocco began in the nineteenth century and culminated in the establishment of French and Spanish Protectorates over the country in 1912 that lasted until 1956. This period is perhaps the best known in Moroccan history and has received much scholarly attention. But in its Jewish formulation, this history is often presented in black-and-white terms—

recalling the Tunisian Jewish writer Albert Memmi's dictate of colonizer or colonized—with limited results.[48] Greater subtlety is surely possible in this area, and indeed recent scholarly work has helped to revise our view of Moroccan Jewry in the context of European colonialism, however piecemeal.[49] A reading against the grain reveals the complicated situations Jews found themselves in as they struggled to find their footing in a quickly changing political landscape and the often makeshift solutions that they cobbled together.

Closely linked to Morocco's experience as an informal empire and eventually a Protectorate, the subject of Chapter 4, is the Moroccan struggle against colonialism and the creation of the independent Moroccan state in 1956, the subject of Chapter 5. The transition from dependence to independence was a grueling process for both Jews and Muslims, but Jews alone did not survive it and began emigrating en masse during and after the independence period. Having lived for two millennia in North Africa, their departure was not somehow inevitable. Rather, it was the culmination of a series of events played out in an atmosphere of great insecurity, while still other events helped to stem that tide, if only temporarily. Complicating the process was the construction of independent Morocco as an "Arab" nation. To be Arab was of course nothing new in Morocco, for Jews or for Muslims. But Arabness as a unifying idea for political mobilization—our last pillar of Moroccan identity—was only embraced by Moroccans in the twentieth century and grew increasingly exclusive as it became a rallying cry for Moroccan nationalists. In such tenuous political circumstances, a contracting definition of Arabness impeded full Jewish participation in the Moroccan independence movements, though there were important exceptions. At the same time, Jews' experience of Vichy rule made them duly wary of who their real protectors were. Finally, Zionism and the creation of the state of Israel in 1948 had a profound impact on both Moroccan Jewish identity and on shifting Arab consciousness in Morocco and the larger MENA region.

Why tell the story of a place from the perspective of a minority's experience? And why the Jewish minority, in particular? Do Jews warrant such a central role in the Moroccan historical narrative—or, by foregrounding a single group, are we skewing that very narrative beyond what would be recognizable to most Moroccans? As these questions suggest, the terrain ahead is rocky, at least for the historian, who is professionally obliged to ground conjecture in evidence. But hopefully it is worth the effort, given all there is to gain from a history that uses generalized categories to articulate Jewish specificities (and vice versa), that implicitly argues against stereotypes, generalizations, misconceptions, and even simple misunderstandings about Jews living in Muslim contexts, and lights a way toward seeing the Moroccan past through the widest possible lens.

Chapter 1: Timeline

647–709	Arab conquest of North Africa
698	Arab settlement of Tangier
711–795	Lifetime of Malik b. Anas, founder of Malikism
740	Great Berber Revolt
788–974	Idrisid Era
859	Founding of al-Qarawiyyin in Fez
1040–1174	Almoravid Era
1062/70	Founding of Marrakesh
1147–1269	Almohad Era
1415	Portuguese capture of Ceuta
1430–1508	Lifetime of Ahmad al-Wansharisi, author of *al-miyar al-murib* [the Clear Standard]
1554–1659	Saʿdi Era
1631–present	Alawi Era
1830–1962	French colonization of Algeria
1849–1923	Lifetime of Muhammad al-Mahdi al-Wazzani (Maliki scholar)
1881–1956	French Protectorate over Tunisia
1912–1956	French and Spanish Protectorates over Morocco

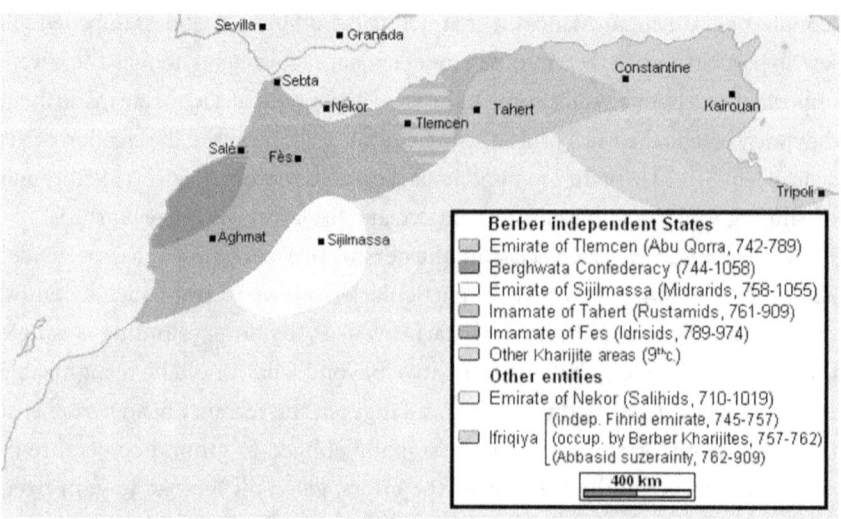

Map 1.1 The Maghrib after the Berber Revolt.

Tounsi, Omar. "Maghreb after Berber Revolt." Digital image. Wikimedia Commons. February 12, 2012. Accessed May 6, 2019. https://en.wikipedia.org/wiki/History_of_Morocco#/media/File:Morocco_and_the_Maghreb_after_the_Berber_Revolt.PNG.

1

Malikism
The Jewish Encounter with Islam in the Far Maghrib (Seventh–Tenth Centuries)

> Islam is the religion of the State, which guarantees to all the free exercise of religion.
> —Article 3 of the Moroccan Constitution, 2011

> It is a national duty and a religious obligation for you to safeguard your identity and remain committed to the Sunni, Maliki rite that the Moroccan people have inherited from their forefathers.
> —Mohammed VI, Throne Day speech, July 30, 2015

> The adoption of Malikism paved the way for the autonomy and moral unity of all North Africa.
> —Abdallah Laroui, *The History of the Maghrib*, 128

> lihoud; lmslmine [Jew, Muslim]
> —The only words appearing in the glossary of Daniel Sibony, *Marrakech, le depart*

Introduction: Moroccan Islam

Islam is Morocco's official state religion, and 99 percent of the country's populace identifies as Muslim. More than 25,000 Christians live in Morocco, but they are legally considered foreigners.[1] Jews, however, are considered indigenous to Morocco; hence they alone in addition to Muslims are eligible for Moroccan citizenship, a legal category invented in 1880 at the Conference of Madrid.[2] And once a Moroccan, always a Moroccan: the *Law of Perpetual Allegiance* stipulates that Moroccans cannot lose their nationality even if they become naturalized to another country. Moroccans' allegiance is not only to the state, moreover, but extends to the monarch himself. This allegiance is likewise considered permanent and indelible, as the motto inscribed throughout the Moroccan landscape insists: "God, Nation, King." Although the Moroccan ruler exchanged the title of "sultan" for "king" shortly after independence, he still maintains spiritual as well as political authority, as encapsulated in his role as *amir al-mu'minin*, the "commander of the faithful," a title he also claims, and which accords him special powers and duties beyond those of any ruler in the neighboring countries of the Maghrib.[3] As *amir al-mu'minin*, the Moroccan ruler is obliged to protect not only the Muslims of his realm but also, explicitly, the Jews. The ability to provide such protection is in fact precisely how a sultan's legitimacy can be measured, according to a view attributed to the eleventh-century Andalusian geographer al-Bakri: a sultan is just only if a Jew or a woman can safely walk alone in the streets of his realm at night.[4]

Moroccan officialdom's protective stance toward its Jewish citizens remains firmly in place today. As we saw in the introduction, the small but highly integrated Jewish community, still the largest in the Arab world, is regularly cited as a prime example of Moroccan "moderation," "diversity," and "tolerance," values that hold great currency at a globalizing moment when the Moroccan state is actively positioning itself as a bulwark against the region's Islamist movements. As a headline in a recent issue of *Morocco World News* put it, "Moroccan Jews and Muslims: A Model of Tolerance for the World."[5] But it would be a mistake to understand this formulation as merely strategic or exclusively contemporary; even the earliest chapters of Moroccan history reveal an intense intertwining of Jews with the majority inhabitants of the country (keeping in mind that historical populations of Jews were much larger than those of today) and a close vertical relationship with the country's rulers. With the arrival of the Arabs in North Africa in the seventh century, the intercommunal relationship was transformed through the introduction of the Islamic principle of *dhimma*, which regulated the lives of non-Muslims under Muslim rule. But it was only in the following centuries, with the institutionalization of the Maliki school of Sunni jurisprudence that Moroccan Islam really began to take form, and with it specific attitudes and guidelines regarding religious minorities. Yet few in-depth studies exist on the history of Malikism in Morocco, and fewer still on the treatment of Jews within its frameworks.[6]

Any discussion of Jewish Morocco must necessarily begin with the question of Jewish origins in Northwest Africa, and it is there, in antiquity, that we begin our story, cognizant of the frequent slippage between history and myth that characterizes these early stages. Jewish Morocco comes into sharper focus with the initial encounter with Islam in the seventh century, a formative moment for both Jews and Muslims in the region. With that scaffolding in place, we will consider a first pillar of Moroccan identity: Malikism, the legal identity based on the school of jurisprudence that first arose in eighth-century Arabia and continued to be elaborated upon as it spread to North Africa, where it became dominant. Malikism is a central pillar of Moroccan identity, as its prominence in the 2011 constitution attests, but what might it count for in the context of Jewish Morocco? The answer lies in how Maliki jurists understood and applied the general legal status of *dhimma* in specific *makan wa zaman*—places and times.

Jewish life in pre- and early Islamic Morocco

Jews, regardless of whether we think of them as members of a tribe, a people, a religion, or a "race," originated in the Middle East, in the place known in antiquity variously as Zion, Cana'an, *Eretz Israel*, and Palestine, with Jerusalem as its focal point. According to biblical genealogies, the identity that would become Jewishness first began to accrue to a specific group of people after the flood, in which all of humanity was destroyed except for Noah's line. It is from Noah's son Shem that the term "Semite" is derived, a linguistic tree that includes both Hebrew and Arabic. A few generations after Shem came Eber, the original Hebrew, as his name implies, and still further on we encounter the father of monotheism, Abraham. It is at the juncture of Abraham's offspring, Isaac and Ishmael/Isma'il, that Islamic tradition inserts itself in the story, with its telling of the sacrifice (*dhabih*) and the establishment of a linkage between Isma'il and the Arabs, leading eventually to Muhammad himself. In Jewish genealogy, however, Isaac is deemed the chosen one, and it is his line that continues to receive God's prophecy. God changed the name of Isaac's grandson to Israel, transforming his descendants thereafter into "Israelites" (a term that is revived in the context of French colonialism, when Jewish/Judaic particularism fell out of favor), with his children constituting the famous twelve tribes. The neo-Assyrian conquest in the eighth century BCE led to the loss of the northern kingdom of Israel, and with it ten of the twelve tribes. This then is the earliest moment that can be proposed for Jewish migration to Morocco: members of the lost tribes of Israel, instead of marching East with the other captives to Mesopotamia, managed to escape Westward, journeying all the way to North Africa. Although lost to history, the mythical reappearance of the ten tribes continues to appear in Jewish historiography, including in Morocco, as we will see.

The Jews—the progeny of the surviving tribe of Judah—enter into historical time after their settlement in the so-called promised land, historical Canaan where they built a Temple in which to perform sacrifices and worship their one God. Twice the Temple was destroyed, first in the sixth century BCE and again in the first century CE, with each destruction resulting once again in the Jews' forced emigration and correspondingly allowing for the possibility that some Jews fled toward North Africa. Perhaps they traveled there on the boats of the Phoenicians (1500 BCE–539 BCE), who ruled in the territory that is today Lebanon, from which they conducted extensive maritime trade between the Eastern Mediterranean coast and North Africa. The ancient and storied Jewish community of Djerba in today's Tunisia is thought to have originated in this early period, and that Jews fleeing the Babylonian conquest of 586 carried foundation stones from the Temple in Jerusalem with which to build their new synagogue in the Maghribi diaspora.

It is only in late antiquity that we find incontrovertible proof of Jewish settlement in Morocco, in the form of Hebrew epitaphs etched on gravestones in the Roman town of Volubilis, near modern-day Meknes, along with ruins of a synagogue dating from the third century CE. There is the theory, based on the arguments of the fourteenth-century North African historiographer b. Khaldun, that Jews in fact never "arrived" in Morocco at all but had been there all along; that is, that Moroccan Jews are actually indigenous (i.e., Amazigh) converts to Judaism from the pre-Islamic era. Begging the question of who converted them, this idea has been rejected by most scholars. Yet it continues to hold currency among Amazigh activists who see an alliance with Jews as a means of distancing themselves from Arab hegemony, against which they continue to struggle for rights and recognition to this day (see Chapter 2).[7] It is also possible, indeed likely, that a looser configuration prevailed, namely that some Jews migrated to Northwest Africa from points further East, bringing with them their Judaism, and upon their arrival encountered a population in which some form of Judaization, or at least monotheism, already had occurred or existed. In any event, Rome annexed northern Morocco in 40 CE, followed by a short Vandal interlude that ended when the Byzantines took over in the sixth century, at which time monotheism of another sort, Christianity, took root in Morocco.

Judaism in pre-Islamic Morocco did not much resemble Judaism as we know it in Morocco or elsewhere today. It may well have been monotheistic, which is to say based on the belief of the existence of only one God, the principle for which Judaism is known. But then again, it is possible that the earliest Moroccan Jews were what are known as henotheists or monolatrists: believers in the existence of many deities over whom one reigns supreme, as some scholars thought was characteristic of Judaism in the time of Moses. Similarly, the nascent Moroccan Jewish community may or may not have had access to the Talmud, the collection and interpretation of Jewish oral law compiled from the third to sixth century CE that lends Judaism its practical and legalistic meaning. After all, Babylon and Jerusalem, where the Talmud was written, are worlds away from Northwest Africa. Elements of Hebrew were probably in North African Jewry's linguistic repertoire, but it is unclear how much and which ones. Though definitive answers to these questions may ultimately elude us, the earliest history of Moroccan Jewry begins to take shape if we consider *when* Jews first came to Morocco. Although written evidence for pre-Islamic Jewish Morocco is all but nonexistent, thanks to the region's strong oral traditions—including legends, myths, folktales, songs, and poems—we are not entirely in the dark with regard to the ancient migrations of Jews to North Africa.

The earliest Jewish communities in Morocco were concentrated in the south, mainly in the Atlas Mountains and pre-Saharan oasis towns of the Sous and Draa valleys. The oldest Jewish community in Morocco is commonly believed to be that of Ifran in the anti-Atlas, which speculatively dates from 361 BCE.[8] Ifran is located between the towns of Guelmim and Tiznit. Its name comes from the Tamazight word *ifri*, meaning cave or cavern, which are numerous in the area. Known to Jews as "Oufrane," it has all the hallmarks of Jewish Moroccan placehood: a remote urban area with its own Jewish quarter (*mellah*) and a connection to the "holy land" by virtue of its purported founding by the descendants of those who fled the destruction of the first temple. According to local lore, these descendants named their new home "little Jerusalem" in its memory and are believed to have established a kingdom there under King Ephrati of the lost tribe of Ephraim.[9]

The Jews of Oufrane were well integrated and deeply rooted in their land, speaking both Tamazight and Arabic. But they also endured bouts of terrible suffering. In the interregnum between the Sa'di and Alawi dynasties in the seventeenth century (periods of political instability were usually bad for Jewish communities), a rebellion broke out, led by the "mad sorcerer" Bu Ihlas. He and his followers marauded through the Sous valley, antagonizing everyone who lay in their path, including a number of Jews from Oufrane. The Oufrani Jews were captured by Bu Ihlas and given the choice of conversion of death, as described below:

> Sixty Jews from Oufrane were at a *suq*. A sorcerer, inspired by Moulay Yazid, arrived along with many armed bandits. The sorcerer wanted to prove his power, to be considered a king. The sorcerer, Bouhalassa, chained up the Jews and tortured them. The local population, who had treated the Jews of the area very well, freed ten of the sixty. Bouhalassa gave the fifty Jews the choice of conversion to Islam or death. He built a great fire. The Jews decided to go as a group into the fire, rather than have even one of them convert. All of them jumped into the fire, one by one. Legend is that a column of fire rose up to the sky. At night, candelabra of fire came down from the sky. Persecutions of Jews stopped. The ten Jews and thirty Muslims gathered up the ashes and brought them to the cemetery in Oufrane.[10]

Although Jews are forbidden by their own traditions from entering the section of the cemetery where the "*nisrafim*" (Heb. "burned ones") are buried, Moroccan Muslims revere it as a holy place. In so doing, they express the syncretistic religious practice typical of Morocco, embodied by the joint veneration of holy figures like the "saint" R. Yehuda b. Naphtali Afriat, the most famous of the Oufrane martyrs.

The Jewish community of Oufrane survived because a more reasonable sultan, Mawlay Slimane (1792–1822), took over and because the skills represented by this community were essential to the town's economic health.[11] Oufrane was an important center for trade, both for Saharan products like ostrich feathers, which were transported to the north and east, and for the redistribution of products from the Atlantic trade originating from Morocco's western coast. The city's economic success continually attracted new immigrants, including Sephardic Jews from the Iberian Peninsula. By the nineteenth century, Jews dominated Oufrane's commercial life and began to set up family members in Essaouira and Illigh to facilitate the movement of goods.[12]

Communities like Oufrane existed throughout Morocco's south. They shared an important characteristic: most were established well before the arrival of Islam in Morocco. As some of the first Jews to interact with members of the new religion, they helped shape the way that Islam would be received in North Africa.

The Islamic conquest of Northwest Africa

The name of Morocco in Arabic, *al-maghrib al-aqsa*, translates into English as the farthest western point of the Islamic world. Morocco was indeed far from the Arab heartlands in the Middle East from which the conquerors came. This distance made Morocco a periphery, for both Jews and for Muslims, which proved to be a significant factor in the development of intercommunal relations. But for the Islamic conquerors, it mostly made for challenging logistics. Getting resupplied with fresh troops, for example, was especially difficult. It took the Muslim armies nearly 70 years to take North Africa, beginning in 647 CE and ending in 709 CE, and required three campaigns by land and sea. All along the North African coast, Arab armies encountered resistance from the vestiges of Byzantine, Vandal, and Roman rule. Many of the inhabitants of these areas were Christians or Jews, presumably speaking Latin, Greek, and/or Tamazight; others were described simply as "Africans" or "Berbers." Resistance and recidivism were especially strong among the latter group.[13] A notable example for our purposes was the mythic Amazigh priestess/sorceress and soldier known as the Kahina, who in the 680s led a fierce albeit ultimately unsuccessful resistance movement against the Muslim armies in the Aurès Mountains, an area located in what is now eastern Algeria. The strength of this resistance was no doubt boosted by the 5 long years it took the caliph in Damascus to send over new troops to relieve the battle-worn ones.

The Kahina's story has appealed to the competing aspirations of various groups in North African society.[14] Depending on whose claims are being buttressed, the Kahina's identity has morphed from Amazigh to Christian or even, ironically, Arab. For Ibn Khaldun, the Kahina was of Middle Eastern descent, which allowed him to see the Arab invasion of North Africa[15] as an act of unification between *maghrib* and *mashriq*. Europeans, not surprisingly, have tended to see her as a Byzantine Christian or proto-Christian in order to justify their own encroachments on the region. Feminists and nationalists have also found her a powerful symbol. Jews, for their part, have long laid claim to her based on her title, which in Hebrew denotes the feminine form of the name of Judaism's priestly caste, the *Kohanim*.[16]

In Morocco, the Arabs established themselves first in the north, around present-day Tangier in 698 CE. But as one territory after another fell to Muslim rule, it became clear that it would be neither economically nor politically prudent to exclude the conquered populations from the new Islamic empire. Who would pay the taxes to allow for continued expansion, let alone cultivate the fields, produce the goods, and perform the administrative functions that were vital to daily life? Islamic tradition clearly forbade the outright killing or expulsion of people who showed no resistance to the invasion. While those who fought back could legally be enslaved, many areas were taken over from local rulers peacefully by treaty and hence were subject to the more lenient conditions of surrender. The only choice left in such circumstances was to integrate the indigenous populations into the new order. But how? Forced conversion was precluded by, among other things, the Qur'anic precept "*la ikraha fi-l-din*" ("there is no compulsion in the religion").[17] The conquered populations would not become Muslims immediately unless they chose to do so themselves. More importantly, the fiscal requirements of the conquests and the concurrent establishment of new administrative structures could best be met by the special taxes authorized for non-Muslims in Islam. Thus there was an undeniable benefit to slow, gradual Islamization, mostly by internal colonization and proselytism.[18] Interestingly, the ultimate criterion for surviving this transition period was submission to Islamic rule, not to the Islamic faith.[19] Indeed in Egypt, both the Copts and the Jews survived the conquests precisely because as minorities with local experience they could fulfill the administrative roles that facilitated the transition from the Byzantine to the new Muslim order.[20] Institutional memory and administrative knowledge had great value in these rapidly changing circumstances and often proved too precious to be sacrificed in the name of religious coercion.[21]

For the indigenous populations themselves, the Islamic conquests were often simply a question of exchanging one overlord for another, and in many cases the new Muslim rulers were preferable to their predecessors. For one thing, the Islamic system of taxation tended to be less onerous and better standardized than the Byzantine one encircling the Mediterranean or Sassanian ones further east in Persia. Moreover, minorities, including non-Eastern Orthodox Christians in the Middle East, were often quite content to get rid of rulers who had oppressed them. In light of this pattern, it took little time before a small Arab Muslim elite found itself at the head of vast masses of non-Muslims, a minority position they would maintain for several centuries before the larger part of the population of the Middle East and North Africa became Islamized.

How could both practical and theological goals be met in ruling over this non-Muslim majority? What might solutions entail religiously, ethnically, socially, and economically, for Muslims and for their non-Muslim subjects? Like all religious traditions, Islam did not develop in a vacuum; it evolved in response to and in dialogue with the practices of non-Muslims it encountered during its formative period, as new rules and principles were articulated to fit new circumstances. The concept of *dhimma* was one such principle to emerge as the definitive guideline for dealing with religious minorities in Muslim-ruled areas.[22]

Dhimma as a mechanism for sustained conquest

The first encounter between Muslims and non-Muslims in any setting constitutes a formative moment that helps to set the tone for the intercommunal relationship that follows. The crucible for Muslim-Jewish relations was without a doubt Medina, formerly known as Yathrib, a small oasis town in Arabia that was the destination of Muhammad's 622 CE *hijra* (migration from Mecca).

There was no permanent Jewish community in Mecca, Muhammad's hometown, and it is unclear whether Muhammad had any contact with Jews during the early part of his life. It is possible that Jewish merchants visited Mecca since it was an important pagan pilgrimage site for Bedouins before it was consecrated to Islam, and hence an important trade center (the two usually went together). But in Medina, there were many Jews to be found; perhaps even the majority of town's population was Jewish prior to the arrival of Muhammad.[23] They were organized into tribes, some exclusively Jewish, some not. Things changed with the arrival of Muhammad and his *ansar* (helpers) from Mecca. Passages in the Qur'an, the *hadith* (the collected words and deeds of the Prophet), and the *sira* (Muhammad's biography) offer a sense of how the intercommunal relationship developed in Medina, at least from a Muslim point of view.[24] A more explicitly historical source for the encounter is the Charter of Medina, a document drafted under the auspices of Muhammad himself, in which we learn that Jews were considered part of the original *umma*, or community, over which Muhammad had been invited to Medina by its clan leaders to govern. As the Charter makes clear, the Jews offered Muhammad their political loyalty in exchange for their religious autonomy, a model that was to endure in the Islamic world for many centuries. The theological basis for this arrangement exists in the famous Qur'anic *ayah* (verse): "*lakum dinukum waliya din*" ("For you is your religion, and for me is my religion").[25] Shortly before he died, however, Muhammad is believed to have said, "Let there be no two religions in Arabia,"[26] leading his followers to expel the Jews (and Christians) from parts of the Arabian Peninsula after his death. The term *umma* itself similarly contracted over time to refer exclusively to the community of *Muslim* believers. Space does not permit a recounting of the vast intervening history that spurred this change in attitude toward the Jewish tribes of Arabia; suffice it to say that the broader theological precepts remained unchanged.

The Islamic conquests further helped define Muslim attitudes toward Jews and Judaism. The all-important concept of *dhimma*, for instance, originates in a peace treaty resulting from the Muslim conquest of Byzantine Syria. The treaty is known as the Pact of 'Umar, named for one of the four rightly guided caliphs who ruled the Muslim community after Muhammad's death.[27] It concerns not Jews but Christians, and, interestingly, it is presented as if it had been drafted not by the Muslim victors, as one would expect, but by the vanquished Syrian

Christians themselves. The Pact set out in writing the rights and obligations of non-Muslim minorities who wished to remain under Muslim rule within the *dar al-Islam*. (It did not apply to non-Muslims living beyond Muslim rule.) They would henceforth be accorded the legal status of *dhimma*. Not all conquered people were eligible, however; *dhimmi*-s had to meet a specific set of criteria. They had to be "people of the book," i.e., maintain a written scripture; they had to be monotheists, believe in one unified god, and their faith had to pre-date Muhammad's prophecy, meaning that the "true religion" had been unavailable to them. The status was eventually extended to include not only Christians and Jews but also Zoroastrians and Sabians (an ancient people of unknown origin mentioned briefly in the Qur'an). To be sure, it was imposed on conquered peoples, and many of its tenets were specifically meant to be humiliating. But at the same time it was also *contractual*: these groups were permitted to remain more or less as they were, in exchange for their loyalty to the state, their humility, and the payment of an annual sliding-scale poll tax known as the *jizya*. What *dhimmis* received in exchange was extraordinarily valuable in that time and place: the right to stay in their homes and the freedom to practice their religion. The idea that non-Muslims could hope to survive at all in the new Islamic order, let alone maintain their rites and practice their rituals, is testimony to the Pact's—and by extension the new Islamic empire's—versatility.

Many of the Pact's provisions reflect the circumstances of the time the document was drafted. A prohibition on abetting spies, for example, was a nod to the ongoing war with the nearby Byzantine Empire. Certain items of clothing that *dhimmis* were required to wear were unfamiliar in later centuries, like the coarse cord or belt known as the *zunnar*.[28] The conical hat known as the *qalansuwa*, which *dhimmis* were *not* allowed to wear, also lapsed into obscurity in later years. Other restrictions had more staying power, however, and became basic tenets of *dhimma* status that were known to all. These included the prohibition against restoring or building new sites of worship, public displays of religious symbols or rites, proselytizing, riding horses, selling alcoholic beverages, or building houses taller than those of Muslims.[29]

Ironically, much of what we know about *dhimma* status in Morocco comes from reports about lapses in protocol. To give just one of many such examples, at the turn of the twelfth century a *qadi* (judge) in Tangier was presented with a complaint against a local Jewish doctor because he "wears a turban and a ring, rides on a saddle on a beautiful riding animal and sits in his shop without a distinguishing mark and without a belt, and he also walks around in the market streets without a distinguishing mark which would allow him to be recognized [as a *dhimmi*]. Rather he [wears] the most exquisite [clothing], like the Muslim notables or even better."[30] In a similar vein, the sixteenth-century traveler Leo Africanus describes Jewish mercenaries roving through the countryside on horseback and carrying arms, two activities explicitly forbidden to Jews.[31] The perceived flouting of *dhimma* regulations could sometimes lead to a serious backlash, as in the case of Touat (see below). The Spanish historian Mercedes García-Arenal sums up the particular combination of rights and restrictions of *dhimma* thus:

> The dhimmi pact provided the group with reasonable security and autonomy, while imposing a ceiling to limit its social mobility. In times of stability, the guarantees were maintained; in times of tension or social disruption, the discriminatory aspects of the pact were accentuated. In general the population did not covet the minority role which was in any case stigmatized, but in times of economic crisis or of recession, the prosperity of certain Jewish groups, or their control over certain sources of economic power, produced resentment and it was argued that contrary to the pact, the dhimmis had been elevated over Muslims.[32]

Some *dhimma* restrictions were adapted from preexisting Byzantine or Sassanian laws.[33] As in those empires, Jews' status as nonconforming minorities was seen by the conquerors as a temporary problem that would eventually disappear, either by conversion or emigration. In North Africa, at least, the indigenous Christian population did in fact become extinct under Islamic rule, though not as a result of the original invasions but rather in the wake of the spectacularly harsh rule of the Almohads (1121–1269). But the indigenous Jewish population survived even the Almohad years. Unlike the Christians, they did not have a powerful ally like Europe nearby to welcome them, but for that same reason they may have been less of a target for Almohad retribution. With the disappearance of the Christians, Jews became the only *dhimmi*-s in Morocco.

The challenge of creating forms of governance that adhered to Islamic principles while accommodating a deeply entrenched Jewish minority was common throughout the MENA region but was especially acute in Morocco given its demographic patterns. In all the places to which Islam spread, tensions between theological directives and practical imperatives on the ground were worked out by Muslim jurists. In the Sunni world, these jurists coalesced into four distinct schools: Hanafis, Hanbalis, Shafi'is, and Malikis, each named for its founding jurist.[34] Schools varied by region: west of Egypt, the area of greatest interest here, the Maliki school dominated. Distinguished by its methods of reasoning, modes of argumentation, and foundational principles,[35] Maliki rulings have profoundly contributed to Morocco's particular religio-legal identity.[36]

Many centuries and miles separate Byzantine Syria from contemporary Morocco, yet the exclusivist Islam of the Pact of 'Umar that presupposed the eventual disappearance of non-Muslims eventually transformed into a "Moroccan Islam" that not only recognized the rights of Jews but, as we will see, actively encouraged Judaism's continuation.[37] How, for instance, are we to understand the 2013 dedication of the newly rebuilt synagogue of Fez, the *Slat al-Fassiyin* by none other than Morocco's Islamist prime minister at the time, Abdelilah Benkirane? Speaking on behalf of the palace, Benkirane extolled the continued existence of the synagogue as an "eloquent testimony to the spiritual wealth and diversity of the Kingdom of Morocco and its heritage"; he further called for the renovation of all Jewish sites in Morocco.[38] Just as the Qur'an and hadith must be read against the background of late antique Arabia in order to understand the foundational moment of Muslim-Jewish relations, so too must we read contemporary attitudes toward Jews in Morocco, like the statement of Benkirane, against the longer Moroccan historical sweep.

Malikism, Moroccan Islam, and Moroccan Jewry

Abu Abdullah Malik b. Anas (711–795) was not himself from North Africa, though the school of jurisprudence he founded flourished there. In fact, Malik was a native of Medina, a place he so esteemed—due to its connection with the Prophet—that he considered the consensus of the early Islamic community there a valid source of Islamic law (*'amal ahl al-madina*). Though begun in the Middle East, Malikism's path to Morocco became assured when it was adopted by the scholars of the Qayrawan, the world's first university, located in Fez. Qayrawan's scholars mobilized Maliki orthodoxies to oppose the growing Shi'i influence in North Africa that stemmed from Fatimid Cairo. In the 1050s, the more austere elements of Malikism caught the attention of a tribe of veiled men (*litham*) from the Sahara. These were the Almoravids (*al-murabitun*), Sanhaja Imazighen who founded Marrakech in 1070 and went on to conquer the whole of Muslim Spain, applying their version of Islamic rule. We will return to them in the next chapter, but for now, we might note that it was only under Almoravid rule that the whole of Morocco was brought under the sway of Islam, since neither of the two ruling dynasties that preceded them, the Umayyads or the

Idrisids, had managed to fully conquer Morocco's southern regions, which also happened to be the regions where the bulk of Jews who first settled in Morocco lived. Hence it is likely that the majority of Moroccan Jews first encountered Islam in its Maliki manifestation, the form in which they were to know it best throughout their collective history.[39]

Though no more inherently liberal than any of Sunni Islam's other schools of jurisprudence, Malikism is nonetheless based on a pragmatic interpretation of the Qur'an and the Prophetic tradition. In addition to its acceptance of the Medina model, it posits both local custom (*'urf*) and public interest (*al-maslaha al-'amma*) as foundations of law, which lend it special sensitivity to its immediate environment. One sees this, for example, in the fact that the Maliki jurists had a much more difficult time dealing with the Imazighen than with the Jews, even though the former had adopted Islam: Imazighen generally kept a tight hold on their customary law, which posed particular challenges to Islamic rule.[40] Other key features of Malikism are a firm rejection of innovative religious practices (*bid'a*), and a confirmation that the duty to "command the right and forbid the wrong" is incumbent upon all Muslims. Again, these tenets are not unique to Malikism, but their emphasis reflects the broader variety of foundational sources at its disposal.

The plethora of sources on which it draws, combined with the particular ethnic and religious makeup of Morocco, has helped to steer Malikism along a "middle way." This path has also been determined from above. In the 2004 annual Ramadan lecture given in the presence of the Moroccan king known as *al-durus al-hasaniya*, a senior *shaykh* from the Fez scholarly establishment extolled the moderate virtues of the Maliki school, with especially high marks for its "balance and temperance":

> [This is manifested] in its judgments, stances, fundamentals, and branches that are removed from excess and neglect, extremism and strictness, strangeness and irregularity, rigidity and complexity, rebelliousness and accusations of unbelief. [...] Consequently, the scope of the openness of the Maliki jurisprudence compared to others becomes clear; as does its conciliation and coexistence with them in peace, understanding, and accord; as well as the possibility of taking and borrowing from them. This is what agitated the womb of the Moroccan community historically to make it this tolerant and open community that makes room for opposition from those who hold opposing views.[41]

The idea of Moroccan moderation is reinforced through less official channels in the Princeton anthropologist Lawrence Rosen's recent ethnography of "two Arabs, a Berber, and a Jew." One of the two Arab protagonists, Yaghnik Driss, is identified as being "a man of the middle." He follows a "middle road of man's freedom and God's own omniscience," in line with the "midmost nation" in which he lives. But as Rosen astutely points out:

> Holding to a middle path is, however, hardly unproblematic. On its face it sounds as though being positioned at the middle must be the easiest of paths. By avoiding extremes one can avoid difficult choices; by dodging pitfalls to either side one can easily prevaricate; by eschewing attachments on either hand one can claim as the high ground an imagined neutrality. In fact, the very opposite is closer to the truth. For the middle path is in fact the most difficult of passages ....[42]

One reason why the "middle path" may be the most difficult is that it is constantly shifting. There were two moments in Moroccan history during which it was particularly hard to find. The first occurred as Morocco was becoming entangled with various European powers, primarily Spain and Portugal, who were encroaching on Morocco's Mediterranean and Atlantic coasts in the fifteenth and sixteenth centuries. The second occurred in the nineteenth century, when Moroccan independence was again being threatened, this time mostly by the French and English. While these junctures will concern us more in the coming chapters, here we may simply locate within them the work of two of Morocco's most outstanding jurists. Their responses to the major questions of their day lend special insight into the enduring, evolving importance of Malikism in Morocco and, in turn, its impact on Moroccan Jews.

Ahmad al-Wansharisi (1430–1508) is Morocco's leading jurist of any period. As the mufti of Fez, he collected thousands of legal rulings (*fatawa*, sing. *fatwa*) from Morocco and al-Andalus that he assembled into a massive work of jurisprudence. Known as *al-mi'yar al-mu'rib* [the Clear Standard], it became the authoritative source for Maliki jurisprudence for centuries to come.[43] Al-Wansharisi's masterful work served to redeem the Moroccan ulema, who had fallen out of favor for having failed to protect Morocco from Portuguese invaders on Morocco's coasts. In 1415 the Portuguese captured Ceuta. Though now held by Spain instead of Portugal, it has never returned to Moroccan sovereignty. Tangier, Alcazar al-kabir, Arzila, and Safi also fell to Portugal in the fifteenth century, followed by Azzemor in the early sixteenth. Al-Wansharisi's *mi'yar* is deeply concerned with the European threat. The author devotes a significant portion (125 out of 6,000 fatwas) to the topic of "*jihad*," meaning here how to relate to non-Muslims, both those of *dar al-harb*, like the Portuguese and Spanish Catholics, as well as locally residing *dhimmis*.[44]

Four centuries later, al-Wansharisi's ideas were collected and repurposed by a talented religious scholar (*'alim*) from the Moroccan city of Wazzan in the Middle Atlas, Muhammad al-Mahdi al-Wazzani (1849–1923). The new *mi'yar* of al-Wazzani was meant to articulate a new Malikism for a new age, one in which European encroachment was again a grave concern. Shortly before al-Wazzani was born, in 1830, France had invaded and annexed neighboring Algeria, and in 1881 took Tunisia. Morocco was surely next on the list, but interference by England and other European powers kept France from creating an imperial triumvirate in the Maghrib until the twentieth century, though this did not mean that Morocco was left unmolested (see Chapter 4). Some scholars blamed Islam itself for the growing European influence, asserting that the religion's own weaknesses were what had left Morocco and the rest of the Middle East and North Africa so vulnerable to European influence and control.[45] But al-Wazzani resisted the idea that Islam was inherently at fault. As an Islamic reformer, he instead sought to bridge the gap between *shari'a*, as it had been traditionally understood, and the social reality facing Morocco. For him, Jews—and their close relationships with Europeans, as helpmates in various forms—were very much part of that reality. The legal rulings of al-Wansharisi, al-Wazzani, and other prominent jurists form the basis of the discussion of Jews in Maliki jurisprudence to follow.

Linkages, contingencies, parallels

Although Malikis were criticized by other Muslim jurists for their "Judaizing tendencies" with regard to their preference for following Jewish kosher laws relating to certain cuts of meat as being unfit for consumption despite their being fully permitted by Qur'an,[46] the treatment of actual Jews and Judaism occupies an infinitesimal place in the history of Malikism in Morocco. Yet by isolating even that small part, we can begin to move beyond the generalities of *dhimma* to a more detailed view of intercommunal life in Morocco. Jews came into the jurists' peripheral vision in a number of areas: discussions of *halal* dietary laws, behavior in the *hammam* (bathhouse), and issues related to sex and marriage involved Jews as a matter of course. The question of whether converted or non-Muslim wives, though permitted in Maliki law, carried residual impurity (*najas*) was a matter of great contention.[47] The bathhouse was a place where the usual markers of external difference could not be maintained for the simple reason that people were undressed. This raised a number of complications for Muslim jurists. It was also one of the few jurisprudential areas where Jews and Christians are treated as two separate cases rather than simply as the collective "*ahl al-dhimma*" since Jews, like Muslims, practiced circumcision, whereas Christians did not, making only the latter distinguishable when naked.[48] (Women in bathhouses were presumably indistinguishable from one another in terms of religion).

Jews were also present in Maliki jurisprudence when it came to issues of commerce and trade—which is not at all surprising given that this was the arena in which intermingling, including formal partnerships, was most common. As a geographic crossroads boasting a huge variety of natural and artisanal products, Morocco was a major trade hub with an intense merchant economy. Many Maliki jurists were troubled by the fraternizing that went on between Jews and Muslims on long caravan trips between Morocco and *bilad al-Sudan* (lit., "land of the blacks," meaning sub-Saharan Africa), which could last for months. Maintaining strict distinctions between Muslims and *dhimmi*-s on these long and arduous journeys across the Sahara was difficult. The ban on *dhimmi*-s riding the same animals as Muslims or using similar saddles was especially hard to enforce, since it would slow down the whole caravan. Moreover, Maliki jurists also generally forbade direct commerce with Europeans.[49] Thus, in order to pursue important exchanges—Moroccan sugar for Italian marble in al-Wansharisi's day; in the colonial period, raw materials like beeswax, animal hides, and apricot kernels for cheap manufactured goods—Jewish intermediaries were a necessity. The founder of Malikism himself, Malik b. Anas, had frowned on the *commendas* (limited liability contracts) between Muslims and Jews that made such exchanges possible, but if conditions for Muslim participation were adequately met, they were nonetheless considered legal.[50]

In the local economy as well, Maliki attitudes had great influence on Jewish lives and livelihoods. Metalwork, for example, was heavily dominated by Jews in Morocco, both because of long Jewish traditions but also because of Malikism's strong aversion to it as a pastime for Muslims. Jewelry making and embroidery with fine metallic threads were seen as especially problematic activities for Muslims; selling such items for more than the intrinsic value of the weight of the metal used to make them was seen as akin to usury, which is forbidden in Islamic law.[51]

In other instances, Jews moved from the periphery to the center of the Islamic legal arena. It is from such cases we can draw a more detailed picture of Jewish life in a Maliki context. In the final part of this chapter, we will briefly examine three such areas. Not only do they illustrate a range of outcomes for Jews—from wholly negative to relatively positive—they also touch upon important markers of Moroccan Jewish identity along the way. On one extreme lies the destruction of the Jewish community of Touat following a heated legal debate over their right to maintain a synagogue. At the other lies the permissive legal attitude toward the cult of saints, a hallmark of both Moroccan Judaism and Moroccan Islam, which has led to the co-veneration of certain figures by both groups in a phenomenon unique to Morocco. Between these two extremes, the payment of the *jizya* tax and its variations over time reveal the particularly Maliki tenor of governance as it pertained to Morocco's Jews.

Touat and the limits of "tolerance"

The very first point outlined in the Pact of 'Umar is a prohibition against building new synagogues or churches or repairing old ones. In the language of the Pact (which, recall, is written in the voice of conquered Christians): "We shall not build, in our cities or in their neighborhood, new monasteries, Churches, convents, or monks' cells, nor shall we repair, by day or by night, such of them as fall in ruins or are situated in the quarters of the Muslims." Yet as anyone who has visited a synagogue or church in the Islamic world surely knows, none of those extant today, whether in Casablanca or Cairo, Istanbul or Isfahan, date from prior to the seventh century. This, then, would appear to be an area where the Pact's rules were loosely applied or, to put it more accurately, where non-legal considerations and contextual circumstances were taken into account by the jurists in their application of the law, such that *dhimmi*-s were often given special dispensation to maintain their places of worship. One infamous exception to this rule occurred in the Saharan oases of Touat.

Touat is a chain of fortified settlements (*qsur*) located several hundred miles south of Tlemcen in what was historically considered the Moroccan Sahara and is today located in Algeria. In the late fifteenth century, when the events under discussion took place, it was located on the frontier of the Marinid-Wattasid empire. Following a familiar pattern, the earliest epigraphic evidence for Jewish settlement in Touat comes much later than the probable origins of the community: Hebrew gravestones found in the area date from the fourteenth century, but Arab geographers have indicated that Jews had lived in the area since the dawn of the Common Era.[52] Jews were no doubt attracted to Touat's location at the northern end of the Tanezrouft route of the trans-Saharan trade that originated in Timbuktu and Gao.[53] From Touat, caravans carrying gold and other valuable items would continue on to Tlemcen or Sijilmasa, the latter one of Morocco's oldest and most important trade entrepôts, where a community of Jewish merchants was ready to receive and redistribute goods.[54] The spread of the Maliki doctrine and the Arabic language across this expanse during the Almoravid period (1040–1147) greatly facilitated this trade. A coherent legal literacy provided the mechanism for recordkeeping, for example, contracts, ledgers, and lists, and just as importantly, helped establish guidelines for pursuing trade relations with non-Muslims like sub-Saharan Africans and Christian Europeans. (Contracts exclusively involving Jews were generally adjudicated by Jewish courts.)

The case against the Jews of Touat was initiated by a *qadi* from Tlemcen, Muhammad 'Abd al-Karim al-Maghili (d.1508, the same year as al-Wansharisi) in 1490.[55] Muslim-Jewish relations were tense in Tlemcen during this period. The Jewish community constituted 4 percent of the population and included relatively wealthy and educated exiles from the Iberian peninsula. The Jews of Tlemcen were doing quite well. So well, in fact, that they attracted the attention of the town's authorities, who felt they were flouting *dhimma* rules and regulations. Both the chief *qadi* of Tlemcen, Qasim b. Sa'id (d.1450), and his grandson, Muhammad b. Uqbani (d.1467), issued fatwas condemning the Jews for what they viewed as their flagrant disregard of *dhimma* humility. Jews were said to be dressing in clothing restricted to Muslims, riding on horseback, and, most interestingly, cultivating relationships with Muslims so loyal to them (the Jews) that they would risk their lives to save them.[56] Al-Maghili arrived in Touat in the late fifteenth century, filled with resentment of Jews. He was outraged by what he saw and heard in Touat, or claimed he saw and heard: a Jewish baker kneading a louse from her head into the bread she was baking for a Muslim, a Jewish launderer urinating on his patron's clothes. He brought his objections to the local *qadi*, who, because he did not share al-Maghili's views on the Jews, followed common practice and sent a query on the matter to several Maliki muftis throughout North Africa asking for their opinions. Seeking justification for his own position, al-Maghili did the same. He also composed a treatise condemning the Jews for their supposed behavior, in which he called them demons, monkeys, and pigs. By their own actions, al-Maghili argued, the Jews of Touat had abrogated their rights as *dhimmi*-s. The principal complaint was against the existence of a synagogue in the settlement of Tamantit, one of the oases in the Touat region, but it was clear that al-Maghili was challenging Jews larger right to protection, thus inviting, indeed requiring, an attack on them by Muslims.

A great juridical debate ensued around whether the existence of the synagogue of Tamantit was lawful, and if was not, what should be done about it. Much of the debate focused on issues related to settlement rights: Had the land been received by the Jews as a gift, by sale, by lease, or as part of a peace treaty? Was the area in which it was located isolated enough so as not to bother Muslims? What were the original conditions of surrender to Islamic rule by the town's inhabitants?[57] The Maliki jurists all seemed to believe that the Tamantit Jews arrived in the area after the Muslims. This gave rise to a discussion of the larger issue of whether the *dar al-Islam* was one unit, i.e., whether the Jews' right to maintain a synagogue can be transferred from one place to another (Muslim) place, as the *qadi* of Tlemcen argued was the case. Historical and economic issues also played a role in the debates, even a defining one, as John Hunwick suggests: "Everything depended upon the time and the place and, above all, on the prevailing economic conditions."[58] Hunwick goes on to discuss the immigration to North Africa of tens of thousands of Sephardic exiles from Spain during this time and the concern their arrival caused among Muslims who feared increased competition in the gold trade.

Overall, the scholarly consensus of the day was against al-Maghili. Many authoritative voices from the Maliki school of jurisprudence issued opinions opposing the destruction of the synagogue. They included the muftis of Tlemcen, Fez, and Tunis, and the *qadi* of Touat itself, whom al-Maghili accused of being an unbeliever and an antichrist.[59] Even those who agreed that the synagogue's existence was not lawful nonetheless did not advocate its destruction, which was seen as an act of injustice (*zulm*) greater than the Jews' original infraction.

Despite the lack of any clear mandate, al-Maghili, on the basis of just one *fatwa* (issued notably by a historian, not a *qadi*), decided that he had sufficient legal standing to move against the Jews. He rounded up enough supporters to destroy the synagogue; any Jews who tried to defend the synagogue were killed. Al-Maghili offered seven *mithqals* [coinage equivalent to the gold dinar] to anyone who killed a Jew for him.[60] As if that were not enough, al-Maghili went on to lead subsequent attacks on Jews in the area.[61] The survivors fled to northern oases, with reverberations from Touat felt as far south as Timbuktu and the Songhay Empire, where al-Maghili convinced the ruler to forbid any Jews to settle or for any of the local merchants to do business with them.[62] Jews stayed away from these areas until the late eighteenth century.

Appalling as they were, the events in Touat were not reflective of Maliki attitudes vis-à-vis Jews. No legal proof was ever produced that supported the destruction of the Tamantit synagogue, let alone of the entire community.[63]

Al-Maghili's views are more aptly located in the puritanical strain of Islamic law influenced by Ibn Taymiyya, the Hanbali theologian of Damascus known for his uncompromising views on *jihad* and non-Muslims, than in Maliki traditions.[64] Even within that tradition, al-Maghili took an especially activist approach to principles like eradicating foreign influences, commanding the good and forbidding the bad, and the principle that to truly love the Prophet one must hate his enemies. More of a polemic than a *fatwa*, his opinions (not to mention his actions) suggest he was driven by a personal hatred of Jews and Judaism that motivated him to seek out like-minded partisans.

Despite its ultimate failure to secure a legally sanctioned outcome, the Touat case nonetheless suggests how the juridical process may have worked in Morocco with regard to Jewish-related matters. First, the Pact of 'Umar served as a crucial starting point on which all jurists to some degree based their decisions. But as the Touat case also shows, decision-making could be done on a very abstract level. Problematically, it holds up two principles at once, without making their relative weight clear: what do *dhimmi*-s owe the Muslim societies in which they live, and what do those Muslim societies owe the Jews? Applying the relative weight of these precepts was left to the jurists, and it is in their application of the law that we start to see the outlines of a Maliki attitude toward Jews. But at the same time, as the outcome in Touat shows, the very strength of a consultative, discursive, and interpretive tradition can leave the door open to its own subversion, in this case by way of a powerful individual propelled by the most basic of hatreds. Maliki flexibility worked to the Jews' disadvantage in Touat, but that was not always the case.

Jizya: Disruptions and continuities

Fundamental to the *dhimma* system is payment of the *jizya*, the annual per capita tax/tribute levied on the so-called people of the book who have submitted to Islamic rule.[65] In Moroccan history, taxes are a very sensitive subject. The introduction of taxes not mandated by Islamic tradition could cause a revolt, whether by tribal populations whose allegiance to the *makhzan* was already shaky or by urban merchants who resented the imposition. But even if Jews were in a position to revolt (which they were not), the *jizya* had indisputable Islamic credentials, directly derived from the Qur'an: "Fight those of the People of the Book who do not (truly) believe in God and the Last Day, who do not forbid what God and His Messenger have forbidden, who do not behave according to the rule of justice, until they pay the tax and submit to it."[66] Most Muslim scholars agree that the *jizya* was originally formulated as a tax to be paid in exchange for protection; later jurists added that it was paid in lieu of military service, which, since it was conceived of as *jihad*, was restricted to Muslims. In addition, there were stipulations as to how the *jizya* was to be paid and by whom. As a poll tax, each male adult was obliged to pay it in person; exhibiting humility—the hallmark of *dhimma*—was part of the process. The pageantry around the act of payment fascinated European observers, as we see in this account from 1894:

> The Governor, as well as the 'Cadi' (judge), pitch their tents at the *mellah* gate, accompanied by secretaries, a dozen soldiers, and the Sheik of the Jews. They send for the Jews, who are inscribed on the list of contribution, four at a time. The rule is, that a Jew cannot send his tax by a friend, clerk, or servant, but must come himself, even if he is ill! Then, when his name is called out, he takes off his shoes, uncovers his head, enters the tent, and crouching before the Governor, puts down his contribution, besides 25 per cent extra, for the Governor and the Cadi's perquisites. He then receives three blows, more or less hard, on the head, from a soldier, with the palm of his hand … He then kisses the hands of all the Arabs who are there, and retires, saying, "May God prolong the life of our Sultan, and give him victory over his enemies!"[67]

Despite capturing the prurient interest of foreigners, the application of the *jizya* and arrangements around its collection were actually quite irregular in Morocco, at least in the periods for which we have records. Displays like the one described above appear to have been the exception. In many areas, it was not the individual but one or a handful of the town's Jews who came up with the required sum and personally delivered it to the pasha. As a rule, if the community did not have the wherewithal to pay its full allotment, the wealthiest members paid it themselves. This pattern is consistent with class stratification among Moroccan Jews, particularly in cities, where there might be a few wealthy families within a community that was otherwise impoverished. Although we find many examples of a leading figure paying the *jizya* in the nineteenth century, when certain Jews grew rich from trading as the protégés for European firms, the ultimate responsibility for payment of the *jizya* lay with each community's *shaykh al-yahud* [*shaykh* of the Jews], the lay leader of the Jews appointed by the sultan. This was established practice dating back to at least the early Alawi period.[68] The *jizya* was a terrible burden, but it could also function advantageously for individuals as a means of demonstrating authority both within the Jewish community and to the Muslim authority.[69] In some cases, aspiring Jewish leaders entreated the sultan to give them the responsibility of collecting and delivering the *jizya*, as they then had the coercive power to collect from poorer Jews in the form of goods and services, if not money.[70] A particularly powerful *shaykh al-yahud* could even use his influence on behalf of other communities, as "the millionaire of the *mellah*," Yeshoua Corcos of Marrakech, did for the Jews of nearby Demnat in 1884.[71] The *jizya* was also preferable to some of the unorthodox arrangements made by the Moroccan government to replace it with other methods of maximizing revenues. This happened in Marrakech, the royal capital where the sultan was in residence at least half the year. As observed by the French doctor William Lemprière during a visit in 1790:

> Those [Jews] of Morocco [Marrakesh] were excused by Sidi Mahomet [Muhammad b. 'Abdullah, 1757–1790] from this tax [*jizya*], upon condition of their taking off his hands, certain articles of merchandize, of which they were to dispose in the best manner they could, paying him five times their original value; by which they become far greater sufferers than if they had submitted to the annual tax.[72]

Such flexibility could also be turned to the Jews' advantage, as when they were able to pay the *jizya* in installments, rather than annually. For example, the *jizya* for Marrakech of 1865–1866 was only partially paid during that year, with the remainder being paid in 1867.[73] Then in the summer of 1887, for reasons that remain unknown but may be connected to an earlier famine, Sultan Mawlay Hassan forgave the *jizya* altogether for 7 years and also excused a debt of grain owed him by the Jews.[74] In 1894, with the cost of reform increasing (see Chapter 4), the *makhzan* demanded that the *jizya* be paid retroactively, and the sultan's local representatives made sure the Jews got a thump on the neck when they delivered it.[75] But the next sultan, Mawlay 'Abd al-'Aziz, seems never to have collected the *jizya* at all, preferring instead to receive "gifts" from the Jews on special occasions.[76]

Despite the centrality of the *jizya* to the finances of the kingdom, special arrangements, accommodations, and even improvisation seem to have been the rule when it came to its enforcement, and not strict adherence to *dhimma*.[77] Although Moroccan officials might have complained when the Jews did not pay it, and, by the nineteenth century at least, European observers complained when they did, there did not appear to be criticism of the improvisation itself by the jurists, which they treated as the prerogative of the ruler. Even if *jizya* can be seen as an example of flexibility on the part of religious authorities, it is still indicative of which way power flowed in the intercommunal relationship between Jews and Muslims in Morocco. The phenomenon of joint saint veneration offers a different view.

The veneration of Jewish Saints in Morocco

Sol (Solika) Hatchuel is a Moroccan saint. There are many versions of her story, but all of the Jewish ones follow the same basic outline: Sol was born in 1817 to a Jewish family in Tangier, a city without a *mellah*, in which Jews and Muslims lived interspersed with one another. Sol had an unhappy family life; she served her mother (or perhaps stepmother) like a slave. She often took refuge from her mother's beatings with her Muslim neighbor and friend, Tahra. During one such instance, Tahra denounced Sol to the authorities, claiming that Sol had converted to Islam but then reverted back to Judaism, which constituted apostasy, a crime punishable by death. Sol denied the charges, but Muslim witnesses contradicted her. Sol sat in the women's prison in Tangier, where she continued to refuse to renounce her Judaism. She was then sent to Fez. There, the sultan himself, having heard of her great beauty, took an interest in her case. (According to a Jewish traveler to Morocco in the mid-nineteenth century: "never had the glowing sun of Africa shone on more perfect beauty."[78]) In Fez, Sol was given every incentive to accept Islam. She was housed in the palace harem and offered sumptuous jewelry and clothing. A rabbi was sent to persuade her to convert to avoid a backlash against the Jewish community; converted Jewish women in the harem tried to persuade her of the wonderful life she could have if she weren't so stubborn. But Sol continued to refuse and was eventually decapitated in a public square in Fez, a scene imagined by the French Orientalist artist Alfred Dehodencq in his 1862 painting "Execution of a Jewess in Morocco." Her remains were returned to the Jewish community, and she was buried in the cemetery of Fez.

Given the circumstances of her martyrdom, it is somewhat surprising that Solika is venerated by Muslims, perhaps even more so today than she is by Jews. Sol, in fact, is the most popular female saint in the entire country. Muslims visit her gravesite in the Jewish cemetery to pray to her; they believe she can cure barrenness, heal sick children, and perform other miracles. As a martyr to her faith, Sol is seen as having *baraka*, a divinely inspired beneficence that connotes special power in Morocco, which Jewish saints are believed to have in abundance. Jewish saints can also be Torah scholars, emissaries from the holy land, or especially pious figures. Nearly every *mellah* has a story of how a rabbi or other leader protected the Jewish quarter from attack: in one case the would-be invaders were turned into dwarves, in another, a swarm of bees or wall of flames suddenly materialized, blocking the entry of the *malfaiteurs*.

Saint veneration picked up considerably in the Protectorate era, thanks to the creation of new infrastructure that made travel between different regions easier. Below is a 1933 description of the pilgrimage to the tomb of Rabbi David Halevi Draa, one of Morocco's most revered saints believed to have died in the fifteenth century:

> A number of Jews knelt and prayed fervently; a large quantity of candles burned slowly. An old man is lying on the ground. He has been in the same place for eight days. He arrived here completely paralyzed. Today he can move. He hopes and expects to make a full recovery. What great faith! Near the tomb is a palm tree, onto which every sick pilgrim ties a piece of cloth which carries the illness. If unfortunately you undo the fragment, you contract the disease another was trying to discard. [… I offered] a short prayer and a bunch of candles, as is the custom.[79]

The tradition of joint saint veneration runs deep in Moroccan culture, but it is a curious tradition on many levels. First and foremost is the matter of sainthood itself within a Jewish or Muslim context, where the legitimacy of the practices surrounding it has been debated with great rigor in the religious discourses of both religious traditions. Both Islam and Judaism are defined by their strict monotheism, whereby God has no intermediaries. Saints are called *wali allah* in Arabic—*wali* for short—meaning one who is a friend of God, a notion that, according to some observers, hints at idolatry.[80] Western scholars used to explain this apparent contradiction by making a distinction between "popular" or "folk" religion and formal religion. In reality, however, the lines were often blurred. Saintly Jewish *piyyutim* [liturgical poems] and other mystically oriented materials fully made their way into Moroccan Judaism to such an extent that they have become defining elements of that tradition. This is obviously a complicated topic, but one is reminded of the distance between canonical ideals and lived experience, both between religions (as in application of *dhimma*) but also *within* religions.

A second puzzling aspect of joint saint veneration is the issue of subverted power differentials. Within the *dhimma* contract, Jews were to be tolerated but were hardly seen as objects worthy of veneration by Muslims. Nonetheless, a detailed study from 1998 shows exactly that. It counts 126 Moroccan Jewish saints that are venerated by Muslims, 36 of whom are jointly venerated by Jews. Not only did Muslims recognize Jewish figures as saints that Jews themselves did not, but they also were more ready to acknowledge venerating saints across religious lines than Jews were (Jews would insist upon Jewish origins of Muslim saints).[81] Saints with a verifiable Muslim identity venerated by Jews were much less common.[82]

This situation may be partly explained by the historical development of Moroccan Islam. As we will see in coming chapters, the rise of the Moroccan state in the sixteenth century was only made possible once Sufism had been weakened enough to fuse it with the traditional religious authority of the ulema,[83] abetted by the well-known saying by Imam Malik: "He who practices *tasawwuf* without learning sacred law corrupts his faith, while he who learns sacred law without practicing *tasawwuf* corrupts himself."[84] The inclusion of Sufism as a defining characteristic of Moroccan Islam had several important effects on Moroccan Jewry. Because Sufism was often a rural phenomenon, it allowed for inroads to be made by Islam in areas that were resistant, namely the southern countryside where Jews were most abundant. It also helped create a religious atmosphere that was highly amenable to the phenomenon of sainthood, where again Jewish traditions were strongly represented. Last, it allowed for traditional power arrangements to occasionally be set aside. According to the folklorist Issachar Ben-Ami:

> Sacred sites possess laws of their own that must be obeyed by all; violation of these laws always evokes punishment. This religious-traditional outlook characterized both Jewish and Muslim society in Morocco, and encouraged everyone to obey those laws irrespective of religious, social, or legal status. Thus it is immaterial that a Jew was a *dhimmi* or disdained and humiliated. The holiness of Jewish saints, particularly when proven to be useful and effective, was itself enough to prompt the Muslims to avail themselves of these saints.[85]

Jews in turn did not hesitate to promote the veneration of their own saints because it helped contribute to their survival in an environment that was sometimes hostile.[86]

It is tempting to view joint saint veneration as a key illustration of Muslim-Jewish symbiosis, particularly given the direction in which influence tended to flow, Jew to Muslim rather than vice versa as is usually the case in majority-minority relations. And to an extent, it is. But there are also mitigating factors that complicate this phenomenon and may make it less romantic, though no less meaningful. To begin with, the joint veneration of saints is typically based on conflicting narratives that turn on the question of whether the individual is "really" Jewish or Muslim. According to Maliki tradition, persuading a non-Muslim to convert to Islam is among the most highly regarded deeds. For Muslim adherents, then, Sol and many others like her are understood to have completed their conversions and died as Muslims. Such hagiographies are plentiful. In one notable example, a Jewish man with a beautiful voice is forced by the sultan to be a *muezzin*, or one who recites the call to prayer. According to the Jewish tale, he throws himself off the minaret *before* reciting the *shahada* (proclamation of faith); in the Muslim telling, he jumps just after, hence dying as a Muslim. The disagreement over narratives is so severe that committed Muslims have been known to steal the remains of saints from Jewish cemeteries and have them reburied in Muslim ones—or even murder a living saint so that he may be given a Muslim burial.[87]

As Jews began leaving Morocco in the 1950s, they faced a very real threat of losing their saints as the latter were subsumed into Muslim culture. That trend has been slowed by the regular return of many Jews to Morocco as pilgrims. The annual *hillula* (pl. *hillulot*), as the pilgrimage is called, usually takes place around the Jewish holiday of Lag b'Omer or on the birthday of a particular saint.[88] Pilgrims camp out at the saint's tomb to pray, sing, eat, drink, and sleep. In the absence of Jewish pilgrims the rest of the year, Muslim caretakers preserve these sites. They maintain the cemeteries where the saints are buried and open the gates to visitors. (Many of these *"gardiens"* speak smatterings of Hebrew and are familiar with the prayers and practices of the *hillulot*.) The economic (and spiritual) benefits that accrue to them as a result are likely to keep the tradition going for some time to come.

In the three cases discussed above—the destruction of the Touati Jews, *jizya* payment, and joint saint veneration—the flexible attitude of Malikism in Morocco was complemented by the Jewish *halakhic* precept *dina de-malkhuta dina*: the law of the land (in which one lives) is binding, even if, in some cases, it contradicts Jewish law. In contrast to the Maliki imperative for Muslims to emigrate from non-Muslim lands, Jewish law gave its adherents unambiguous permission to adapt, as is consistent with their minority position.[89] In the legal sphere, this willingness to adapt ran deep in Morocco, where Jews regularly availed themselves of the Islamic courts, particularly when they did not agree with the rulings of the Jewish courts. Women were especially prone to seek justice where they could find it, since Islamic rules on divorce and inheritance were often more beneficial to them than Jewish ones. Over time, these patterns of "court shopping" developed into a true legal plurality, whereby Jewish and Islamic courts were joined by *makhzan* and European consular courts to create a wide arena of legal and in turn social possibilities.[90]

Conclusion

In the century following the death of Muhammad in 632, the Muslim community spread in all directions to create one of the largest empires known to the late antique world. Despite their many triumphs, the Muslim conquerors were tested repeatedly as they extended their realm. Chief among the challenges they faced was how to deal with the conquered peoples themselves, who for centuries would remain in the majority. Islamizing the conquered peoples was far from a top priority (popular conceptions to the contrary, there is no evidence of a concerted effort or plan to do so). They were more absorbed with preventing their own adherents from acculturating to the new, sometimes quite attractive, societal norms they encountered in foreign territories. Economically, meanwhile, they had to find ways to exploit the conquered people enough to provide for communal needs, but not past the point of subsistence so as to ensure continued economic growth. Under the evolving rules of the new religion, Jews (and other specified religious minorities) were accorded the status of "*dhimma*," a legal identity denoting a "tolerated" minority with specific rights—including the right to practice their own, pre-Islamic religions—that were also subject to a certain set of restrictions. *Dhimma* was discriminatory in the truest sense of the word: it was intended to distinguish (*ghiyar*) between Muslims and non-Muslims. While the former were clearly the more privileged, *dhimma* was still a relatively progressive framework compared to other majority-minority arrangements of the period. *Dhimma* represented a worldview in which Muslims and Islam were clearly superior, with the added expectation that Jews and Christians would eventually come around; hence the non-Muslim "other" was to be tolerated until that time came. That tolerance became permanent.

Well into the twentieth century, the term *dhimma* was a common refrain in Muslim discourse concerning Jews in Morocco. However, *dhimma* as a legal device did not function the same in all times and places in Morocco, let alone across the vast Islamic world. It was subject to interpretation by individual jurists and varied widely in its application. As Islam established deeper roots in Morocco, there was a discernible move away from a generalized practice of *dhimma* toward a specifically Moroccan one, characterized by flexibility toward Jews. Within that flexibility lay the potential for lapse. These moments are often interpreted as a positive event for the Jews, as when the *jizya* could be ignored or postponed. But we should not lose sight of the fact that, in the pre-Protectorate period, *dhimma* functioned as a bulwark against institutionalized persecution, something European Jews mostly lacked much to their detriment. When the Almohads came to power in the twelfth century and (temporarily) abolished *dhimma* along with many other aspects of the Maliki tradition, religious minorities were put in extreme danger; the indigenous Christians did not survive. The reestablishment of *dhimma* can only have come as a great relief.

In the late fifteenth century, the Tlemceni *qadi* al-Maghili based his decision to destroy the Tamantit synagogue on his claim that the Jews there had abrogated the Pact of 'Umar. Maintaining the Pact was clearly to Jews' advantage in this case as well. There is little doubt that in fully historicized, comparative terms, *dhimma* in its Maliki manifestation proved to be a useful mechanism to ensure the continuation of Jewish life in Morocco.[91]

Moving from Morocco back to the larger Islamic context with which this chapter began, we can conclude that the lands of the Middle East and North Africa were not construed as mere "host" societies for Jews, the way that Europe is sometimes described in Jewish histories. Jews were not simply "tolerated" strangers in Islamicate societies; they were fully embodied members, whose rights and obligations were deeply encoded in scripture and regularly articulated in legal procedures and social situations. To be sure, Jews were not "equal" members of these societies (another term that held little meaning at the time); they were to be discriminated against for having been shown the truth of Islam and yet refused it, but they were not to be barred from practicing their religion or forced to convert. Although this was a narrow window, it proved wide enough to allow Jewish life to continue to develop, and in many cases flourish, under Islamic rule.

Chapter 2: Timeline

740	Great Berber Revolt
744–1058	Barghawata independent state
1047	Almoravids establish capital at Aghmat
1062/1070	Almoravids establish capital at Marrakech
1145	Fall of Almoravids
1147–1269	Almohad Era
1160	Moses Maimonides settles in Fez
1244–1465	Marinid Era
1464	Aaron b. Battash named Marinid prime minister
1472–1554	Wattasid Era

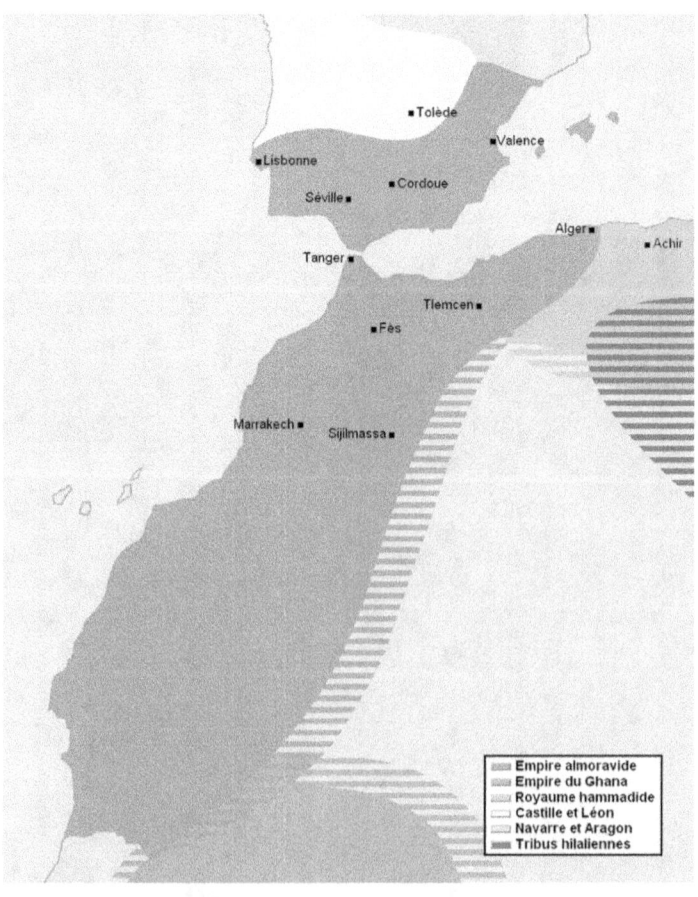

Map 2.1 Almoravid era Morocco.

Tounsi, Omar. "Map of the Almoravid Empire at Its Maximum Extension." Digital image. Wikimedia Commons. February 19, 2012. Accessed May 6, 2019. https://fr.wikipedia.org/wiki/Histoire_du_Maroc#/media/File:Empire_almoravide.PNG.

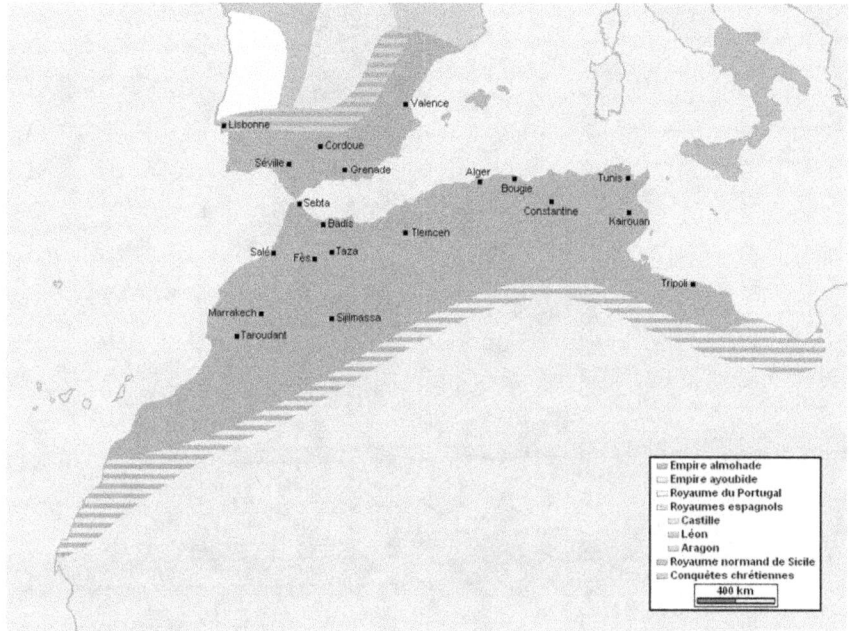

Map 2.2 Almohad era Morocco.

Tounsi, Omar. "Map of the Almohad Empire." Digital image. Wikimedia Commons. February 19, 2012. Accessed May 6, 2019. https://fr.wikipedia.org/wiki/Histoire_du_Maroc#/media/File:Empire_almohade.PNG.

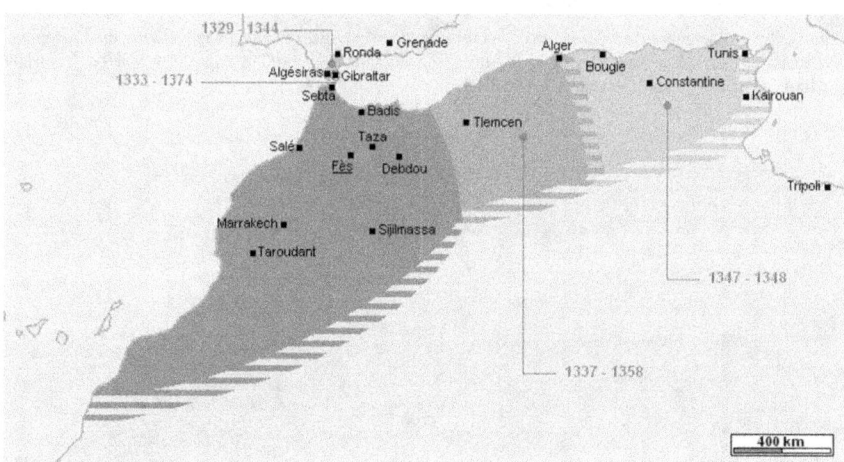

Map 2.3 Marinid era Morocco.

Tounsi, Omar. "Map of the Merinide Empire and Its Extensions." Digital image. Wikimedia Commons. February 14, 2012. Accessed May 6, 2019. https://fr.wikipedia.org/wiki/Histoire_du_Maroc#/media/File:Empire_mérinide_-_XIVe.PNG.

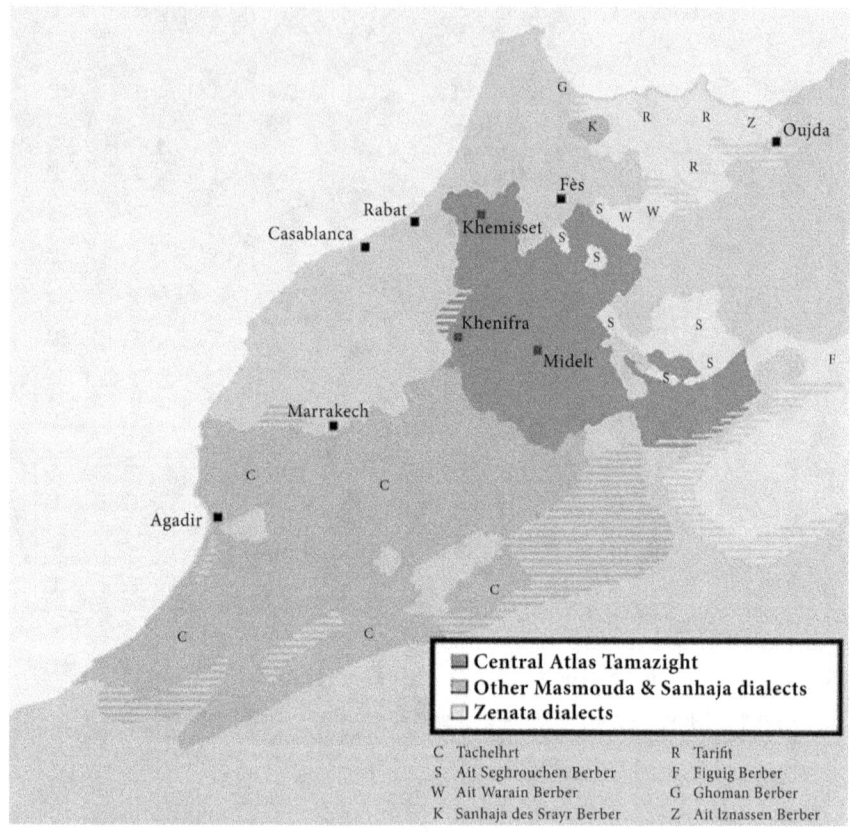

Map 2.4 Central Atlas Tamazight.

Tounsi, Omar. "Language Areas in Morocco—Tamazight Central Atlas." Digital image. Wikimedia Commons. December 25, 2011. Accessed May 6, 2019. https://ca.wikipedia.org/wiki/Tamazight_del_Marroc_Central#/media/File:Central_Atlas_Tamazight_-_EN.PNG.

2

Amazighity
"Berber" Morocco—A Jewish History (Eleventh–Fifteenth Centuries)

> Arabic is the official language of the State. […] Likewise, Tamazight constitutes an official language of the State, being common patrimony of all Moroccans without exception.
>
> —Article 5 of the Moroccan Constitution, 2011

> Scratch a Moroccan, find a Berber.
> Scratch a Berber, find a Jew.
>
> —David Hart/Berber activist[1]

Introduction: "Righteous Berbers"

In November 2009, a group of Moroccan schoolteachers of Amazigh background made an official visit to Israel. They went in order to take part in a holocaust education program formulated specially for them. Their trip was funded by the Adelson Family Foundation, an American Jewish organization known for its conservative views on American and Israeli politics. According to the Moroccan group's leader, "The purpose of the seminar—the first of its kind—was to get to know the history of the Jewish people and to renew the close connections between Jews and the Berbers, a relationship that dates back more than 3,000 years."[2] The eighteen Moroccans who traveled to Israel met with journalists and politicians, including government ministers who were themselves originally from Morocco or of Moroccan heritage. The highlight of the teachers' trip was a visit to *Yad Vashem*, the holocaust memorial museum in Jerusalem. At the museum, the Moroccans were told the stories of

Albanian Muslims who risked their lives to save Jews during the Holocaust. The museum calls such non-Jewish heroes "righteous gentiles" and memorializes them in a special section dedicated to their actions. As the director of the International School for the Study of the Holocaust remarked, "Teaching about the Holocaust to citizens of Muslim countries is an absolutely critical task of the International School." This attitude on the part of Israeli officialdom is not difficult to understand. On the one hand, the Islamic world is the main locus for overt expressions of anti-Semitism today; hence identifying and promoting sympathetic Muslim emissaries is a logical way to combat it.[3] At the same time, there are strategic interests at stake for Israel in cultivating citizen-to-citizen diplomacy among countries not normally considered potential allies. With most Arab countries (except Morocco) politically out of range for its diplomatic entreaties, Israel has long compensated by concentrating its efforts on other regional powers, from prerevolutionary Iran to contemporary Turkey, as well as to certain MENA minorities (Kurds, Yazidis, etc.) to offset the official antipathy toward Israel of many Arab-Muslim governments.

Given the above considerations, Israel's support for the visit is easy enough to comprehend. But what about the schoolteachers themselves? Why have some Amazigh Muslim activists gone out of their way to make overtures to Israel, often at considerable personal and professional risk?[4] Like their Israeli counterparts, the actions of these Amazigh Muslims are probably motivated by a combination of humanistic impulses and realpolitik expedience. Many Amazigh Muslims are quick to express a shared cultural legacy with Moroccan Jews, and even a shared ancestry, lending an emotional resonance to the forging of these links. Many Amazigh groups also lean toward secularism.[5] At the same time, for the Amazigh activist, Israel is a convenient ally in the struggle against a common enemy. Arab-Islamic hegemony—once resisted by the Berber Queen Kahina—today takes the form of Islamist currents like those of Morocco's Justice and Development Party (PJD) on the one hand and pan-Arabist supporters of the *makhzan* on the other. An alliance with Jews, and by extension with Israel, helps counterbalance these threats. To invoke a Middle Eastern cliché, the current rapprochement between Amazigh activists and Moroccan Jews is a case of the enemy of my enemy being my friend.

In the winter of 2010–2011, against this background of Amazigh interfaith conciliation, the so-called Arab spring burst into being, catapulting Amazighity to the forefront of North African politics for the first time since the colonial period. The centrality of Amazigh demands to the revolts in North Africa caused the very term used for the uprising to be called into serious question.[6] In Tunisia and Libya, Amazigh activists pushed back against the Arab hegemon in the form of Zine El Abidine b. Ali or Muammar Qaddafi respectively, both of whom had repeatedly denied that Berbers even existed in their countries.[7] In Morocco, the February 20 movement demanded that the government implement old promises to end Amazigh marginalization once and for all. In 2001, some early moves in this direction had been made with the establishment of the Royal Institute of Amazigh Culture in Rabat (IRCAM). In 2003, IRCAM introduced the Tifanigh alphabet to transcribe the Tamazight language, which began appearing on public signs; shortly thereafter a census was held in which Tamazight speakers could identify themselves as such for the first time. Tamazight began to be taught in public schools at this time as well. But it was only with the 2011 uprising and the new constitution it inspired that Tamazight became "an" official language in Morocco (compared to Arabic, "the" official language), and the country's Amazigh patrimony "in which we all share" was duly recognized.

While much progress has been made, the full measure of "dignity and justice" demanded by the Imazighen activists has yet to be achieved. Heavily Amazigh areas of Morocco, like the Rif Mountain area, remain egregiously underserved and underdeveloped; this situation led to violent protests in the summer of 2017. The entrenchment of the Amazigh struggle in Morocco has served to redouble interest in Jewish compatriots who can be enlisted as potential allies. Moroccan Jews' perceived success at raising awareness about their history, culture, and values is a model for Imazighen. And indeed, the "Jewish question" and the "Berber question" are to a great extent two sides of the same coin when it comes to the recalibrations of Moroccan identity taking place in the wake of the so-called Arab spring.[8]

While Moroccan Jews have generally been receptive to the entreaties of the Amazigh activists, the meaning of Amazighity in Jewish Morocco is ultimately of a different nature. Though by no means devoid of political content for Jews, Amazighity for them is less about obtaining rights than it is about where one situates oneself amidst the panoply of available ethnic ascriptions in Jewish Morocco: Amazigh, Arab, Sephardic/Andalusian, and/or European, each with its own set of social connotations and, in all but the last category, Muslim counterparts. Above all, for Moroccan Jews, Amazighity is a way of grounding their identity in the Moroccan soil, both literally, in the sense that the Imazighen are generally a rural population and Morocco is one of the few places where Jews in large numbers were rural dwellers too, but also, perhaps especially, in the sense of Amazigh autochthony. Regardless of whether they personally identify as *toshavim* [indigenous, non-Sephardic] or not, Moroccan Jews are quick to point out that Judaism arrived in

North Africa well before the Arabs brought Islam to Northwest Africa and that Jews commingled with the indigenous populations in the pre-Islamic era. What benefits accrue to this origin story? What does it reveal about how ethnicity functions in Jewish Morocco? These questions will guide the inquiry into Amazighity and its significance to Jewish Morocco of the present chapter. At the same time, a focus on Amazighity moves our chronology forward from the Arab conquests treated in the last chapter to the five centuries of rule by Amazigh dynasties [c. 1060–1554] that followed, preceded by a brief foray into pre-Islamic Morocco.

For complex historical reasons, North Africa's Imazighen were unable to completely resist the Arabization that came along with Islam, at least not as effectively as did the major ethnic groups in the Middle East, like the Turks and Persians, who managed to retain their ethnic identities even while submitting as Muslims. And yet, Morocco until today has never been fully Arabized. It remains endowed with an indelible Amazigh character, reflected in all manner of local beliefs and practices and in the fact that Tamazight never disappeared as a spoken language.[9] The Islamization of Morocco is itself commonly understood as having taken place not via the Arab conquests but through a sort of internal colonization by successive Amazigh dynasties: the Almoravids (1060–1147), the Almohads (1145–1269), and the Marinid-Wattasids (1248–1465). As one scholar has noted, Islam's very success was "because the vehicles of transmission were Berbers, authentic members of the Maghrib, not groups derived from the Middle East and thus linguistically and culturally alien."[10] Though they mostly resisted Islamization, Jews, as an autochthonous population, nonetheless share this identity as "authentic members of the Maghrib." They too helped form and in turn were formed by changing conceptions of Amazighity in Morocco, as much as by changing attitudes toward Jewish Morocco under four centuries of Amazigh rule.

Origin myths (and countermyths) in Jewish Morocco

Amazighity is foundational to North Africa; it is arguably the single socio-ethnic characteristic that most distinguishes the Maghrib from the Middle East. Amazigh settlements stretch from the Atlantic coast of Northwest Africa to the Siwa oasis in Egypt and exist nowhere east of the Nile. Within this area, Imazighen live in the highest concentrations in Morocco, where they are commonly divided into three main groups: Masmuda, Sanhaja, and Zenata. They have come to be known collectively by the term "Amazigh/Imazighen," meaning free person, with the related term "Tamazight" denoting the Amazigh language,[11] and "Tamazgha," a geographic imaginary covering much of northern Africa including everywhere Imazighen are thought to have lived. The Roman word "Berber," while common, is considered pejorative.[12] While the overwhelming majority of Moroccans are of Amazigh descent, officially, approximately 40–60 percent of the population identify as Imazighen. Out of a total of 35 million Moroccans, 12 to 13 million people speak Tamazight as their first language. The majority of those also speak some Arabic or are fully bilingual, while a small minority are monolingual Tamazight speakers.

Jews and Imazighen come together in local reckonings of humanity's most distant past. Some myths tie the Imazighen to biblical history in the holy land, either as the supposed progeny of the patriarch Noah who fled West before the flood or as Philistines who absconded from Canaan after Goliath was defeated by David.[13] Other stories place Jews in North Africa much earlier than the historical evidence currently supports: the Jonah story is sometimes relocated to the coasts of Morocco; Joab's tomb is believed to be in Tazzarine in southern Morocco.[14] A more plausible if still unsubstantiated origin story is that Hebrews arrived in North Africa in the ninth century BCE in the company of Phoenicians from the Levant, who built a capital in Carthage (today's Tunisia) and set about establishing trading outposts along the Mediterranean coast. Conservative assessments based on archeological finds of a Jewish candelabrum and Hebrew gravestones in Volubilis, just outside today's Meknes, place Jewish settlement in North Africa with certainty by the second temple period, ending in c. 70 CE. Thus one of the few definitive stories related to Jewish origins in Morocco is that Jewish settlement most certainly predated the arrival of Islam in Morocco, keeping in mind that what constituted Judaism and Islam were not as clearly defined in that era as they are today.[15]

Unfortunately, information about the initial Jewish encounter with the indigenous population of Morocco is very slight. In the absence of conclusive evidence, various myths have arisen to fill the void. A particularly tenacious one is the idea that Moroccan Jews are in fact Imazighen who converted en masse to monotheism/Judaism during the pre-Islamic period.[16] In some iterations, this population then converts to Islam with the arrival of the new religion, while in others they remain Jews. Either way, Jews and Judaism are given local roots inextricable from the Imazighen. The myth of a common origin appeals to the Amazigh activists pursuing common cause with Zionists, as mentioned at the beginning of this chapter; it is also useful to proponents of Muslim-Jewish coexistence as an ancient undergirding for the contemporary idea of Moroccan "tolerance" and diversity.

Despite its persistence, there is little if any concrete evidence for the idea of a shared origin between Jews and Imazighen in the pre-Islamic period. Arab Muslim authors asserted the possibility of Judaized tribes in North Africa from at least the fourteenth century, often basing their claims on still earlier accounts. According to the author of the 1326 chronicle *rawd al-qirtas*, Jews were members of the (Amazigh) Banu Zanata during the time of Idris, founder of the city of Fez (r. 788–791).¹⁷ Likewise writing a good seven centuries after the fact, Ibn Khaldun offered a more detailed, if cautious, proposition:

> It is also possible that some of these [tribes of] Berbers adhered to the Jewish religion, which they had adopted from the Children of Israel at the time of the expansion of their kingdom to the vicinity of Syria and their rule over it. This may have been the case with the Jarawa, the people of the Aures mountains, the tribe of the Kahina, who was killed by the Arabs at the beginning of the conquest. This may also have been the case with the Nafusa, of the Berbers in Africa, and with the Fandalawa, the Madyuna, the Bahlula, the Ghayata, and the Banu Fazaz, until Idris the Great, who shone in the *maghrib*, of the Banu Hasan b. Hasa, wiped out all the remnants of the religions and communities that were in the region.¹⁸

But there is a countermyth to consider as well: the supposition that Moroccan Jews arrived from the Middle East at a given moment in the distant past but remained entirely endogamous, and did not mix with the local population.¹⁹ The idea of Jewish "purity" helps account for the small number of Jews overall in Morocco and also preserves the ideal (if not necessarily the reality) of Judaism as a non-universalist, non-proselytizing religion. It may also appeal to some elements of the urban Moroccan Jewish elite, who would not relish being associated with rural peoples, reflecting the larger anti-Amazigh bias in the Moroccan urban population. Significantly, nowhere in the early Jewish sources is there any mention of a common Jewish-Amazigh origin.²⁰ Despite that glaring absence, the idea of a shared origin was readily picked up in the European literature. Based on the problematic work of the Jewish scholar Nahum Slouschz in particular (see Chapter 4), colonial ethnographies repeat the idea of shared origins *ad nauseum*. This is not surprising when one considers its usefulness to colonial policy. That is, the idea of a pre-Islamic shared origin of Jews and Imazighen provided corollary support for France's *politique berbère*, which sought to divide and conquer Morocco by separating Imazighen from Arabs on the one hand and Jews from Muslims on the other. The "Berber Jew" served both goals simultaneously.²¹ With this linkage, the idea of Amazigh authenticity and indigeneity could be reinforced at the expense of the Arab-Muslim "interloper."²² Nor was this simply a romantic notion based on Orientalist fantasies; the separating out of the Imazighen was also concretely institutionalized under the French Protectorate. In 1927, the College of Azrou was founded in order to help form an Amazigh elite that would help France implement its divide and rule policies.[23] We might recall that separate Jewish schools had likewise existed in Morocco since 1862 via the Alliance Israélite Universelle, including many in the rural south where the Imazighen were concentrated. In contrast, only a small number of Franco-Muslim schools existed for the children of "Arab notables." France's *politique berbère* culminated in the so-called Berber *dahir* [edict] of 1930, which sought to establish a separate legal system for Imazighen based on the assumption that their attachment to customary law was deeper than their attachment to *shari'a* and that their ethnic identity trumped their religious allegiances.[24] In May of 1918 a similar type of *dahir* reorganizing Jewish legal institutions had been promulgated (See Chapter 4).[25] Although the "Jewish dahir" caused nothing like the backlash that the "Berber dahir" did, both edicts worked to institutionalize Jewish and Amazigh separateness to the detriment of social and political cohesion.

Moroccan Jewish ethnicity

The lack of a definitive shared origin does not preclude a deep ethnic identification between Jews and Muslims in Amazigh areas. "Ethnicity" may be a loose amalgam, but it is not reducible to one's origin or, in contemporary terms, one's DNA. According to Susan Gilson Miller and Katherine Hoffman, ethnicity in Morocco is "a historically contingent construct whose characteristics fluctuate but may include such factors as shared language, expressive material culture, beliefs, customs, social organizations, norms, or shared ancestry."[26] There is every indication that Jews shared in Amazigh cultures of the Atlas, the Draa, the Sous, and the Rif in most if not all of these terms. Yet we would do well to remember that Moroccan Jews were not always one "community" in the sense that the term conveys today; rather, Moroccan Jews cohered into a semi-unified whole over time, with difficulty, and with the persistence of many local specificities. It is this diversity that gives Moroccan Jewish culture its richness, as can be seen in the delicate Berberisca dresses worn by Jewish women in Tetuan, Tangier, and Larache or the horsehair wigs worn by brides in the Atlas or the heavy silver jewelry and headpieces of the Tafilalt; in the *Hakétia* spoken in the north of the country as opposed to the Tamazight spoken in the Atlas Mountains and the Arabic in between and all over. Roughly drawn, these differences correspond to the division between the *megorashim* and the *toshavim*; in ethnic terms, Sephardic and Amazigh/Arab. But like many binaries in Jewish history, this one can use some unpacking.[27] The arrival of Sephardic Jews to Morocco will be treated in the next chapter; for now, our focus will remain with the *toshavim*, and among them the Jews whose participation in Amazigh culture provided the foundation for Moroccan Jewish ethnicity.

Language

The ethnic identity of Jewish Morocco prior to the arrival of the Sephardim was expressed on the most basic level in shared language, though the linguistic situation of Jewish Morocco was shifting and dynamic, with most Jews having at least some familiarity with at least two if not three or four languages, using an admixture of expressions from each as needed. The main language groups of Jewish Morocco were Hebrew, Tamazight, and Arabic (Spanish and French would come later).

As elsewhere, Hebrew was the liturgical language of the Jews, the language of the Torah, parts of the Talmud, and the prayer book. It was the language used by the rabbis to answer intricate and sometimes arcane legal queries (*takkanot*), like whether an unmarried daughter could inherit from her parents or under what circumstances a widow was required to marry her late spouse's brother.[28] Hebrew was the language of marriage contracts (*kettuba/kettubot*) and amulets;[29] its very letters were endowed with sacredness; anything written in Hebrew could not be thrown away but must be deposited in a *geniza* and buried like a human body.[30] Hebrew was usually written using the semi-cursive Rashi script. Though it was taught to men exclusively, in oral usage it extended to women and children. Sacred poetry like *mizmor l'david* were known and sung by the whole household on Shabbat and other occasions, as they are throughout the Jewish world today. As the language of high religious culture, Hebrew publications were imported to Morocco from Europe and the Middle East, and for a short time in 1516 Morocco even had its own Hebrew printing press. (Hebrew printing was revived in Tangier in the late 1890s, when it was used by the Moroccan *maskilim*, the poets and writers of the Jewish renaissance.[31])

Hebrew could also be used in a pinch to communicate with Jews in other parts of the world, and not only about religious matters. Business and marital arrangements could be contracted using Hebrew between Moroccan Jews and those in far-flung places. The Cairo Geniza collection offers at least two such examples. The first concerns a silversmith named Ephraim

b. Ishaq, originally from Ceuta, in northern Morocco, but who had fled to Egypt when the Almohads came to power. Ephraim describes himself as a "foreigner" in Egypt despite having lived there for 15 years. In the letter in question, he asks the addressee, also of Moroccan origin, for charity. The letter dates from 1181. It opens in Hebrew, and includes a poem (lines 3–8), before switching to Judeo-Arabic.[32] In a second such example, from 1228, a doctor from Fustat (Cairo) named El'azar ha-Levi b. Tiqva ha-Levi requests that power of attorney be granted to a local judge to ask a woman in Marrakesh, one Yamun bat 'Eli b. Joseph, for her hand in marriage on his behalf.[33] The letter is in Hebrew, the signatures in Arabic. From these few examples, it is clear that Hebrew had utility beyond the religious sphere for Moroccan Jews.

Significantly, Moroccan Jews' knowledge of the Hebrew script also afforded them a path to literacy in Moroccan Arabic (*darija*) that Muslims themselves generally lacked. Though they did so with a Jewish accent,[34] the majority of Moroccan Jews spoke *darija* as their first language, even in Amazigh areas.[35] They called it "*al-'arabiya diyalna*" ("our Arabic") as distinct from the Arabic of the Muslims. Spoken Arabic was an essential tool for Jews conducting commerce and petty trade in Morocco's cities and towns. But using the Hebrew script, Jews also wrote in *darija*. Literate Muslims, meanwhile, did not write in Arabic dialect. Instead, they mostly obeyed the diglossic nature of the Arabic language and spoke in *darija* but wrote in classical or standard Arabic, a language with which most Moroccan Jews would be unfamiliar since it was traditionally taught in religious settings, using the Arabic script.[36]

The Judeo-Arabic that resulted from this interpenetration was much more than a vernacular; it was also the language of serious intellectual production. One of the earliest and most famous works in Maghribi Judeo-Arabic is the ninth-century *risala* [letter] to the Jews of Fez by Judah b. Quraysh. The text is an ambitious comparative philology of Semitic languages, including Arabic, Aramaic, and Hebrew. And to the extent that his brief sojourn in Fez allows him to be categorized as Moroccan, Maimonides wrote almost entirely in Judeo-Arabic, including his monumental *Guide of the Perplexed*. As the social anthropologist Oren Kosansky points out: "For centuries, written Judeo-Arabic had functioned alongside Hebrew as a medium of philosophical speculation, rabbinic regulation, hagiographic narrative, jurisprudential opinion, legal judgment, personal correspondence, commercial transaction, liturgical composition, and communal governance."[37] To that list one can add modern literary works, at least from the late nineteenth century, when Judeo-Arabic presses in Morocco flourished alongside Modern Standard Arabic and Hebrew ones as the MENA region as a whole experienced the Arabic literary renaissance known as the *nahda*.[38]

Tamazight, or "Judeo-Berber" ("Tamazight-Tudayt" in Tamazight), was an oral language of the Jews in Morocco's mountainous regions and pre-Saharan oases. It was used widely in many of the same ways that Moroccan Arabic dialect was used in non-Amazigh areas: for commerce, for some prayers, for oral explanations of religious texts, for songs, poetry, and storytelling. Despite their knowledge of Tamazight, Jews in Amazigh regions were rarely if ever monolingual Tamazight speakers. A few isolated communities in the area of Tifnout below Mount Toubkal appear to have been the exception that proves the rule.[39] Nor did Jews who spoke Tamazight *write* in Tamazight. Before the arrival of Europeans in Morocco, Judeo-Arabic was the primary written language among all Moroccan Jews who wrote, not just those of Arabic-speaking regions.

The linguistic portrait of Jewish Morocco is in no way an orderly one, where each group speaks its "own" language. Instead, there is so much overlap and so many surprising patterns that linguists have sometimes been left scratching their heads, beginning with the question of where Tamazight itself originates.[40] As for surprises, the folklorist Sarah Levin has found that Jews in certain Amazigh contexts purposely used Arabic, the language of Islam, as a means of differentiating themselves from their (Amazigh) Muslim neighbors, thus marking Arabic as a specifically Jewish as opposed to a Muslim language in those regions.[41] Jewish Morocco was a place of multilingual code-switchers in a linguistic context that freely mixed orality with literacy and sacred with profane. A testament to its ethnolinguistic diversity can be seen on the tombstone of one of its best-known products, the writer Edmond Amran El Maleh (1917–2010). El Maleh was born in the coastal town of Safi and spent much of his adult life in France but returned to Morocco and began writing at the age of 63. Although he wrote in French, the themes he dealt with most often reflected his multidimensional heritage. His grave lies in the old section of the Jewish cemetery of Essaouira, closest to the wall and the Atlantic Ocean just beyond. As he himself described this cemetery "all these graves which, exposed to the rank growth, the wind, and the ravages of the ocean, silently enclose the Hebrew inscriptions and mysterious symbols."[42] Following El Maleh's instructions, his tombstone is inscribed in the letters of four languages: Tamazight, Hebrew, Arabic, and French (Latin).

Ethnicity in Jewish Morocco was also expressed in a variety of material and nonmaterial ways that complement language. Again, these expressions—

foodways, music, and artisanry—typically constituted variations on the broader Muslim theme rather than separate cultural practices.

Foodways of Jewish Morocco

Moroccan Jewish foodways shared many characteristics with the preferences, ingredients, preparations, and consumption patterns of Moroccan Muslims. To begin with, the country they shared was extremely fertile. Depending on the region and weather, all manner of produce was available. In terms of fruit, grapes, apples, pears, peaches, melons, figs, dates, and citrus of all kinds might be ripe; grazing grounds for animals was ample; nuts, sugarcane, and olives were widely used; and all the vegetables of the Mediterranean were plentiful. Herbs and spices were in wide usage everywhere: cumin, cinnamon, paprika, turmeric, pepper, and coriander, plus preserved lemons and cilantro ("Arab parsley") for added taste. Still, each region had its specialities: Tangier and Tetuan's cuisine had more Spanish influence, and, as with the entire coastal region, more fish; dried meat (*khlii*) was common in rural areas where food preservation was challenging. Both Jews and Muslims ate couscous on special occasions, lamb on holidays, and relied on legumes as well as chicken and beef for protein. Meat was often prepared with dried fruit, and both Jews and Muslims abstained from eating pork. With the exception of the Sabbath bread, which was chewier from the use of extra water, they baked the same breads and enjoyed the same cookies and cakes on festive occasions. Mint tea, that quintessentially Moroccan beverage (at least from the late eighteenth century when green gunpowder tea and refined sugar became widely available), was enjoyed by all who could afford it.

But foodways could function as a barrier as well as a bridge; indeed that was the implicit purpose of *kashrut*, Jewish dietary law. The laws of *kashrut* enforced a clear line between Jews and non-Jews on a daily basis. They required that the meat Jews consumed be slaughtered and butchered according to religious specifications: salting, draining the animal's blood, saying special prayers, and so on. Although some schools of Islamic law make exceptions that allow Muslims to eat kosher meat if *halal* meat is unavailable, the reverse was not the case: Jewish law does not permit the consumption of *halal* meat expept perhaps in matters of extreme scarcity. (In conversations with Moroccan Muslims, this habit of their former neighbors is well remembered.) Certain distinctively Moroccan dishes like *seffa* that mixed butter with chicken or other meat could only be found in Muslim homes. This is because Jews were also uniquely prohibited from mixing meat and milk together in a single meal. Even if the meat was kosher, it could not be mixed with dairy products of any kind. Moroccan Jews' most characteristic dishes were the result of the rules of the Sabbath when no active cooking could take place for twenty-four hours, like the famous *dafina* (alt. *t'fina*; also called *skhina*, "hot"). This slow-cooked stew would be buried in coals or left at the neighborhood oven before sundown on Friday to cook overnight and be picked up in time for lunch on Saturday (Muslims would kindle the fire). As Claudia Roden notes, the Sabbath stew in all its varieties was famous throughout the MENA: "Every community had its own special recipe using meat (often meatloaf), chicken, stuffed intestine, calf's foot, potatoes, sweet potatoes, chickpeas, beans, broad beans, rice, and hard-boiled eggs in their shells. Some very original dishes resulted: for example, in Morocco a chicken stuffed with dates and marzipan, or with quince."[43]

Although the differences in cuisine were slight in terms of ingredients and preparations, the underlying strictures were significant enough that Jews and Muslims generally did not eat together. But their foodways still contributed to their interdependence. Jews relied on Muslims to help them surmount some of the restrictions of the Sabbath and the holidays; Muslims tended the cooking fires for Jews when they were forbidden to and supplied Jews with leavened foods for their first meal after Passover (Mimouna). Muslims were less dependent on Jews, but, as we will see in later chapters, Jews supplied them with certain imported foods and, significantly, with alcohol. Moroccan Jews made and consumed alcohol and Muslims did not, at least according to religious and social prohibitions. Moroccan Jews were especially famous for their *mahiya*, a strong eau-de-vie distilled from figs or other fruits. Jews also blessed and drank wine in accordance with many religious ceremonies. (Vineyards became a key component of colonial agriculture in North Africa.) If Muslims wanted to consume alcohol in Morocco, it was no secret that they went to the Jewish quarter to find it.[44]

Music in Jewish Morocco

As the historian Chris Silver has noted, "There is no North African history without music and there is no Maghribi musical past without Jews."[45] Music punctuated all stages of life in Jewish Morocco, and it is often what Muslims most remember about Jews.[46] Like all other cultural artifacts of Jewish Morocco, however, music was never static in either form or function. It accompanied activities from the most mundane—housework, toiling in workshops, cooking—to the most exalted: the singing of psalms for the Sabbath or the accompaniment of an Andalusian orchestra at a wealthy couple's wedding. As in many areas of Jewish Moroccan culture, Sephardic elements came to dominate the musical scene.[47] Certainly the liturgical poems of Andalusian luminaries like Judah Halevi, Solomon Ibn Gabirol, and Moses Ibn Ezra were deeply ingrained in the musical repertoire. But Amazigh areas maintained distinctive musical forms as well. Sung poetry duels were an important conduit for communication and easing tension in Amazigh villages in the Atlas Mountains, with Jews trading insults with Muslims in ways that could never be risked in other contexts.[48] A special musical event in Amazigh areas was the *ahwash* a large communal dance performed out of doors.[49] The *ahwash* involved all the men and women of the village. They were accompanied by singing and drumming to celebrate rites of passage of the villagers, like weddings or circumcisions.[50] There is evidence from several Amazigh areas in Morocco (Tifnout, Tidili, Ait Bou Oulli, Ighil n'Ogho) that Jews participated in the *ahwash* alongside Muslims as both spectators and as participants.[51] They sang, danced, and improvised lyrics alongside their Muslim neighbors. According to some Imazighen, the presence of Jews—particularly Jewish women dancers—was a requirement for a successful *ahwash*.[52] Amazigh influence is also present in the cantorial practices of Moroccan Jewry, as noted in a recent interview with the ethnomusicologist Samuel Torjman Thomas:

> Perhaps the most apparent musical element illuminating an Amazigh past is found in the Moroccan *ḥazzan*'s [cantor's] approach to rhythm. An incessant, driving twelve-beat cycle has found its way into many places during synagogue services. For example, during the *kedushah* prayer, or for one of the many performances of kaddish, the *ḥazzan* regularly taps out the rhythm. Listen closely and you'll hear the characteristic *tek, tek-dum*. Even when a *ḥazzan* lets loose on a melody clearly borrowed from the classical Arab-Andalusian genre, or borrows a more recent composition from Israel, it is quite common to hear the pulse of the Amazigh. But not only Amazigh rhythms: melodies borrowed from *chaabi* or folk songs work their way into the prayers, unearthing the influence of Morocco's Amazigh foundations even more.[53]

Artisanry of Jewish Morocco

Morocco is a country known for its handicrafts: painted ceramics, embroidered babouches, carved *thuya* wood, multilayered silk caftans; the list of handmade goods is long. Although the market for local consumption was less luxurious than what tourists find in the *suq*-s of Fez, Tangier, and Marrakech today, the work was still of notable quality. Jews were active in all areas of Moroccan artisanry and renowned as specialists in more than a few. The latter included leatherwork and saddle making, but above all, jewelry and metalwork design. Jews were so deeply connected to this industry that in Tashelhit (the Amazigh language spoken in the Sous), the word for "Jews" *is* "Jewelers," i.e., "Iskaken."[54] Jews' omnipresence in gold and silver work in Morocco (and in the Islamic world more broadly) was predicated, as we have seen, on Muslims' avoidance of the same, for fear of inadvertently engaging in usury, which is forbidden by Islam.[55] Moroccan Jews involved in the goldthread trade were among the most mobile of merchants, selling their wares as far away as India and Taiwan.[56] Moreover, the extensive involvement of Jews in the gold trade as well as in buying and selling luxury goods like cloth, silk, spices, pearls, and corals shows that they were in no way restricted to "lowly" or despised trades, as is sometimes suggested.[57]

In sum, Jews and Muslims in Amazigh areas may not have shared a common origin, but they did share enough elements of a common culture to accurately ascribe an Amazigh ethnicity, however loosely construed, to those among the *toshavim* who lived in Amazigh areas.[58] (We will take a closer look at Moroccan Jews and Arab identity in Chapter 5.) In addition to being an ethnic marker for the *toshavim*, Amazighity also functions as a broader historical paradigm for Jewish Morocco. As mentioned above, Morocco was ruled by a succession of powerful Amazigh dynasties from the eleventh–sixteenth centuries. In tracing the relevant events of that period, we now shift our focus away from Amazighity as one form of ethnic identity within Jewish Morocco to the experience of Moroccan Jews under Amazigh rule.

Jewish Morocco under Amazigh rule

Islam was firmly established in Morocco by 709. But it did not take long for the indigenous populations to begin chafing against the administrative structures that came along with it. Particularly vexatious was the conquerors' Arab-centric practice of restricting Imazighen to the role of *mawali*-s [clients] of the ruling Arab elites and not allowing them to be full members of the new society despite Islam's promise of equality among all Muslims.[59] In 740, independent-minded Imazighen in the area of Tangier grew tired of this discrimination and overthrew their Arab overlords in what is known as the "Great Berber Revolt." This was the first successful secession from the Umayyad caliphate, and it portended well for Morocco's continued independence: Morocco would not be conquered by outside forces again until the establishment of the French and Spanish Protectorates more than a thousand years later.

The Tangier rebels were later joined by the Barghawata "sect" of the mid-Atlantic coastal region of Morocco. The Barghawata were a group of Masmuda Imazighen who, in the ninth and tenth centuries, established a veritable "Berber Islam," featuring a Tamazight Qur'an, Amazigh prophets, and a set of revelations. It is at this fascinating juncture that Jews first enter into the post-conquest historical narratives of Morocco. According to some medieval Arab historians, the leader of the Barghawata, Salih b. Tarif (749–795), was himself Jewish. His genealogy is noted by the eleventh-century Andalusian geographer al-Bakri as "Salih, son of Tarif, son of Simeon, son of Jacob, son of Isaac." While subsequent Maghrib chroniclers tended to accept Salih's Jewish origins, modern historians are more divided on the issue.[60] But Salih himself fully embraced it. His prophecies overtly combined Islamic, Jewish, and other astrological elements, and he gave himself a Hebrew name in addition to his Arabic and Amazigh names; Salih literally embodied the complicated ethnic patterns of early Islamic Morocco.

By all estimates, the Barghawata were successful rulers. From the plains of Tamesna they ruled over their own state for a good three centuries. Notably, with the Barghawata firmly ensconced in the middle of the country, the Arabs were never able to expand southward to fully conquer central or southern Morocco. It was up to subsequent tribal dynasties—all Amazigh until the rise of the Sa'dis in the sixteenth century—to introduce Islam to these regions. While theirs was not the "Berber Islam" of the Barghwata, it nonetheless was an Islam deeply imbued with Amazigh values and meaning.

Almoravids (1040–1147)

The Almoravids [al-murrabitun] were the first Amazigh dynasty to rule Morocco. They were Sanhaja tribesmen originally from the Sous and the Draa who in the course of the 1050s conquered not only Morocco but also western Algeria and al-Andalus to create a huge Morocco-based empire, one that was short-lived but powerful. The Almoravids began their conquests in Sijilmasa, Morocco's oldest city, which proved to be a fortunate starting point. Sijilmasa was Morocco's most important trading center at the time, which gave the Almoravids the economic base they needed to continue their expansion.[61] Sijilmasa's wealth largely came from trade. It was the gateway to the *bilad al-sudan* (routes led to Mauritania and Ghana), hence an important stop on the caravan route. Like all important trading cities, Sijilmasa had a sizeable Jewish community. Many of its Jews were merchants who were active in the trans-Saharan gold trade.[62] Jews from Sijilmasa also traveled eastward as far as Baghdad and Cairo for the purposes of trade or contracting marriage.[63] Sijilmasa was also a center of rabbinic learning, referred to as "the city of the *geonim* [Talmudic sages]" by Abraham b. Ezra in his famous elegy, lending additional credibility to the claim that Sijilmasa was indeed "the last civilized place."[64]

Despite Sijilmasa's many advantages, the Almoravids had their eye on a different location for their capital. When they came down from the Atlas Mountains and saw the great plains of the Haouz, they knew they had found the ideal site. According to local lore, the Almoravid leader Abu Bakr b. 'Umar is said to have bought the land from the widow who owned it for a fair price, and that a date pit he spat out took root and was the beginning of the Palmeraie, the great palm tree forest. In 1070 the Almoravids declared their new capital, Marrakech.[65] In time it would grow into Africa's largest city and home to the Arab world's largest Jewish community.

Jews began moving to the new capital upon its founding. The first Jewish settlers came from Aghmat, a small village to the southeast of Marrakech that had served as a waystation for the Almoravids since 1058 and was home to a sizeable Jewish community. Marrakech was attractive to them precisely because it was the Almoravid capital: center of wealth, power, administration, and hence opportunity. It helped that Marrakech ranked even above even ranked above al-Andalus for the Almoravid sultans: Yusuf b. Tashfin may have conquered Spain but he chose to rule from Marrakech. The new settlement also appealed to Jews because of the presence of Europeans there. The early European population of Marrakech consisted mostly of slaves or prisoners of war who had been captured in the Almoravid conquest of Spain, and Jews often acted as intermediaries in their ransoming and care. Despite having a new capital at their disposal, the Almoravids still maintained some administrative structures at their former base in Aghmat, and many Jews of that town stayed on to serve the administration. For example, the mint where Almoravid coins were struck was in Aghmat and run by Jews.

In all, Jewish Morocco flourished under the Almoravids. We know that Jews paid the *jizya* during this time, indicating that they were integrated into society with the recognized protected status of *dhimma*. This was also a period when the limitations placed on Jews by that same status were often contravened or ignored. Jews who normally would not be allowed to bear arms or ride horseback are known to have accompanied the armies of the Almoravids in their conquests in Europe and Africa. In fact, Jewish soldiers went to great lengths to keep the Sabbath during these military expeditions.[66] Although some Jews left Morocco for Spain during Almoravid rule—including the famous rabbinical scholar Isaac al-Fassi of Fez—it is unknown whether they were fleeing persecution or the fighting more generally, or simply exercising their newfound mobility under a united realm. Two figures whose biographies have survived down to our times can even be said to have enjoyed an elevated status under the Almoravids. Solomon b. al-Muallim and Me'ir b. Qamni'el were both invited to relocate to Marrakech from Spain in order to serve Sultan 'Ali b. Yusuf at court as his personal physicians. We might also note that the mosque built by that same sultan was oriented toward Jerusalem rather than Mecca in the manner of Jewish prayer (for which reason it was later destroyed).[67]

The Almoravids represent something of a victory for Amazighity in Morocco. Just as the Crusaders were conquering Jerusalem, these tribesmen from the remote Sahara united the whole of the Islamic west. Moreover, they managed "to scale the heights of power and authority with no Arab or descendant of the prophet to raise him up."[68] They did so while continuing to protect the Jewish minority as dictated by Malikism, whose dry legalism the Almoravids enriched with local practices and culture, including mutually beneficial cooperation with Jews. The dynasty that ruled after them would have a very different attitude toward Jewish Morocco.

Almohads (1121–1269)

Jews didn't fare nearly as well under the second Amazigh dynasty to take over Morocco: the Almohads [*al-muwahhidun*, "unitarians"]. The Almohads originally came from high up in the Atlas Mountains, an area abounding with small Jewish communities. But during their century-and-a-half-long rule (1121–1269) they showed little sympathy for their non-Muslim neighbors.[69] Indeed, the Almohad period constitutes the first recorded instance of serious persecution of Jews in Morocco, including massacres and forced conversions.[70] The persecution was not anti-Jewish *per se* but anti-*dhimma*, insofar as Christians were also targeted.

The Almohads' intolerant attitude was dictated by their doctrinal innovation. They were "unitarians" who followed a new doctrine of *tawhid* that emphasized certain elements of shi'i, Sunni, Mahdist, and Ghazzalist Islam and totally neglected others, such as Malikism, the principle of *dhimma*, and the obligation of *jizya*. They gave preference to a simple and clear delineation between right and wrong. Allowing the presence of *dhimmi*-s to dilute the purity of the Muslim *umma* fell on the wrong side of that divide.

The Moroccan chronicler 'Abd al-Wahid al-Marrakushi notes that both churches and synagogues were destroyed under the Almohads. While Christians could flee to Europe, Jews were more limited in their options. In some cases forced conversions led Jews to outwardly embrace Islam while inwardly waiting for the persecution to end in order to revert back to Judaism: "The Jews make a show of Islam, and pray in the mosques, and make their children learn the Qur'an, acting according to our creed and practice, but God knows what their breasts conceal, and their houses contain."[71] The phenomenon of dissimulation would again become common among Sephardim in later years under Christian rule, leading to the Spanish Inquisition, which was aimed at rooting out "false converts." But Jewish dissimulation under the Almohads received a controversial if humane measure of support from Maimonides, himself a victim of Almohad mistreatment (his family was forced to flee Cordoba in 1160 for Fez and then Egypt). Maimonides's famous *Epistle on Forced Conversion* posited that saving one's life was the highest value and that martyrdom should be avoided at all costs. This lenient attitude by Maimonides and subsequent Sephardic rabbis contrasted with the generally harsher verdicts of their Ashkenazi counterparts and reflected Maimonides's further argument that Islam was not an idolatrous religion; hence conversion to it under duress was not an irredeemable act. This episode suggests that some Jews may have remained Muslims permanently, since leaving to a place where one could safely revert to Judaism was not always possible. In any event, the "converso" phenomenon among Jews troubled the Almohads enough that in 1199 they decreed that new Muslims of Jewish origin whom they suspected of backsliding had to wear a "grotesque and distinctive" attire.[72] The required uniform was not much different from what was outlined in the Pact of 'Umar: a yellow and/or canonical hat (*qalansuwa*), a black robe, and a distinctive belt (*zunnar*). Other Jewish communities were destroyed altogether by the Almohads. The Andalusian poet Abraham Ibn Ezra included a list of the places where Jews were eliminated, including Marrakech, Fez, Tlemcen, Ceuta, Meknes, and the Draa.[73] In Sijilmasa, 150 Jews who refused to convert to Islam were martyred.[74] (Jewish learning in Sijilmasa briefly revived in the post-Almohad period, though the town as a whole never fully recovered and soon disappeared off the map.)

Somehow, the Almohad years still had a silver lining: it was a period of great intellectual flourishing for Jews, Muslims, and Christians alike. We have already spoken of Ibn Ezra and Maimonides, two intellectual giants of the period. To that list one could add Isaac al-Fassi (d. 1103), a great legal scholar who lived in Fez for 40 years and established a yeshiva there that attracted students like Joseph Halevi, author of the famous work the *Kuzari*. Among Muslims, Ibn Tufayl and Averroes (Ibn Rushd) completed their greatest works under Almohad rule in Spain.[75] The cross-pollination of ideas between individual members of religious groups is a hallmark of the so-called *convivencia*, and it endured even under

Almohad rule. Maimonides himself can be seen as having internalized certain aspects of Almohad doctrine. His firm stance against anthropomorphism as incompatible with monotheism, his affinity for certain legal methods above others, and, in a particularly striking parallel between Jewish messianism and Almohad Mahdism, his model for what constitutes a righteous king, are all highly redolent of the Almohad context.[76]

Later Almohad rulers repudiated the initial rejection of *dhimma* and allowed Jews to openly practice their religion, and Judaism began to rebound in Morocco. Christianity, however, was ultimately not revivable, even though a church existed in Marrakech for a short while under the Almohad ruler 'Abd al-Mu'min (r. 1130–1163). By 1269, the Almohads were replaced by a new dynasty.

Marinids (1244–1465)

In the waning years of Almohad rule, a third Amazigh dynasty, the Marinids [*Banu Marin*], began moving westward from what is today Algeria and Tunisia to stake their claim in Morocco. These nomadic Imazighen were members of the Zenata tribal confederation, which Ibn Khaldun (and later French scholars) believed had experienced significant Judaization in the past. The Kahina, the semi-mythical Berber priestess who had resisted the Arab invasions of the seventh century, was a member of the Jerawa branch of the Zenata.[77] In the first half of the thirteenth century, the Marinids began taking over the *jihad* against the Spanish Catholics from the Almohads and establishing themselves as the new rulers of Morocco.

Whether because of their own supposed proximity to Judaism or for reasons unknown, their attitude toward Jews was in direct contrast to that of the Almohads, going well beyond the bounds of simple tolerance toward a mutually beneficial relationship in which Jews and Judaism once again flourished in Morocco. Under Marinid rule, Fez eclipsed Marrakech as the political and intellectual capital for both Jews and Muslims, a position it would maintain until the Sa'dis moved the power back to the south in the sixteenth century. The Marinid sultans went on a building spree in their new capital. They adorned Fez with exquisite schools, mosques, administrative buildings, and palaces. They even built a "new city" [*fas jadid*] a short distance away from the *madina* [Muslim residential quarter]. It was there, just south of the royal kasbah, that they created Morocco's first walled Jewish quarter, an architectural and social innovation that would literally shape Jewish life in Morocco for centuries thereafter. The quarter was called the *mellah* after the salty marsh area in new Fez in which it was built. (With the creation of similar entities in Marrakech and Meknes, the term would become generic for Moroccan Jewish quarter, much like the pattern seen with the Italian term "ghetto."[78]) The 12.5 acre enclosed space had previously been inhabited by a special corps of Syrian archers in service to the Moroccan monarchy. At first, only Jews employed by the palace lived there. Over time, Jews from old Fez migrated to the *mellah*, until 1438, when it became the exclusive residence of all the city's Jews.[79]

The location of Morocco's first *mellah* was of great symbolic significance: Fez was the second oldest city in Morocco after Sijilmasa, the largest city in the world just prior to Marinid rule,[80] and the royal capital. The new city (*fas jadid*) contained just two important urban institutions: the kasbah for the sultan and his entourage and the *mellah* for the Jews. The *mellah* in many ways became the physical representation of the close connection between Morocco's rulers and its Jews that existed from this period forward. With only a few stumbling blocks along the way, a strong vertical relationship developed between the two parties that allowed Jews to receive the protection of the sultan in exchange for the special services they provided.[81] Principal among these were tasks related to financial administration and execution, like tax collection, currency exchange, moneylending, gold- and silversmithing, and administering the royal treasury and overseeing the royal mints. Jews provided similar services to the elites associated with the *makhzan* as well. As a Spanish observer commented: "No noble household was complete without a Jewish majordomo in charge of day-to-day affairs."[82]

One of the most influential Jewish families of the Marinid period was the Banu Raqusa who rose to prominence at the end of the thirteenth century. Two of its members served as palace attendants, making them some of Morocco's earliest "court Jews," privileged individuals, often bankers, doctors, or merchants, who served as special advisors to the monarchies in both Christian and Muslim Spain as well as in Ashkenazi lands (where they were known as *hofjuden*) and in the Ottoman Empire. In Morocco, the "court Jew" tradition became firmly established under the Marinids, but it also directly led to the dynasty's downfall. In 1464 Sultan Abu Muhammad 'Abd al-Haq named a Jew, Aaron b. Battash, to the position of *wazir* (prime minister). Battash used his position to secure high posts for his relatives, one of whom—Shaul Battash—was accused of assaulting a Muslim woman.[83] Aaron himself was known for riding on horseback and carrying a sword engraved with Qur'anic verses, both of which are forbidden by the Pact of 'Umar. Placing Jews in positions of authority over Muslims was deeply problematic from the perspective of *dhimma*, which the Marinids adhered to unlike their Almohad predecessors, and whose strictures the Moroccan public was likewise keenly aware of. When Jews were perceived as breaking the Pact, backlashes were not uncommon. In 1335, for example, Jews were banned from all economic activities following accusations of fraud.[84] The backlash was decidedly more violent when it came to the figure of Battash. In 1465 a popular revolt erupted among the Muslims of Fez, a notably conservative group. It ended with the assassination not only of the Jewish vizier, but of the Marinid sultan himself, followed by the destruction of most of the Jews of the city, now easily locatable by the angry mob in the new *mellah*.

Life in Jewish Morocco in the Marinid period was unpredictable; periods of great prestige and influence for Jews fluctuated with anti-Jewish violence. The beneficent extremes of Marinid rule are obvious when compared to the anti-*dhimmi* policies of the Almohads. The Marinids also had more freedom to chart an independent course because the Maghrib was divided into three separate political entities at this historical juncture. There was also greater diversity in Moroccan society as Jewish and Muslim newcomers fleeing the Reconquista in Spain arrived in Morocco, and mobility between Europe and the Maghrib increased in general.[85] But even before the Battash affair, the Marinids had begun to grow weak. Portuguese and Spanish attacks on the coast, economic crises, and the black death all took their toll, until finally a related dynasty, the Wattasids [Banu Wattas] took over, ruling from 1472 to 1554. The Wattasids oversaw the arrival of Sephardim from Iberia in 1492, which will be discussed in the coming chapter. They would be the last rulers of Morocco for whom Amazighity would be a defining characteristic.

Conclusion: Philosemitism and the fetishization of the Amazigh Jew

Every year on the Muslim holiday of 'Ashura a special carnival is held in Goulmima, an Amazigh village in southeastern Morocco in the Tafilalt/Akka region. Goulmima was once home to a sizable Jewish community; today, no Jews live there. But each year, the carnival brings them back to the village, at least figuratively. It is a strange phenomenon viewed from the outside: Muslims masquerade as "Jews" by assuming a grotesque, often sexualized version of Jewish costume; some men dress as Jewish women; others wear masks and quasi-hasidic outfits. In what Islamist critics call a pagan bacchanalia, the "Jews" then parade through the streets of the village carrying signs emblazoned with nonsensical Hebrew writing and stars of David. They sing songs and greet each other in a made-up Jewish language and finally make a pilgrimage to Goulmima's abandoned *mellah* and cemetery.[86]

The display of "*Udayn n acar*," or "Jewish Ashura," is risqué on several levels. First, it is an occasion for cross-dressing and homoerotic expression among men, as well as a time of open flirting between the sexes.[87] Politically, the unrecognizability of festival participants gives them free rein to slander local officials; so disguised, they can even risk an oblique, hence just tolerable, critique of the *makhzan* itself. Finally, Jewish Ashura is an example of Amazigh philosemitism, the phenomenon with which this chapter began and which most concerns us here. Whether in the form of normalized relations with Israel or the fetishization of its symbols, Amazigh philosemitism easily slips into an embrace of Zionism and a concomitant rejection of the Palestinian cause as an "Arab issue."[88] Amazigh philosemitism also serves to reinforce the (mythic) idea of shared origin of Moroccan Jews and Muslims discussed above, thus strengthening the indigenous voice overall and wedding Amazighity to a "successful" minority.

In many ways, the philosemitism on display in Goulmima reverberates with the current policies of the *makhzan* itself: while the Moroccan government does not maintain official diplomatic or economic ties with Israel, it has long been active behind the scenes in the peace process and receives many Israeli visitors each year. It also has longstanding security arrangements with the Israeli government. Yet the *makhzan* has shown itself to be much more willing to accommodate the claims of Amazigh Jews—mostly better off, mostly gone—than it has the claims of Amazigh Muslims, mostly worse off, and mostly present.

Ultimately, our Jewish Moroccan lens on Amazighity allows us to triangulate a major point of tension in contemporary Moroccan politics. On one side lies the *makhzan*, trying to control the aftermath of the "Arab spring" by carefully monitoring the degree and kind of inclusivity it will proffer and to whom; on the other side lies the Amazigh movement, pushing for faster and more radical change; on the third side are the Islamists, the main threat to the King's power and the Amazigh vision of secularism. One is reminded of Aomar Boum's idea of Jews as a "present absence" that continues to exert influence on contemporary Moroccan politics and society despite (or perhaps because of) the relative absence of actual Jewish Moroccans.[89]

All of this is to say that the Amazigh question has never stopped being relevant in Jewish Morocco, nor by the same token has the Jewish question ever stopped being relevant in Amazigh Morocco, though the respective forms and functions have changed over time. On the one hand, shared autochthony suggests a closeness so intimate as to be seen by some as part of same root. But the historical reality in the Amazigh regions was more ambiguous. Jews were not quite Imazighen, insofar as they consistently used Arabic as their first language among themselves and maintained strong communal barriers. As elsewhere in Morocco, Jews and Muslims in Amazigh areas generally did not eat together, did not pray together, and did not reproduce together, yet a common ethnic identity nonetheless developed on the local level within (and well beyond) the shared experience of Amazigh rule.

The current chapter has attempted to go beyond easy symmetries to embrace Amazighity in all its complexity and even contradiction in Jewish Morocco, from its function as an ethnic identity within Moroccan Jewish society to the experience of Jews as subjects of Amazigh dynasties. Given the timeframe, our attention has rested with the *toshavim*. In the next chapter, covering the early modern period, we find Amazighity receding in Jewish Morocco, both internally, as the Sephardim arrive from the Iberian peninsula in the late fifteenth century and begin to overwhelm the local populations, and externally, in the sixteenth century, as the Muslim rulers assume a new political ideology, Sharifism, which privileged Morocco's Arab-Islamic identity over its Imazighen roots.

Chapter 3: Timeline

1416–1511	"Maraboutic crisis"
1492	Jews expelled from Iberian Peninsula
1438	Creation of *mellah* of Fez
1509	Sa'di principality established in Draa Valley
1541	Sa'dian army expels the Portuguese from Agadir, Azzemor, Azafi, and Arzila
1554	Muhammad al-Shaykh overthrows Ahmad al-Abbas, the last Wattasid Sultan
1557	Creation of *mellah* of Marrakesh
1578	Battle of the Three Kings
1603	Death of Mawlay Ahmad al-Mansur
1603–1627	Civil War
1608	Mawlay Zaydan wins limited victory
1609	Muslims expelled from Iberian Peninsula
1627	Death of Mawlay Zaydan
1630s	Dila'iya zawiya begins revolt
1641	Muhammad al-Haj conquers Fez
1666	Conversion of "false Messiah" Shabbatai Tsvi to Islam
1666	Mawlay Rashid overthrows Dila'iya zawiya
1670s	Second phase of Moroccan Sabbateanism
1672	Ascension of Mawlay Isma'il as sultan
1679	Creation of *mellah* of Meknes

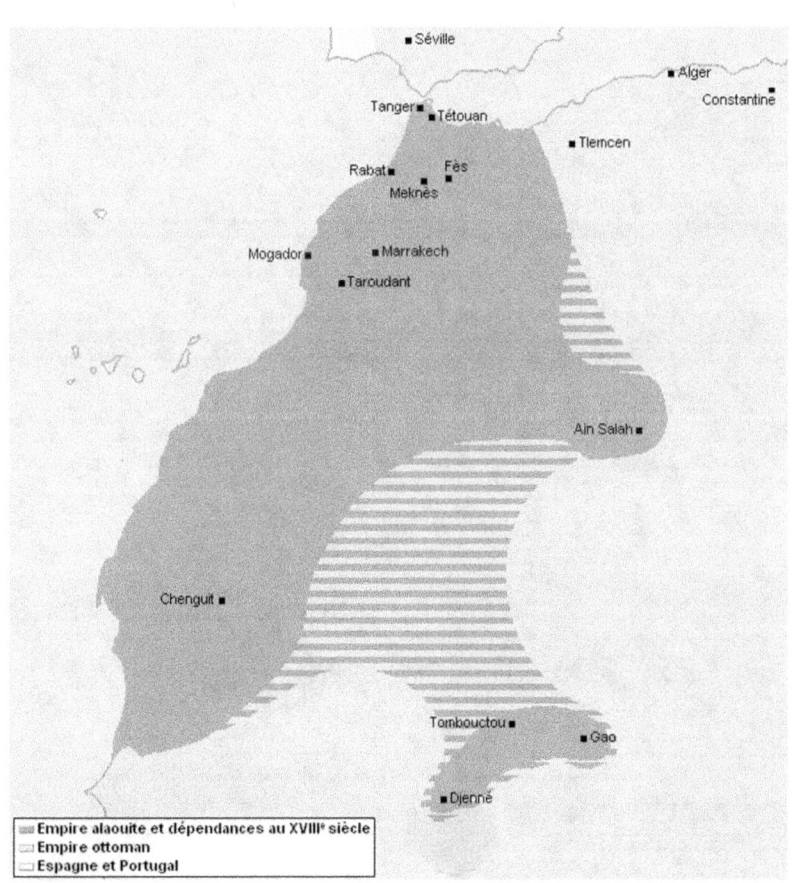

Map 3.1 Saʿdi era Morocco.

Tounsi, Omar. "Saadian Era—Maximal Extension." Digital image. Wikimedia Commons. February 16, 2012. Accessed May 6, 2019. https://commons.wikimedia.org/wiki/User:Omar-toons#/media/File:Maroc_-_fin_XVIe_siècle.PNG.

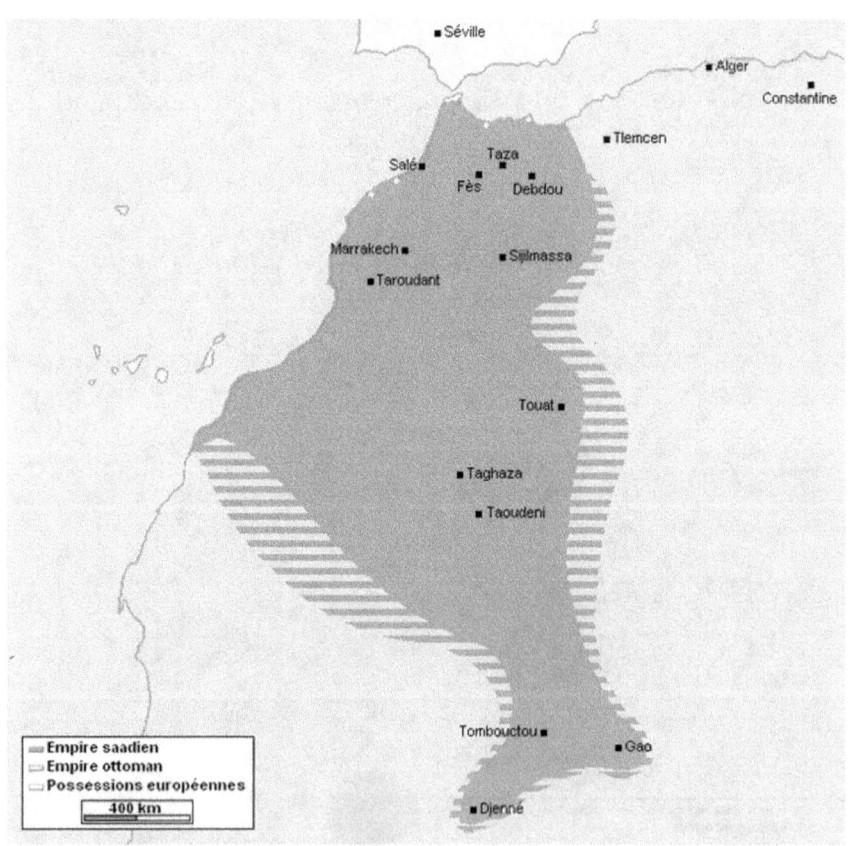

Map 3.2 Alawi era Morocco.

Tounsi, Omar. "Alaouite Era—Maximal Extension." Digital image. Wikimedia Commons. February 21, 2012. Accessed May 6, 2019. https://commons.wikimedia.org/wiki/User:Omar-toons#/media/File:Empire_alaouite_-_XVIIIe_s.PNG.

3

Sharifism
Religious Authority and the Rise of the Moroccan State (Sixteenth–Eighteenth Centuries)

The person of the King is inviolable, and respect is due to him.
—Article 46 of the Moroccan Constitution, 2011

The *mashriq* is for Prophets, the *maghrib* is for Saints.
—Common Moroccan saying

Introduction: Of Messiahs and sultans

The period from the fifteenth to the seventeenth centuries is known in Moroccan historiography as the "maraboutic crisis," so called for the Sufi lodges and their adherents—"*marabouts*" in French, *al-murabitun* in Arabic—who struggled to fill the power vacuum left by the collapse of the Berber dynasties discussed in the previous chapter.[1] Sufis from the Jazuli order had helped the Sa'di family from the Sous to establish themselves as the country's new, putatively Arab rulers in 1524. Despite the Sa'dis many triumphs, including a successful *jihad* against the Portuguese, conquests deep into West Africa, even a bold gesture toward new world discovery,[2] they were ultimately unable to break out of the Khaldunian cycle of limited rule.[3] Morocco's political crisis in leadership came to a head in 1603 with the death of the Sa'di sultan Mawlay Ahmad al-Mansur. For the next 6 years a civil war raged as his three sons fought each other for control, causing the fledgling political structures of the Sa'di state to collapse. According to a Moroccan historian of the time, the tumult was enough to turn the hair of a nursing baby gray.[4] The internecine struggle was mostly centered in Marrakech, where Mawlay Zaydan finally won a limited victory in 1608. This localization did not prevent the *fitna* [uprising, political chaos] from spreading throughout the country, however, a situation that was readily taken advantage of by various pretenders to power. On the banks of the Bouregreg river dividing Rabat and Salé, an all but independent state emerged, populated by Muslims and *moriscos* (former Muslims coerced to convert to Christianity) exiled from Iberia as well as many Sephardic Jews, and ruled by a tense coalition of corsairs and Sufis. In Fez and areas throughout southern Morocco (Illigh, Marrakech) still other Sufi groups were fighting for control, increasing the political fragmentation. Taking advantage of the distraction, European powers entrenched themselves more deeply along the coasts, forcing Moroccans to retreat to the interior. Following the death of Mawlay Zaydan in 1627, Morocco slid even further into anarchy. The chaos was finally brought to an end in the 1660s. Relief did not come as the result of any one of these groups—marabouts, *moriscos*, or Europeans—rising above the fray to dominate the others. Rather, it came from previously quiet quarters: an unknown family in an obscure area of Morocco reviving a timeworn, if not quite mundane, doctrine with which to stake their claim to power: Sharifism.

As indicated above, Sharifism was not a new idea in seventeenth-century Morocco; in a sense, Sharifism has existed as long as Islam has existed. In Islamic tradition, there is no doubt that Muhammad is considered a man. Despite his role as God's final messenger, no divinity accrues to him personally (or to any human being, animal, place, etc., which would be considered idolatry). But even if only a man, Muhammad is still a man above all others. This attitude can be witnessed in the fact that the things he did and said during his lifetime form an important part of Islamic law, that his birthday is celebrated as a holiday (*mawlid*) by many Muslims, and, especially important for our purposes here, individuals who can demonstrate an ancestral link to him are accorded a special status, as indicated in the Qur'anic verse: "God intends only to remove from you the impurity [of sin], O people of the [Prophet's] household, and to purify you with [extensive] purification."[5] An entire genealogical science has evolved around this idea. Those whose bloodlines can be traced back to Muhammad's line are known as *shurafa* (sing. *sharif*) in North Africa. They have long existed as a social elite and were given special treatment depending on the time and place. They might receive tax exemptions, special gifts at the Mawlid, preference for certain high positions, and so on. But the elevation of Sharifism to a creed whereby political leadership was predicated on it is fairly unique to Morocco. The dictate that *only* a *sharif* should rule the Morocco dates back to the time of the Idrisid founders of Fez (788–974), who were themselves descendants of the

Umayyads, hence imminently eligible for the position.[6] During the rule of the subsequent Amazigh dynasties, Sharifism lay dormant beyond the local level since the Almoravids, Almohads, Marinids, or Wattasids, as non-Arabs, did not have much to gain from it. The transformation of Sharifism into a potent political doctrine began under the Sa'dis. Despite a lack of consensus on their genealogical qualifications,[7] the Sa'dis assumed the title of *sharif* and used it as a cudgel against their opponents. In the name of Sharifism, the Sa'dis successfully took over the *jihad* against the Portuguese invaders, toppled the last Wattasids in Fez, and pushed back the non-Arab Ottomans encroaching from Algeria. If the Sa'dis laid the foundation for Sharifism, it was up to the Alawis to mobilize it as the primary source of political legitimacy.

Where do Jews fit into all of this? On a microcosmic level, the process by which "Jewish Morocco" was created occurred both in parallel with and contingent to the birth of the Moroccan state itself. As the Sa'dis and Alawis demarcated a new form of political authority in Morocco, they also sought to redefine their relationship with the country's Jews, which, as we can recall from the earlier quotation by al-Bakri, was a fabled yardstick for measuring legitimacy among Moroccan rulers. All the while the Jews themselves were changing, absorbing new immigrants from the North and new ideas from the East and, with considerable difficulty, combining these into something like a corporate identity for the first time. As we will see in the current chapter, the consolidation of the Moroccan state and the consolidation of Moroccan Judaism were not only concurrent processes but also contingent. In both cases, powerful mystical forces had to be neutralized in order for the new entities to emerge. For the Moroccan state, this entailed reducing the role of the *zawiya*-s as political actors who could pose a threat to established authority. Over the course of the seventeenth century, the Alawis worked to weaken Moroccan Sufism through their assertion of their even more formidable religio-political ideology, Sharifism. For Moroccan Jews, cohering into a community meant coming to terms with a new messianic incursion from the Ottoman Empire known as Sabbatenism, the false messianism of Shabbatai Tsvi and its troubling antinomian ideology, and subsuming *it* into an emerging normative Moroccan Judaism. Consolidation on all levels of Moroccan society during this period was made all the more elusive by the rifts that had resulted from the influx of exiles from the Iberian Peninsula. Among the immigrants were tens of thousands of Sephardic Jews expelled from Spain by royal decree in 1492. Receiving, understanding, accommodating, and assimilating these people was the defining event of the early modern history of Jewish Morocco.

The spiritual climate of Jewish Morocco in the early modern period

On October 16, 1666, a dramatic event unfolded in the Royal Palace in the Ottoman capital of Edirne: the Messiah converted to Islam—or at least the man whom most of the world's Jews at the time thought was the messiah, one Shabbatai Tsvi of Izmir. Shabbatai Tsvi[8] (1626–1676) was the leader of the most important messianic movement (Sabbateanism) to arise from within Judaism since Christianity. His antinomian teachings of "redemption through sin" completely disrupted—in some cases irrevocably—Jewish life the world over, including in Morocco.[9] Shabbatai's career was cut short when he ran up against the Ottoman authorities, who had come to realize that the eccentric rabbi was not simply a nuisance but the leader of a potential religious insurrection with a large, excitable following and a treasonous message. When Shabbatai was brought before the imperial council in Edirne, under the searing gaze of Mehmed IV, he was induced, probably on the pain of death, to convert to Islam.[10] The Ottoman Empire had once again reasserted its supreme authority. World Jewry would find it much harder to overcome the event and re-cohere.

Several factors contributed to the reception of the Sabbatean movement in Morocco. Some of the seeds for the movement were planted centuries before Shabbatai's birth; others took root in his lifetime, while still others grew into a "second wave" of messianic fervor after his death. Jewish mysticism, in particular, the "practical kabbalah" formulated by Isaac Luria in sixteenth-century Safed (Tsfat), in northern Israel, was central in all stages of the development of Sabbatianism. Luria's teachings, while too complicated to go into in any detail here, focused on the need to redeem divine sparks that became trapped in impurity when the world was created. In Lurianic terms, Shabbatai's antinomianism and ultimate conversion were part of a necessary descent into evil to rescue the godhead. Among Moroccan Jews, Lurianism is said to have been the dominant trend during the Sabbatean period,[11] but it is difficult to know if this was in fact the case. Jewish ideas certainly traveled with relative ease throughout the early modern Mediterranean world, often through the mechanism of trade,[12] but it should be noted that Morocco also had a deeply rooted local mystical tradition that was not Lurianic *per se*. The *Zohar*, the central text of the kabbalah, was composed in Spain in the thirteenth century and spread quickly to nearby Morocco, that is, well before the Lurianic period.[13] The transmission of mystical ideas to Morocco intensified with the expulsion of Sephardic Jews from Spain in 1492, leading scholarly families like the Azoulays to help establish kabbalah in Fez and Marrakech. Thus, long before the Zohar raised expectations, messianism was already pervasive in Morocco. Moses Maimonides, the great rationalist who lived in Fez during the twelfth century, was fiercely opposed to it. We learn from his *Epistle to Yemen* that a false prophet named Moses (Mushi/Moshe) Darʻi was active in Fez during his father's time. Despite having been warned against him by the rabbis, people still flocked to Darʻi because of his "piety, virtue, and learning," as well as his many successful predictions. Once Darʻi had won over the majority of the people, he made his most important prediction that the Messiah would come on the next Passover and that Jews should begin their preparations:

> He advised the people to sell their property and contract debts to the Muslims with the promise to pay back ten dinars for one, in order to observe the precepts of the Torah in connection with the Passover festival, for they will never see them again, and so they did.[14]

When the messiah failed to appear, "the people were ruined as most of them had disposed of their property for a trifling sum, and were overwhelmed with debt." The Moroccan Muslims understood this as a "hoax" and would have killed Darʻi had they found him, but he quickly escaped to Palestine.

In the Ottoman Empire, Jewish messianism was mostly an urban phenomenon, which, in its Sabbatean form, appealed primarily to Sephardic Jews in urban centers (Izmir, Salonica, Istanbul). In Morocco, the pattern was different. Outside of Fez, the main centers for the teaching and spread of esoteric studies were in fact situated in the rural south of Morocco: in the Sous, the Draa, and the pre-Saharan oasis towns (Taroudant, Tamagrout, Erfoud, etc.). This pattern is consistent with the topography of Moroccan Sufi institutions: the Moroccan ulema tended to be based in the madrasas of the cities, while the *zawiya*-s, though they may have maintained urban outposts, were headquartered in the countryside, usually at or near the location of the founder's grave. In a further parallel, an important Mahdist (eschatological) movement emerged in seventeenth-century Sijilmasa led by the charismatic *shaykh* Ibn Abi Mahalli (d. 1643) who called for a rebellion against the Saʻdis. Not only have the Mahdists been identified as a possible precedent for Sabbateanism in Morocco,[15] but this region, the Tafilalt, is precisely where the most famous Jewish saint Baba Salé and his Abihatsera clan trace their roots. As with Shabbatai Tsvi, belief in Ibn Abi Mahalli as an occluded *Mahdi* persisted long after his death (which was particularly gruesome, involving his decapitation and the exhibition of his head on the ramparts of Marrakech). The Draa valley, from which Moshe Dar'i originally hailed judging from his name, was another hotbed of messianic mysticism in Morocco.[16] According to an early twentieth-century Hebrew source, "The Draa region in southern Morocco ... was a center of kabbalah studies, and many took pride in Elijah having been revealed to them and in being able to foresee the future."[17] With the rise of Lurianic kabbalah, many Jews from Morocco, including a large contingent from the Draa, moved to Eretz Israel to immerse themselves in practical kabbalah. Moroccan scholars including Mas'ud Cohen, Mas'ud Azoulay, Avraham al-Maghribi, and Sulayman Ohana settled in Hebron, Jerusalem, and Safed. Such migrations ensured that books, ideas, and manuscripts flowed in both directions, carried eastward by Moroccan scholars and westward by Palestinian emissaries. Livorno provided an important link midway, where Jewish publishers maintained an active Hebrew printing press by which they disseminated the seminal texts of the period.

Shabbatai never personally came to Morocco, nor anywhere further west in Africa than Egypt. In his absence, the single most important figure in the introduction of Sabbateanism to Morocco was Elisha Ashkenazi, the father of Shabbatai's "prophet" and public relations guide, Nathan of Gaza. Elisha was not himself Moroccan, but he had a close relationship to the place. He served as a *shadar* (Heb. emissary) to Morocco, collecting funds for the Jerusalem community off and on throughout his lifetime. Upon leaving Israel for the Maghrib, he entrusted the upbringing and education of his son Nathan to one Jacob Hagiz. Hagiz was originally from a prominent family of Fez and had moved to Jerusalem in the 1650s to open his own yeshiva to take advantage of the revitalization of the city under Ottoman rule. Although not a Sabbatean by any means (he opposed the movement), Hagiz was still a node in the network through which ideas passed from the Maghrib to the *mashriq*, and he must have had considerable influence on Nathan as his main caretaker. Another node in this network was the figure of R. Jacob Pallache of Marrakech. Unlike Hagiz, Pallache clearly was a Sabbatean, having been excommunicated by rabbis in Cairo for the offense of being one of Shabbatai's three main accomplices in that city.[18]

Another important contributor to the heightened spiritual environment of seventeenth-century Jewish Morocco was the rumored reappearance of the ten lost tribes of Israel, an ancient sign that the messianic age was imminent. Reports of the ten tribes resurface regularly in Jewish Morocco; as can be recalled from Chapter 1, they featured in some of the origin myths of the community. But the seventeenth century was a high point for reported sightings, with both

Muslims and Jews heavily engaged in the transmission of such stories.[19] As we know, Nathan first publicly proclaimed Shabbatai's messianism in Gaza in the summer (mid-Sivan) of 1665. Just as Europeans were receiving the first reports about the strange goings-on among Jews in the Ottoman Empire,[20] a flurry of letters was sent from Morocco to France describing the sudden appearance of tens of thousands of strange men in the Sahara. The letters were written by one Monsieur Monet of Salé to his patron Le Comte de Merode, whom he kept informed about matters of interest. One of the letters, dated August 6, 1665, tells of no fewer than 8000 groups, each numbering between 100 and 1000 men, marching up from the Sous valley. They were said to be speaking the "holy tongue," i.e., Hebrew, and had conquered several towns in their path, where they killed everyone except the Jews.[21] Such stories continued to spread throughout the seventeenth century, paving the way for Sabbateanism.

Sabbateanism and the Sephardic factor

An overarching feature of Jewish Morocco during this period was the sharp division between the Sephardim, known as *megorashim* (Heb. exiles) or *rumiyin* (Ar. Romans, i.e., Europeans), who mostly lived in the northern cities (Tangier, Tetuan, Fez, etc.) and the older Amazigh and Arabized Jewish communities, known as the *toshavim* (Heb. natives) or *bildiyin*[22] (Ar. natives), the autochthonous Jewish population of Morocco, who were concentrated in the south and interior of the country. As in the Ottoman Empire, Moroccan Sephardim were highly susceptible to Sabbateanism. Although the Sephardim had been officially welcomed by the Wattasid ruler of Fez, Mawlay Muhammad al-Shaykh (as they had been by Mehmet II in the Ottoman Empire), they still had difficulty settling in. Because refugees were known for carrying concealed wealth, they became easy marks for criminals, especially upon arrival to Morocco before they had acquired the ability to defend themselves. Although the Wattasid sultan sent emissaries to greet the Jews (probably at the beach known until today as "wad al-yahud," "the Jews' river") and bring them to Fez, many stragglers were left to their own devices. Reports from the period tell of multiple instances of harassment, theft, rape, and violence committed against newly arrived Sephardic Jews. In some instances, these experiences were so miserable that the Sephardim preferred to return to Christian countries than stay in Morocco. The Sephardic rabbi Judah Hayyat reports that when he first arrived in northern Morocco he was immediately denounced by a Muslim he had known in Europe and was sentenced to death by stoning. His life was spared only when the Jews of Chefchaouen redeemed him. He repaid them in books, indeed his entire library. The rabbi then went to Fez, where there was a terrible famine. He had to eat grass to survive and at night he slept in a ditch made of dung. Having had enough of Morocco, he left to Naples.[23]

While the local Moroccan Jewish community usually came to the Sephardim's rescue, as in Chefchaouen, this was costly, and the relationship between the two communities grew tense. It didn't help that the Sephardim were snobbish in their attitude toward the indigenous Moroccan Jews. However traumatized they may have been by the experience of expulsion, the Sephardim were still extremely proud of their heritage and customs. For many decades after their arrival they resisted mixing with the *toshavim*, whom they looked down upon as "*foresteros*" (Sp. foreigners; outsiders; in Judeo-Spanish this term has negative connotations). The cultural gap was wide. Outside of the Hebrew used in synagogue, the two groups generally did not speak the same language; the *toshavim* were Arabophone and Berberophone, while the Sephardim in Morocco developed their own form of Judeo-Spanish, known as *Hakétia*. They also differed in terms of ritual, liturgy, dress, communal organization, lineage, and so on. In larger cities like Fez and Marrakech, the two groups lived in separate neighborhoods, rarely intermarried, and for a period did not share the same *shkhita* (Heb., practices of ritual slaughter), making it impossible for them to eat together, let alone intermarry and thereby integrate.[24] Another impediment to intermarriage was the differences in *kettubot* (marriage contracts). Sephardic *kettubot* were known for having much more favorable terms for the brides than those of the *toshavim*, so Sephardic families resisted having their daughters marry into local families. Even their tombstones looked different: the Sephardic ones, like those of Andalusi Muslims, often featured human shapes.

The separation between the two communities was underlined by the *converso* experience of some Sephardim, those who had converted to Christianity under duress in Europe.[25] The rabbinical authorities established reconversion centers in Fez and Marrakech to help *conversos* return to Judaism, but this group remained spiritually vulnerable. The experience of having lived outwardly as New Christians (in some cases for generations) had left them with a tenuous grasp on Jewish law and ritual, which they knew in an amalgamated form if at all. Their knowledge of Hebrew was equally shaky. Presumably they also possessed well-honed dissimulation skills, which, in the Ottoman Empire, facilitated their outward conversion to Islam in emulation of Shabbatai's conversion. (There is no evidence of this phenomenon having existed in Morocco.) The *toshavim* were wary of this group of Sephardim and worked to prevent them from holding public positions or enjoying the privileges of the priestly cast, the *kohanim*.

Spanish exiles were especially numerous in northern Morocco, so it makes sense that northern cities like Salé, and to a slightly lesser degree Meknes, were main centers of Moroccan Sabbateanism. The two towns were linked by the figure of Elisha Ashkenazi himself, who spent many years in Salé in the mid-1650s, and when he died in 1673 was buried in Meknes. Jacob b. Sa'adun, one of the movement's most zealous local leaders, likewise had roots in one town (Meknes) and lived in the other (Salé), often moving back and forth between them.[26] Jacob Sasportas, the anti-Sabbatean polemicist who is the main source for the Sabbatean movement in Morocco, though born in Oran and professionally active in Europe, also spent time in both places and was married to the daughter of a prominent Meknes rabbi. During his time in Salé, even he supported Nathan's prophecy, an inconvenient fact he later denied and left out of his anti-Sabbatean treatise, *Sisat Novel Tsvi*.[27]

Sasportas openly rejected the movement once Shabbatai converted to Islam, but other Jews in Salé were slow to follow suit. In fact, enthusiasm for Sabbateanism seems to have grown there after 1666. The fast of Tisha b'Av was celebrated with a feast by Sabbateans in Salé just after Shabbatai's conversion.[28] In 1668 and 1669 the fast was also not observed.[29] The Sabbateans did not practice their faith passively: anyone caught fasting was ordered to be boycotted and ostracized by the community.[30] Germain Mouette, a French writer on his way to the New World captured by corsairs and held in Salé from 1670 to 1681, describes an outbreak of Sabbatean activity:

> When I was in Salé, a Dutch ship arrived from Amsterdam bringing prophecies from Holland to the Jews in the first-mentioned place. The contents of those prophecies were, inter alia, that the Messiah, for whom they had been waiting for such a long time, would be born in Holland at the beginning of the following year, i.e. 1672. On hearing these glad tidings, the Jews celebrated a second Feast of Tabernacles, rejoicing and revelling for eight days.[31]

The story continues with a description of a bet over the imminent arrival of the Messiah made between a visiting French merchant named L'Aubia and one "Jacob Bueno de Mesquita, the wealthiest of those dressed after the manner of the Christians who had fled from Spain because of the Inquisition." From this description, we can confirm that some Moroccan Sabbateans were definitely *conversos*. The story's denouement is also relevant when at the end of the year it became clear that Mesquita had lost the bet, the Frenchman called on him to pay up. Mesquita thought the whole affair had been in jest, but L'Aubia would not relent, and sought the intervention of the local governor. The two men apparently split the 400 pesos they were finally able to extract from Mesquita, who was given no right of appeal. For neither the first nor the last time, messianic enthusiasm had cost the Jews the goodwill of local rulers.

The ordeal of expulsion made the Sephardim particularly susceptible to Sabbateanism: the more miserable their situation, the more plausible magical solutions seemed. European and Ottoman Jews had their distress compounded by the Khmelnitsky uprisings of 1648–1657, when Cossacks and Tatars rose up against their Polish overlords and massacred tens of thousands of Jews in the process. (The Cossack term "pogrom" enters into our vocabulary from this event.) Streams of Jewish refugees fled from destroyed towns in Eastern Europe to the Ottoman Empire bearing the psychological wounds of Khmelnitsky. Among them was the woman who would become Shabbatai's wife, Sarah, a mystic in her own right who was responsible for galvanizing the movement. Although there is no indication that Moroccan Jews as a whole were aware of the Khmelnitsky massacres, or received any of its refugees, there were certainly other types of trauma experienced by Moroccan Jews during this period that may have predisposed them to a messianic reawakening.

When considering these events it is important to note that Moroccan Jews rarely suffered alone; regardless of whether the disasters were man-made or natural, Moroccan Muslims usually underwent the same or similar travails. For example, Morocco repeatedly experienced terrible droughts, particularly in the periods 1603–1606 and 1662–1669, which resulted in widespread hunger and famine. And while Jews may have been subject to extortionate taxation imposed on them by the various contenders jostling for power, this was hardly unprecedented in times of political turbulence and would not in itself be a cause of acute religious foment. Moreover, such practices were localized in particular cities (e.g., Fez) and not in others. (An important exception was the heavy and even extortionate taxation imposed on Jews during the interregnum between the Sa'di and Alawi dynasties.) Rather than accepting the lachrymose assertion that Moroccan Jews turned toward Sabbateanism because they "smarted under almost continuous oppression and persecution,"[32] and the corresponding thought that their lives were equivalent to those of "their brethren in Poland,"[33] let us instead look for clues in the sociopolitical climate of seventeenth-century Morocco, which will bring Sharifism and its relationship to mysticism back into the picture.

Moroccan Jews and the rise of the Sharifian state

In their rise to power, the Alawis encountered domestic rivals of many different orders. The northern "pirates" were relatively easy to dispose of given the *moriscos'* general indifference to politics. After a short battle, the warlord Ghaylan fled Morocco in 1669, first to Algiers and a few years later, ironically to the same English garrison in Tangier that he himself had previously attacked. The powerful Sufi orders shared none of the *moriscos'* indifference to political life, however. To the contrary, as an armed and formidable enemy to the centralizing state, the *zawiya*-s were a constant thorn in the *makhzan's* side. In their time, the Sa'dis had dealt with the Sufi threat through co-optation. They took over the *jihad* themselves and merged their opponents' maraboutic credentials with their own authority. They even exhumed the *shaykh* al-Jazuli's body to bring to Marrakech and reinter in a specially built mausoleum. The Alawis, however, were not so quick to join forces with the Sufis. Perhaps wishing to avoid the compromises of the Sa'dis,[34] they were determined to rise to power without the help of the brotherhoods and thereby put an end to the "maraboutic crisis" once and for all. In addition to its short-term political significance, the Sa'di approach also had broader ramifications in terms of helping to establish what constituted legitimate rule in the Maghrib. It dictated the terms for the state-sponsored Islam that is being propagated in Morocco today, an Islam tied slightly more tightly to the Orthodoxy of the ulema than to the mysticism of the *zawiya*-s and to the Arab *sharif*-s than the Amazigh shaykhs.

Jews were often caught in the crossfire between the rulers and the Sufi challengers, though their allegiance was usually to the established authority, a fact that was not lost on the members of the *zawiya*-s. Already in the Sa'di period, some Sufis had made known their resentment of the fact that Jews in the sultan's court had been given favorable positions as ambassadors and agents. It was on these grounds that Yahya b. 'Abdallah, an important Sufi *shaykh*, rebelled against Mawlay Zaydan in Marrakech in 1614. He claimed that the Sultan maintained too close a relationship with the Jews Abraham Wa'ish, who was in charge of the treasury, and Samuel Pallache, the well-known ambassador.[35] Amidst the increasing fragmentation of the interregnum period, another *zawiya* made a bold move: the Dila'iya invaded and occupied Fez.

The Jews of the Zawiya

The Dila *zawiya* was founded in the late sixteenth century in the Middle Atlas south of Khenifra, strategically located in the middle of the country near or on what is today Ait Ishaq.³⁶ The brotherhood (*ikhwan*) of the Dila'iya comprised Sanhaja berbers who followed the teachings of al-Jazuli. In the early 1630s, the Dila'iya *zawiya* began to flex its political muscle in its home region. Muhammad al-Haj, the grandson of the founding *shaykh*, had grander ambitions. In 1641 he conquered Fez and declared himself sultan. The response to this provocation from Muhammad b. al-Sharif of the nascent Alawi dynasty was nothing less than scathing:

> You are not cut out to handle the flames of discord that you have stoked up. In any case the Moroccan people have not perceived in you Dila folk any aptitude beyond serving dishes of gruel to each other—for you eat gruel when we eat couscous. You vie with each other in verses impossible to listen to, so horrible are your dirges. As for the sciences, we allow you their practice in the name of fairness, just as long as you don't set your sights beyond the study of the law or a teacher's salary.³⁷

But the Dila Sufis did not bow. Instead, they the captured Salé, giving them control of the Bouregreg, and thus the profits of piracy, an economic sector that expanded significantly under their rule.³⁸ The period from 1641 to 1660 marked the apex of the Dila'iya's power in Morocco.³⁹ For Jewish Morocco, this corresponded to the very worst part of what was known as the "forty years of chaos," so named by a Jewish source of the period the Ibn Danan chronicle. The Dila'iya's occupation of Fez, where the chronicle was written, was indeed a terrible time for Jews. As the chronicle recounts:

> In the year 5406 [1646], for our great sins, all the synagogues were closed and sealed by order of the sodomite of the *zawiya*, Sidi Muhammad al-Haj. They were closed on Wednesday, the 11th of Elul, and on Sunday, the 15th of Elul, the enemies entered our sacred glorious house, defiled our sacred temple, laid our synagogue in heaps. Woe to the eyes that see such things, woe to the hands that record them. [...] On Thursday of the said week they wrecked the lectern and the women's pews. Their work of destruction was like the destruction of the Temple. [...] On the Eve of Yom Kippur, they destroyed the old house of study and the new house of study, and there were none left of the synagogues except that of Saadia b. Rabuh and R. Yaakov Rute, and these were saved only by bribes.⁴⁰

Given the treatment of Fassi Jews by the Dila'iya, it is easy to see why Jews might support Sharifism as a means of reining in certain Sufi groups.

In their original quest to expand, the Dila'iya had encroached on Alawi territory in the Tafiliat, which was probably a fatal mistake, as it galvanized the political ambitions of this group of *sharif*-s who had been quietly living in the oases since the thirteenth century. The Alawis repulsed the Dila'iya from the heart of the Tafilalt in 1638, and then they themselves began to expand toward the northeast (Tlemcen). In 1650, the aforementioned head of the Alawi family Muhammad b. Sharif was moved by an appeal from the people of Fez to rid them of Dila'iya rule, but after a brief siege he was not able to hold the city and the Dila'iya reestablished control. The Dila'iya's chaotic rule eventually led to fighting between the new and old quarters of Fez. Again, the unrest took an especially terrible toll on the Jews, whose *mellah* was located in *fas jadid* [the new city], which was ruled by al-Duraydi, a rebel from among the Dila'iya. According to the same source:

> The Jews who were in the *mellah* were utterly consumed with hunger and with the taxes imposed on them by Sidi Adridi [al-Duraydi]; the tax collectors would take flour from the jar which a woman had kneaded and would take the robe from her body too. And the Jews would flee, and he who left the city lost his livelihood. And there were those who threw themselves from the city walls.[41]

The rescue of Fez and the final overthrow of the Dila'iya *zawiya* fell to Muhammad b. Sharif's brother, Mawlay Rashid. This heroic act marked him as the true founder of the Alawi dynasty. Following two unsuccessful raids on the city, on June 6, 1666, Mawlay Rashid finally was able to enter Fez through a breach in the walls of the *mellah*[42] and save the city. The people of Fez, with the support of local Idrisid elites who shared the Alawis' sharifian credentials, proclaimed Mawlay Rashid sultan.[43]

Two years later, Mawlay Rashid was ready to move against the Dila'iya *zawiya* itself: "Mawlay Rashid swore that he would not leave the city of *al-zawiya* until he destroyed and shattered the houses and walls and desolation is left, and so he did, he exiled the 'plishtim' ['Philistines', i.e., Imazighen]."[44] By this time, Hajj Muhammad had grown old and blind and put up little resistance. The period of Dila'iya domination was finally over.

The Alawi destruction of the Dila'iya *zawiya* brings us back to the Sabbateans and allows us to link the rabbis' and the *sharif*-s' struggles against mystics more closely together. For not only did a Jewish community live in the area of the Dila'iya *zawiya*, but it seems to have been comprised of practicing Sabbateans.

One can only guess whether any mutual influence existed between them and the members of the *zawiya*; though we know that there is precedence for cross-pollination among Kabbalists and Sufis in the Ottoman Empire and elsewhere.[45] Unlike the Jews of Fez, the Jews of the *zawiya* did not suffer at the hands of the Dila'iya. It was only with the destruction of the *zawiya* by the Alawis that they were forced to flee to Fez and Meknes. According to the Ibn Danan chronicle, the Dila Jews were given three days to leave and were allowed to take some small amount of gold and silver with them:

> On the third day, the people took their dough before it was leavened, their kneading troughs, etc., and nearly all were wealthy people, and their houses were full of all good things: silver and gold vessels, countless quantities of grain, and immeasurable amounts of wine, oil, honey, and butter, and they left everything behind, except such silver and gold as they could carry, and the whole community of the *zawiya* came here, to Fez.[46]

The authors of the chronicle make no mention of the Sabbatean controversy in connection with the events at the Dila *zawiya* or for that matter at all.[47] But a letter from the anti-Sabbatean activist Aaron Sibony reveals that the Dila'iya refugees had to be physically forced into confinement by the Jews of Fez so that they would have no choice but to observe fast days, thus proving that they were Sabbateans who had to be reformed in order to reenter the Jewish community.[48] There are several additional elements to this story. First, suffering does not appear to be the reason for the Dila Sabbateans' clinging to their antinomian behavior, as was the case for the Sephardim. On the one hand, the Dila Sabbateans were clearly wealthy: "their houses were full of all good things." Even their relocation to Fez does not seem to have diminished their fortunes. When the larger population of Fez was subsequently squeezed by drought and inflation, we are told that "the Jews were rich and did not feel the high prices."[49] Second, the persecution of the Jews of Fez appears to have been short-lived and not widespread. In trying to justify their non-observance of the fast of Tisha b'Av, the Sabbateans staked their position on the grounds that fasting is not mandatory in situations where there is no active persecution. Indeed Jacob b. Sa'adon lists Morocco, Amsterdam, Hamburg, and England as places where "there is no persecution" and hence "the people [...] may choose not to fast if the majority does not wish to."[50] This evidence suggests not only that the Dila'iya Jews *were* Sabbateans, but that the Jews of Fez, who had clearly suffered the most from the forty years of *fitna*, were *not* (or at least not to the degree of the Jews of the Dila'iya *zawiya*,

Meknes, and Salé were, to which one could also add those of Marrakech and Tadla). We are told that a contingent of Jews from Fez was assigned responsibility for bringing the Dila'iya Jews back into line. In the same letter, Aaron Sibony reaffirmed that the wise people of Fez "had not changed," i.e., had not become Sabbateans.[51] Despite the pressure from normative Judaism to view Sabbatean behavior as the result of suffering, that was not always the case.

The Moroccan Jewish response to Sabbateanism

Normative Moroccan Judaism's best weapon against the Sabbateans was the aforementioned Jacob Sasportas, a brilliant if harsh man (his image in a famous portrait has been likened to that of a "Jewish Inquisitor"[52]) who devoted his entire career and considerable intellectual gifts to fighting the Sabbatean movement. Sasportas was born in Oran and served as a rabbi in Fez, Salé, and Marrakech, and as a diplomat for the Moroccan sultan. But his real forte was the poison pen letter: carefully crafted polemical attacks on the supporters of Shabbatai Tsvi. The following is a typical response sent to a Sabbatean sympathizer:

> I received your confused letter, which slithers like a snake, your scroll which is rolled up with the blood of the innocent, written front and back showing its back to the Temple, in spite of the great ones in the eyes of others, and at first I thought to disregard it and its crimes ... and whether you respected me or looked down on me, you did not impress me and only worsened your situation. For I will only accept respect from respectful people and will only accept disgrace from the rabbis and not by people who have not reached that status.[53]

Other times Sasportas did not even deign to respond himself but instead instructed one of his students to reply on his behalf: "I responded to him through one of my students so that he would be disgraced in reading it."[54] In the latter case, directed at the aforementioned Ya'akov b. Sa'adon, the leader of the Sabbateans in Salé with whom Sasportas was in constant conflict, the insult apparently stuck: in 1670 Ben Sa'adon publicly regretted his attempt to cancel the traditional fasts.[55]

Sasportas's epistolary responses to the incidents at the *zawiya* further underline the Dila Jews' practice of Sabbateanism. In another letter to Ya'akov b. Sa'adun, he wrote: "And there in Salé itself they did not have a house of worship due to a royal decree, and in *zawiya*[56] their entire Jewishness was hidden, and even observing Shabbat was denied to them."[57] He goes on to say that the Jews regarded this as a sign that the messiah was near. In a letter to the leader of the Livorno yeshiva, also a Sabbatean sympathizer, he introduces his argument that repressive measures against the Jews by the authorities were the fault of the Sabbatean movement itself and the unrest it caused:

> And from the city of Salé (may the Most High preserve it) it was written that they were almost in great danger due to their excessive enthusiasm for that creed [Sabbateanism] and the evildoer Ghaylan had arisen against them and had decreed death and destruction against them, and only the mercy of heaven and bribery alleviated the fierce wrath in the bosom—and I wrote to you at length on this matter and called your faith into doubt.[58]

For Sasportas, the Muslim authority—whoever it may be at the time—was as a force that could potentially be marshaled in the battle against Sabbateanism.[59] The threat of a backlash by the authorities was in fact used by many opponents of the movement as a tactic. Avraham Sibony of Salé fought the Sabbateans using this method both in their stronghold and throughout Morocco. He described his entreaties to the adherents in Marrakesh:

> And I wrote to them about the synagogues that were destroyed by order of the *khalifa* [governor], and I cried out, and I had a letter that I had written to them concerning the fasts [recalling that Sabbateans feasted on fast days] so that they might return from their straying to the ways of their fathers and the conduct of the prophets, so that we do not divide in two.[60]

Yet all was not coercion and harshness. Sasportas had actually left Morocco in 1664, before the announcement of Shabbatai's messiahship, for London and then Hamburg. Although his missives continued to arrive regularly from abroad, the local rabbinical authorities were largely left to deal with the practical management of the movement on their own. (Sasportas's ties to Morocco are often overemphasized by scholars, to the point that Oran, where Sasportas was born, is sometimes considered to be part of Alawi Morocco, which it was not.)

Despite Sasportas' urging the harshest possible treatment of the Sabbateans, as the movement developed, the indigenous rabbis took a more conciliatory approach, allowing for the incorporation of some aspects of Sabbateanism into Moroccan Jewish practice where they remain to this day. Whether this was a conscious tactic or merely an act of acquiescence to popular sentiment is unclear. Yet certain prayers and supplications from Sabbatean works were allowed to enter into the Moroccan Jewish liturgy and prayer books, specifically those in the controversial *Hemdat Yamim*, which, by the eighteenth century, had become a mainstay of Moroccan Jewish religious texts. Similarly, in many Moroccan Jewish communities, it is common to offer toys or money to children on Tisha b'Av, mimicking the Sabbatean practice of celebrating rather than mourning on this holiday. It was likewise from North Africa that an important ideological modification came from within the ranks of the movement that allowed for greater flexibility and toleration. The highly influential Sabbatean figure Abraham Miguel Cardoso (alt. Cardozo), who was originally from Spain and lived in Tripoli and Tunis during the Sabbatean period in Morocco (c.1663–1674), publicly opposed Shabbatai's calls for mass conversions on the grounds that what is allowed for the messiah is not allowed for the masses.[61]

The messianic strivings of Jewish Morocco also registered on the state level. According to a seventeenth-century author, Sabbatean Jews were scolded by the sultan himself:

> Above thirty years have I been amused with an idle tale of the coming of your Messiah. For my part, I believe him come already; therefore, if you do not now tell me the precise day on which he is to appear, I will leave you neither property nor life. I will be trifled with no longer.[62]

The Jews were made to pay the *makhzan* a sum of money instead of accepting the wager. "The emperor bade them begone, and told them to beware, and not invent any more of their fabulous tales." Even the homegrown Sabbatean prophet Joseph b. Sur (see below) invoked the threat of official retribution for Sabbateanism, though he did so to buttress his own claims: "And if you wish, I shall walk in the streets of Fez and announce that Shabbatai Tsvi is the Messiah of Israel, and you will see that no harm will befall me or anyone from Israel."[63] We should also keep in mind that the peculiar behavior of the Jews, and the ultimate failure of their messiah to come, caused them to be harassed and ridiculed in the streets by their Muslim neighbors.

Despite the strategic use of threats, Sabbateans were in reality treated quite leniently in Morocco. (By way of contrast, in Yemen the movement's very public failure has been linked to the expulsion of the Jewish community from the capital Sanaʿa and their relocation to the distant coastal town of Mocha, where they floundered and many died.[64])

Mawlay Isma'il and Jewish Morocco

The 1672 ascension of Mawlay Isma'il as sultan reinforced the strong vertical relationship between the sultan and Morocco's Jews, as we have seen exemplified in the Sa'di institution of the *tujjar al-sultan*, whereby prominent Jewish merchants conducted trade on behalf of the *makhzan* to great mutual benefit.[65] For this and other reasons, Mawlay Isma'il's poor reputation in European sources does not extend to Jewish accounts of the era. During his more than five decades of rule, Mawlay Isma'il often relied on Jews and appointed them to high positions as counselors and diplomats. Joseph Toledano, the son of Mawlay Isma'il's advisor, was such a figure. Under his auspices, an important peace treaty between Morocco and Holland was negotiated. Moroccan merchants, including many Jews, benefited greatly from the increased trade that resulted. Mawlay Isma'il's rule also had an important impact on how Moroccan Jews lived their daily lives. He rebuilt many ruined synagogues and constructed a new capital in the city of Meknes, which attracted Jewish immigrants from throughout the country. His urban projects also included the construction of a Meknes *mellah* in 1679, the third walled Jewish quarter in Morocco after those of Fez (c. 1438) and Marrakech (c. 1557). As in the preceding instances, the motivation for building the Meknes *mellah* included the need to establish municipal order, the ambitions of a new sultan reflected in a new capital with all the requisite attributes of a royal city, the facilitation of *jizya* [poll tax] collection at a moment of fiscal need, and so on.[66] But the timing of the creation of the Meknes *mellah* raises the possibility that Sabbateanism was also a factor. Mawlay Isma'il came to power in 1672 just as Sabbateanism was entering its second stage, centered in his own capital of Meknes.[67] The advantages of building a *mellah* in this context include the possibility it offered for surveillance and monitoring, its location next to the kasbah allowing it to function as a panopticon that could be used to control a restive population. Along similar lines, we might recall that the construction of the *mellah* of Marrakech was motivated in part by the need to resolve demographic pressure and social instability caused by the influx of immigrants from Spain.[68] As there were even more *megorashim* in Meknes than in Marrakech, this was likely also a factor in Meknes. Finally, we might also recall that some of the Sabbatean exiles from the Dila'iya *zawiya* were sent to Meknes as well as to Fez. Not only did they help to increase the number of *toshavim* there, but for these Sabbateans, the imperial capital held great symbolic significance: Shabbatai set sail to Istanbul for the express purpose of taking the crown off the Ottoman sultan's head and putting it on his own as proof of his messiahship. The urge to usurp power, which constituted a capital offense for Ottomans (to the extent they took Shabbatai seriously), was a constant feature of Sabbateanism.[69] The creation of a *mellah* might have helped to quash any similar fantasy in Meknes.

Finally, it is in Meknes where Joseph Bensur, the locally-grown prophet who ushered in the second phase of Sabbateanism, appears in the 1670s. Joseph Bensur is a pivotal figure in the history of Moroccan Sabbateanism. It is the texture of his prophecy, and local reactions to it, that finally Moroccanize the Sabbateanism. He stands apart from other Sabbatean figures in several important ways. First and foremost, in clear contrast to other Sabbateans, including Shabbatai himself, Bensur was known for his *lack* of scholarship; indeed it was the spectacle of a previously ignorant man espousing Torah and kabbalah that convinced people of his prophetic status. His story also contains a strong element of magic, a common characteristic of Moroccan Judaism, particularly as articulated through kabbalah.[70] Aspects of Bensur's prophetic career appear in the testimony of Baruch of Arrezo, the author of the earliest surviving biography of Shabbatai Tsvi. According to Baruch, a "spirit guide" appeared to Josph Bensur on Rosh Hashanah in 1673. He had come to purify Joseph, using "a single pitcher that flowed so copiously he was obliged to change his clothes." He was then shown "in heaven, Our Lord and King, Sabbatai Sevi" and told that he is the messiah and that Nathan is the true prophet, and that Joseph himself is "messiah son of Joseph."[71] The news of Bensur's "good tidings" spread quickly, and Jews from throughout Morocco flocked to him. When he told them that the redemption would occur on Passover eve in 1675,[72] many prominent Jews believed him. According to Elie Moyal, who has studied the religious output (poems, *piyyutim*, prayers, etc.) associated with Sabbateanism in Morocco in detail, "The awakening was indeed stronger in the second revelation than in the first."[73] This is an important observation, indicating that Sabbateanism had its greatest impact when it was expressed in a local idiom.

Although Bensur was more interested in mystical rearrangements of the alphabet and predicting ever later dates for the coming of the messiah than he was in actually overthrowing the *makhzan*, it is nonetheless significant that he made his appearance in the new Alawi capital, where it would carry the greatest symbolic importance.[74] Meknes was also where Elisha Ashkenazi finally settled when he returned to Morocco after having spent several years in Europe.[75] He was buried in its cemetery in 1673. Meknes again became a center of messianic agitation when a repentance (*teshuva*) movement with strong Sabbatean overtones took hold there in 1713–1714.

The legitimate exercise of authority

The Alawis responded to the threat of *fitna* in three main ways: by reinforcing their dynastic authority through the creation of a royal capital, by quashing their enemies using brute force, and by fostering the religious ideology of Sharifism, thus asserting "the supremacy of the genealogical view of the basis of *baraka* over the miraculous."[76] The Alawis found that they could contain and control the bloodlines of the sultans much more easily than the miracles of the Sufis. In a parallel development, the Moroccan rabbis saw to the consolidation of Moroccan Judaism by asserting their own authority and linking it to Alawi authority.[77] In order to achieve their goals, the rabbinical institutions had to find a way to cope with Sabbateanism before it destroyed the Jewish community, just as the *makhzan* had to meet the challenges of a Mahdi coming from the *zawiya*-s.

Internally, within Jewish society, Sabbateanism was deeply problematic for traditional authorities. Where Shabbatai first emerged in the Ottoman Empire, the rabbis found themselves powerless to curb a charismatic movement. They issued writs of excommunication and banished him, but the arsenal available to normative religion was not enough to stop the movement from spreading. Sabbateanism was also a great disturbance externally. The Ottoman sultan, though originally indulgent of the Jews, eventually saw Sabbateanism not as a spiritual phenomenon taking place within an unimportant *millet* but as a rebellion against his authority and hence used the state's conventional tools of force and coercion to put an end to it.

In Morocco, with its different religious and political climate, the rabbis were able to control and ultimately assimilate the movement into a normative Moroccan Judaism without ever actually destroying it. Sabbateanism arrived in Morocco fully formed, and the rabbis understood immediately what was at stake, their own authority included. Although they had little access to brute force, they did not hesitate to harness that of the *makhzan*, using the threat of retribution to calm social unrest. Milder forms of coercion also seem to have worked, as in the confinement of the Dila Jews in Fez, boycotts of individual Sabbateans, or polemical attacks of figures like Sasportas. On their end, local Sabbateans also helped integrate Sabbatean themes into Moroccan Jewish life by promoting a more benign form of the movement, one that harmonized with its surroundings. Based on Cardoso's arguments, the strong messianic yearning in Sabbateanism was consciously separated from the rest of the theology as an acceptable tenet of Judaism and allowed to persist, while apostasy itself seems to have been completely avoided. In contrast to Sabbateans in the Ottoman Empire, those in Morocco, including the Sabbatean prophet Joseph Bensur, did not convert to Islam. Even Joseph Bensur's messianic message, which condoned Shabbatai's conversion, was not otherwise antinomian; he did not seek to subvert any legal conventions or cancel any fasts. For this reason the rabbis could just tolerate him. They, in turn, lost none of their authority; indeed it was buttressed by the emergence of a new Jewish elite of merchants and diplomats in service to the Alawi sultan.

Late-stage Sabbateanism proved to be less of a threat in Morocco than elsewhere thanks to the strategic intervention of the rabbinical authorities and the growing coercive power of the surrounding Moroccan state toward upstarts. By weakening the movement enough to assimilate acceptable aspects of it into normative practice, the Moroccan rabbis were able to avoid anything resembling the three-way split between the traditional *halakha*-based Judaism of the so-called *mitnagdim*, the mystical *hasidim*, and, eventually, the advocates of Jewish enlightenment (*maskilim*) that so fractured European Jewish society, which has been traced back to the destructive forces of Sabbateanism.[78] The assimilation of aspects of Sabbateanism into Moroccan Judaism also facilitated the integration of the Sephardim into Moroccan Jewish society; the total rejection of Sabbateanism would have likely perpetuated the social rift. Their actions served to reinforce Moroccan Jewish identity in situ rather than dislodging it, as was the case with assimilation trends in later periods, which bound Moroccan Jews more closely to European culture. The actual mechanisms by which this occurred are not well known, but the split between the *toshavim* and *megorashim* appears to have been mended by the onset of the modern period, though social distinctions remained in force. Just as Moroccan Muslims routinely make claims to Sharifism, many Moroccan Jews continued to claim or create Sephardic genealogies to bolster their status.[79] The rationalist Maimonides was accepted as the ultimate legal source by Moroccan Jews, but strong mystical tendencies are still apparent in many aspects of Moroccan Jewish practice, not least of all in the widespread practice of "saint" veneration discussed in Chapter 1. Vestiges of Sabbateanism specifically were still found in Morocco as late as 1826 but were no longer indicative of a religious rift.[80]

Conclusion

The upheaval caused by the arrival of the Sephardim in Morocco and the transformation of Moroccan Jewish society as a result was an important milestone in the history of Jewish Morocco. It was closely tied to the arrival of Sabbateanism from the north and the east and the subsequent need to assimilate strong messianic urges into normative religious practices. All of which occurred in the context of the institutionalization of a strong and direct vertical relationship between the Jews and the Sharifian sultan, representative of an emerging Moroccan state in which Sufism had been brought to heel.[81] Throughout the early modern period, developments among Moroccan Jews, even when explicitly religious in nature, still moved in tandem with developments in the surrounding society, even moving directly in parallel with those developments on a microcosmic level at times.

While the details of Jewish Morocco's trajectory are unique, the linkage between state formation and the consolidation of Jewish communal identity during this period is not. Europe is often held up as the model for this process, but a better point of comparison for Morocco in this regard is the Ottoman Empire. In Europe, Jewish assimilation and integration went hand in hand with the erasure of Jewish corporate identity: Jews could only become a part of European societies as individuals "of the Mosaic faith." In the Ottoman Empire, however, a fully Ottoman Jewish identity came to replace the myriad distinct communities that were characteristic of Jewish life in previous periods. The cultural and legal changes undergone by the Jews of the Ottoman Empire as part of the *Tanzimat* process were not intended as a means of integrating Jews into a homogeneous society, but rather worked to solidify Jews' communal identity within a distinctive legal framework known as the *millet* system. The Ottoman Jewish community was henceforth able to participate with other groups within a schema of "communal egalitarianism." In Morocco too, Jewish communal formation was a gradual process. Rather than alienating Jews from the societies in which they lived, the process of consolidation they underwent during this period put them squarely within the trajectory of Moroccan society as a whole, so much so that it suggests an early modern periodization comprising in equal, dialectical parts Jewish communal and Moroccan state formation. It was only later, with direct colonial intervention, that Jewish communal coherence began to have very different ramifications and that Jewish history in Morocco begins to diverge.

Chapter 4: Timeline

July 5, 1830	Algeria falls to France
August 14, 1844	Battle of Isly; Treaty of Tangier signed
1856	Mawlay 'Abd al-Rahman signs unfavorable maritime trade treaty with England
1859–1860	War of Tetouan with Spain
1860	Alliance Israélite Universelle (AIU) established in Paris
1862	AIU opens first school in Tetuan
December 1863	Moses Montefiore visits Morocco
1864	Royal *dahir* promising the protection of Jewish and Christian minorities in Morocco
1879	Sultan calls for end of the protégé system
1880	Treaty of Madrid grants Europeans more privileges in Morocco
1883–1884	Charles de Foucauld explores southern Morocco
March 30, 1912	Treaty of Fez establishes French and Spanish Protectorates over Morocco
1918	Royal *dahir* establishes local Jewish councils along the lines of those in France
1924	AIU given official responsibility for educating Moroccan Jewry under the Protectorate

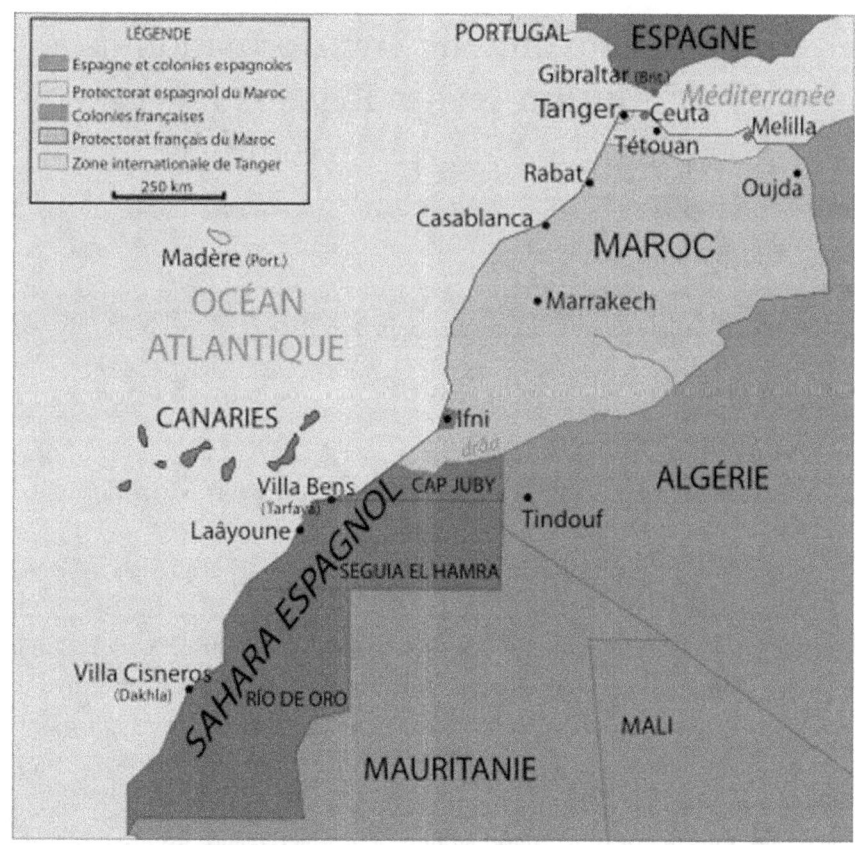

Map 4.1 French and Spanish Protectorates.

Map of the different parts of colonial Morocco (1912–1956): French and Spanish protectorates, Tangiers international zone, territories directly annexed. Digital image. Wikimedia Commons. December 1, 2006. Accessed May 6, 2019. https://fr.wikipedia.org/wiki/Histoire_du_Maroc#/media/File:Marrocoprotectorate.png.

4

Europeanization
Imperialism and the Transformation of Muslim-Jewish Relations (the Long Nineteenth Century)

> Every part of the empire more or less abounds with Jews
> —Dr. William Lemprière, 1791

Introduction: Charles De Foucauld's Jewish Morocco

"There were only two religions in Morocco. It was necessary at all costs to be one of those. Would one be Muslim or Jew? Wear a turban or a black skullcap?" Such was the question that Charles de Foucauld, French army officer and explorer, later priest and martyr in the Algerian Sahara, asked himself as he prepared to venture to southern Morocco in 1883–1884 on a mission of *"Reconnaissance."*[1] Foucauld's remarks were prompted by his recognition that he would have difficulty passing as a Muslim among North Africans, so he took the advice of his friend, the curator of the national library in Algeria, and disguised himself as a Russian Jew instead.[2] Foucauld congratulated himself on the tactical advantages of his choice: the voluminous "half-Algerian, half-Syrian" Jewish costume he adopted would perfectly conceal his compass, watch, barometer, and other equipment, and he assumed that no one would bother him in the "shadows of the *mellah*" as he wrote up his findings each evening.[3] Foucauld completed his preparations by employing a Moroccan rabbi, one Mordechai Abi Serour of Akka, as his guide. The two men posed as *shelakhim* [Heb. emissaries] from Jerusalem, characters that enjoyed even greater freedom of movement than would a local. Such "wandering Jews" were a common sight in nineteenth-century Morocco, certainly more common (and less disruptive) than the sight of Christians would be in these areas. In 1867, the Moroccan sultan had lifted the requirement that Europeans seek his permission in order to enter the interior of the country, but given the fate of some earlier visitors, Christians were still few and far between in the areas beyond Marrakech by the time of Foucauld's arrival.[4]

Foucauld was far from the first European to make such a journey, however. Morocco has had a long history of attracting foreigners to its shores, with the Mediterranean acting as much as a bridge as a barrier between the two continents (prior to postcolonial migration patterns, most of the traffic was one way).[5] Some Europeans even settled permanently in Morocco. Among the earliest of these were five Franciscan missionaries who lived in Marrakech in the thirteenth century. They were famously martyred in 1220, an event that led the Almohads—not generally known for their tolerance of non-Muslims (see Chapter 2)—to accede to the establishment of a church in their capital a few years later.[6] The Franciscan church provided an important base for missionaries who came to Morocco to care for the Christian captives held there, generally European sailors captured at sea by Moroccan corsairs, who automatically became property of the Moroccan sultan. Many of these men stayed in Marrakech for years; some stayed their whole lives. Foreign merchants were also attracted to Morocco. A group from Marseille established the country's first foreign-run *funduq*-s (hostel/warehouse), in Ceuta in 1236, from which they conducted trade. Later came the large trading houses like the Barbary Company in Morocco, which set up shop on the Atlantic and Mediterranean coasts; with them arrived various consulates to support trading activities. In addition to merchants, diplomats, and refugees, Morocco also attracted Western writers and artists, including, in the modern period, such figures as Edith Wharton, George Orwell, Paul Bowles, William Burroughs, and many others, who synchronized their own rhythms with those they found in the Maghrib.

Although part of this continuum, the European "discovery" of Morocco by explorers during the nineteenth century was its own beast with its own characteristics. Foucauld ostensibly came to Morocco independently: his trip was self-financed and he was not an employee of the French government at the time. Yet it is impossible to disentwine the purportedly "neutral" explorer from the imperial ambitions of his (and in some cases, her[7]) country. Wittingly or not, journeys of the sort Foucauld and many others undertook, particularly in the latter half of the nineteenth century as the Ottoman Empire faltered, were closely linked to the process of European powers establishing control over North Africa. The perception of European encroachment is well borne out by the historical record.[8] By gathering important information about the land and its people, European explorers, scientists, and doctors helped pave the way for increasing levels of foreign intervention in Morocco, beginning with control of Moroccan fiscal and political affairs and eventually culminating with the establishment of a French Protectorate (with Spain holding territories in the North) that lasted from 1912 to 1956.

Foucauld's voyage to Morocco not only fits into those larger patterns, it is also telling is on the microcosmic level of Jewish Morocco, insofar as a similar process attended to Foucauld's relationship to his guide, Mordechai that was likewise particular to the precolonial context: it indicated a new kind of attention being paid to Moroccan Jews in certain sectors of European society, one that recognized Jews' potential utility to the imperial project at the same time as it mobilized contemporary ideas about "race" and Orientalist attitudes toward the Middle Eastern and North African "other," including Jews. But first, who was Mordechai?

Mordechai Abisrour was Originally from the small oasis of Akka in southwestern Morocco.[9] At the age of 9 he left home to study at a yeshiva in Marrakech and later went to Jerusalem to continue his education. Upon his return to Morocco, he went into business with his brother, Isaac. In 1863 the two joined a trans-Saharan caravan to *bilad al-Sudan* (lit. "land of the blacks," meaning sub-Saharan Africa) to set up their own outpost for long-distance trade. The brothers established the first Moroccan Jewish community in Timbuktu since Jews had been chased from the area by al-Maghili and his followers (see Chapter 1).[10] Mordechai reported about his experiences to the *Société de Géographie de Paris*, earning himself the title "*le rabbin voyageur*," "the traveling rabbi."[11] The same organization later brought him to Paris, and he eventually secured the directorship of a Jewish school on the Algerian coast. It was from Oran that Mordechai and Foucauld set off on their Moroccan adventures in 1883.

Mordechai was Foucauld's constant companion during the trip south. He was responsible for making all the arrangements; locating housing, materials, and meals; and conducting all communication with the locals, including explaining the reason for their voyage, which sometimes required some quick thinking. They often pretended to be medical doctors or scholars. Despite Mordechai's obvious talents, Foucauld was not fond of his guide. Tellingly, Foucauld neglected to mention Mordechai or any other Jews for that matter, though they were almost always his hosts, when acknowledging the support he received for his journey, citing only two clearly demarcated groups as praiseworthy in this regard: European Christians and Moroccan Muslims.[12] As *Reconnaissances* makes clear, Foucauld needed Mordechai, but he didn't much like him. His feelings are laid out in a section devoted specifically to Mordechai's biography, in which Foucauld disparages his companion in the same breath as he admits his usefulness: "Even if I received such services, he who rendered them was, at the same time, by his ill will, a constant and considerable obstacle to the execution of my voyage. Just as he contributed to my success, he also, from the first day to the last, did all he could to cause me to fail."[13] According to Foucauld, Mordechai's two great faults were that he wanted to proceed at a slower pace than Foucauld and that he did not agree to follow the itinerary Foucauld had set. Foucauld attributes these faults to avarice and laziness in the first case (Mordechai wanted to get paid for a longer period of time that included more rest) and cowardice in the second (Mordechai was fearful of visiting areas with which he was not familiar).[14] An alternative reading might be possible, however. Perhaps Mordechai's behavior was indicative of a broader reticence—even a premonition—on the part of Moroccan Jews about cooperating with Westerners in their quests for imperial influence. The ambivalence and mistrust that constantly clouded Foucauld and Mordechai's partnership can be seen as a harbinger for the fraught relationship that developed between French colonizers and Moroccan Jews more generally over the following decades, a relationship characterized as much by mutual exploitation as by mutual misunderstanding.

Europe's *mission civilisatrice* in Jewish Morocco

Meanwhile, a different sort of ambivalence about the colonial enterprise had begun to spread in mainland France. Despite the financial and other benefits the metropole received from its overseas territories (which were negligible compared to the benefits the *colons* themselves reaped), the French public required convincing to continue its Moroccan explorations. The so-called pacification of Algeria (1835–1903) was costing France dearly in terms of resources, not to mention lives (Algerian as well as French, though the former were not necessarily being counted in France at the time). French citizens were not eager for a repeat performance in Morocco. But what was largely a political and economic question was answered by French officialdom, divertingly, with a *moral* argument: Morocco was in dire need of a "*mission civilisatrice*": European society had a responsibility to elevate the world's more "backward races" to their level of "civilization."[15] In England, this argument was articulated in terms of the "white man's burden." Orientalist, patronizing, and racist as such thinking is by today's standards, no doubt many Europeans involved in the colonial project and their counterparts in the region really believed they were fulfilling a moral duty by intervening in Morocco's domestic affairs. As evidence, for colonialism's success advocates could point to increased literacy and the advantages of bilingualism, access to better healthcare and modern medicine, and the education of girls (though they did so out of context and often based on erroneous data). However cynical the motives and damaging the results, the civilizing mission nonetheless had its gray areas, and the experience of Jewish Morocco is one of them. The reasons were complicated, but partly because Jews were more familiar to Europeans than were Muslims, who did not have established communities in Europe at the time, Moroccan Jews came to constitute their own subgroup within the *mission civilisatrice*, with its own goals and methods for achieving them. The "situation of the Jews," as it was branded, was thus an early target for "improvement."

Those Europeans who heeded the imperial call became experts on Jewish misery in Morocco, which, to be sure, was rife. Foreign visitors in the precolonial period rarely failed to comment on the overcrowding and its attendant ills (poverty, disease, prostitution, etc.) they witnessed in the Jewish quarters. The *mellah*-s of the interior had grown especially dense by the late nineteenth century. Normal population increases were difficult enough to accommodate in the circumscribed space of the *mellah*, but they also had to absorb huge influxes of rural Moroccans to the cities, including rural Jews. But even if their descriptions of Jewish misery were not necessarily inaccurate, most European observers nonetheless failed to notice either the condition of the Muslim masses, which was equally appalling, or the tenuous foothold of the Jewish communities back home in Europe, where emancipation had only partially delivered on its promises. Moreover, even as it lamented the Jews' circumstances, European travel writing about Moroccan Jews was rarely devoid of the anti-Semitic tropes of the time. The practice of lending money at interest, forbidden by Islamic tradition but allowed within certain limits by Jewish law, was frequently singled out for scorn. The following account was written by the English journalist Walter Harris in the 1880s:

No doubt the Jews have been, and are still, to a small extent persecuted; but it is not in the least to be wondered at, for they swindle, on every possible opportunity, the slow, thick-headed Moors, who borrow money from them without the least understanding at what interest they are repaying it, which is generally something like fifty percent per month. When one arrives in the country of Morocco, just as when one first sees the Jews of Russia, one is apt to pity; but experience of a few days teaches one differently, and one learns that, after all, it is more their fault than that of the Moors, whom they despise, and make the victims of their hardhearted usury. I do not at all mean to say that all the Jews in the country are the same. I am speaking now of towns like Morocco and Fez, where they are in the same state of civilization as the Moors themselves, only dirtier.[16]

Foucauld also had less than kind things to say about Jews. A lengthy section of his work is titled "The *Israélites* of Morocco." Invoking both the term for Jews and a bifurcation of which French observers were especially fond (despite the more fluid reality), he divided the "Israelites" into two groups: those falling under the sultan's authority, i.e., those of the "*blad al-makhzan*," and those of the "independent" arcas, the "*blad al-siba*."[17] The former, he wrote, "live decadently, are lazy and effeminate, with all the vices and weaknesses of civilization and none of its delicacies. Lacking any [positive] qualities or virtues, they seek well-being in the satisfaction of their senses, and stop at nothing to achieve it. Once contented, they think themselves wise." The second group of Jews he considers "no less contemptible," simply more miserable: "Lazy, greedy, gourmands, drunks, liars, thieves, hateful above all, without faith or kindness, they have all the vices of the Jews of the *blad al-makhzan*, save their cowardice."[18] Attitudes like those of Harris and Foucauld were far from atypical, giving Moroccan Jews good reason to be ambivalent about European plans for their country. A 1907 report concerning the Jewish community of Marrakech makes this point clearly, stating that "the Jews, as much as the Muslims, fear European intervention":

> What advantage has the European presence brought? Has it improved the moral situation? No, quite to the contrary. The European has only been jealous of the Jew, he has always disdained him and treated him like a pariah. The commercial epicenter of Morocco, Casablanca, is a well-known locus of anti-Semitism and the French consul himself has no tenderness [for the Jews]. In other towns, the movement is less visible because Europeans there are less numerous and the Jews are still useful. The Jews themselves are perfectly aware of this.[19]

Indeed Moroccan Jews probably were "perfectly aware" of what was in store for Morocco as European encroachment continued. But their calculus of the potential gains or losses that might result from cooperation was also perfectly understandable given the particular circumstances of Morocco in this period. This chapter will explore the cultural and other shifts that Moroccan Jews underwent as they struggled to position themselves individually and as a newly cohered and officially recognized community in an imperial context,[20] and how the choices they made (or were made for them) created a separate path for them away from their Muslim neighbors for the first time.[21]

From European exploration to French encroachment

Precolonial Morocco had a population of just 5–6 million people, most of whom lived in the countryside. Trade was limited to what was needed to satisfy domestic requirements. The state structure was correspondingly modest: the sultan stood at the head of the government, surrounded by ministers mostly without specific portfolios (a *na'ib* [deputy] was appointed in 1845 to deal with foreign affairs on behalf of the sultan). The cities were ruled by *amil*-s (agents) and pashas, while the countryside was under the control of rural chieftains (*qa'id*-s). The economy was one of subsistence. In a year without drought, locusts, or other environmental calamities, Morocco's natural resources were sufficient to meet the basic needs of its people. The taxes people paid were both Qur'an based and directly linked to the success of harvests, making them less onerous. Moreover, taxes were usually paid in kind, not in cash, which was hard to come by throughout the region. Grain and other agricultural goods were especially difficult to convert to liquid assets. The limited trade with Europe that did exist was undertaken by the *tujjar al-sultan* (royal merchants). In exchange for providing an important buffer between the *makhzan* and foreigners, they were given generous tax benefits and allowed to monopolize the import and export of certain products. Since there was no banking system to speak of in premodern Morocco and the collection of interest was forbidden for Muslims, Jewish *tujjar* offered loans and credit, including to the government itself.

This political and economic system began to change in 1830, when Moroccans saw their worst fears realized with Algeria's fall to France. Moroccans were deeply affected by the plight of their neighbors, as Algerians were transformed into *indigènes* without rights in their own country; their labor, natural resources, and markets were all levied for the benefit of the metropole. Popular support for the Algerian resistance soon gave rise to a more generalized anti-foreign sentiment among Moroccans. When the resistance fighter 'Abd al-Qadir sought refuge from the French in Morocco in 1842, the Moroccan authorities were obliged to provide him with shelter or risk a serious revolt. This traditional act of offering *hurm* [*haram*; sanctuary] to a *mujahid* ended up having terrible consequences for the Moroccans, however. The French navy reacted to Morocco's sheltering of 'Abd al-Qadir by bombarding the coastal towns of Casablanca and Mogador (Essaouira) in August 1844. Shortly afterward, the French army routed the more numerous but disorganized Moroccan forces fighting under the command of the sultan's son near the Isly River on the Algerian-Moroccan border. This was a watershed event that made Morocco's relative weakness painfully apparent to all concerned; the French general even made off with the Moroccan commander's tent and umbrella, traditional symbols of Alawi dynastic rule. The Treaty of Tangier signed by a humiliated Sultan 'Abd al-Rahman (r. 1833–1859) in late 1844 recognized French colonial rule in Algeria and led to the permanent ban of 'Abd al-Qadir from Moroccan soil. European influence in Morocco grew by leaps and bounds thereafter. In 1856, Mawlay 'Abd al-Rahman was again coerced into signing punitive treaty, this time with England, which liberalized the rules for maritime trade, including reducing the customs duties paid to the *makhzan* and provisions for greater European commercial infiltration. The pattern continued. Just a few years later, in 1859, Morocco entered into a disastrous conflict with Spain over the borders of Ceuta known as the "*harb titwan*," the war of Tetouan, so named after the northern Moroccan town where most of the fighting took place.

Morocco's loss in the Tetouan war resulted in yet another imbalanced treaty. This time it included a war indemnity so crushing that the *makhzan* had to borrow money from England in order to pay Spain. This arrangement continued throughout the following decades such that until 1884, two-thirds of the country's daily customs revenue had to be diverted to pay off foreign loans and war indemnities.[22] Under the rule of 'Abd al-'Aziz (r. 1894–1908), Morocco's financial situation went from bad to worse. His unbridled spending brought the Moroccan economy to the brink of collapse. Observers of the *makhzan* during this time noted that the roads to the palaces were literally littered with packing crates that delivered all the newest European gadgets to the young ruler: motor cars and bicycles (sometimes ridden around the palace grounds by women from the royal harem[23]), cameras, exotic animals, corsets, fireworks, wigs, and even an elevator, though the palace comprised only a single story.[24] The sultan even forsook his traditional white horse, instead riding from the palace to the mosque for Friday prayers in a coupe given to him by the Queen of England.[25] To explain how to actually use this bounty, experts were summoned from abroad who cultivated the young ruler's every whim. The cadre of foreign specialists at court included, among others, an American portrait painter, a German lion-tamer, a French soda-water manufacturer, and a Scottish piper.[26] Still more loans had to be taken out by the Moroccan government to pay for it all, accelerating the cycle of dependence and exploitation.

The Protégé system in Jewish Morocco

As foreign influence spread both within and beyond the *makhzan*, European colonialists seeking to establish a foothold in Morocco found themselves in need of points of contact within the local population. Like Charles de Foucauld, explorers in the hinterlands needed translators who were familiar with the terrain and could speak Arabic or Tamazight in addition to European languages. The European trading houses on the coasts needed middlemen to help them establish a presence in the Moroccan interior, where they could obtain desirable goods like apricots, dates, wax, animal skins, and rose petals, as well as to sell their manufactured products, many of very shoddy quality. As foreign post offices and consulates opened in Morocco, a multilingual staff was needed to staff them. Local proxies were highly sought after to fill all these positions. More than any foreigner, local partners could help extend a given government's reach into Morocco without risking direct confrontation with either a competitor or the *makhzan* itself.

Throughout North Africa, this role often fell to native Jews.[27] They were known for their reliable international networks, their high degree of mobility, and their knowledge of foreign languages—skills and attributes that had long made them popular with those in power (if not always with their fellow subjects). The *makhzan* had long cultivated Jews as intermediaries, thanks in part to the Moroccan authorities' traditional aversion to dealing with Europeans directly. Seeing such contact as contaminating, or at least below their station, they were only too happy to leave these tasks to select *dhimmi*-s, particularly after the humiliating defeat at Isly. By the second half of the nineteenth century, the Moroccan government had new and urgent dealings with Europe, covering everything from treaty negotiations to the purchase of firearms.

While Jews continued to provide their traditional services to the *makhzan*, for the first time their service to foreign powers (European countries, primarily, and, to a much smaller degree, America) began to outpace it. The status of these local agents became institutionalized in the form of the protégé system. This system granted an individual a patent of protection from a specific country for a set term in exchange for the kinds of services described above. The patent guaranteed its holder immunity from taxation and the local system of justice, including the Jewish courts (Heb. *batei din*), the *makhzan* courts, and the *qadi* court. First established by a treaty between France and Morocco in 1767, such "protection" was originally intended as a form of legal extraterritoriality to French merchants residing in Morocco in order to encourage long-distance commerce that would boost the Moroccan economy. But the system was also closely related to the capitulations of the Ottoman Empire, which had a clear punitive edge. There, "protection" was extended collectively, usually over a particular religious community in order to weaken the sultan's hold on his ethnically and religiously diverse population. Often the beneficiaries were the empire's Christian minority groups, who were understood as having a "natural" allegiance to the Christian powers. Thus when the Russians defeated the Ottomans in the Crimea in 1774, the terms of the Küçük Kaynarca peace treaty extended the Czarina's gains by establishing Russian protection over Eastern Orthodox populations deep within the Ottoman Empire, including the provision to build a Russian Orthodox church in Istanbul (though it never came to fruition). Similarly, France's historic protection over European Christian pilgrims and missionaries in the Middle East was extended to indigenous Catholics of the Ottoman Empire, including the Maronites of Lebanon.

Jews were largely left out of the capitulation scheme. Britain and Germany at one point attempted to establish protection over Ottoman Jewry, but this was met with fierce resistance from the Sublime Porte. Only in Algeria was a European power—France—able to extend a claim of protection over the Jews as a single community. In fact, the Crémieux decree of 1870 granted not just protection but actual French citizenship to Algerian Jews.[28] It was named for Adolphe Crémieux (born Isaac Moïse), a successful liberal Jewish politician in France who had worked to abolish slavery in the French colonies and the death penalty at home. Toward the end of his career, he turned his attention toward the Jews of Algeria, seeking to raise their legal status to equal that of the *colons*. Fortuitously for the supporters of the liberals, Crémieux's initiative coincided with the 1870 elections in France: the decree instantly created 80,000 new voters exceedingly grateful to the French Republicans. Blanket French nationalization of this sort would remain beyond the collective grasp of Moroccan Jews, however, due to French resistance to the idea.[29] And despite French promises of equality between natives and settlers in Morocco (the latter group less numerous in Morocco than in Algeria, but still significant), that was never the case.[30] Under these circumstances, the protégé system was seen as the best option for upward mobility by many Moroccan Jews.

"From the *dhimma* of Muslims to the *dhimma* of Christians"

France, England, and Spain held the greatest numbers of protégés in Morocco, followed by smaller numbers held by the United States, the Netherlands, Portugal, Brazil, Belgium, Germany, and Italy. While the majority of the protégés serving these countries in Morocco were, in fact, Muslims, Moroccan Jews were disproportionately represented in the protégé system as a whole.[31] Jews' usefulness as intermediaries for both European firms and governments and for the Moroccan authorities has been noted above. But what were Jews' own motives for collaboration, if such a word is apt, particularly given their apparent cognizance of the potential risks of being associated with the despised colonizer? While it is true that minorities throughout the Middle East and North Africa were generally more welcoming of European intervention than was the Muslim majority, the reasons for this were complex.[32] In a premodern context, *dhimma* status was preferable to the status of Jews in Christian Europe, where the looming possibility of persecution, oppression, and expulsion made life much less secure.[33] But by the late nineteenth century, the tables were starting to turn; Europe itself had changed. Jews constituted the only significant religious minority remaining in Europe after Muslims were expelled from the Iberian Peninsula. Beginning in the eighteenth century, France's *Declaration of the Rights of Man* and similar legislation in other countries granted Jews equal rights and eventually citizenship. This should not be confused with assimilation and acculturation, which, it could be argued, were still stronger in the Muslim world than in Europe at the time, but the French Revolution and its offshoots established regular, codified legal rights for Jews and new avenues of recourse against abuse that were by and large not available in the Middle East and North Africa. By comparison, the legal status of *dhimma*, though always fluid in application, was still a far cry from citizenship and as such less appealing to Moroccan Jews. For them, ties with European governments and businesses were seen as offering a way out of their inferior position, an opportunity for economic gain and the chance to be on what appeared to be the "winning" side. In this situation, Jews also had less to lose than Muslim elites, who, though also not citizens in any sense, were more heavily invested in traditional hierarchies. As a representative of the Anglo-Jewish Association put it, "The Jews abandoned the *dhimma* of Islam [...] for the *dhimma* of the Christians."[34]

Particularly successful at obtaining patents of protection were *tujjar al-sultan*,[35] the elite corps of royal merchants charged with handling much of the kingdom's long-distance trade on the behalf of the *makhzan*. Their already high status was reinforced by becoming protégés; indeed, one of the many ways that the protégé system weakened Morocco was by exacerbating preexisting class differences.[36] The biography of Haim Benchimol is typical in this case. A wealthy banker, Benchimol, was active in both the Jewish community and the larger circles in Tangier. He is beloved in Tangier to this day for having endowed Morocco's only Jewish hospital, which functioned until it was abruptly torn down in 2010. He began his service to France as a translator and acting French consul in Larache, from which he advanced to become the "auxiliary dragoman," or translator, for the French Legation at Tangier. His achievements multiplied thereafter. He founded and served as president of the city's masonic lodge, as director of a French maritime bank, as editor of an important newspaper (*le Réveil du Maroc*), and as a commercial agent for a French steamship company. For Haim's many services, the Benchimol family was given the special privilege of French protection in perpetuity.[37] Thanks to the protégé system, the rich became richer. Beyond his obvious elite standing, two aspects of Benchimol's protégé status are telling: one, his patent had originally been granted to Haim's father, and was later extended to Haim's entire family, not just to him personally; and two, it was granted in perpetuity. Neither of these were original provisions of the protégé system, which, according to the 1863 *Regulation of Tangier*, was intended to be both temporary and individual. But the system had expanded in scope far beyond what had originally been envisioned. Eventually it involved nearly all the European powers as sponsors, with hundreds, if not thousands, of indigenous Moroccans operating as their protégés. Unauthorized practices abounded: in addition to being passed on to one's heirs, protégé status was extended to family members, associates, and so on; sometimes it was simply auctioned off to the highest bidder (who may or may not have been employed by a foreign power) or acquired by out-and-out bribery of a corrupt official. Once it had been obtained, the abuses often continued. Protégés were known for all kinds of bad behavior, knowing that they had little to fear from the Moroccan authorities. Among their more vexing privileges was their right to submit lists of unpaid debts to the consular powers protecting them, who could in turn demand that the sultan himself pay them, with the understanding that he was ultimately responsible for all his subjects.[38] Protégés also tended to invoke their rights of protection at the least provocation. A letter from the French Legation asserted that no fewer than 2000 claims had been made by Moroccan Jewish protégés over the course of a single year, resulting in thousands of Muslim defendants being pursued by the authorities and put in jail, where some died.[39]

In 1879, the Moroccan sultan called for an international conference to try to stem the abuses of the protégé system. It took place in Madrid and was attended by representatives of all the major European powers as well as the United States. But instead of curtailing the protection racket, the Treaty of Madrid that resulted on July 3, 1880, granted foreigners even more privileges in Morocco, including the right to own land in the countryside. They had previously gotten around this prohibition by owning land in partnerships with Moroccans, but now they could buy land outright in their own names. Major agricultural areas like the Haouz around Marrakech started to fall into the hands of French and other landholders, leading to the slow disenfranchisement of Moroccan peasantry.[40] At the same time, a provision for limiting the number of Moroccan protégés, which the European powers had originally offered to the Moroccans in exchange for the right to buy land, was summarily ignored. A provision establishing the principle of perpetual allegiance, which required naturalized Europeans (in practice this meant Moroccan Jews who had obtained French naturalization in Algeria under the Crémieux decree and then returned home) to revert to their Moroccan nationality if they stayed in Morocco for longer than three years, also went unheeded. Over the Moroccan government's vociferous objections, the protégé system succeeded in giving the European powers a particularly powerful means by which to divide and conquer Morocco.

In the short term, on an individual level, protégé status was surely welcomed by Moroccan Jews as a boon. For the protégé, it meant a job and a salary—already huge advantages—that furthermore came with tax relief and something akin to diplomatic immunity. The protégé had every reason to welcome such improvements in his daily life. For the *makhzan*, however, the ultimate victim of this arrangement, the protégé system was far from benign, as it weakened the Moroccan state by decreasing tax returns and diverting endless energy and resources to addressing irregularities.[41] The damage also spread beyond the immediate lands of the *makhzan* to the hinterlands. Jews in those areas had long been part of a complex system of protection whereby for a payment (*zattata*), tribal leaders of the rural areas would insure the safe passage of Jewish peddlers from town to town.[42] Protégés were increasingly able to bypass these arrangements by substituting European protection for the *qa'id-s'* guarantees.

Moreover, the French had long had trouble "pacifying" such regions. As their reach extended into the Moroccan hinterlands through the use of protégés, they made allegiances with the so-called Grand Caids, or Great Lords, of the Atlas, most notably the chiefs of the Glawa, Goundafa, and M'tougga clans. Thus even in these remote areas, traditional hierarchies and arrangements were disrupted by the protégé system, paving the way for the establishment of European colonial control.

But perhaps the most harmful aspect of the protégé system for Jewish Morocco was its impact on Muslim-Jewish relations. For Muslims, it was shocking to witness the swift elevation of *dhimma* status. After centuries of living severely restricted public lives, suddenly protected Jews could be seen owning slaves (including Muslim slaves), wearing European clothing, and openly flaunting their connections to those in high places that allowed them to engage in such behavior.[43] Some Jews were able to acquire great wealth and influence. Nonetheless, Jews were still expected to project an image of subordination, at least in public. This was getting harder and harder to enforce however. As the Moroccan historian Mohammed Kenbib has noted, intercommunal tensions ran especially high when Jewish protégés were placed in positions of authority directly over Muslim protégés—an order that stood the traditional notion of *dhimma* on its head—or over ordinary Moroccan subjects engaged in complaints or lawsuits against Muslim protégés.[44] For regular Moroccans, ancient hierarchies had been upended, privileges lost, the world as they knew it had been turned upside down. For those granting the patents, however, such subtleties were lost in translation.

European Jewish intervention and the Alliance Israélite Universelle

Overarching such changes in legal status was the cultural transformation of Jewish Morocco. The "*regeneration*" of Moroccan Jews was high on the list of priorities for newly international-minded European Jewry, who had started paying attention to events in the region in the wake of the French bombardments of 1844, when thousands of Jews fled from Morocco's coasts to Gibraltar and Algeria. Deeper involvement in Moroccan Jewish affairs came with the visit of the prominent British philanthropist Moses Montefiore to Morocco in 1863. By then, two decades had passed since the Damascus blood libel, which instigated Montefiore's last intervention in the region.[45] Montefiore's Moroccan trip was likewise motivated by reports of the false arrests of his coreligionists. In the

Moroccan case, some local Jews had been involved in a dispute with Spanish merchants in Morocco's north and were being imprisoned. Again, Montefiore's intervention was successful: the surviving prisoners were released, and a subsequent visit to the sultan in Marrakech resulted in the issuing of the *dahir* of February 5, 1864, promising justice and the protection of Jewish and Christian minorities in Morocco. The *dahir* was not seen as particularly significant in Morocco, insofar as it didn't represent a change in policy: traditional *dhimma* status already contained these provisions. So what was Mawlay Muhammad b. 'Abd al-Rahman's motivation for issuing the *dahir*? Was he placating the British? The Moroccan historian Mohamed Kenbib calls attention to the inclusion of Christians in the *dahir* incongruous because Morocco had no native Christian population at the time. Based on that observation, he argues that the formulation proposed by Montefiore was in fact directly modeled on capitulation treaties in the Ottoman Empire, which weakened Ottoman independence by granting various European powers legal authority over specific *millet*-s.[46] Apparently Montefiore's Jewish humanitarianism also had a political agenda. This is underlined by the extensive involvement of the British Foreign Office and the British Legation in his visit, who rightly perceived it as a possible means of increasing British influence in Morocco.

Following Montefiore's visit, many European Jews grew concerned with the "distressed" condition of Moroccan Jewry.[47] Motivated no doubt by a strong sense of solidarity with their fellow Jews, such concern was as sincere as it was complicated; Moroccan Jews may or may not have needed help, yet one cannot ignore the potential strategic value for European Jews of being cast as their brothers' helpers. On the one hand, European Jewish intervention into Moroccan Jewish affairs could and did further the colonial imperative to divide and conquer. But such "help" could also be useful to European Jews' efforts to disguise or displace questions about their own capacity for acculturation at home. This observation may require some further explanation.

Only recently emancipated themselves, "enlightened" Jews in Europe dreaded few things more than the possibility that European gentiles, who, in the name of imperialism, were probing ever further into the Islamic world, would "discover" the "backward" Jews of Africa and Asia and draw a connection between them and the Jews back home. Such an amalgamation would weaken European Jews' chances at full acceptance in European society.[48] European Jews worried that Moroccan Jewish culture was all too similar to that of the Muslims among whom they lived and whose own rights to freedom were quickly diminishing in Europeans' eyes. An 1876 report from the southern capital Marrakesh by the

Orientalist scholar Joseph Halevy urged that something be done for Moroccan Jewry before it was too late: "In sum, the Jews [...] have unconsciously copied the manners, faults, and superstitions of the Muslim population in whose midst they live; it must be admitted that among the poorer classes, which are the most numerous, conversion to Islam is frequent."[49] Whatever else may have motivated European Jews—they could not be accused of the same anti-Semitism as European gentiles and their Orientalism was complicated, to say the least, by their own status as perennial outsiders in Europe[50]—it was in their self-interest to transform Moroccan Jewish culture along European lines. Not surprisingly, European Jews became the most ardent defenders of their Moroccan counterparts, urging the latter's "regeneration" and integration into "modern" civilization to both European and Moroccan governments at every opportunity. Their efforts would indeed help transform Moroccan Jewish culture, but few at the time could have guessed at what cost.

Several international Jewish aid groups were established to address the perceived plight of non-Western Jewry, including in eastern and southern Europe. The best known of these organizations were the Anglo-Jewish Association, the Jewish Joint Distribution Agency, the (British) Board of Jewish Deputies, and the *Alliance Israélite Universelle* (AIU). Of these, the AIU had by far the greatest impact on Jewish Morocco.[51] The AIU was established by a group of French (mostly Alsatian) Jews in Paris in 1860. It was conceived of as an activist organization to fight for Jews' political rights worldwide at the same time as it sought their Europeanization, in part so that metropolitan Jews themselves could fulfill the promise of emancipation. The AIU claimed to represent world Jewry, speaking in its name at both the Congress of Berlin in 1878 and the Paris Peace Conference in 1919. (Such a program would eventually put the AIU at odds with Zionism, which also sought to speak for world Jewry but promoted Jewish separation, not assimilation, see Chapter 5.) The leadership of the AIU was exclusively European, including the above-mentioned Adolph Crémieux, one of its early leaders, along with members of the French Jewish intellectual elite (many were from the Alsace region). Its primary mission—the term is especially apt here—was to provide education and vocational training to young Jews.[52] At its height it maintained a network of nearly 200 schools in the Islamic world and the Balkans, but Morocco was its most important site of operations. It opened its very first school there, in Tetuan, in 1862, and many more followed before the century drew to a close, including in Tangier, Mogador (Essaouira), Fez, Casablanca, and Marrakech.[53] Ultimately, the AIU would operate more schools in Morocco than in any other country. Its girls' schools were the first of their kind in Morocco, or indeed anywhere in the Middle East and North Africa, where a system of education for Jewish girls had been nonexistent until their arrival.

The AIU provided Moroccan Jewish children with a "modern" French primary and lower secondary education that combined both secular and Jewish learning, the latter somewhat reluctantly (see below).[54] AIU students learned French and other European languages (sometimes too many to juggle) in addition to other subjects,[55] with a strong emphasis on vocational training. Deeply intertwined with this academic curriculum was a social program. Jewish pupils were strongly encouraged to adopt European habits, especially in the area of hygiene, dress, and religion, and to bring these new habits home to their families. The wearing of headscarves was discouraged, and girls were urged to uncover their heads or wear European hats.[56] As two sociolinguists of the French scientific mission in Morocco observed: "Whether boy or girl, every child taught in school leaves behind their traditional clothing. Every young woman who in her youth dressed in the black apron worn by young students of the Alliance Israélite refuses to hide her hair beneath a scarf. Every young man who knows how to speak French refuses to wear the black skullcap."[57]

Special attention was paid by the AIU to sexual matters; prostitution, promiscuity, sexually transmitted diseases, and homosexuality were the bane of the AIU's existence in Morocco. The organization worked especially hard to combat child marriages, so-called *mariages précoces*, which were traditionally contracted (though rarely consummated) between very young girls and older boys/men, usually for the purposes of sealing alliances between families. To that end, married girls were banned from attending the AIU girls' schools, which were first opened in Tetuan in 1866, just 4 years after the founding of its first boys' school there.[58] The education of Jewish girls may actually have been the AIU's most revolutionary and consequential act,[59] aimed at creating a new type of Jewish wife and mother to serve as handmaidens to the new Jewish man.

As radical as the AIU's attitude toward gender issues may have been, their program for girls was nonetheless not in and of itself the source of greatest friction with the local communities. When girls stayed away from a school opened in Marrakech in 1901, a report from the *directrice* identified the main stumbling block as financial, not moral. A child needed clean clothes to go to school, which cost money. In such cases, boys always came first.[60] Although the AIU would over time create a Europeanized elite, its target demographic was, in fact, the poor. As Susan Miller has written in the context of Tangier: "More than half of the students at the Alliance schools were not paying. Jewish street urchins entered the school at age seven, unwashed and undisciplined, and emerged seven years later, speaking, reading and writing in French, Spanish and English, adept at math and accounting, and gorged on the *Alliance* dogma vis-à-vis the limitless capacity of the human spirit."[61] The availability of food, clothing, and medicine also attracted students to the AIU.

Jewish Morocco's attitude toward the AIU, to the extent one can generalize, was ambivalent.[62] On the one hand, the students themselves were enthusiastic early adopters of Europeanization. When the Marechal Lyautey visited the AIU schools in Marrakech in 1912, he received the following message from the students:

> We are very happy and honored to wish you our sincere welcome to this building which to us is the house of France. It is here that we learn the French language [which is] useful and indispensable for everyone everywhere. It is here that we are taught to know our duties and our rights which will be easily recognized—thanks to the new regime implanted by the country that, since our entry to the school, we consider as our own homeland.
>
> We dare to hope that after the establishment of the French Protectorate our schools will be enlarged so that we can continue our studies there. One could go to France [for education], but only the affluent have the resources necessary to do so; those who lack the resources ardently deserve to be as educated as others. We ask you, Mr. Resident General, to accept our respectful homage and to trust in our complete dedication. [signed] The Students of the Schools of the Alliance Israelite Universelle.[63]

But whenever its program pushed up against explicit religious norms, there was great resistance. While gender relations can certainly be subsumed in that category, in practice this usually meant AIU's secularizing program, which was squarely aimed at Jewish learning and ritual. The AIU never lacked for chutzpah, as it were, in this area. From the outset, the AIU made no secret of its wish to replace traditional Torah learning with secular studies. When it did concede to teach Judaism, usually under pressure from local Jewish communities, it was refracted through a French Enlightenment lens. Arguments broke out constantly between the Jewish elders and the AIU directors, as when prize ceremonies were scheduled for the Sabbath or when European languages took up time that could be devoted to Hebrew.[64] This is not to say that the religious/secular divide was the only source of conflict. Outbreaks of anti-AIU feelings could also arise from personal conflict, as in Tetuan in 1874, when the AIU director entered into a very public feud with the town's chief rabbi, the director publicly mocking the rabbi for his kabbalistic leanings, resulting in the schools being closed down for several months.⁶⁵ Pro-British leanings among the *evolués* in Mogador (Essaouira), where the Anglo-Jewish association operated its own schools, also helped foment anti-French and hence anti-AIU feelings among local Jews.

The legacy of the Alliance Israélite Universelle

Without denying any of the AIU's achievements, the educational and cultural norms it sought to instill—known collectively as *alliancism*—often came at the expense of traditional Jewish education and culture in Morocco. The two worldviews proved difficult to truly bridge; advances by the AIU usually entailed the retreat of local practices, particularly among the youth. The AIU schools displaced rabbinical authorities and eroded traditional learning, which in Morocco had a long and distinguished history that included some of Sephardic and Arab Judaism's greatest luminaries.⁶⁶ It is not a coincidence that this venerable tradition remained most vital in areas where the AIU made the fewest inroads. For example, the Tafilalt, deep in rural southeastern Morocco, was the home of the Abuhatsera clan, one of Morocco's most influential rabbinic families of the modern period. Scions of this family include Rabbi Ya'qub, buried in the town of Damanhur in Egypt's Nile delta, and the even more famous Baba Salé, a.k.a. Israel Abuhatsera buried in Netivot, Israel, where he is widely venerated as a Moroccan Jewish "saint." In the adjacent Draa valley, world-renowned kabbalists were active for a good thousand years until their departure in the twentieth century. Their brand of knowledge, however, was not especially valued by European Jewry at the time. It only survived because of limited European Jewish interference in these regions.

Nationalist historians have tended to view the AIU as part and parcel of French imperialism in Morocco, but its trajectory is more complicated than that. Jonathan Katz has identified three distinct phases in the AIU's involvement with Jewish Morocco that can help us recapture some of the missing nuance: prior to 1914 ("*les temps heroïques*"), in which the AIU took no government funding at all and could claim full independence; between 1914 and 1924, when it became more closely aligned with the French government and received a partial subvention; and the third phase, from 1924, when the AIU was given official responsibility for educating Moroccan Jewry under the Protectorate, and teachers were "de facto state employees."⁶⁷ But even within each of these stages, there was always a countervailing tendency toward cultural amalgamation, whereby resilient cultural patterns meshed with, but were not replaced by, imported ideas.[68] There were also many instances of outright resistance by the local communities, notably in Sefrou,[69] and in Marrakech,[70] stemming both from specifically Jewish concerns mentioned above but also because a minority of Jews shared with the majority of Muslims true consternation at the prospect of European control over Morocco. This same sentiment would carry into the anti-colonial period, when a small number of Jews rejected *alliancism* and allied themselves with the Moroccan independence movement.[71]

Moroccan state reform and the Jews

All this activity on the part of Western powers and European Jews on behalf of Moroccan Jews does not mean that the latter were ignored by the Moroccan authorities. As the Montefiore-inspired *dahir* of 1864 shows, Jewish issues never strayed far from the *makhzan-*'s attentions. These efforts can be best understood within their proper context, however, namely the larger program of reform undertaken by the Moroccan state.

In the nineteenth century, *nizam* ["order"], or *al-nizam al-jadid* ["the new order"], was developed as a conceptual framework for various programs of Western-style reform and modernization that political leaders throughout North Africa and the Middle East experimented with, implemented by the Ottomans as *tanzimat*. The thinking behind *nizam* was defensive: by revamping certain sectors of society and government along European lines, local rulers hoped that total colonial encroachment might be forestalled.[72] In their struggle to become more orderly, or less "Oriental," governments throughout the Middle East and North Africa began sending their cadets to Europe for military training or importing foreign officers, creating their first foreign ministries, promoting the education of girls, and developing modern bureaucracies with Western-style fiscal and administrative practices.

Following the Ottoman example, Mohammed IV (r. 1859–1873) was the first Moroccan leader to embark on an ambitious program of reform. The sultan was adamant about keeping Britain, Spain, and France—which from 1849 on were in a heated competition for Morocco—at a safe distance. Although Mohammed III's grandson 'Abd al-'Aziz was, as we have seen, much less competent, the reforms of this period nonetheless helped keep Morocco independent longer than any other country in the Maghrib. The professionalization of the administration and the creation of new ministries, the modernization of the Moroccan army, and the regularization of taxes can be counted among the pre-Protectorate *makhzan*'s major achievements, implemented against a backdrop of increasing foreign incursion into Moroccan territory, not to mention environmental disasters like famine, drought, and epidemic.[73]

Urban planning, including the creation or enlargement of several of Morocco's Jewish quarters, was one mechanism of reform that had a particularly significant impact on Jews. Morocco's first modern census, a symbol of *nizam* if ever there was one, had the Jewish quarter of Marrakech, the country's largest, as its subject.[74] After determining that the *mellah* had become overcrowded as a result of population growth and rural influx to the city, the government proceeded to enlarge it to build new housing and thus ease the crowding. The *mellah* of Essaouira was also enlarged during this period, though a small number of Jews in that town were also allowed to live in the kasbah alongside Muslims and foreigners, probably owing to their elite status as merchants.[75] As part of a similar effort, new *mellah*-s were built in several coastal towns where none had existed before, including Rabat, Salé, and Tetouan. In these cases, the Jewish quarters were created in order to control and monitor native Jews' interaction with Europeans, who were concentrated in Morocco's ports. The only city with a significant Jewish population to remain without a *mellah* was Tangier.[76]

But it was too little too late. Whatever reforms the *makhzan* could muster were insufficient to counter the combined onslaught of the protégé system and the AIU. While the Europeanizing efforts that had begun in the nineteenth century never fully succeeded in transforming Moroccan Jews into Europeans, they nonetheless reinforced the position of a Westernized elite whose habits trickled down in a limited way to the masses. For a small minority, the protégé system completed the process by offering a new legal status to match the shift in culture. As foreign encroachment became more visible, and more unwelcome, the heightened status of Europeanized Jews did not go unnoticed by other Moroccans. But it is important to keep in mind that Jews' tacit support for colonialism was rarely ideologically motivated. Moroccan Jews were pawns in the imperial game and, to the extent that they knew it, took advantage of the new opportunities that arose where and when they could. But being identified with what were increasingly perceived as negative forces was not conducive to Jewish integration into the growing sense of a Moroccan nation, and Moroccan historiography has retrospectively, and often unfairly, castigated Jews as collaborators for taking such an active part in the protégé system in particular.[77] But Jews themselves would also suffer the consequences of Europeanization: by taking members of this minority community out of the more than thousand-year-old framework of *dhimma* while leaving them physically in place, the protégé system put Moroccan Jews on a path toward existential crisis, while the cultural inroads made by the AIU reshaped their sense of self, community, and nation.

Jewish Morocco under the Protectorate

Morocco was able to remain officially independent into the twentieth century, the only Maghribi country to do so. But in 1904, France, Spain, and England, whose rivalries prevented any one power from dominating, finally worked out a secret bilateral deal. Despite Napoleon's watershed campaign into Egypt in 1798–1801, the French would give Britain a free hand there in exchange for the British offering the same to France in Morocco. (Spain got territory in the north and the far south of the country.) Less powerful rivals including Germany and Italy were also neutralized. Worn down by political crises, military interventions, and crippling loans, Mawlay 'Abd al-Hafidh was obliged to sign the Treaty of Fez on March 30, 1912. It established French and Spanish Protectorates over Morocco, with Tangier as an "international zone." Morocco thereby joined Algeria and Tunisia to form the French colonial trinity of *"le maghreb."*

The 44-year period of foreign control that followed may not have been the total rupture it was once thought to be,[78] but it was still a deeply unsettling turn of events for Moroccans. New patterns of land ownership, trade, employment, legal status, education, and cultural orientation often cut off access to older ones, which had the overall effect of worsening the living conditions of ordinary Moroccans. Protectorate rule in Morocco was characterized by a policy of "association," whereby the trappings of sultanic authority were carefully maintained but the real political and financial power of the state was transferred to France. This stood in contrast to the policy of "assimilation" France had followed in Algeria, which entailed direct control of the country and development of its resources with little regard for its people or existing social structures. Despite a keen desire to avoid the missteps of *Algérie Française*, the French resident-general was still the ultimate authority in Morocco beginning with the highly influential Louis Hubert Lyautey, who served in that role during the formative period 1912–1925. The power of the Moroccan sultan, so hard-won by the Alawis in the precolonial period, was reduced to little more than the proverbial stamp, though wielded with acuity.

Early in the Protectorate period, the French resident-general sought out the advice of the Jewish scholar Nahum Slouschz on how to better organize, and in turn utilize, the Jewish communities in Morocco to the advantage of the Protectorate. Slouschz was another unique character. Born in Vilna and raised in Odessa, Slouschz studied Semitic languages in France. In 1905 he was invited to become a member of the *Mission Scientifique du Maroc*—a proto-colonial research project that published the highly influential journal *Archives marocaines*.[79] With the sponsorship of the *Mission* as well as support from the AIU and the Semitic Commission of the *Academie des Belles Lettres*, Slouschz undertook a detailed study of North African Jewry based on extensive travels from the Atlantic coast to the Libyan desert. To Lyautey, Slouschz was the ideal person to provide the Protectorate with much-needed information about Morocco's Jews. Motivated as always by the determination to avoid the mistakes of Algeria, Lyautey was desperate to find an alternative to the French "*consistoire*" system that placed Algerian Jews under the direct control of the chief rabbi of France (who from 1808 until today is a government appointee).[80] He asked Slouschz to make a formal study of the Jews of Morocco as a first step.

Slouschz's forays into the Jewish communities of the far reaches of the Moroccan hinterlands resulted in many valuable findings, though his close descriptions of Jewish life have withstood the test of time much better than the theories he extrapolated from them. Slouschz was also a committed Zionist. The ideological inferences in his work clashed with both French Protectorate and AIU positions (the former encouraged Jews to become westernized Moroccans; the latter wanted them to become naturalized Frenchmen and women). Although the aims of Slouschz's nationalism shifted—he at one point traveled to Libya to explore the possibility of establishing a Jewish colony there—it was sufficiently ardent to bring him to loggerheads with the French authorities, and Lyautey did not keep him in his employ long. Lyautey knew that whatever plans lay in store for Morocco's Jews, the governing powers would have to straddle a fine line between French Jews who were agitating for a Crémieux decree for Morocco[81] and Moroccan Muslims who would presumably be against such action, all against the backdrop of the struggle for Jewish emancipation and civil status in Europe and the colonies.[82] Above all, Lyautey did not want to see a repeat of Algeria, where the granting of French citizenship to (most) Jews sparked a violent anti-Semitic backlash among European settlers (and fear of the same from Muslims, though it never materialized). Indirect rule was Lyautey's answer for Morocco, but what did it entail for Moroccan Jews?

For a small elite,⁸³ French rule in any form was a welcome development. This was certainly the case for the descendants of Jews who in the nineteenth century had already begun moving from the Moroccan interior toward port cities to gain access to coastal Morocco's growing economic opportunities. The corridor between Marrakech and Essaouira was especially well traveled, given both the density of the population in Morocco's south and the southern capital's appetite for luxury items, especially when the sultan was in town. Foreign goods like sugar and tea would arrive in Essaouira from Europe, where Jewish merchants arranged for them to be sent to the interior. From Marrakech, Jewish merchants exported goods like almonds, olive oil, wax, and apricot kernels to the coasts.

A prominent Jewish family with branches in both cities were the Corcos, Sephardic Jews who first arrived in Fez after the 1492 expulsion and were well established in Marrakech by the eighteenth century. The Corcos family boasted some of the country's most notable royal merchants, property owners, community leaders, and financial advisors. Yeshoua Corcos (1832–1929) was known as "the millionaire of the *mellah*" of Marrakech; Stella Corcos, the wife of the Moroccan merchant Moses Corcos, ran a successful tuition-free school for Jewish girls in Essaouira, which by 1907 was educating more pupils than the local AIU school. Both Essaouira and Casablanca grew from small fishing villages to Morocco's most active ports in the colonial period, thanks in large part to the activities of Jewish merchants like the Corcos.⁸⁴ And in Tangier, Jewish businessmen crossed communal lines to join forces with other entrepreneurs and developers in order to create a new capitalist core from which to modernize the city.⁸⁵

French influence also catalyzed Jews' involvement in the intellectual developments of the period, which included the establishment of a vigorous Jewish press, which published Benchimol's *le Réveil du Maroc*.⁸⁶ French language publications existed alongside new Arabic language newspapers, among them *nahda* journals from the Levant that regularly featured the work of Jewish thinkers.

Despite the gains of a small minority, however, the masses of Moroccan Jews remained poor or became poorer during the Protectorate period, as did the majority of Muslims. Lyautey had promised benign neglect: "The Arab and the Jewish quarters, I will not touch them. I shall clean them up, restore them, supply them with running water and electricity, and remove the waste, but that is all."⁸⁷ But his approach was deleterious in practice. Under the Protectorate, the *mellah*-s grew impoverished and more overcrowded than practically any other part of Moroccan cities. The wealthier Jews simply abandoned them for the *villes nouvelles* built by the French, leaving the poor to fend for themselves.

Poverty in the inland capitals (Marrakech, Fez, Meknes) was so acute, however, that even when restrictions on Jewish residency outside the *mellah* were finally lifted in 1912, Jews were slow to leave. In Marrakech, the largest *mellah* in Morocco, not a single Jewish family actually resettled in the new city (Gueliz) until 1927.[88]

Moreover, the rise of Jewish merchants in the port cities often came at the expense of the Jewish communities in the interior, whose livelihoods were severely threatened as industrial imports from Europe supplanted local crafts in the *suq*-s, and the artisans who had lived off their production for centuries were reduced to poverty.[89] Jewish craftspeople who specialized in leather, metallurgy, embroidery and sewing, in addition to those involved in peddling and commerce, were negatively impacted by the new mercantile pressures placed upon them. Even the wealthy merchant class of Fez, many of whom were Jews, were sorely disappointed when new contracts and trade development failed to appear as had been promised.[90] Although few Jews were large landholders in Morocco, it was not completely unknown for Jews to own and work in rural agriculture. Hence European land speculation in the countryside, and the resulting increase in the price of land, hurt Jews as well as Muslims.[91] The broad exploitation of the countryside by European settlers brought rural refugees from the *bled* to the *hadariya* [civilized] cities, who quickly took the place of elites moving out to the coasts, causing even more overcrowding of the interior urban *mellah*-s. As elsewhere in the Middle East and North Africa, the "modernization" that occurred under colonial auspices raised birth rates but did not improve the standard of living or increase economic resources for the majority of the population.[92] These trends, moreover, must be considered alongside the fact that Morocco had the largest population of Jews of any Arab country in the twentieth century. In 1912, between 110,000 and 120,000 Jews lived in Morocco. By the 1950s, that number grew to a quarter of a million.

Under the French Protectorate, the protégé system was eliminated and protégés reverted to the status of "natives." But even with that particular wedge removed, the sense of separation and alienation between Jews and Muslims continued to widen. The French had created an autonomist apparatus that deterred Jews from intermingling with Muslims on a number of levels that was never really dismantled. A 1918 *dahir* established local Jewish councils and committees along the lines of those in France as well as a central rabbinical court in Rabat. Jews no longer had recourse to the *shari'a* courts, which had functioned as a much-used alternative, and instead found themselves under the combined jurisdiction of rabbinical and Moroccan *makhzan* courts. The position of inspector general of Jewish institutions was created at the same time to serve as the compliant representative of the Jewish communities to the French Protectorate authorities. Various pro-French Moroccan Jews filled this position, beginning with Yahya Zagury and Maurice Botbol. The Jewish community forfeited some of its autonomy, but failed to gain equality in exchange due to the inherent inequalities of the colonial system.[93]

Conclusion

With the establishment of the French Protectorate over Morocco in 1912, political and economic processes that had been set in motion during the preceding decades accelerated and consolidated. The gap between rich and poor widened, Jews began to leave the *mellah*-s for the European quarters, and Jews increasingly dressed, worked, and spoke like Europeans, with the result that Jews' alienation from the surrounding Muslim society continued to grow. As one scholar deftly put it: "The Jew under colonization became synthetically French, a product of a laboratory, who, in claiming to be exclusively French, assimilated to a non-reality."[94] Their unique position is exemplified by the fact that Jews were the only group in Morocco to have members in both the native and European sectors of colonial society.[95] Although Albert Memmi deemed it impossible, Moroccan Jews were, in fact, both "colonizer" and "colonized" *à la fois*.

Despite the tumultuousness of the Protectorate period, it was nonetheless unforeseeable to many at the time that French North Africa would not endure. This belief made the struggle to adapt to the new colonial reality even more crucial for Jews given their minority status. But the French would indeed depart, leaving the Jews behind. By the 1930s, with the early rumblings of decolonization and calls for independence growing, Morocco's Jews were confronted with their most wrenching choice yet.

Chapter 5: Timeline

August 1907	French troops enter Oujda; Bombardment of Casablanca
March 30, 1912	Treaty of Fez establishes French and Spanish Protectorates over Morocco
April 1912	Fez riots, French soldiers bombard Fez *mellah*
1917	Balfour declaration promising Jews a "homeland" in Palestine
1921–1925	Rif war
1923	Tangier designated an "international zone"
1930	*latif* prayer in Salé instigates popular revolt
May 16, 1930	Berber *dahir* signed by Mawlay Muhammad V
1931	Moroccan delegation travels to Jerusalem to take part in the General Islamic Congress
1934	Founding of the *Comité d'Action Marocain* (CAM)
1940–1942	Vichy occupation of Morocco
December 10, 1943	Founding of *Istiqlal*, Morocco's main nationalist organization, under the leadership of 'Allal al-Fassi
November 14, 1945	Founding of the Moroccan Communist Party under Léon Sultan
May 1948	Creation of the state of Israel; First Arab-Israeli War
June 1948	Anti-Jewish riots in Oujda and Jerada
1956	Creation of *al-wifaq* ("entente") to foster nationalist sentiment among Moroccan Jews
March 2, 1956	Declaration of Moroccan independence
October 29– November 7, 1956	Suez Crisis (Second Arab-Israeli War)
1961	Egyptian President Gamal 'Abd al-Nasser visits Casablanca
1961	Sinking of the Pisces ship carrying clandestine Jewish emigrants; rules against emigration relaxed
June 1967	Six-day War
October 1973	Fourth Arab-Israeli War
July 10, 1971	Attempted coup against Hassan II at Skhirat Palace
August 16, 1972	Second attempted coup against Hassan II
November 1975	Green March on Western Sahara
1980s	Israeli invasion of Lebanon
July 23, 1999	Death of Hassan II
July 30, 1999	Ascension of Muhammad VI
March 11, 2007	Casablanca bombing

Map 5.1 Modern Morocco.

"Morocco Political Map." Accessed May 06, 2019. http://www.mapsopensource.com/morocco-political-map.html.

5

Arabness

Nationalism in an Old-New Key (Twentieth Century)

> A sovereign Muslim State, attached to its national unity and to its territorial integrity, the Kingdom of Morocco intends to preserve, in its plentitude and its diversity, its one and indivisible national identity.
> —Preamble to the Moroccan Constitution of 2011

> 'The Jew, the Arab,' that is to say also, between the Jew and the Arab the passage or the impossibility of a passage from the Jew to the Arab, the possibility or impossibility of the Arab, the Jew, and the Arab Jew.
> —Gil Anidjar, *The Jew, the Arab: A History of the Enemy*

Introduction: Arabness and Jewishness in the Moroccan struggle for independence

Morocco would not remain under foreign control forever. But if the country was not to be European, what exactly would it be? Too much had changed in the Maghrib and the surrounding world to revert back to precolonial ways of being. Jews, for their part, would not be returning to the *mellah* nor to the status of *dhimma*. What had historically been an advantageous status became unacceptably retrograde when compared to the new standard set in Europe of full emancipation. Not only Jews, but Moroccans as a whole had become politicized in new ways through their encounter with colonialism and began to seek answers to questions that they had never before thought to pose: not only whether independent Morocco would be a monarchy or a republic, but who actually counts as "Moroccan" and based on what criteria?

The preceding chapters have traced the historical development of four central pillars of Moroccan identity—Malikism, Amazighity, Sharifism, and Europeanization—from the perspective of Jewish Morocco. During the interwar period, these phenomena were joined by a fifth powerful force for national cohesion: Arabness. Needless to say, Arabness was not new in Morocco. It was the Arabs who brought Islam to North Africa in the first place and the Arab Bedouin (hillali) invasions of the late medieval period that solidified the new religion's hold. In cultural terms as well, Morocco was mostly Arabized by the twentieth century. Although Tamazight and its variations were spoken widely, Arabic was the country's primary written language. The Sharifian claims on which the early modern Moroccan state was built were by definition based on Arab lineages. But a new type of Arabism arose in the 1930s in the context of anti-colonial resistance that would cast Moroccan identity in a new light. Known as pan-Arabism and closely tied to Arab nationalism and Arab socialism, it drew sharp lines of division where previously only rough sketches had existed, including between Muslims and Jews.

Pan-Arabism arose in the Middle East as a rallying cry for revolt against Ottoman rule in the midst of the First World War. Its main tenet was that all Arabs are part of the same nation and should organize politically and culturally along unified lines. With the loss of the war by the Axis powers, however, the former Ottoman territories of the Arab Middle East were not made into the independent Arab state that the pan-Arabists had hoped for and had been promised; instead, they were divided into European mandates. Pan-Arabism shifted at that point to become part of the ideological arsenal of anti-colonial thought and action, particularly in the Levant, where the European powers had concluded contradictory and often secret pacts. But if the pan-Arabists were clear about their goal of ousting European colonial powers from the MENA, they were less decisive when it came to the role of minorities in that struggle. On the one hand, the movement billed itself as a secular alternative (or, more accurately, complement) to pan-Islamism, a slightly earlier ideology that sought to unite all Muslims against European colonial incursion and would be central to Moroccan nationalism.[1] To that end, pan-Arabists were careful to use inclusive language and gestures. At the first Arab Nationalist Conference in Paris in 1913, one of the delegates declared that "for us every Arabic speaker is an Arab: we do not differentiate between Muslims and non-Muslims."[2] Christian minorities were particularly well situated to take advantage of pan-Arabism's openness and became some of the movement's best-known proponents, like Michel Aflaq, the co-founder of the Syrian Ba'ath party or Edmond Rabbath of the Syrian nationalists' bloc under the French mandate. The situation was different for Jews. A small number of Iraqi, Egyptian, and Syrian Jews likewise flourished in the literary expression of pan-Arabism, through the movement known as the *nahda* [renaissance]. But cultural gains did not necessarily translate to political gains. By the 1930s, for reasons to be explained below, the modern definition of "Arab" narrowed at the same time as the line between Arabs and non-Arabs became fixed.

It was not at all clear how welcome Jews would be in the emerging nation-states of the region. They were often seen by the nationalists as collaborators or beneficiaries of colonialism rather than comrades. At the same time, Jews were associated with Zionism, the bête noire of the pan-Arabists, particularly after the Balfour declaration of 1917 promised Jews a "homeland" in Palestine despite the presence of another people on that same land. In short, the idealized theories of pan-Arabism dating from the period of anti-colonial resistance rarely survived the realities of institutionalization. Ultimately, and perhaps surprisingly, Jewish belonging proved to be more elusive in a pan-Arab context than in a pan-Islamic one. In theory, this can be explained by the inherent amorphousness of Arab identity compared to the clearly defined legal status of the *ahl al-kitab* in Islamic legal tradition; "Who is an Arab?" remains one of MENA history's great unanswered questions. But the very real politics of nationalism, both Jewish and Arab, also got in the way.

The appeal of pan-Arabism as a catalyst for national independence is not immediately obvious in a Moroccan context. The Arab heartlands are located far from this corner of the Maghrib—a good 3000 miles away—and quotidian Arab culture—narghila smoking, falafel and hummus, belly dancing, and so on—is foreign to most Moroccans as a result. Rather than identifying as "Arabs," Moroccans were historically known, and named, by dint of their hometown, village, or tribe, which might or might not reveal an Arab or Amazigh origin. Jews, meanwhile, might additionally be identified as *dhimmi*-s, *ahl al-kitab*, or simply *al-yahud*.[3] Cultural norms around Arabness in Morocco slowly began to change only after 1931, when a small Moroccan delegation traveled to Jerusalem to take part in the General Islamic Congress, which was held in conjunction with the Palestine National Congress.

Despite its name, the congress was equally devoted to pan-Arab ideas, which thereafter began to flow freely from the *mashriq* to the Maghrib.[4] Egypt was an important hub in the *maghrib-mashriq* pan-Arab network, a distinction that would only grow with time. The connection was sustained through an important community of Moroccan students and merchants who lived in Cairo and also by the fact that Egypt was a traditional stopping place for Moroccans on pilgrimage to Mecca.⁵ The central components of the pan-Arab platform at the time were strong support for the Palestinian cause and the end of colonial control of all Muslim countries. A small radical element of Jewish Morocco embraced this anti-Zionist and anti-European stance and sought to advance the cause of Moroccan independence, either assimilating to Morocco's revised Arab identity or simply ignoring it on their way to larger goals. Often they worked through the communist party, though a few—Marc Sabbah, Albert Aflalo, Jacques Dahan, and Joseph Ohana among others—took more direct action through their participation in Morocco's independence movements.⁶ Theirs is a lost history that has fallen between the cracks of these competing nationalisms, Moroccan nationalism on the one hand and Zionism on the other, which, like many conformist ideologies, have together written out these small but significant exceptions to the rule. Leftist Jews were fighting against the tide, regardless. The larger Moroccan Muslim community was understandably not attuned to the views of this minority within a minority but also increasingly associated Jews with the colonial power rather than with the resistance to it despite these individual examples to the contrary. Jewish Morocco's previously uncomplicated attachment to Arabness (or lack thereof) quickly became fraught with new meanings and urgency in this period, with stakes that could not have been higher.

A separate path for Jewish Morocco known as "alliancism" had been paved in the nineteenth century with the creation of institutions like the Alliance Israélite Universelle and the protégé system. But it was only in the twentieth century that Moroccan Jews found out where that path actually led, once they reached a tipping point whereby their sense of alienation became stronger than their sense of belonging. They reached that tipping point only at the culmination of an accelerating process that began well before the Protectorate was even established. It started with Jews' and Muslims' divergent experiences of anti-colonial resistance, was reinscribed during the cruel period of Vichy control, and reached its apex with the rise of Arab and Jewish nationalism, a zero-sum game for all involved. Jewish Morocco, which had painstakingly cohered over the preceding millennia, would not emerge intact from the events of the twentieth century.

Primary resistance from the perspective of Jewish Morocco (1907–1926)

It rarely took long for foreign intervention to spark a local reaction in Morocco. This was true from the earliest periods of Moroccan history, as in the eighth century when the Imazighen revolted against the Umayyads in the great "Berber revolt." Once Islam became firmly established in the Maghrib, resistance often took the form of *jihad*. *Jihad* not only targeted the foreign invader; it was also an important means for registering criticism of the sultan for not fulfilling his oath of office (*bay'a*) to keep Moroccans safe from outside interference. Thus in the fifteenth century, when Portuguese and Spanish merchants tried to muscle their way into the trans-African trade via the Atlantic coasts, the main resistance they met came from the Sufis of the al-Jazuli order who had taken the defense of the country into their own hands. This is not to say that resistance did not come also from the *makhzan* itself, though the sultan often had his hands tied by pre-existing treaties and alliances. Foreign encroachment followed by local resistance is a pattern that weaves, Yet it is also true that this active, almost spontaneous resistance to incursion was much more common among Moroccan Muslims than among Moroccan Jews. Known as "primary resistance," this form of anti-colonial activity was followed in the interwar period by "secondary resistance," which allowed for marginally greater Jewish involvement.[7] Why were so few Jews involved in the anti-colonial resistance compared to Muslims? The Muslim elites who benefitted from the French Protectorate system, and hence tended to support it, constituted only a small minority of the overall population; the majority of Moroccan Muslims suffered under colonial rule and were keen to be rid of it. In contrast, a small but still disproportionate number of individual Moroccan Jews tended to benefit from colonialism, making the larger Jewish community as well as the Muslim community *perceive* that they did too, due to the special attention they received from the French as part of the latter's colonial strategy to divide and conquer. The ministrations of the AIU to the country's Jews were especially obvious to outsiders, even if the AIU was not formally part of the French government. In reality, Jewish gains under colonial rule were quite meager. The Protectorate authorities never officially abolished *dhimma*—that would only happen with Moroccan independence 1956—they merely let it fall into disuse. True, Jews' status had improved under French rule and certain degrading measures had been abolished, but they had not been granted equality. Jews' legal position was ill-defined and in some cases contradictory, and their prospects of acquiring French citizenship were dim. In more social terms, French settlers had never accepted Europeanized Moroccan Jews as their equals, and they along with many Protectorate officials did little to hide their anti-Semitism.[8] Seen in this light, the generally pro-French stance of Jewish Morocco was largely unrequited.

Although the anti-colonial struggle in Morocco never reached the levels of violence seen in neighboring Algeria, it still was a time of immense insecurity and fear.[9] Muslim nationalists who threw their own bodies into the struggle faced the greatest danger, of course. Yet Jews of all political inclinations also had their lives put at risk as they once again found themselves caught between opposing forces, this time precariously wedged between a determined colonizer and an equally, if not more determined colonized population. The mass emigration of Moroccan Jewry that took place in waves during the two decades surrounding Moroccan independence (1947–1967) is often attributed to the general instability of the period.[10] Many Jews felt abandoned by the French and simply didn't know whether or how they would survive the transition to Moroccan independence and statehood. They were also being pushed and pulled in different directions by groups with starkly different agendas—Zionists, nationalists, colonialists—all of whom made promises that would be difficult to keep in the calmest of circumstances. Certainly these factors contributed to a heightened sense of insecurity. But rather than generalize further about the chaos of the period, it may be useful to investigate a few specific instances of primary resistance from the standpoint of Jewish Morocco in order to break down the process of Jewish alienation and identify some of its mechanisms before moving on to evaluate Jewish participation in certain facets of secondary resistance. To that end, three moments in the dawning struggle against European control in Morocco are instructive: the murder of the French doctor Émile Mauchamp in Marrakech in 1907, the promulgation of the Treaty of Fez in 1912, and the Rif war of 1920–1926. Jews were mostly bystanders in these events when viewed from afar. Seen from within Jewish Morocco, however, they reveal the eventmental underpinnings of the developing vision for independent Morocco and raise important questions about the place of Moroccan Jews within it.

The murder of Dr. Emile Mauchamp in Marrakech

Émile Mauchamp (1870–1907) was not a well-liked man.[11] Described variously as haughty, hypocritical, and incorrigibly racist, he did little to ingratiate himself with the people of Marrakech, where he was sent by the French government to open a medical dispensary in 1905. Mauchamp had previously served in Brazil and Jerusalem and was maneuvering for a new post in Egypt upon leaving the Levant, but that was not to be.[12] In Morocco, he hoped to be placed in Rabat where he might try to gain the ear of sultan, but that also was not to be. Mauchamp went unhappily to Marrakech. In the short time he was there, he earned a reputation for constantly complaining to whatever authority would listen, whether about his lodgings, the insufficient resources at his disposal, and especially the "backwardness" and hostility of Moroccans.[13] All of that made him an annoyance, but it is not what got Mauchamp killed.

On March 19, 1907, Emile Mauchamp was murdered by a crowd in front of his medical dispensary in the *madina* of Marrakech. He was stabbed and stoned multiple times and his body was mutilated. The immediate cause for the attack was that the townspeople thought Mauchamp was a spy. While this was technically incorrect, it was also not entirely untrue. As Edward Said, Franz Fanon, and others have shown, medicine and colonial conquest worked hand in glove in the imperial incursion into the MENA, and European doctors acted with particular impunity in precolonial Morocco. As Mauchamp's obituary in the *British Medical Journal* duly recognized: "His professional work among the natives was doing much to extend French influence in Morocco."[14] "Men of science" like Mauchamp used their professional positions to provide cover for gathering information, affording them access to places and bodies that few others had.[15] Tellingly, they were often sent by and reported back to military or geographic societies rather than by medical organizations. Mauchamp, we may recall, was an employee of the French government. Doctors of German, Belgian, and other nationalities also practiced in Morocco at various times. But in medicine as in politics, the main rivalry in Morocco was between the English and the French. And among the latter group, few took their political role more seriously than Emile Mauchamp.

In Marrakech, Mauchamp meddled in diplomatic affairs and claimed authority he didn't have. His most fervent hope was to ingratiate himself with the *makhzan*, but he found himself blocked in his efforts by the fact that the sultan already had a personal physician, one Judah Holzmann. Holzmann had a complicated, nineteenth-century identity: he was born an Ottoman subject in Jerusalem in 1867 and a Jew. He studied medicine in Berlin in the 1890s. More recently, he moved to Morocco where he married a Moroccan Muslim woman and was said to have converted to Islam. French diplomats referred to him as an "Ottoman adventurer," but Mauchamp suspected him of more nefarious activities; he was certain that Holzmann was a spy, in league with the German consul in Marrakech. This suspicion proved Mauchamp's undoing. In the spring of 1907, Mauchamp returned to Morocco following a visit home to France. He brought with him several packages. Back in Marrakech, Mauchamp installed what appeared to be wireless telegraph equipment on his roof. His timing was poor.

The pasha of the southern capital had just recently warned the townspeople to be on the lookout for spying devices, and whatever was on Mauchamp's roof seemed to fit the bill. Early reports suggested that it was a flag or surveying equipment. But the reality was more embarrassing and exposed Mauchamp's petty nature: it was in fact a fake antenna—a pole with four wires dangling from it—meant to provoke his German rivals in the city.[16] As an angry crowd gathered in front of the dispensary, Mauchamp conceded and agreed to take down the apparatus. The melee in the narrow street escalated quickly however, and Mauchamp did not act fast enough. As his translator ran for safety, the first of many knife blows plunged into the French doctor's body.

According to the historian Ellen Amster, Mauchamp's murder was a political act—a *jihad* of the type mentioned earlier—in protest of the failure of Sultan 'Abd al-'Aziz to protect his people and ensure their well-being: "In the Moroccan political imagination, Mauchamp came to embody internal and external threats to the body politic and was made to suffer 'many deaths'— for a crumbling Moroccan state, for foreign influence, and for the social and economic crisis in Morocco."[17] But all the colonial lobby (known as *le Comité du Maroc*) saw was a dead Frenchman, urban unrest, and a complicit pasha. Their response was as swift as it was devastating. Using Mauchamp's murder as justification, they successfully pushed for the military occupation of the eastern Moroccan city of Oujda. The invasion came just days after Mauchamp's death. It was led from Algeria by Marshal Hubert Lyautey, the man who would be France's first resident general in Morocco. Although Morocco was ruled as a Protectorate and was never made into an official colony, the French troops that entered Oujda in 1907 would not depart from Morocco for fifty years.[18] As Jonathan Katz explains,

> Mauchamp's death provided the catalyst for changes that would irrevocably seal Morocco's fate. The retaliatory occupation of Oujda and, a few months later, the French naval bombardment of Casablanca abruptly put an end to the gradualist approach. The military had trumped the diplomats. In place of peaceful penetration, France would opt for a program of military conquest, euphemistically called "pacification."[19]

As noted above, the French occupation of Oujda was soon followed by the bombardment of Casablanca: on July 30, 1907, the French cruiser Galilee flattened the city. The French went on to occupy large parts of the surrounding hinterlands known as the Shawiya. Again, the French attack had been precipitated by violence against Europeans. As protests against the occupation of Oujda erupted throughout Morocco, nine European quarry workers who were building a new port were murdered. This time, the anti-European *jihad* succeeded in hitting its ulterior target: with Morocco under siege on both its Atlantic and Mediterranean flanks, Mawlay 'Abd al-'Aziz was forced to step down to make way for his more militant brother, 'Abd al-Hafidh. But there was little more he could do to stave off the coming Protectorate.

The implications of the Mauchamp affair for Moroccan independence are clear. But what impact did the murder of a French doctor by a Muslim crowd have on Jewish Morocco? A significant one, as it turns out, when the causal role of guilt by association is taken into consideration. Such guilt was both a logical fallacy and a factual mistake, but that did not stop it from being fully internalized by certain sectors of Morocco's Muslim population. The association arose from a triangular framework in which Jewish Morocco had existed since the nineteenth century. Local Jews formed one leg of the triangle, the AIU the second, and non-Jewish Europeans the third. By the twentieth century, there was no escape from this structure, partly because it was physically manifest in space. The AIU schools were located either in or adjacent to the Jews' residential quarters, for obvious reasons. Less obvious may be the fact that historically, all European visitors to Morocco were required to stay in the *mellah*-s so as not to disturb the Muslim population. This practice began centuries before the precolonial period and continued even after *villes nouvelles* for European settlers had been built in the larger cities. The intimacy Europeans felt with Jewish space could be seen in the newly invented picture postcards that featured images of Jews as "native types"[20] or in Eugene Delacroix's famous painting *Jewish Wedding in Morocco*, now hanging in the Louvre in Paris. For reasons mentioned above, many of the European visitors to Morocco were in fact doctors. They were interested in domestic space less for its aesthetic values but as a locus of health and hygiene; they also shared the typical Orientalist fascination with indigenous women. Since Jewish homes were generally the only ones to which they had access, some of the most detailed descriptions of Moroccan homes and their female inhabitants come from European doctors. Consider the following account from William Lemprière:

> The dress of the Jewish women consists of a fine linen shirt, with large and loose sleeves, which hang almost to the ground; over the shirt is worn a caftan, a loose dress made of woolen cloth, or velvet, of any colour, reaching as low as the hips, and covering the whole of the body, except the neck and breast, which are left open, the edges of the caftan being embroidered with gold. In addition to these is the geraldito, or petticoats, made of fine green woolen cloth, the edges and corners of which have sometimes a gold ornament; this part of the dress is

fastened by a broad sash of silk and gold, which surrounds the waist, and the ends of it are suffered to hang down behind, in an easy manner; when they go abroad, they cover the whole with the haick, the same used by the Moorish women. The unmarried Jewesses wear their hair plaited in different folds, and hanging down behind; and to this they have a very graceful and becoming method of putting a wreath of wrought sild round the head, and tying it behind with a bow. This dress sets off their features to great advantage, and distinguishes them from the married women, who cover their heads with a red silk handkerchief, which they tie behind, and over it place a silk sash, leaving the ends to hang loose on their backs. None of the Jewish women have stockings, but use red slippers, curiously embroidered with gold. They wear very large gold earrings at the lower part of the ears, and at the upper, three small ones set with pearls or special stones; their necks are loaded with beads, and their fingers with small gold or silver rings; round each wrist and ankle are fixed large and solid silver bracelets; and the rich have gold and silver chains suspended from the sash behind.[21]

Lemprière must have studied Jewish women up close and at length in order to convey such information, something that would never have been permitted with regard to Muslim women.[22] The presence of Europeans in Morocco's *mellah*-s contributed not only to the stigmatization of Jewish space, but also to the sense of Jews themselves as colonial collaborators.[23] The association between Jews and European doctors in particular was reinforced beyond the spatial level by the fact that Western medicine was accepted by Jews in Morocco much more readily than it was by Muslims. Inoculations are a case in point. Muslims tended to resist the needles used for inoculations, fearing they caused permanent markings or even Christianization.[24] Jews did not share that fear and vaccinated widely. In Marrakech, for example, the aforementioned Dr. Holzmann worked directly with the AIU to vaccinate the children of the *mellah* in 1900 and again in 1903.[25] Trachoma was another major health problem in the southern capital, due to the dry and dusty climate. A report from Dr. Ferriol of the French health and hygiene services suggests that 100 Jews for every 120–150 Muslims visited his eye clinic each Saturday, a remarkable statistic given that Jews of that city comprised just a tiny fraction of the city's overall population.[26] In Meknes, meanwhile, the local Jewish community replaced their traditional midwives with French trained midwives with diplomas early in the Protectorate period.[27] Finally, the pride of the Moroccan Jewish community was to be found in Tangier: the Benchimol Hospital. Built in 1904 with the private funds of the Jewish banker Haim Benchimol and his wife Donna, it functioned for over a hundred years as modern hospital and old-age home.

Jewish Morocco and European doctors were connected in still other ways. Jews often held the monopoly over the importation of medicine into Morocco, which put them in contact with doctors. In 1885, for example, the *makhzan* intervened with local officials to make sure that exclusive rights to the importation and sale of drugs and medicine were given to "the *dhimmi* Ya'qub b. Fillah."[28] Jews also worked for European doctors, often as translators, but also as medical assistants. Mauchamp himself had a Jewish translator who later became his pharmacist. He also had a Jewish maid. Mauchamp was actually one of the few members of the European "colony" in Marrakech not to live in the *mellah*, though he had stayed in the Jewish quarter immediately upon his arrival while a house was secured for him. Mauchamp treated thirty to forty patients in his practice, most of whom were Jews.[29] He visited the *mellah* three times per week on average. He also visited the classes at the AIU, whose students he found to be "weak and puny."[30] He even represented the local Jews' interests to the magistrate when access to freshwater was cut off to the *mellah* in the midst of a typhus epidemic.[31]

The third leg of the triangle, connecting the AIU with European gentiles, should be obvious given their common origin, but in the case of Mauchamp it was not. Mauchamp simply did not like Jews. If pushed, however, he preferred European Jews to Moroccan ones. And he was indeed pushed; the expat community of Marrakech was tiny and he was desperate for European company.[32] As Katz explains: "Despite his antipathy to religion in general and his anti-Semitism in particular, the lack of alternative society drew Mauchamp into the social circle of the Alliance and its teachers. Indeed, because of the [AIU] school's association with France, Mauchamp's fate and that of the city's Jews became entwined."[33] The director of the AIU school in Marrakech, Nissim Falcon, was a particularly close associate of Mauchamp. He lived in the *mellah*, as did Louis Gentil, a French geologist. The three men maintained a close friendship. There was some suspicion that the pole on Mauchamp's roof was in fact meant to connect him to Gentil's house in the *mellah*.[34]

With this triangulation in mind, the aftermath of the Mauchamp murder and its repercussions for Jewish Morocco can be better understood. The French occupation of Oujda sparked outrage among Moroccans. Adding insult to injury in Marrakech, the *makhzan* bowed to French pressure and recalled the pasha who had been in charge of the city during the Mauchamp events. On April 25, violent anti-European demonstrations broke out in the southern capital. At first, Europeans hunkered down in the Jewish quarter for safety, locking the huge gates from within. But on May 8 a large group of them fled to the coastal city of Safi. *Yeshou'a* Corcos, the *shaykh*-s *al-yahud* of the Marrakech *mellah*, urged Nissim Falcon, director of the

AIU, to close the schools and flee along with the others, not only for his own safety but for the safety of the local Jews: "Mr. Corcos revealed to me that our presence in the *mellah* was rather harmful to our coreligionists, since the [protest] movement is strictly anti-European, and that the vexations to which the Jews have been subjected are uniquely the result of their sympathy for foreigners."[35]

With the Europeans gone, the Jews left behind in the *mellah* came under intense scrutiny. It was not the local townspeople but members of the region's rural tribes who most gave Jews cause to fear. In the pre-Protectorate era, the main source of political power lay in the countryside.[36] For this reason, primary resistance of the type being examined here is sometimes referred to as "tribal nationalism."[37] The Rehamna tribe around Marrakech were among the most unrestrained, constantly challenging the *makhzan's* authority in the southern capital by conducting raids on the city. They also victimized the *mellah* any chance they got.[38] They would not pass up the opportunity presented by the Mauchamp murder to invade Marrakech and contest the *makhzan's* authority. A report from AIU director Nissim Falcon describes the Rehamna entry into the fray and their quick conflation of Jews and Europeans in their attempt to reestablish "correct" Muslim authority:

> The most insolent of the Kabyle[39] tribes, those who consider themselves to be the masters of all the Haouz, the R'hamma [Rehamna], claim to govern the city. Three days ago, during the festival of Mouloud, they demanded that no European or Jew be allowed to circulate in the streets of the medina ... Today soldiers are in *mellah* to forbid our co-religionists from wearing yellow babouches. All commerce is interrupted and our poor brothers dare not leave their neighborhood. I must inform you that more than any other European, the teachers of the alliance are considered by the Arabs as very dangerous agents of France. "They do trade," they say, "and they spend crazy sums to feed and clothe the children, to give relief to the Jews, who sends them, who pays them, why do they always take the defense of the Jews?" "France sent these people (the teachers)," they conclude. "To corrupt the Jews and arm them against us." The population of the capital sympathizes with the Kabyle tribes.[40]

As the report confirms, Mawlay Hafidh complied with Rehamna conditions for peace in Marrakech, including the release of all Rehamna tribesmen in the town's prisons, the vacating of Europeans from real estate owned by Rehamna, and the reimposition of harsh *dhimma* rules.[41] The Rehamna didn't hesitate to enforce these rules themselves, as when a German agent attempted to intervene on the behalf of his Jewish clerk. The clerk had been ordered to remove his slippers by a Rehamna tribesman. When his German boss tried to stop him from obeying, the tribesman pulled his rifle on the foreigner.[42] Developments in Casablanca followed a similar trajectory. Just after the European quarry workers were fatally attacked, tribesman of the Shawiya laid siege to the Jewish quarter.[43] In Oujda and Fez as well, the riots that took place targeted Jews and were led by tribes.

The Treaty of Fez

Guilt by association proved to be a powerful mechanism for isolating Jews from Muslims and precluding their participation in acts of primary resistance. The patterns of resistance seen in Marrakech with the Mauchamp murder and its aftermath resurfaced five years later in the northern capital of Fez, where a different sector of Moroccan society, the military, joined in the pairing of Jews with European colonists.

After decades of successfully staving off European rule, on March 30, 1912, Mawlay 'Abd al-Hafidh signed the Treaty of Fez establishing a French Protectorate over Morocco. France subsequently granted northern Morocco as a sublease to Spain, while Tangier became an international city ruled by a "committee of control" starting in 1923. Though the sultan maintained his title as *amir al-mu'minin* in the new arrangement, in practical terms, the *makhzan* was reduced to an empty shell. The kingdom's finances were controlled by France, and all edicts [*dahir*-s] originated from and were enforced by the Protectorate authorities even if they still bore the sultan's stamp.

Moroccan Muslims viewed the treaty of 1912 as a personal betrayal by the sultan. Suspecting as much, 'Abd al-Hafidh signed it in secret and quickly escaped to Rabat, and then France, in fear for his life. The Moroccan soldiery (*'askar*) soon learned of the sultan's capitulation. The troops were already undergoing a rigorous and difficult reorganization under European tutelage. They were not pleased to hear about the new, more stringent military regulations that would go along with the Protectorate treaty, which included what looked to them to be a pay cut. On April 17 the soldiers revolted. They killed their French military instructors and went on a rampage, summarily shooting any Frenchmen they encountered. French troops responded by surrounding the *ville nouvelle* where Europeans lived and the French consulate was located. Deflected away from their original target, the soldiers—by then joined by a popular insurrection—headed to the *mellah* in *fas jadid*. Was this a tactical move, given the *mellah*-'s placement between the European quarter and the royal kasbah, or were the soldiers intending to attack the Jews as proxies for the Europeans? Were they searching for Europeans known to frequent the *mellah*? In any event, the French authorities were put in an awkward position. Despite the distinct possibility of a rebellion, they had insufficient troops within the city, and they had also recently removed all arms from the *mellah* so the Jews could do nothing to defend their quarter. A French relief force eventually arrived from its garrison outside the city and entered into a pitched two-day battle against the mutinying soldiers who were by then firmly ensconced in the *mellah*. According to the Moroccan historian Mohamed Kenbib, the French forces incorrectly believed that the Jews were collaborating with the Moroccan soldiers, which in their eyes justified the use of brutal force.[44] The French soldiers attacked the *mellah* with heavy artillery, killing and wounding large numbers of people and destroying a huge section of the quarter. Reports on the final death toll vary, but it seems that 46–51 Jews, up to 66 Europeans, and as many as 1,000 Muslims lost their lives in the battle. In addition, upward of 10,000 Jews—nearly the entire Jewish population of Fez—fled the *mellah* to seek refuge from the battle on the palace grounds. They were so terrified they hid in the animals' cages in the royal zoo. Local brigands and tribesman took advantage of the Jews' absence to rob the *mellah*'s homes and shops. According to the director of the AIU school in Fez, the French authorities did nothing to stop the looters.[45]

The Fez riots were the first instance of anti-Jewish violence that had occurred in the city for over a century. Even during sensitive moments of interregnum or tribal rebellion, the Jewish community of Fez, one of Morocco's oldest and most respected, had remained unharmed.[46] But something had shifted with the signing of the treaty of Fez. The scale of possible violence and the price of resistance were made known on both sides; the upheaval had also served to further divide Jews from Muslims as well as to cultivate fear and general antipathy. The divergent experience of the events in Fez that spring is reflected in the very names used to describe them. For Moroccan nationalists, it was an *intifada*, a popular uprising. French colonial historians call it "the bloody days of Fez" (*les journées sanglante de Fès*.) In Judeo-Arabic, it is known simply as *al-tritl*, the pillage.[47] Although French shelling was responsible for most of the damage, in the wake of the Fez riots administrative authority over the Fassi Jewish community was taken away from the *makhzan* and handed over to the Protectorate authorities as part of a reorganization of the administration of the city.[48] The country's capital was also moved from Fez to Rabat, indicating that the old way of doing things was over.

The Jews of the Spanish zone and the Rif War (1921–1926)

In November 1912 Spain was given a small territory in the Sahara as well as the entire northern coastal region, with the exception of Tangier, which was made into an international zone in 1923. Spain based its claims to Moroccan territory on the fact that Ceuta and Melilla had been part of the Spanish empire for centuries (they still belong to Spain today). Spanish Morocco constituted just 10 percent of Morocco's total territory and 5 percent of its total population. The Jews of Spanish Morocco were correspondingly few in number compared to the rest of the country. They were concentrated in Tetouan, the only city in the north and the capital of Spanish Morocco, where under the Protectorate they constituted approximately one-sixth of the town's population.[49] There were also Jewish families in the formerly Portuguese held towns of Larache and Arzila, like the famous Pariente family, which for centuries produced some of Jewish Morocco's most illustrious religious scholars, diplomats, royal merchants, and bankers. Moses Pariente was the founder of Morocco's first bank, *Banque Pariente*, established in 1802. Deeper in the Rif Mountains lies the picturesque town of Chefchaouen, which also had a substantial population of *megorashim* [exiles from Spain]. According to popular lore, the Jews were originally responsible for painting all the town's buildings blue to resemble the color of their prayer shawls, a custom maintained today by its Muslim inhabitants.

The Jews of Spanish Morocco were a relatively new community, comprised entirely of exiles from the 1391 and 1492 purges of Jews from the Iberian peninsula. With no significant Arab or Berber roots, they were a "pure" Sephardic community in terms of language, culture, and domestic life. In this sense they were distinct even from the Sephardic Jews of Fez, who may have shared the same origins (and often came from the same families) but had incorporated many elements from the *toshavim* over centuries of living together. The Jews of northern Morocco remained much closer to their Andalusian customs. The Spanish novelist Pedro Antonio de Alarcón saw them almost as a historical time capsule. Alarcón was from Andalucia and served in the 1859 Spanish-Moroccan war. On encountering the northern Moroccan Jews, he was fascinated by their use of the old Castilian language and their preservation of the finest details of Andalusian life, elements that barely existed in the Spain he knew.[50]

Like many Sephardic Jews, the Jews of Spanish Morocco comprised a diaspora within a diaspora, yearning for their former paradise in al-Andalus with a fervor usually reserved for Jerusalem. In the words of the novelist A. B. Yehoshua, "It is as if they had said to those who drove them out: you succeeded in expelling us physically from Spain, but you will never succeed in expelling Spain from inside of us."[51] Their affinity for what lay to the north was buttressed by their aversion to what lay to the south, at least in terms of their distinctly negative experiences with the Rif tribes. They also suffered a painful collective memory of a short but bitter episode of acute victimization by Sultan Mawlay Yazid (1790–1792), who punished them ruthlessly for their failure to provide him with funding in order to overthrow his father.[52]

Spain was close enough to see with the naked eye, but still out of reach for Jewish Morocco. At least it was until the first Rif war. In 1859, a Spanish garrison in Ceuta was invaded by some tribesmen from the Rif. The Spanish used this minor act of aggression as an excuse to enter into the colonial competition for North Africa (France and England were already ahead in the Great Game) and launched a war with Morocco, which they quickly won. For the *makhzan*, the loss was another disaster heaped on top of a growing pile of misfortune, following as it did on the heels of the defeat at Isly and a punishing trade treaty with England. The loss cost Morocco both territory—Spain would occupy Tetouan for two years—and a huge war indemnity that the sultan would have to borrow half a million pounds from England to pay off.

In the course of the fighting, the *mellah* of Tetouan had been badly abused by the Riffian tribes taking advantage of the chaos.[53] But once the dust settled and the Spanish occupation began, it became clear that the war would be a major turning point for the Jews of northern Morocco. They would finally be reunited with Spain; Spanish sources state that Jews opened the gates of the city for the occupiers.[54] Jews viewed the Spanish troops as their protectors and welcomed their presence in the city, crying "Viva la reina!" as they entered the city. In their enthusiasm they created a special (and ironically named) "Purim de los Cristianos," dedicating the Jewish celebration marking delivery from persecution in ancient Persia to the Spanish crown.[55] The Spanish reciprocated by modernizing the city and increasing Jewish representation in its governance. A Jewish mayor, a Muslim mayor, and five representatives from each community sat on the municipal council.[56] At the same time as their representation increased, Jews' proportional power did as well. The Spanish conducted a census of Tetouan during their occupation of the city. Taken into account with other sources, it reveals a Muslim exodus from the city during Spanish rule such that the Jewish population became by far the largest demographic group. According to a letter from the Spanish Consul dated July 17, 1861, out of Tetouan's total population of 11,000, 5,000–6,000 were Jews, 1,000 were Muslims, and the remainder were Spaniards and other Christians.[57]

Accounts from this period register a change in the mentality of the Jews of Tetouan and northern Morocco. As a coastal population and an exilic one, they had long been accustomed to living among foreigners, but from 1860 the world outside Morocco grew even more dazzling. Tetouan, as we may recall, was the first Moroccan city to establish an AIU school in 1862. Through it the Jews of the north were introduced to French culture, but they still gravitated toward the Hispanic world. It became increasingly fashionable for educated Jews to migrate abroad, especially to Latin America, where they established communities in Buenos Aires, Caracas, Lima, Montevideo, and Rio de Janeiro. After 1880, when the demand for rubber from South American rainforests boomed, Moroccan Jewish merchants began organizing its extraction and exportation.[58]

With the establishment of the Spanish Protectorate in 1912, the historical longing of the Jews of northern Morocco was once again satisfied. The reunion with Spain led to another Sephardic revival. Spanish-Jewish institutions began popping up, like the Spanish-Hebrew association. The Spanish themselves found it difficult to consolidate their gains, however, due to the rough terrain of the north and strong tribal resistance especially in the Rif. Their attempt to pacify the mountainous region once and for all led to the third Rif war (the second having been a minor skirmish in Melilla in 1909). At first, it was an embarrassing defeat for Spain. The northern Amazigh (Riffi) tribes unified and managed to beat back the Spanish troops, causing them to lose 18,000 men. The defeat eventually helped topple the Spanish government, but it was a great victory for the indigenous people of northern Morocco, at least while it lasted (1921–1926), that is until French forces under the command of Marshal Petain joined the Spanish side in 1925.

The brief Riffian victory was decidedly less advantageous for Jewish Morocco. Not only were Jews' eternal enemies—the tribes—not vanquished, but the hero who emerged from the war turned northern Morocco away from Spain and toward the Middle East and pan-Arabism. He was the famous 'Abd al-Karim al-Khattabi, popularized as "Abedlkrim," whose success made him a model for guerilla fighters of the time including Che Guevara and Ho Chi Minh. (Even Mao Tse Tung invoked his name in a meeting with a Palestinian delegation in 1971.[59]) After having been captured and exiled by the French, Abdelkrim eventually made his way to Cairo where he quickly allied himself with hardline Arab nationalists. Despite his Amazigh roots, Abdelkrim took on the position of chair of the Maghrib Arab Liberation Committee and became active in pro-Palestinian causes.[60] He cautioned Morocco against entering into the Arab-Israeli war, insisting that in time Israel, like all colonial states, would inevitably disappear.[61] Originally trained as a *qadi* and a journalist, Abdelkrim fought against Western influence in Morocco until his demise in 1963. He died in Cairo, but his politics reverberated back home to northern Morocco. In the postcolonial period, many of the street names in the Tetouan *Juderia* were changed to distinctly Palestinian names: Gaza, Nablus, and Ramallah.[62]

The three instances of primary resistance to European colonialism in Morocco described above show how Jewish Morocco not only became caught in the middle of the burgeoning anti-colonial struggle, but how Jews were increasingly pushed toward the colonists' side as the French policy of "assimilation" gave way to the more flexible policy of "association."[63] One way that Moroccan Muslims registered their dissatisfaction with the sultan for his failure to protect them from European incursion was through acts of *jihad*. Their targets were Europeans or, in their absence, those who had come to be seen as their proxies: Jews. Guilt by association made Jews into targets for Muslim frustration and anger. Still, violence against Jews was concentrated within the tribes, who had a history of hostility toward urban populations in general and urban *mellah*-s in particular. (Rural Jews were much harder to victimize since they were usually under the protection of a specific tribal *qa'id*, and attacking them would have been equivalent to attacking the tribe itself.[64]) In the wake of the Mauchamp murder, the Rehamna redirected the insurrection toward the Jews of Marrakech. In Fez, the French military was largely responsible for the physical destruction, but the surrounding tribes led the looting of the *mellah*, as they did in Oujda as well (and as the Rif tribes had also done years earlier in Tetouan). As was often the case, some of the local townspeople took advantage of the situation to join the victimization of the Jews, while others sought to protect their Jewish neighbors. Either way, an anti-colonial consensus was being reached from the north to the south of Morocco. For reasons that were often beyond their control, Jewish Morocco increasingly appeared to be on the wrong side of history.

Secondary resistance

Resistance to European colonialism in Morocco began with "primary" acts like those described above, when Moroccans reacted immediately and instinctively to imperial provocations. The secondary resistance that followed in the interwar period was connected to primary resistance but was more concerted and organized and entailed a certain amount of deliberation that slowed down the process and resulted in less overt violence. This in turn allowed for more productive Jewish participation than was the case with primary resistance. Secondary resistance was often channeled through organized political movements.[65] Moroccan Jews were in fact leaders of secondary anti-colonial resistance in the form of communism. A few also joined Morocco's nationalist movements. Still, republicanism remained the main political trend in Jewish Morocco during these years or, in its Jewish form, alliancism. These different ideological impulses, to which one can also add Zionism, were not necessarily contradictory. Up until the Second World War, these ideologies were remarkably fluid and could exist alongside other political affiliations, even in a single person. Such ideological fluidity did not last. The Vichy interlude (1940–1942) severely tested Jewish Morocco's Francophilia; soon after, the establishment of the state of Israel and the ensuing Arab-Israeli war strained Jewish-Muslim relations nearly to a breaking point. With competing nationalisms on the rise, what once had once been fluid became solid, and the choices demanded by the circumstances became even harder.

Jews and the Moroccan independence movement

In 1925 a group of Moroccan students from the Qarawiyyin university in Fez gathered together to study ways in which the colonial regime might be reformed. They were influenced by both *salafi* ideas as well as by pan-Arabism, a synthesis that Moroccan nationalism would maintain throughout its existence.[66] Initially, they saw themselves as reformists. Their goal was to limit French power and expand the sultan's authority under the Protectorate, not necessarily to end the Protectorate altogether. Soon similar groups formed in Rabat-Salé, Tetouan, and Tangier. With the signing of the Berber *dahir* in 1930, however, their reformist restraint was drowned out by more maximalist calls for a total French withdrawal from Morocco. The *dahir*, it might be recalled, attempted to place Imazighen majority territories under a separate administrative and legal structure, which among other French goals would also facilitate the colonial confiscation of rural land. The nationalists correctly perceived the *dahir* as a further attempt to divide Morocco. It also rankled as an attack against the authority of Islamic law and the sultan, both of which the treaty of Fez had promised to protect. Once the contents of the *dahir* became known, protests erupted in Fez, Rabat, and Salé. It was a galvanizing moment for Morocco's young nationalists.

In 1934, Morocco's first nationalist organization, the *Comité d'Action Marocain* (CAM), was founded. Among its first acts was to issue a 150-page plan for reform. The plan discusses the Muslim, Arab, and Amazigh aspects of the Moroccan nation at some length but makes no reference to Jews as partners in the nationalist struggle.[67] That would change in later iterations of the nationalists' platform. The Moroccan independence movement was highly fragmented. Many different groups broke off from original *Comité d'Action Marocain*. The *istiqlal* emerged in 1943 as the most important of the group, under the leadership of 'Allal al-Fassi, one of the original Qarawiyyin group. It too submitted a plan for reform to the sultan. The anti-colonial manifesto of 1944 is a document of enduring significance for all Moroccans. It guaranteed "freedom of belief and of thought for all. All Moroccans should enjoy equality before the law; they should enjoy equal rights and assume equal obligations, without discrimination on account of religion or race." With regard to Jews specifically, it went on to note: "The Jewish question is non-existent in Morocco because the Jews of the country are members of the Moroccan family as are the Copts in respect to Egypt; they would continue to enjoy, as before, their religious freedoms, and particularly those pertaining to the jurisdiction of religious courts, as is the case with other Moroccans."[68]

Yet, in practice, Jews were an afterthought for the nationalists. They were not partners in the nationalist struggle except for during key moments when it was strategically beneficial for the nationalists to emphasize Jews' native status.[69] Not a single Jew was a signatory to the *istiqlal* manifesto. The neglect was mutual: Jews by no means flocked to the nationalist movements. Partly, they were put off by their *salafi* orientation. The nationalists met in mosques and required their members to swear an oath of loyalty on the Qur'an, which made it difficult for Jews to participate (although the activists might have made an exception had any Jews actually tried to join them). Excluding Jews was not the purpose of the nationalists' *salafi* tendencies, however. They were really directed at the Sufi brotherhoods who were seen as collaborators with the French. Jews didn't matter enough in the big picture for the nationalists to bother actively excluding them. But the effects were the same.

The Islamic orientation of the independence movement was set in stone with the mobilization of the *latif* prayer in response to the Berber *dahir*. In Islamic tradition, the *latif* prayer functions as a communal invocation to God, often for rain. In the wake of the Berber *dahir*, the *latif* prayer was invoked as a rallying cry to unite Imazighen and Arabs against the colonial power. It began in the great mosque of Salé and quickly spread to other towns. Over the summer it spread to the Middle East where Muslims continued to recite it on Morocco's behalf. The *latif* prayer marks the first mass manifestation of modern nationalism in Morocco. It was extremely effective, if limited by its singularity. The religious articulation certainly surprised the French, who thought they'd stemmed that particular tide by having co-opted much of the religious establishment. This seminal moment of Moroccan nationalism may have returned the Imazighen to the fold, but it did little to increase a sense of belonging among Jews.

Jews reflexively rejected the Islamic coloring of Moroccan nationalism. Yet, in the long run it was precisely this inherent conservatism that allowed Jews to maintain their position as the longest-lasting religious minority in Morocco.[70] That is, the enduring model of *dhimma* and the protection of the sultan it afforded prevented a total break between Muslims and Jews seen in places where secular nationalism—i.e., pan-Arabism—came to fully dominate. In contrast, Moroccan independence movements cultivated a national identity that stressed the Islamic past of Morocco, supported the Alawi monarchy, and focused its attention on urban populations. These were not necessarily barriers to Jewish participation—quite the opposite. But the Moroccan nationalists were Arabists as much as they were Islamists, and, ironically, therein lay the barrier to Jewish integration. Given current debates surrounding the "Arab Jew" as a conceptual category, it is perhaps important to clarify that the current discussion has little to do with whether or not Moroccan Jews either were or were not Arabs in a historical sense.[71] Rather, it is meant to distinguish between the two forms of Arabness confronting Jewish Morocco at this moment: the traditional Arabness that had been introduced with the arrival of Islam in the seventh century and continually flourished in terms of language primarily but also culture, shared history, and linkages to the Middle East, on the one hand, and the newly configured twentieth-century notion of pan-Arabism that reworked the meaning of Arabness for an age of nationalism by linking it to secularism, anti-colonialism, and the Palestine issue on the other. Although these two forms could be treated as a continuum for Muslim Arabs, for Jews, the newer articulation of Arabness proved to be more exclusionary of Jews than the more capacious Arabness of tradition, which existed, indeed was exalted, in Islamicate culture. The Palestine issue was particularly difficult for Jewish Morocco to transcend. The *istiqlal* and the other nationalist groups were created against the backdrop of the growing conflict in Palestine: the 1929 riots in Jerusalem followed by the Palestinian revolt of 1936–1939 were formative experiences for many Moroccan nationalists. After 1948, its leaders held that the Zionist movement, not just the

Israeli state, had declared war on Palestinians and the rest of the Arab world. 'Allal al-Fassi promoted Morocco's Arab-Muslim identity with special fervor. In 1963, when he was a member of the government, he instigated a trial against a group of Moroccan Baháʾís that ended in their conviction and sentencing to death for their deviant religious practices.[72] Jewish Morocco surely took notice.

The growing emphasis on pan-Arabism in Moroccan nationalism worked to the detriment of not only Jews but also of Imazighen. Both groups faced barriers to fully identifying as Arabs. Language was the most important of these. Even if Moroccan Jews were more likely to speak Arabic than Amazigh Muslims were, rarely were they able to write in Arabic. Whatever Arabic skills they might have had were sacrificed in the schools of the AIU, where as many as four European languages might be in use (English, French, Italian, German), but Arabic was generally not taught despite sporadic attempts at the local level. This was a disability in an increasingly Arabized political context. Moroccan nationalists sought to avoid the sad irony of Algerian nationalism, in which the *Front de libération nationale* (FLN) often had to publish its pamphlets in French because even the most radical Algerian nationalists' Arabic skills had been decimated by 130 years of colonial rule. In the interest of political expediency, the Amazigh issue was temporarily shelved thanks to the nationalists' strategic deployment of the *latif* prayer that extended Moroccanness to all of the country's Muslims.[73] (The Amazigh issue was taken off the shelf in the late twentieth century and is still being hashed out today.)

The emphasis on Arabness within the nationalist movement and in the country at large continued to grow in the 1930s and 1940s. In April of 1947, Sultan Mohammed V gave a speech in Tangier during which he for the first time publicly embraced nationalism and associated the Moroccan struggle with the newly established Arab League and pan-Arab solidarity. A month later, a few days after the state of Israel was founded, he gave another speech in which he affirmed Jews' traditional protected status in Morocco but also warned them not to demonstrate any solidarity with the Zionist cause. Just a few weeks later, anti-Jewish violence broke out in Oujda and then in Jarrada in northeast Morocco. These towns lay near the Algerian border and were launching pads for Jews to cross over into Algeria. From there they would travel to Marseille and then Israel where, in the eyes of many Moroccans, they would join the ranks of enemy combatants against the Arab armies. The Oujda and Jarrada riots claimed the lives of 47 Jews and one Frenchman; many more people were injured, and property was destroyed. The door to Arabness was quickly closing for Jews. But unlike the Imazighen, who still had Islam through which to claim belonging, Jews had no back way into the Moroccan nation.

Despite these many challenges, a small number of Jews resisted the pressure to Europeanize or accept Zionism's claims to Jewish separatism and instead worked toward an inclusive Moroccan nation. Recognizing the potential advantages of having a cadre of Moroccan Jewish sympathizers, the nationalists put aside their usual ambivalence toward Jewish Morocco and set about cultivating this group in a serious way for the first time. In January of 1956 members of the two main nationalist movements, the *istiqlal* and the *parti democratique de l'independence* (PDI), created a special wing known as *al-wifaq* ("entente") whose goal was to foster nationalist sentiment among Moroccan Jews and discourage them from emigrating. The establishment of *al-wifaq* was announced in the chamber of commerce of Casablanca, a hive of Jewish activity; other chapters soon popped up in Rabat, Meknes, Fez, and Safi. Some of *al-wifaq*-'s program was purely social and meant to demonstrate the possibilities for Jewish-Muslim coexistence, like the galas it organized with both Jews and Muslims in attendance. It also sought to familiarize Muslims with Jewish culture by arranging for the broadcast of Jewish songs on Moroccan national radio and television, adding Hebrew to the language offerings in the Arabic Department at the University in Rabat and organizing public lectures about Moroccan Jewish civilization throughout the country.[74] Another part of its program sought to prepare Jews for undertaking the responsibilities of citizenship in independent Morocco. This primarily meant teaching Jews to read and write in Arabic, a necessity as Moroccan nationalists sought to purge their country of the colonial culture. But these efforts met with only limited success. The Jewish journal *La Voix des communautés* ("the Voice of the Communities") was published with an Arabic supplement, but only once. Jews also wrote for some of the nationalist publications (in Arabic), but no Muslims wrote for the Jewish ones. Ultimately, Arabic literacy was a failure in Jewish Morocco, partly because the French language was never fully expunged from Moroccan life. Until today, many Moroccan Jews speak *darija*, perhaps with a Jewish inflection, but the vast majority are unable to read or write in Modern Standard Arabic. French remains the language of literacy in modern Jewish Morocco.

Marc Sabbah was one of the main leaders of *al-wifaq*. He had close ties to the *istiqlal* leader Mehdi Ben Barka and was also a devoted subject of Sultan Muhammad V. (The *istiqlal* itself maintained a complicated pro-monarchy position.) Sabbah's attitude toward the colonial power and the Jews who supported it was less forgiving. He is known for having attacked the Moroccan Jewish leadership in a major editorial in the *istiqlal* newspaper for their pro-

French leanings in the wake of the exile of Muhammad V to Madagascar. The editorial included the critique: "There was a Jewish mass ... restless, bewildered, and misinformed about its own problems because those who retained the name and privilege of leaders were courageous only when their old positions were at stake, and energetic only in clinging to those positions."[75] Intra-Jewish disputes like the one fomented by Sabbah were rife in *al-wifaq* and were part of the reason that the organization lasted only 2 years. Attitudes toward Zionism were especially divisive, both within the membership of *al-wifaq* and between it and the larger *istiqlal* organization, where slippage between "Jew" and "Zionist" was not uncommon. In the wake of the 1956 Suez war, *al-wifaq* published a pamphlet in French, Judeo-Arabic, and Arabic calling on Moroccan Jews and Muslims to unite:

> Despite all international laws, the British, French and Israelis have declared war on Egypt. The Moroccan people, in its entirety, rises up against this aggression and condemns this premeditated act of war by the imperialists in order to subjugate the Egyptian nation and to strip it of its freedom and independence. Current events demand, therefore, dear brothers, to maintain and reinforce among us, Muslims and Jews, cohesion, friendship, unity and understanding which alone can ensure the independence of our Country. The colonizers are trying to divide us as they always have and will use all provocations to turn us against one another. Here in Morocco, there are only Moroccan citizens: Moroccans of the Muslim faith and Moroccans of the Jewish faith, but all Moroccan. All Moroccans without distinction of religion must consider themselves as mobilized in order to assure calm and order. Moroccans, dear brothers, we must be united, we must be vigilant. From our Union, from our Vigilance and our Confidence without any reservation in SM the King and his Government, on which the future of our country depends. Don't listen to those who would disassociate us. On the contrary, denounce them! Thus mobilized, you will participate in the most glorious activity there can be, the preservation of our Independence. All of this is in support of King Mohamed V's words. Long live the King! Long live Morocco![76]

Just a few years later, the leaders of *al-wifaq* themselves would have their loyalties questioned. In 1961, several Jewish members of the organization were castigated in the Moroccan press for attending a meeting of the World Jewish Congress in Geneva that had a pronounced pro-Israel agenda.[77] The accused responded with a "Communiqué by Patriotic Jews" in the daily newspaper *al-Tahrir* signed by thirty "intellectuals and professionals" declaiming their anti-Zionism.[78] It ended with the statement "Our attitude is not meant to be in harmony with any one person or group, nor is it presented as a challenge. It stems from our feeling as loyal citizens who recognize Morocco as their only home."[79] Albert Aflalo, another leader of *al-wifaq* and the nephew of Marc Sabbah, promoted Jewish non- or anti-Zionism in Morocco not only by affirming Jews' Moroccanness but by calling attention to inequalities in Israeli society and the poor treatment that awaited any potential Moroccan Jewish immigrants there, particularly after the Wadi Salib protests (1959) that gave rise to the Israeli Black Panther movement. The anti-Zionist tradition has been carried forward by leftist Moroccan Jews into the current century, most notably by the former political prisoners Abraham Serfaty (1926–2010) and Sion Assidon (1948–). Although leftist activists were mostly rejected by the more mainstream Jewish community, Jewish proponents of Moroccan nationalism did receive the occasional boost from international Jewish organizations, which at the time were less uniform in their commitment to Zionism than they are today. The same World Jewish Congress that had extolled the Zionist movement and raised funds for Israel at their 1961 meeting in Geneva had previously opposed large-scale *aliyah* for Moroccan Jews and advocated for their integration and assimilation into the new Morocco. In September of 1955, its representative Meir Toledano published an article in *Le Monde* arguing for Jewish participation in what he called the "natural and irresistible" Moroccan nationalist movement. Toledano wrote that "instead of thwarting a natural and irresistible movement, France would facilitate the political development of Morocco, the grateful Moroccan people would never be able to contest the established rights of France in Morocco, the exercise of which was essential to France's role as a great world power. Moroccan Jewry too, had to rally behind the idea of a free Morocco."[80]

Sabbah, Aflalo, Toledano, and a few others were the exception, however; Jewish Morocco as a whole never embraced the nationalist movement. True, *al-wifaq* was seen by many Jews as elitist and unrepresentative of the Jewish masses.[81] But their reticence can be traced to other causes as well. First, Jews had a deep allegiance to the Moroccan sultan, both to the office and to Mohammed V in particular, preventing them from taking any radical positions. The Sultan's role as protector of the Jews, which was reified under Vichy, had strong religious undertones that spoke directly to his legitimacy as *amir al-mu'minin*, a status few Jews were willing to challenge. The *istiqlal* was ostensibly pro-monarchy but also was in open competition with the king to see who would hold the reins of power once independence came, and Jews knew better than to take sides against their protector. Second, Zionism was no longer simply another ideology that could coexist with others after the creation of the Israeli state in 1948; it was a real option.

Moroccan Jews were increasingly looking toward emigration, not integration, as a solution to their problems. Third, despite whatever public position the nationalists or the king took regarding minorities, there were countervailing attitudes among the broader population that boded ill for Jewish inclusion. When Jews left their stores open during an *istiqlal* strike in Petitjean (today's Sidi Qasim) in 1954, apparently on French orders, they were brutally attacked by the protesters and seven Jews were killed. Finally, Jews began to doubt the sincerity of the leadership of the *istiqlal* itself. As tensions from the first Arab-Israeli war spilled over into Morocco, the nationalists did not hesitate to scapegoat Moroccan Jews in order to gain the support of their fellow Muslims against the French.[82] After the attacks on Jews in Oujda and Jarrada in 1948, the *istiqlal* was quick to publically distance itself from the violence, but privately it raised funds to support the defense in the criminal trial against the perpetrators.[83] Nor did the *istiqlal* do much to resolve its inconsistencies in the following years. In 1955 it adopted a motion that Jews and Muslims should benefit from the same rights, "with no distinction of class, religion, or race."[84] Yet at the same time, the nationalist press it controlled criticized Jews as traitors, unpatriotic, and outside the nation. As a minister in the Moroccan government, 'Allal al-Fassi was quoted as saying that Jews in Morocco were not regarded as Moroccans but as residents enjoying Moroccan protection.[85]

Jews were granted full equality with Moroccan independence in 1956. In a particularly promising sign, Dr. Léon Benzaquen, a Moroccan Jewish doctor, was made minister of posts and telegraphs in the first government. Jews also served in the consultative council, ministries, and government agencies. Individual Jews were also elected to local city councils in Moroccan towns and appointed by the government to positions in Moroccan embassies overseas. But their collective belonging in the Arab nation as such was still undecided as Morocco's pan-Arab agenda continued to gain steam. Morocco joined the Arab League in the fall of 1958 after much urging by member states (there was no love lost between the Egyptian leader Gamal 'Abd al-Nasser and 'Allal al-Fassi, hence the delay). At Nasser's urging, the Arab League asked the Moroccan government to put an end to all Jewish emigration to Israel. In early 1960 the Moroccan king and Nasser issued a joint statement calling for "non-stop, joint struggle against Israel until Arab Palestine is liberated."[86] All postal and telephone connections between Morocco and Israel were cut in accordance with Arab League policy. Life became more stressful for Moroccan Jews, but worse was yet to come. In January of 1961, the king convened the "Casablanca conference" ostensibly to deal with the crisis in the Congo. Nasser participated in the proceedings by giving a speech that incited Muslims against Jews. Anti-Jewish articles started to appear in the press, several Jews youth were arrested and beaten by the Moroccan police, and a strike was called against the Jewish wholesalers of Casablanca. Just a week later, even greater tragedy stuck when a clandestine emigration operation organized by the Israeli Mossad failed. A ship meant to carry Moroccan Jewish emigrants to Israel via Spain capsized, killing all forty-four people on board.[87] A month later Mohammed V died suddenly after complications from surgery. Jewish Morocco had lost its bearings.

Alternative nationalism: Zionism in Morocco

For that section of Jewish Morocco for whom neither *alliancism* nor Moroccan nationalism was the answer, Zionism was another alternative in the ideological marketplace whose attractiveness grew over time. In the pre-Protectorate period, Zionist activity was extremely limited in Morocco. Only in north of the country and on the coasts was there any Zionist infrastructure: Zionist offices opened in Tetouan in the late 1890s and in Mogador (Essaouira) in 1900, but they could do little to penetrate deeply entrenched AIU networks and win Jewish souls over to non-assimilation and emigration. The AIU was adamant in its opposition to Zionism in this period. It advocated for the assimilation of French norms within Jewish Morocco, but not for emigration, and certainly not to Palestine. Rather, the AIU sought French naturalization for Morocco's Jews along the same lines as the Crémieux decree of 1870 in Algeria or at least an easing of the path to French citizenship for Jews as eventually happened in Tunisia under the Protectorate. But the idea was for Jews to stay put in Morocco. Only after the Second World War did the AIU's position change to embrace Zionism under the leadership of Jules Braunschvig.

The situation became somewhat more fluid during the Protectorate period, but the growth of Zionism was still hampered by opposition from French authorities. The French had good reason to discourage Zionism. Not only did they not want to do anything to upset the majority Muslim population, but they also strongly associated Zionism with the British, who held the mandate for Palestine from 1920 and had issued the Balfour declaration. Lyautey's own resistance to Zionism stemmed from his suspicion that it was a British plot. Lyautey wrote a report to the Zionist fund-raising group *keren hayesod* defending his position by arguing that the French Protectorate had ameliorated the material, social, and moral situation of Jews sufficiently for them to have no reason to leave Morocco. As evidence, he cited the Protectorate's reorganization of Jewish institutions, the creation of rabbinic tribunals, the admission of a Jewish representative to municipal commissions and to the indigenous section of consultative chambers of commerce, industry, and agriculture, and finally the indemnities paid to Jews for their losses during the Fez uprising of 1912.[88] In its goal of removing Jews from the traditional Moroccan social structure, Zionism violated the French policy of preserving traditional society in Morocco, a policy that the Protectorate had adopted after having seen the price for failing to do so in Algeria. Jewish Morocco was an especially valuable sector of Moroccan society for the French to want to maintain in place given its consistent support of the Protectorate.

Zionism in Morocco got a boost with the Balfour declaration of 1917. In 1919, the Protectorate authorities decided to allow Moroccan Jews to join the French Zionist movement as long as they did not form their own local organizations or disseminate Zionist propaganda. Zionist offices were soon set up in Fez, Meknes, and Marrakech. They were often staffed by Zionist intermediaries from outside Morocco, including members of the *mossad le-aliyah*, the organization that facilitated clandestine Jewish immigration to Mandate Palestine. They organized scouting activities, collected subscriptions (through the purchase of shekels), and quietly helped Jews organize themselves for emigration. The opening of the Marrakech office finally gave the Zionists access not only to one of Morocco's largest Jewish communities, but also to the hundreds of Jewish communities of the south that lay in and beyond the Atlas Mountains. It was able to attract over 700 subscribers, though it never sent any delegates to any of the Zionist congresses.[89] It also ran into some trouble with plots of land they had sold to Moroccan Jews in Palestine. When the buyers sought to settle in Israel, they were informed that their plots had been reserved for Eastern European Jews.[90] The privileging of Ashkenazim over so-called *mizrahim* in housing and other areas was to become a persistent pattern in Israeli society that deeply hurt Moroccan Jewish integration there. The reports that started trickling back to Morocco from earlier emigrants were not reassuring. In fact, many of the first Jews to leave Morocco for Palestine ended up coming back.[91] Zionist activity died down again by mid-1920s in the face of renewed opposition from all sides. The rabbis had long been opposed to Zionism because of its secular bent. The middle class was mostly not interested thanks to the new upward mobility they had under the Protectorate. With their European educations, they served as administrators, agents, merchants, middlemen, bankers, and so on: they were hardly the factory workers of Europe and had little interest in working the land.[92] Even the Jewish communists and socialists rejected it, as they tended to be intellectuals, not laborers *per se*. In 1926, the Zionist periodical *l'avenir illustre* was founded in Casablanca by a Polish Jew, but its message was challenged by assimilationist Jews in the pages of *l'Union marocaine* and by Muslim nationalists in *l'Action du peuple*.[93] By this point, the French Protectorate authorities were careful to discourage nationalist expressions of any type, correctly perceiving them as a threat to peace in their empire.

Moroccan Jews may have been reluctant Zionists, but they still felt an undeniable emotional affiliation with *'Am Yisra'el*, the people of Israel in the Biblical sense, that did nothing to lessen their allegiance to Morocco. A letter by Marc Sabbah and David Azoulay to the *istiqlal* newspaper *al-'alam* defended their participation in World Jewish Congress in Geneva in precisely such terms: "The Arab nation of Morocco always understood that the Jewish religion was more than a mere cult, and demands contact among Jewish communities so long as this does not interfere with our duties as loyal Moroccan citizens."[94] Zionist ideology never made much headway in Morocco. And yet, as we will see below, the historical trajectory of Jewish Morocco was permanently altered by the emigration of the majority of Morocco's Jews to Israel, making them *ex post-facto* Zionists, intentionally or otherwise.

The Vichy interlude

When France fell to Germany in 1940, the collaborationist regime based in Vichy in the unoccupied south of France took control of France's colonial holdings, including in Morocco and Algeria in North Africa. (Tunisia was directly occupied by the Germans for 6 months.) Although Morocco's Jews were spared the disaster that befell European Jewry, they were still marginalized, stigmatized, and made to suffer under Vichy rule. The war brought great economic hardship to all Moroccans, but Jews were subject to special discriminatory laws. Vichy ordered the full implementation of a quota system and the "Aryanization" of Jewish property and assets. It was decreed that only 2 percent of medical doctors and lawyers could be Jewish and 10 percent of secondary school teachers. Léon Sultan, future founder of the Moroccan communist party, was disbarred from practicing law. Similar restrictions were imposed on other professions, like real estate agents and pharmacists. There was even a quota on how many Jews could work as cinema operators. Jews were also ordered to vacate their properties in the European quarters of Moroccan cities and return to the *mellah*-s.[95] Given the nature of these restrictions, they hit the educated elite the hardest, i.e., those with European educations, jobs, and property. In practice, however, Vichy laws could only be effectively applied and enforced in Casablanca.[96] The Protectorate administration was notoriously understaffed, especially in the southern part of the country. Most local officials were not hostile to Jews and were lax in their application of the new laws. For them, peace and order via the status quo was preferable to disruption or *siba*. It was especially difficult for Vichy to enforce its statues in the tribal areas. The *qa'id*-s protected "their" Jews from outsiders as they always had.

Undergirding the Vichy regime, the Protectorate apparatus still existed and needed the *makhzan* to function in order to justify its existence. Hence anti-Jewish discrimination, like all new laws, had to be promulgated by royal *dahir*. The Vichy laws of October 3, 1940, that had established a new legal status for the Jews of France were transferred into a *dahir* to be presented for the sultan's approval and published in the *Journal Officiel* in November 1940 and August 1941.[97] But the anti-Jewish laws contained therein posed certain unique contradictions in a Moroccan context. How could the commander of the faithful be considered a legitimate ruler if part of his flock was under the control of outsiders? How could he protect the *dhimma* as was his God-given duty? Against the combined power of Vichy, backed by Nazis, and French imperialism, the Moroccan king had very little room to maneuver. He met with members of the Jewish community privately to reassure them, but publicly he was obliged to sign anti-Jewish legislation and exclude Jews from places they had traditionally been included, like the annual Celebration of the Throne. Another contradiction that has been pointed out by Daniel Schroeter involves the question of how Jewish identity would be determined in Morocco in the first place.[98] As the film *Casablanca* has popularized, this was a time when thousands of Ashkenazi Jewish refugees were streaming into Morocco to escape the Nazis. Between June 1940 and February 1941, 7700 refugees, the majority Jewish, were registered by the Protectorate as having arrived in Morocco.[99] A *dahir* of October 1940 ruled that the identity of such non-Moroccan Jews in Morocco would be determined according to French (i.e., Nazi) criteria, namely via the existence of at least one Jewish grandparent. But the identity of Moroccan Jews, in contrast, was still to be determined as it had been traditionally, i.e., by religion, not by "race." Any other arrangement would have challenged the authority of the sultan as *amir al-mu'minin*, as explained above, and in turn challenged the legitimacy of the French Protectorate. Equally problematic, a racial definition would have caused Jewish converts to Islam to revert back to their Jewish identity. This would have constituted apostasy under Islamic law, whose authority in such cases the Protectorate was also obliged to protect. A 1941 *dahir* attempted to resolve this issue, applying the same racial definition to both groups but not specifically targeting converts. It is unlikely this stop-gap measure would have held had the war continued any longer than it did.

The Vichy era came to an end with the Allied landing in Algiers in 1942. It is worth noting that Operation Torch was preceded by a local insurgency in Algeria that was comprised in its majority of Jewish fighters: 85 percent of the 377 insurgents were Algerian Jews who were fighting to reclaim their right to French citizenship.[100] But the liberation of Algeria did not mean restoration of the status quo ante. Instead, it led to a new battle—Algerian Jews had to wait a full year to get their rights restored. In Morocco, the effects of the Vichy interlude were more subtle. Previously, as noted above, *alliancism* existed alongside other affiliations. Leon Sultan, for example, was simultaneously a communist, a Zionist who organized a Moroccan team to compete in the Macabbee games, a Moroccan nationalist, and a French citizen. He was as fluent in Arabic as he was in French; he wrote in both languages for leftist magazines. But Vichy put an end to such fluidity and hybridity. The anti-Jewish decrees they issued via the *makhzan* had no precedent or parallel in Moroccan history. Even as scholars continue to uncover the actual extent of their enforcement, anti-Jewish laws had a symbolic effect that was undeniable. For decades, Moroccan Jews had been told that France would save them. All they needed to do was obtain a French education, adopt French laws, and embrace French habits. The Protectorate itself was established under the fiction of "protecting" Morocco. The Vichy regime betrayed that rhetoric. Its actions bore no resemblance to what France had announced to the world that it would do for Morocco, nor to what the French regularly congratulated themselves for having accomplished in its colonies. Both Muslims and Jews suffered under Vichy rule. But Jewish vulnerability was particularly highlighted: Vichy had cast doubt not only on the quid pro quo Jews had thought they were entering into by assimilating French values, but onto those values themselves.

Even if many Moroccan Jews tried outwardly to pass Vichy off as an anomaly, they were still deeply shaken by the experience; they were also impelled to action. It was clear that they could no longer hope to wait out the chaos, recede to the background, or be politically passive. Their choices had narrowed to three options, none of which really overlapped anymore: They could continue their allegiance to France, despite the fact that the country had betrayed them and its days as a colonial power were clearly numbered, not to mention that France still refused to naturalize Moroccan Jewry even after the Second World War. In 1945 the Protectorate created the Council of Moroccan Jewish Communities in an effort to provide Jewish Morocco with coherent representation, but the body was seen as representing only the (diminishing) pro-French element of Jewish Morocco. Second, Jews could take their chances by staying in Morocco when independence inevitably came, where a much-weakened sultan remained their protector but where the criteria of belonging was constantly shifting, and it was unclear whether the promises of the independence movements could be kept even if they were sincere. Jews were loyal to the sultan, but it was unclear if he would reign supreme as the *istiqlal* was accruing more power by the day. Or they could leave Morocco altogether. Before resorting to departure, however, a new activist strategy emerged in Jewish Morocco.

Communism and socialism in Jewish Morocco

What would it mean to be a Moroccan citizen in newly independent Moroccan state? The question was surely foremost in the mind of Leon René Sultan as he set about establishing the Moroccan branch of the French communist party (*Parti Communiste Marocain* (*PCM*)) in 1943 and became its first secretary general. Sultan served in this position for two years, after which he was replaced by a Muslim, 'Ali Yata. Although Sultan had lived and practiced law in Casablanca since 1929, he was originally from Algeria, where he had obtained French citizenship under the Crémieux decree. His French credentials were essential, as the Protectorate authorities forbade Moroccan Jews and Muslims from attending leftist meetings in hopes of keeping both groups under control.[101] But European leftists could attend other types of gatherings with Moroccan Jews and Muslims present. There they discovered an audience predisposed to communism, with well-developed anti-racist, pro-human rights views. They would form the kernel of the Moroccan communist party.

Throughout the MENA communism was a crucial outlet for politically active Jews.[102] Communism allowed colonized Jews in cities from Casablanca to Baghdad to join together in common resistance to imperialism (which to them included Zionism), anti-Semitism, and racism. In places where Islam was often a prerequisite for political action, the leftists' secularism was a major attraction for minorities. The PCM, with its staunchly secular program, provided an enduring and important venue for Jewish supporters of Moroccan independence. It attracted both Muslims and Jews, Europeans and "natives." It comprised lawyers, teachers, and laborers united in their call for Moroccan independence from France.

Even if the PCM was not made up of factory workers, its members were still attuned to the economic climate and the rights of workers. Morocco had faced an economic downturn in the early 1930s as a result of the great depression, and another one during the war years. Under the Protectorate, the move toward automation and a mercantile economy damaged many traditional crafts. If Fez, for example, the traditional craft of making gold thread, founded and dominated by the Jews of Fez for centuries, nearly collapsed completely. The effects of industrialization were most dramatic in Casablanca however, where the building and operation of phosphate mines, ports, and railroads transformed the city and its economy. The PCM was based in Casablanca. Though Rabat was the governmental capital, Casablanca was the economic center of the country, and as such had been a target of Jewish migration from the countryside ever since the French began developing it in the nineteenth century to compete with Morocco's traditional Atlantic ports like Essaouira, Azzemor, and Safi.

Although the PCM welcomed everyone, it held special appeal for urban educated elite; almost all of Morocco's prominent Jewish intellectuals joined the party at one time or another, people like Simon Lévy, who would in 1971 become a professor of Spanish at Mohammed V University in Rabat and later go on to open the Arab world's first Jewish museum; Germaine Ayache, a founder of modern Moroccan history and editor of the esteemed periodical *Hespéris*; the world renowned novelist Edmond Amran El Maleh who gave a narrative voice to many of the dilemmas facing Jewish Morocco in the twentieth century; Abraham Serfaty, who studied the labor laws around mining and worked in the economics department of the national administration before his career was cut short when he was arrested for his political activities.

As was also the case among the nationalists, the Zionists, and the alliancists, there were deep splits in and around the PCM. Its relationship to the French communist party, the PCF, was an area of particular concern. During the Protectorate period, many PCM members resented the French group's colonial attitude toward the Moroccans. The crisis among French communists when Stalin's abuses became known also made its way into Moroccan circles. When the goal of independence was finally achieved, the *makhzan* itself became the communists' greatest obstacle as they continued to fight for workers' rights and other social justice issues. The PCM was legally disbanded by court order in 1960 but reemerged in 1963 as the PLS (Parti de Libération et Socialisme). In the student uprising in March of 1965, Simon Lévy was arrested and tortured by the Moroccan authorities. The Soviet Union hosted him during his convalescence. Despite the communists being a "crucible of solidarity" in Lévy's words, in 1970, the more radical elements of the PCM broke away to form the Maoist group *Ila al-Amam* (Ar. "Forward"), led by Abraham Serfaty. In 1972, several of its members were arrested for possession of anti-government leaflets, including the Jewish mathematician Sion Assidon, who would spend thirteen years in prison. In 1974 Serfaty would also be arrested for his political activities and spend seventeen years in prison. Both men refused any appeals by Jewish organizations on their behalf that did not also embrace their fellow (Muslim) political prisoners. In 1974 the remaining members of the PLS changed their name to the PPS (Parti du Progrès et Socialisme), by which they are still known today.

Simon Lévy remained loyal to the PLS. But even for him, the question of why Léon Sultan was the only Jew ever to head the party remained a painful one until his death in 2011. (El Maleh served as de facto leader for a short while, but no other Jew was ever elected to the position.) Lévy ran for the position of secretary general in the late 1990s but was not elected. His opponent, Nabil Benabdallah, won the election using the slogan: "Vote for the *sharif*, not the *juif* [Jew]!"[103] This loss was a source of great bitterness to him and helped turn him toward the more overtly Jewish endeavor of creating a Jewish museum.

Emigration and the end of territorial Jewish Morocco

Despite the tepid beginnings of Zionism in the MENA, the movement grew by leaps and bounds in the wake of the Second World War. Jews who had either rejected Zionism or been rejected by it in earlier periods ended up fleeing to Israel in the aftermath of Arab countries' independence and the Arab-Israeli wars of 1948, 1956, and finally 1967, especially those of lower economic rungs who required the social services of the Israeli state and international Jewish organizations working on its behalf. This is also the period when the Zionist movement itself turned its attention back to MENA Jewish communities after several decades' respite. The masses of Eastern Europe Jews whom the Zionists thought would people Israel were gone forever with the Shoah. The only "human material" left was in the Islamic world, and one of the largest groups was in Morocco. Between 1948 and 1964, 220,000 Moroccan Jews settled in Israel.[104]

The process of illegally transferring such a large number of people from the furthest corner of North Africa to western Asia was haphazard and dangerous. Under the Protectorate Jewish emigration to Israel was illegal but the law was inconsistently enforced. Various deals were brokered between the French authorities and the Zionist agents that allowed for the discrete emigration of groups of Jews. The process accelerated in April 1949 when "Kadima," an organization for *aliyah* operating under the Jewish Agency, was allowed to open a headquarters in the European section of Casablanca, soon followed by branches elsewhere in the country. Kadima operated under the guise of providing social services and a library.[105] Between 1949 and 1951, it facilitated the departure of 30,000 Jews, mostly from the poorer communities. Poverty was exploited by the agents of *mossad le-aliyah* to motivate poor Jews to leave, though their economic situation would not improve much in Israel.[106] Demand to leave stepped up in the last 2 years of the Protectorate. Nonetheless, 200,000 Jews still remained in Morocco at the moment of independence in 1956, roughly two-thirds of the country's total Jewish population.[107] The early years of independence would be crucial for determining their fate.

Jewish emigration to Israel was outlawed by the new government which feared that Jews would join the Israeli army. Zionist activity was banned. But a new, poorly trained police force marred by corruption made it easy enough to evade detection. Between 1956 and 1961 the Jewish Agency facilitated the illegal emigration of 66,503 Jews to Israel. Many of these were Jews from the countryside who had only recently made their way into the overcrowded *mellah*-s of the interior. A Jewish eyewitness to this wave of departures saw it as "an exodus that no one truly desires," adding, "the people are not fleeing Morocco, but their own misery."[108]

In 1957–1958 the Moroccan government attempted to clamp down on clandestine emigration. They held a show trial of Jewish families in Tetouan and Tangier who were caught trying to make *aliyah* illegally. Emigration remained officially restricted until 1961, until the sinking of the Pisces. Thereafter, one wave of Jews after another left the country. By 1962, Morocco retained about a quarter of its pre-independence population of Jews. They tended to be the wealthier, Westernized Jews who had the most to lose by leaving. Whatever political and economic constraints they were subject to, Muslims were subject to equally. Communal institutions continued to run well. Jews reported that they did not feel discriminated against and that they had a meaningful role to play in independent Morocco.[109] Nonetheless, between 1962 and 1990 another 130,640 Jews left Morocco. Most went to Israel but also to other destinations. In sum, of the 250,000–300,000 Jews who had lived in Morocco at the start of the twentieth century, only 170,000 remained by 1956, 60,000 by 1967, 22,000 by 1975.[110] Today there are fewer than 5,000 Jews living in Morocco.

Three caveats regarding the twentieth-century mass emigration of Jews from Morocco are warranted given our particular lens: First, the departure was never total. Unique in the Arab world, there remains in Morocco a small but vital Jewish community. Casablanca is the center of Jewish Morocco and boasts Jewish communal associations, schools, clubs, and synagogues. Second, not all of the Jews who left Morocco settled in Israel or remained there. The Moroccan Jewish diaspora is well represented in France, Canada, the United States, and South and Central America.[111] Third, each region of Morocco had a different experience of departure, though few were Zionists in the Herzlian sense of the word. Economic concerns were a strong motive for departure.[112] But the notion of *aliyah* also had an outsized spiritual dimension for many of the Jews of southern Morocco, who, as we might recall from Chapter 3, not only had pronounced mystical and kabbalistic tendencies but were also motivated by historical connections to the biblical land of Israel.[113] For them, as for many Moroccan Jews, the connection to *Eretz Israel* was ancient. There had been an established community of Maghribi Jews (and Muslims) in the "holy land" for centuries. Some had gone to fulfill the *mitzvah* (pious deed) of "returning" to Zion, often at the end of their lives. These people were not Zionists—they were neither socialists nor secularists—they were responding to the religious draw of Jerusalem, Hebron, and Tiberias, the land of the Patriarchs. Particularly in rural areas, messianic urges and religious traditions were more compelling than the begrudging inclusion of Jews in the Moroccan nationalist movement.

There is no doubt that the emigration of a quarter of a million people from Morocco would not have been possible without the tacit agreement of the Moroccan government. The United States had given food aid to Morocco during a drought in 1957, and in 1961 it was time for Morocco to pay back the favor. The Israeli authorities hatched "Operation Yachin," a plan negotiated with the Moroccan king and involving the Hebrew Immigrant Aid Society (HIAS), which would act as a cover for the Israeli emigration agents. A half million dollars was paid to Morocco for allowing 50,000 Jews to emigrate, followed by a per capita charge of $250 for each additional departure.[114] In an interview in Kathy Wazana's 2013 film about the Jewish departure from Morocco entitled *They Were Promised the Sea*, Simon Lévy points out that it was Moroccan trucks, airplanes, and so on, that transported the Jews away. The prospect of official complicity makes this chapter of Moroccan history all the more traumatic for everyone involved, following as it does a century of mutual estrangement, hollow attempts to include Jews in the national narrative, and equal citizenship that was more symbolic than real. Susan Miller calls the departure of the vast majority of Jews from Morocco a "monumental national tragedy."[115] Director of the National Archives Jamaâ Baïda suggests that, until very recently, the topic is simply too painful for Moroccan historians to deal with.[116] This unresolved aspect of Moroccan history often turns on the question of whose fault it was that the Jews, acknowledged today on (almost) all sides as "true" Moroccans, left their ancestral land. Though fading from the scene in the twenty-first century, Moroccan nationalists blame the colonial powers for having destabilized the traditional social structures that had long sustained the Jews. The younger generation of Moroccans blames the *istiqlal* for failing to be more inclusive.[117] Popular opinion blames the Zionists for having "stolen" Morocco's Jews.[118] Zionists, meanwhile, tend to blame Moroccan Muslims as a whole for having endangered Jewish lives during tense times. Scholarly opinions are divided but generally grant more agency to Moroccan Jews themselves, such as Michael Laskier's descriptions of the departure of Morocco's Jews as a "self-liquidation process." (Ironically, Islamists' accusations of Jewish treachery likewise grant Jews more agency, however nefarious in nature.) Moroccan Jews themselves seem to still be working it out, with their views depending heavily on their present location and circumstances.

There is an allegorical story about the *mellah* of Tetouan that likens the Jews of that city to a sparrow [*turunji*] in a cage living in a wealthy Muslim merchant's garden. One day the sparrow hears the song of a canary who has alighted on a nearby branch. The sparrow is captivated by the sound of the canary's song and cannot resist it. It tries with all its might to imitate the canary. It jumps around in its cage, oscillating between one bar and the next. It seemed as if the sparrow would outdo himself. It also seemed like this musical performance would go on for a while, because the canary started singing again. For a while the two harmonized, but in the end the sparrow simply couldn't go on. Worn out by its efforts, it tucks its beak under its wing and dies. The canary, according to the author relating the story, is the call of Zionism. The sparrow has neither the strength to withstand the canary nor to follow it. In the end the sparrow, like the Jewish community of Tetouan, is simply gone, and the canary moves off to another branch in another forest.[119]

Conclusion: Allah, al-Watan, al-Malik (God, nation, king)

Among the many new discursive habits to be found in the post–9/11 world is the tendency to describe people and events having to do with the MENA primarily in terms of religion, whether from the standpoint of Islamophobes or the organizations devoted to countering them. The Council on American-Islamic Relations, the Islamic Networks Group, and the Muslim Student Association (to name just a few) all approach Middle Eastern issues from a religious standpoint. The same is true of their nemesis, the far right proponents of "Islamofascism." But in the last century, Arabness ruled the MENA. Arab secular organizations flourished, from the creation of the Arab League in 1945 to the rise of the

Syrian and Iraqi Ba'ath parties mid-century and the radical militancy of the *Popular Front for the Liberation of Palestine* in the 1960s and 1970s. This new formulation of Arabness allowed for a more secular and differently politicized conceptualization of MENA identities, including in Morocco. Pan-Arabism informed both anti-colonial resistance and the construction of the postcolonial nation in Morocco. It was the key to entry in the independence movement. It also worked to exclude Jews from that same entity. Despite the commitment to an inclusive independent Morocco on the part of many individual nationalists, the overall attitude of the Moroccan independence movements toward Jews was one of ambivalence. The Vichy interlude in Morocco (1940–1942) interrupted some of these processes but accelerated others, making Jews all the more aware of their tenuous position in the emerging new nation. Before independence was even won, the idea that Jews would be able to assume the role of equal citizens was severely tested by the creation of the state of Israel in 1948.

Uncertainty was a strong a determinant of Jewish behavior when Moroccan independence came. As Ella Shohat suggests: "Panic and disorientation, rather than desire for *aliyah* in the nationalist sense of the word, was the key factor in the migration to Israel of most Jews who migrated there from the Arab region."[120] But even uncertainty can be unpacked to find its causal components. The form taken by anti-colonial resistance in both its primary and secondary stages had served to either sideline Jews or put them on wrong side of history. Jews were mostly bystanders in the aftermaths of the murder of the French doctor Émile Mauchamp, the signing of the Treaty of Fez, and the Rif war, but were nonetheless deeply affected by the outcome of these events on a collective level. On a personal level, many individual Jews were far from passive or neutral in exercising their political will. Throughout the 1930s and 1940s, Moroccan Jews joined leftist parties; organized boycotts of German, Japanese, and Italian goods; fought against the rise of fascism; supported workers' rights; and provided refuge to Europeans fleeing Nazis.[121] Hélène Cazes Benatar, for example, was a lawyer and a nurse for the Red Cross from Tangier who took great risks to save refugees in Morocco through her founding of the Moroccan Refugee Aid Committee. In partnership with the Jewish Joint Distribution Committee, her group succeeded in improving the dire situation in Vichy labor camps in Morocco. Benatar ensured that prisoners in these camps had food and arranged for them to go to America after the war, even securing them employment once there. Her efforts were one of the most successful operations to save Jews in the Second World War.[122] After the war, when the limits of *alliancism* and integration became all too clear, Jewish Morocco turned to thoughts of emigration.

Questions of who belonged where abounded in North Africa as colonialism gave way to new nation-states. In Algeria, the huge *pied noir* population focused attention on the idea of the settler, raising a issues scholars still struggle with today: When does the settler become a native? After how many generations is one considered to belong to a place?[123] With decolonization, Algeria's *pieds noirs* were officially deemed foreigners despite their 130-year presence in the country. When it came to Jews, however, the question was posed in exactly the opposite way: When does a native become a settler? Despite a millennia-long presence in North Africa, at what point were Jews considered to no longer belong? In Algeria, the moment is easy enough to pinpoint: the Evian Accords that ended the Algerian war for independence in 1962 gave Jews the same status as *pieds noirs*, resulting in their near-total "repatriation" to France (though this was of course preceded by the Crémieux decree of 1870 that already gave Jews French nationality).

In Morocco, where Jews were never granted blanket French citizenship, the process of deciding where they belonged was more slippery, closely tied as it was to the nation's newly redrawn Arab identity. There was no real barrier to considering Moroccan Jews to be Arabs historically, although questions of identity were rarely if ever posed in those terms in Morocco prior to the colonial period. To the extent that facility with the Arabic language determines who is an Arab, it is worth remembering that Jews in Morocco were actually more likely than Moroccan Muslims to be primary Arabic speakers, given the larger number of monolingual Tamazight speakers among the Muslim population. But when the question of Arabness began to be posed in new ways in the twentieth century, Jews no longer met the criteria. Previously Arabness had been implicit; the rise of pan-Arabism rendered it explicit for the first time, marginalizing Jews and Imazighen both. The continual relevance of Islam in the nationalist movements allowed for the Imazighen to make their way back into the Moroccan nation. Jewish Morocco, lacking such recourse, instead responded to the siren call of Zionism. They would then shed their Arabness for good under pressure from Israeli society, where Arab culture was shunned. And yet in the twenty-first century, a small number of Moroccan Jews appear to be reclaiming their Arab identity. Proving once again its inherent flexibility, Arabness is currently in the process of being reformulated, reinvigorated, and reasserted by some of today's most prominent Moroccan Jews, both in Morocco and in the Moroccan Jewish diaspora. This reclaiming of Arab Jewish identity actually began among Middle Eastern Jews who were searching for a corrective to the semantic division created by Zionism on the one hand and pan-Arab nationalism on the other, which, as we have seen, have together conspired to make the term "Arab Jew" seem like an oxymoron.[124] As religious identities continue to gain in prominence, the last Arab nationalists left in the world might just be Jews, many of them Moroccan.[125]

Map C.1 Morocco in the world.

Morocco Guide. "Where Is Morocco Located in the World? Where Is Morocco? Map." Morocco-Guide. January 26, 2019. Accessed May 06, 2019. https://www.morocco-guide.com/information/where-is-morocco/.

Conclusion
Postmodern Jewish Morocco

> There are no Jews in Morocco. There are only Moroccan subjects.
>
> —Saying commonly attributed to Mohammed V

The most momentous event to have occurred in the twenty-first-century MENA so far is the Arab Spring, the popular uprising against autocratic rulers. It began in the Maghrib, sparked quite literally by the self-immolation of the vegetable seller Mohammed Bouazzizi in Tunisia in February of 2011 and climaxed with the toppling of no fewer than three North African regimes. To date, Mohammed VI has survived the cataclysms, attributable no doubt to the monarchy's deep roots and continued relevance in Moroccan society, something the deposed rulers of Tunisia, Libya, and Egypt all sorely lacked. But the Arab Spring did give rise to a newly empowered protest movement in Morocco, called the February 20 movement in commemoration of the date in 2011 when Moroccans first took to the streets in solidarity with their Tunisian brothers and sisters. The *makhzan* appeared to take the protests seriously. It responded with a referendum on constitutional reforms, which passed by a wide margin. The 2011 constitution reinforced the king's religiously mandated authority as *amir-al-mu'minin*, but for the first time it also set limits on his power. Trade unions and grassroots organizations, women's groups, the media, foreign NGOs, elite families, and opposition parties have also helped keep the potential for autocracy in check. A new addition to the mix is political activists. Once taboo, they are now tolerated, at times even accommodated by the Moroccan government.[1]

Older patterns of co-optation and repression still exist alongside, or underneath, the 2011 constitution and the laws it has inspired, however. Moroccans have not entirely recovered from the so-called *Years of Lead*, when political dissidents were mercilessly persecuted by the regime of Hassan II, father of the current king. But these days, it is Islamists rather than radical leftists who pose the greatest challenge to governmental authority and who often pay the price for doing so. Morocco's political stability is closely tied to its economic outlook. Sustained by agriculture, mineral mining, and tourism, the Moroccan economy has mostly weathered the storms of globalization, but the benefits are unevenly distributed. Moreover, even if the king remains popular, his inner circle is seen by many Moroccans as venal and corrupt; a culture of *"wasta"* (connections; nepotism) is pervasive. The 2017 protests in al-Hoceima in the Rif revealed just how much corruption has stymied growth in Morocco's underdeveloped regions, indeed to the extent that a fishmonger would risk his life by jumping into a trash compactor to save his confiscated catch of swordfish. Illiteracy and poverty are deeply entrenched in Morocco's rural areas and are further stumbling blocks to economic growth.[2] Gender equality is another important marker for economic and social progress. The Moroccan family code, known as the *mudawana*, was reformed in 2004 to the general benefit of women, and laws regarding rape and domestic violence have been revised, though in this area as well much work is still needed. Decentralization and the fate of the Western Sahara are issues of top political importance; the Tamazight question also looms large in twenty-first-century Morocco: what language should children learn at school? How many languages can they be expected to know? Moroccan families tend to see learning French and English as a means of upward mobility for their children, but Tamazight is fundamental to coexistence and integration. Either way, weakening the position of Arabic in Moroccan schools in favor of *any* other language is politically risky, as can be seen in the sectarian fracturing that has occurred in Middle East with the rise of Kurdish separatism, to give just one example. Moreover, the dilution of Arabic in the Moroccan curriculum would almost certainly provoke a backlash from the Islamists.

Jews are noticeably absent from the portrait of contemporary Morocco sketched above. Yet passages from the 2011 Constitution, the document meant to guide Morocco into the twenty-first century, have framed the chapters of this book on Jewish Morocco. This raises the question: Do Jews have a stake in postmodern, postcolonial, post-Arab spring Morocco? Or are they merely artifacts of the Moroccan past?

Jewish Morocco's branches began to stretch outward in the nineteenth century with the transformative experience of Europeanization; under the weight of colonialism, nationalism, and emigration in the next century, they started to break, and the majority of Moroccan Jews eventually left their native land. From a height of nearly a quarter million people, today only a few thousand Jews live in

Morocco. Jewish communities are no longer dispersed among the pre-Saharan oases, remote Atlas villages, royal capitals, and Mediterranean enclaves but instead are concentrated in Casablanca, as if poised to leave on the next boat out.

During the uncertain years surrounding Moroccan independence in 1956, Jews began leaving Morocco for what at the time seemed like the safer shores of France and Israel, and later, Canada and the United States. As a history of Morocco from a Jewish perspective, the scope of the present study does not extend to the Moroccan Jewish diaspora. However, any portrait of Jewish Morocco would be incomplete without at least a glance in that direction.

The greatest portion of the Moroccan Jewish diaspora lives in Israel. They and their offspring number 1 million out of the country's total Jewish population of 6.5 million. Despite their large numbers, the initial experience of Moroccan Jews in Israel was indisputably rocky. Arriving in a new country in which the trauma of the holocaust still lingered and the economy was flailing, all new immigrants to Israel in the 1950s faced hardships. But Moroccan Jews faced an especially daunting ordeal. Their struggles began immediately upon arrival, with their housing assignments: Moroccan Jews were initially placed in *ma'abarot* [Heb. transit camps], where they sometimes were made to live in tents for months on end while immigrants from Europe passed more quickly onto permanent housing. When permanent housing was finally available to Moroccans, it was typically located in distant, often desolate areas of the country, like the Negev desert, where their presence could be used to secure contested border regions. As a result, they were often the first victims in skirmishes with Israel's neighbors. (The town of Sderot, near Gaza and often the target of missiles launched from there by Hamas, has a population consisting of 80 percent Moroccan Jews.) Although these sites were called "development towns," they were in fact strikingly underdeveloped—plagued by low levels of education, low wages, and poor healthcare, with economic life centered around a single state-run factory.[3] Moroccan Jews were also concentrated in *moshavim* [cooperative villages], the less romantic (and less subsidized) counterpart of the Ashkenazi-dominated Kibbutz movement; those who were able to settle in urban areas typically lived in slums.

Along with other Jews from the Arab world who immigrated to Israel, Moroccan Jews were subsumed under the general category of "*mizrahim*" (lit. "easterners"). *Mizrahi* identity initially helped galvanize and unify MENA Jews who rejected the more traditional labels of "Sephardim" or the Israeli term "*bnai edot ha-mizrach*" ["children of the communities of the East"]. But the connotations of the term changed as ethnic exclusion intensified in Israel. Underlying their difficult absorption was the fact that, in the eyes of many

Israelis, the *mizrahim* represented the culture of the enemy: they spoke Arabic, listened to Middle Eastern music, produced large families, and so on; they were "Jews in Arabs' Bodies" as the saying went. Israeli films like *Sallah Shabati* (1964) reinforced such stereotypes even as they tried to cultivate empathy among Israelis. The "negation of the diaspora" was a tenet of Zionism that all Jews arriving in Israel were subject to, at least in theory. To become Israelis, Jews from the outside would have to shed all cultural vestiges of their lives as minorities. When it came to Moroccan Jews, however, their "absorption" into Israel was additionally marked by strong anti-Arab cultural biases and Eurocentric ideas of "modernization," not unlike what had already been undergone by these same communities in Morocco with regard to programs of French acculturation in the schools of the AIU.

The sense of an Ashkenazi "us" and a *mizrahi* "them" already existed in Israel prior to the arrival of the Moroccan immigrants, but their particular circumstances exacerbated the divide. Not only was the Moroccan *aliyah* the largest of any from Arab country, but it was motivated less by Zionist sympathies than by disillusionment with the government that came to power with Moroccan independence in 1956, combined with strong messianic fervor among rural populations.[4] None of this harmonized particularly well with the heavily ideological secular socialism of 1950s Israel. The growing poverty and discrimination experienced by Moroccan Jewish communities in Israel gave rise to prostitution, alcoholism, and high crime rates. Social awakening and resistance soon followed. The first public manifestation of Moroccan Jews' frustration with the Israeli system erupted in the Wadi Salib slums of Haifa in 1959, when the police shot a local man for being drunk and disorderly. Riots ensued, and public outrage converged into a mass movement that continued to grow throughout the 1960s, particularly when benefits from the post-1967 war boom were seen as accruing disproportionately to the country's Ashkenazim.[5]

Moroccan Jews had had enough. A group from the Musrara slums of Jerusalem founded the Israeli Black Panthers in the early 1970s. They borrowed their name from the Oakland, California-based Black Panthers in an effort not only to evoke a similarly divided society but also to highlight the parallel condition of the two sets of victims. The Black Panthers were a distinctly left leaning, social justice group. ("Unless everyone shares the cake, there will be no cake" was the motto of one of the original founders of the group, Sa'adia Marciano.) Over the course of the 1970s and 1980s, various members of the Black Panthers entered electoral politics in Israel. Newer political organizations founded on *mizrahi* ethnic bases like the political party SHAS or the social justice organization the *mizrahi* Democratic Rainbow Coalition came to absorb some of the political energies of Moroccan Jews in Israel in the coming years.

The disparities between Moroccan Jews and other Israelis have eased considerably in the twenty-first century. Moroccan Jewish traditions are now a prominent part of Israeli cultural expression. The Chief Sephardic rabbi is Moroccan and every town and city in Israel has its share of Moroccan synagogues, restaurants, and other institutions. At the same time, the radical politics of the Black Panthers has been muted. In fact, with some important exceptions, Moroccan Jews in Israel today are on the whole much more likely to hold hard right positions vis-à-vis the Palestinians and Israeli foreign policy in general. They tend to vote for Likud or SHAS, both of which have grown increasingly hawkish over time, although allegiances could conceivably shift as Moroccan Jews begin to make their way up the Labor list to higher slots, as has Avi Gabbay, who was voted in as leader of the Labor Party in 2017.[6] The right-wing Likud party has never been led by a Moroccan Jew, though David Levy (b. 1937, Rabat) rose high in its ranks beginning in the Menachem Begin era. In addition to their increased visibility in government, Moroccan Jews have also assumed powerful positions in the military (the current Chief of Staff of the Israel Defense Forces, Gadi Eizenkot, is of Moroccan descent: his mother is from Casablanca and his father is from Marrakech) and in business, even as they remain underrepresented in the liberal professions and the academy.

The second largest portion of the Moroccan Jewish diaspora lives in France, which itself is home to the largest Jewish population in Europe, numbering about half a million people.[7] The Moroccan diaspora is dwarfed by France's Algerian Jewish community, however, those who were "repatriated" to France in 1962 with Algerian independence and their offspring. Compared to the total migration of Algerian Jewry to France, Moroccan Jewish immigration to France was only partial. But similar to Algerian Jewry, their transition was nearly seamless, facilitated not only by the geographic proximity of the Maghrib to France, but also by preexisting cultural affinities. France was not a foreign country to Moroccan Jews. They spoke French, dressed like the French, and— thanks to their AIU educations and the many generations they spent under French domination—had perfect knowledge of French history, culture, and geography.[8] Their relatively smooth landing in France was further facilitated by their financial situation, which was generally better than that of their coreligionists who went to Israel. In turn, Moroccan Jews were met by a booming French economy and the amplified generosity of French Jews who perhaps regretted not having been able to do more for the earlier, wartime wave of Jewish refugees from Eastern Europe. Many Moroccan Jewish immigrants experienced a rapid social and economic ascent in France. Several of France's leading public intellectuals and artists are of Moroccan Jewish background, including Audrey Azoulay, former Minister of Culture and current Director General of UNESCO; Nobelaureate physicist Serge Haroche; journalist Pierre Assouline; philosopher Marc Alain Ouaknine; and the well-known comedian Gad Elmaleh. Politically, Moroccan Jews in France tend to concentrate in the center, though concerns about rising anti-Semitism have engendered newfound support for right-wing parties, including the National Front.[9]

Moroccan Jewish immigration to the Americas followed a somewhat different pattern. It began quite early, in the nineteenth century, out of an economic impetus, when Spanish-speaking Jews from northern Morocco began moving to Argentina and Brazil to take advantage of the booming South American rubber industry.[10] With Moroccan independence, some Jews made their way to Canada, attracted by the relatively familiar francophone culture of Quebec in particular. Canada eventually came to have the largest Moroccan Jewish community in North America, numbering 27,000.[11] Approximately 75,000 Moroccans live in the United States according to the 2010 census, though how many of those are Jews is not indicated.[12] This community is largely the result of repeated migrations, often first to Israel, and/or to Europe or Canada, rather than being composed of emigrants coming directly from Morocco. They are concentrated in New York, Miami, and Los Angeles. Some had first been exposed to America in the form of American soldiers who landed in Morocco at the end of the Second World War.[13] Its more prominent members have made a name for themselves in the clothing business, like the Marciano brothers (Paul, Armand, Maurice, and Georges) who grew up in Marseille but are originally from Debdou and founded the *Guess* brand in the 1980s. (Along similar lines, Aldo Bensadoun, the founder of Canada's Aldo Group shoe retail business, was born in Fez.) Even with its smaller numbers, Moroccan Jewish immigration to North America altered the dominant Ashkenazi identity of the preexisting Jewish community and helped cultivate a new appreciation for Jewish multiculturalism.

Despite the many forms the Jewish Moroccan diaspora has taken, in Morocco itself the absent Jews left a void of distinct contours behind when they left. That void is being recognized, rehashed, and rearticulated in myriad ways in contemporary Morocco, both out of genuine nostalgia and, it must be said, strategic interest. Indeed it is rare these days to open a newspaper or turn on the television and *not* find a reference to Jews in Moroccan media. Issues of the popular history journal *Zamane* frequently feature Jewish themes; the cover of the May 2013 issue called out: "Morocco: A Jewish Land." Other issues have considered Moroccan Jews' role in the "discovery" of the Americas, the holocaust, and Jewish music. Meanwhile, the visits of Moroccan officials, including the king himself, to Jewish sites are widely reported on in the Moroccan media. It is not an overstatement to say Morocco is experiencing a wave of philosemitism in some quarters. Leading the charge is the *makhzan*, the Moroccan government, for whom the memory of Moroccan Jews and the positive model of Muslim-Jewish relations has an undeniable utility in the current political climate. Namely, it allows the Moroccan state to position itself as a haven of diversity and progressiveness, thus challenging those elements seen as threatening to its traditional "multicultural" identity, particularly the homogenizing forces of Islamism and Arabism. As conservative ideas flow into Morocco from the Gulf in particular, they are being offset by an official narrative of diversity, transmitted through press articles, interviews, and speeches, as often as not evoking the long history of Jewish Morocco.

Jewish heritage sites in Morocco have been the object of intensive restoration projects. With the palace's help, more than one hundred synagogues, cemeteries, and other Jewish sites have been restored.[14] The king's senior economic advisor, André Azoulay, recently oversaw the creation of a Jewish museum and study center in Essaouira, the country's second such institution after that of Casablanca.[15] A recent exhibit at the Dar el-Basha Museum of Confluences in Marrakech featured sacred sites shared by the three monotheistic religions in Morocco and worldwide. The state's very public stance not only serves to destabilize Islamists internally, it also reassures international audiences, especially in the United States and France, that Morocco is a trustworthy partner with which to conduct politics and business. (Recall that Morocco holds 75 percent of the world's supply of phosphates and that the United States is the largest importer.[16])

The showcasing of tolerance also gives a boost to tourism. Although Morocco has not yet developed a multibillion dollar Jewish tourism industry like Poland's, Jewish-themed tourism is a growing phenomenon within an already large sector of the economy. Judaica and Jewish knickknacks, *mezzuza*-s, Hanukkah menorahs, ceramics decorated with stars of David and Hebrew letters (often nonsensical) pepper the *suq* of Morocco's medinas; shopkeepers call out to passersby in smatterings of Hebrew. In the Marrakech *mellah*, once home to the Arab world's largest Jewish community, tourist groups amble through the newly widened streets. Although this impoverished quarter was in desperate need of renovation and municipal services, many of the changes seem to have been done with tourism rather than historical accuracy in mind: "The Rabbi's Hotel" stands where no such figure lived; the thresholds of buildings on the main thoroughfare are framed in foreign-seeming Damascene wooden structures, cement has been laid over ancient graves to create neat pathways in the enormous Jewish cemetery.

The embrace of Jewish Morocco has also helped the Moroccan government gain important ground in one of its greatest PR challenges: its struggle for international recognition of the Moroccan claim over the Western Sahara. Morocco annexed this area bordering Mauritania and Algeria in 1975 after the Spanish withdrew from their colonial possessions in the south, but a rebel movement known as the Polisario front opposes Moroccan rule there and is fighting for Sahrawi independence. The Polisario has the open support of Algeria; Morocco has the support of the United States, and perhaps Israel. (Pro-Polisario groups have long claimed that an Israeli company built the sand berm surrounded by land mines that encloses the Western Sahara and keeps the Polisario out of Morocco.[17]) In any event, certain sectors of the Jewish Moroccan diaspora have sought to reinforce the Moroccan government's position. When in March of 2016 then secretary general of the United Nations Ban-Ki Moon described Morocco as "occupiers" of the Western Sahara, Jewish groups launched a vocal counterattack. The World Federation of Moroccan Jewry, located in Israel, along with the American Jewish Committee and the Moroccan Jewish community of Toronto, all issued statements to the effect that the Sahara has always been and always will be Moroccan.[18] Jews living within Morocco have also made their position on this issue well known. In 2016, the holiday of Mimouna coincided with the fortieth anniversary of the Green March, the date in 1976 when Morocco lay claim to the Western Sahara. It also came just a month after Ban Ki-Moon's remarks. Moroccan Jews gathered in the coastal city of Mazagan to celebrate the holiday, which they dedicated to the Saharan issue, adding songs about Laâyoune, the capital of the Western Sahara, to their usual Mimouna repertoire.[19] Sam Ben Chetrit, president of the World Federation of Moroccan Jewry, sent his regards to the group. In his remarks, he alluded to the *quid pro quo* behind Jewish Morocco's support of the *makhzan-*'s policy, linking his "utter indignation" at Ban-Ki Moon's remarks to "the Jewish People's gratitude to Morocco's royal house, government and people, who have done more than any other nation in the Middle East and many nations elsewhere to preserve Jewish heritage and protect Jewish citizens."[20]

Though not always nuanced, the official embrace of Jewish Morocco is not necessarily cynical. In many quarters, the belated realization of and regret for Morocco's loss of its Jews is sincere. Without its Jewish component the possibility of a certain type of nation became impossible, even as it is being constantly evoked. As the poet Mois Benarroch has remarked of his native city, Tetouan: "For three hundred years in Tetouan the population was more than 15 percent Jewish, life revolved around the Jews. All the buildings in the city center were built by Jews that had traveled to the Americas and returned to their city. Now it is like a body without kidneys. It doesn't really work."[21]

There is a sad irony in watching references to Jews in official discourse increase as the number of actual Jews declines. What does the image of Islamic pluralism mean in the absence of actual religious minorities? To be sure, Moroccan officialdom is not concerned about other minorities in same way it is about Jews. Jews alone are a model minority community in the Moroccan context; they are not considered "problematic" like Moroccan Muslims who have converted to the Baha'i faith or Christianity and are seen as apostates from Islam. Nor do Jews pose a potential demographic or political threat, as do the Imazighen. With little risk, the embrace of Jewish Morocco allows the state to present itself as diverse, tolerant, and open, a place where the Muslim majority lives in peace with other sectors. The inconsistencies abound, however, given that majority constitutes a full 99 percent of the population, and that Moroccan constitution provides for freedom of religion, but article 220 of the Moroccan penal code mandates prison sentences for undermining the Muslim faith via conversion or proselytizing.[22]

In late January of 2016, King Mohammed VI convened a major international conference to combat Islamist discourses on minorities in the MENA. The conference included important Muslim thinkers of the day from Morocco, Europe, Iran, Turkey, and the Arab world (an Emirati organization served as a cosponsor). Among the conference's outcomes was the "Declaration of Marrakech," which proposed a new legal orientation that merges the Prophet Muhammad's original conception of a community ("*umma*") with the more modern contractual idea of citizenship as a means of counteracting discrimination against minorities.[23] Jews are not explicitly mentioned in the Declaration, but the fact that its model is the Constitution of Medina makes the connection clear. The Constitution of Medina was devised by Muhammad shortly after his arrival to that town following his emigration from Mecca (c. 622). It lays out how the various groups under Muhammad's authority were to cooperate with regard to warfare, ransoming of captives, bloodwite, and other matters relevant to late antique tribal society. In the seventh century, Jewish tribes were an important part of the social structure of Medina. Although the meaning of the term would change over time, the Medinan "*umma*" (community) that is cited in the document is widely understood to have included the local Jews. The

Constitution pays careful attention to their rights and obligations, citing several tribes by name. No Christian tribes are named in the document; presumably they did not live within the limits of Medina at the time. There are probably more Christians living in Morocco today than Jews (no official statistics exist). But they are not invoked, implicitly or otherwise, in the Declaration of Marrakech. Insofar as they are essential for imagining Moroccan society, governance, and national identity in the future, Jews remain a *dhimmi* apart.

On the popular level, however, the official embrace of Jewish identity can be problematic. The reality is most Moroccan Jews in Israel support right-wing governments and policies that are oppressive to Palestinians, with whom many Moroccans sympathize deeply. In the 1977 Israeli elections, it was the so-called *mizrahi* vote, Moroccan in its majority, that put the hawkish Likud party in power for the first time. In the following decades, many Israelis of Moroccan background began supporting SHAS, which has leaned further and further right since its inception. None of this history is lost on Moroccan Muslims. In the age of the internet, Moroccans are subject to influences and messages other than those the state mandates. In 2006, it was a Moroccan contestant who won the prize for the best cartoon denying the holocaust in a contest sponsored by Iran.

And yet, there is no denying the nostalgia for Jews that exists among many Moroccan Muslims, what the Italian scholar Emanuela Trevisan Semi calls the "double trauma" of Jewish emigration from Morocco, encompassing both the Jews who left and the Muslims who were left behind.[24] The texture of that loss has been painstakingly revealed in the work of the Moroccan-American scholar Aomar Boum. He quotes a common expression in the southern oases "A market without Jews is like bread without salt."[25] Indeed certain food preparations were lost with the Jews' departure. So were some artisanal skills. Jews were especially competent metal and leather workers. There are stories of entire villages in the south that are missing their brass door knockers, since the Jews alone knew how to make them and they disappeared. Boum further notes that attitudes toward Jews are strongly generational.[26] Older Muslims remember participating in Jewish holidays, festivals, and celebrations, Mimouna in particular. There are few Mimouna parties in Morocco outside of Casablanca any more, but there is something called the "Mimouna club." Registered as a foundation, the Mimouna club has chapters in Fez, Tetuan, Rabat, and Marrakech. Its membership consists primarily of Moroccan Muslim university students who want to promote the history of Jews in Morocco as part of the larger national history. Nostalgia or simple curiosity about Jewish Morocco can also be seen in a new subgenre of mnemonic literature about Jews by Muslim authors. In the last decade, at least six novels focusing on Jewish themes or characters have been published, by Moroccan Muslim authors five of them in Arabic and one in French. All grapple with the events and structures that "robbed" Morocco of its Jews.[27] Film is another genre that Moroccan Muslims have utilized to understand the absence of Jews. Documentaries like *Tinghir-Jerusalem* by Kamal Hachkar, melodramas like *Goodbye, Mothers* by Mohamed Ismail, comedies like *Where Are You Going Moshe* [More musically rendered in Moroccan Arabic as *"fin mashi ya mushi?"*] by Hassan Benjelloun, even teenager flicks like *Marock* by Laïla Marrakchi have all taken up the question of Jewish Morocco's "present absence" to use Aomar Boum's evocative phrase for this ghostly void.[28]

How has this message been received within Jewish Morocco itself? Many Jews of Moroccan descent, even a generation or two removed from the land itself, remain deeply attached to their ancestral homeland. Their difficult integration in Israel as *"mizrahim"* and, more recently, the economic and social challenges they face in France have served to foster a deep if not uncomplicated appreciation for the Morocco that was and the lives Jews once led there, real or imagined. Many visit Morocco on a regular basis. According to *The Economist*, 50,000 Jews travel to Morocco annually from Israel alone.[29]

Outside of Morocco, Jewish traditions are maintained to such an extent that Jewish Morocco is now a transnational phenomenon that shows no signs of waning. Websites like *diarna* [our homes] and *dafina* [the characteristic Moroccan Sabbath stew] help perpetuate this memory. On *dafina* we are told that Jews once numbered 400,000 in Morocco, a tellingly optimistic figure. The site has sections for posting memoirs, old family photographs, jokes, and the all-important *"rencontres"* ["meetings"]. Moroccan Jews in France, Israel, Canada, and the United States have also told their stories through film. Many of these filmmakers are women, who have brought an awareness of gender to a topic where it has been sorely missing.[30] There is even an entire genre of cookbooks devoted to Jewish cuisine of Morocco, *dafina* taking pride of place: for example, "The Taste of Memory: Grandma Elmaleh's Moroccan Cookbook" specializing in the cuisine of the coastal town of Essaouira. Such elements have created a global Moroccan Jewish identity of surprising force. Though it is still too early to compare the two, it seems that the Moroccan diaspora has been at least as successful at retaining their traditions as the European Jews who migrated to the United States. Regardless of whether these patterns will continue, and what direction they may take in the future, their echoes are being heard across the globe.

Several years ago I was asked to serve on the jury of the San Francisco Arab Film Festival. During one early fall weekend, my fellow jurors and I sat in a small suite of offices in San Francisco's Mission district and watched film after film from Egypt, Palestine, Jordan, and the Maghrib. Never before had I seen so many movies in such a short period of time; it felt as if I had taken several back-to-back transatlantic flights without ever leaving the Bay Area. I was the only North Africanist on the jury that year; all the other members worked on or in the Middle East "proper," that is to say Egypt and eastward, the region known in Arabic as the *mashriq*. One of the featured films was *Casanegra* by Noureddine Lakhmari, a gritty story about street life in Casablanca focusing on a young man, Karim, who steadily loses hope of a better future in the face of unemployment, corruption, and inequality. The film's title perfectly captures Karim's disillusionment. It was made before the Arab spring, but the tenor of Karim's frustration uncannily foreshadows the grievances of Moroccans who would take to the streets on February 20, 2011, demanding justice and accountability. Politics aside, one of the subplots of the film is the crush Karim develops on an unobtainable woman. Although I do not know if the character in question, Nabila, was intended thus (indeed her name suggests otherwise), I immediately read her as a Moroccan Jew: she was a member of the Casablanca elite, managed a store that dealt in Art Deco (i.e., colonial) furniture, wore a bright red dress in a prominent scene, spoke Arabic with an accent that Karim's friends made fun of, and seemed to enjoy a relatively high level of mobility for a Moroccan woman. She is seen going dancing with friends and making her own way through the city. Her putative Jewishness would also serve to advance the film's plot, as it underscored her unavailability to Karim. Interestingly, none of my cojurors had detected the possibility that Nabila might be Jewish and were surprised by my interpretation. In the Arab societies with which they were most familiar, namely those of the Middle East, the markers of Jewishness were not just different from those in Morocco, they were rarely, if ever, so subtly portrayed. (Egyptian television specials during Ramadan are especially well known for featuring grossly distorted Jewish stereotypes.[31]) But in the film *Casanegra*—as in the history recounted in the preceding pages—Moroccanness and Jewishness can be so intertwined as to become at times nearly indistinguishable, as to be one and the same.

Within the Arab-Islamic world, only Morocco can lay claim to this level of entanglement between Jews and Muslims that lays at the foundation of the production of intercommunal memory. The basis for such claims is partly quantitative: Moroccan Jews are the single largest and among the oldest of all Jewish communities in the Arab world; they are also qualitative: Jews are the only indigenous religious minority in Morocco, a position they have held for nearly a millennium, since the disappearance of the last vestiges of Latin Christianity from Morocco under the Almohads. When one thinks of a *"dhimmi"* in Morocco—members of that protected class of non-Muslims under Islamic rule, the so-called people of the book, or *"ahl al-kitab"*—one thinks, definitively, of a Jew. In this way North Africa stands in contrast to the Middle East, where indigenous Christian communities persist into the contemporary period, however precariously. That Jews are largely (though not entirely) an element of the Moroccan past makes their story that much more critical to preserve yet also risks veering toward clichés and generalizations or even strategic mobilization. This is the point at which memory and history often part ways. In this work I have tried to remain true to the historical record while also expanding the boundaries of the communitarian mode of Jewish scholarship to think comparatively, across sectarian lines, and with attention to what Michael Rothberg calls "multidirectional memory."[32] Yet Jewishness undeniably remains at the foundation of this history of Morocco, even if it has not been considered in isolation from broader issues (I leave it to others more qualified than me to write a history of Moroccan Judaism.) The nuanced way in which Daniel Schroeter and Yossi Chetrit have characterized Jewish Morocco in the late colonial period applies across all the time periods covered in this book: "Most Moroccan Jews continued to be intimately connected to both a universal halakhic culture and an increasingly Jewish culture of Morocco that was culturally related to Moroccan practices found among the Muslim population yet always related to the larger world of Judaic practice."[33] This book has explored how Jewish roots stretch deep into the Moroccan soil, finding purchase in the most "authentic" pillars of Moroccan identity: Malikism, Amazighity Sharifism, Europeanization, and Arabness. Having shown Jewish Morocco's stake in the historical development of each of these, I am led to conclude that Jewishness itself may just be a sixth pillar of Moroccan identity, one in which all Moroccans, to some extent, participate.

Notes

Introduction

1. Although precedents for the concept of "toleration" exist in Latin in the medieval period and in other forms even in antiquity, the modern sense of the term is often projected backward in Moroccan history anachronistically, hence is used here cautiously.
2. Elaine Sciolino, "Aftereffects: Morocco. Jews in Casablanca Ponder Meaning of Attacks," *New York Times*, May 20, 2003.
3. According to the Moroccan Minister of the Interior, 1,631 Moroccans have joined ISIS since 2012. Youssef Igrouane, "1631 Moroccans Have Joined ISIS since 2012: Minister of Interior," *Moroccan World News*, May 13, 2017.
4. Amanda Rogers, "Warding off Terrorism and Revolution: Moroccan Religious Pluralism, National Identity and the Politics of Visual Culture," *Journal of North African Studies* 17, no. 3 (2012): 458.
5. *Wikipedia* apparently shares this stance. It categorizes the targets of the 2003 Casablanca attacks as being of just two possible types: "Western" or "Muslim," the former encompassing a hybrid "Judeo-Greco-Christian civilization" to which Moroccan Jews would apparently belong. "2003 Casablanca Bombings," Wikipedia. Accessed September 5, 2017.
6. As neatly conceptualized by Jewish community leader Serge Berdugo in the wake of the attacks, "by attempting to kill Jews, these criminals wanted above all to harm the whole Moroccan society and affect the way of life of moderate Moroccan Muslims. Islam in Morocco is an open and tolerant Islam." *Maghreb Arab Press* (MAP) website, September 6, 2003.
7. Sophie Wagenhofer, "'We Have Our Own History': Voices from the Jewish Museum of Casablanca," in *Memory and Ethnicity: Ethnic Museums in Israel and the Diaspora*, eds. Emanuela Trevisan Semi, Dario Miccoli, and Tudor Parfitt (Cambridge: Cambridge Scholars Publishing, 2013).
8. See the formulation in Benjamin Barber, *Jihad vs. McWorld* (New York: Ballantine Books, 1996).
9. A wide variety of sources including those authored by Jews, Muslims, Christians, and others is used to reconstruct this history.
10. Note that Jewish communities in non-Arab Iran and Turkey were quite large as well, though not as large as those in Morocco: Approximately 200,000 Jews lived in

Turkey at the turn of the twentieth century, and 140,000–150,000 Jews lived in Iran in the mid-twentieth century. Today, both countries have larger Jewish populations than any still living in the Arab world, numbering 20,000–25,000 in Iran and 17,000–18,000 in Turkey. The putative Arabness of Morocco will be taken up in Chapter 5, though here I note that Morocco is a member of the Arab League.

11 Though some scholars have tried to do just that. See, for example, the work of the nationalist historian Abdallah Laroui, *The History of the Maghrib: An Interpretive Essay* (Princeton, NJ: Princeton University Press, 1977), in which the author makes fleeting reference to Jews in a general way (e.g., pages 75, 86) but never considers them as an organic part of the larger national narrative. Even in his discussion of the mythic Amazigh warrior known as "the Kahina," no mention is made of the popular (if unsubstantiated) claim that she was Jewish.

12 See Jonathan Boyarin and Daniel Boyarin, *Powers of Diaspora: Two Essays on the Importance of Jewish Culture* (Minneapolis: University of Minnesota Press, 2002).

13 Some exemplary works in this genre include: Julia Cohen, *Becoming Ottomans: Sephardi Jews and Imperial Citizenship in the Modern Era* (New York: Oxford University Press, 2014); Katie Fleming, *Greece: A Jewish History* (Princeton, NJ: Princeton University Press, 2008); Devin Naar, *Jewish Salonica: Between the Ottoman Empire and Modern Greece* (Stanford: Stanford University Press, 2016); Mark Mazower, *Salonica, City of Ghosts: Christians, Muslims and Jews 1430–1950* (New York: Vintage Books, 2006); Michelle Campos, *Ottoman Brothers: Muslims, Christians, and Jews in Early Twentieth-century Palestine* (Stanford: Stanford University Press, 2010); Joshua Schreir, *The Merchants of Oran: A Jewish Port at the Dawn of Empire* (Stanford, CA: Stanford University Press, 2017).

14 On Essaouira, see Daniel Schroeter, *Merchants of Essaouira: Urban Society and Imperialism in Southwestern Morocco, 1844–1886* (Cambridge, UK: Cambridge University Press, 2010). On Tangier, see Susan Gilson Miller, "The Beni Ider Quarter of Tangier in 1900: Hybridity as a Social Practice," in *The Architecture and Memory of the Minority Quarter in the Muslim Mediterranean City*, eds. Mauro Bertagnin and Susan G. Miller (Cambridge, MA: Harvard Univ. Press, Harvard Univ. Graduate School of Design, 2010), 138–173; Miller, "Apportioning Sacred Space in a Moroccan City: The Case of Tangier, 1860–1912," *City & Society* 13, no. 1 (2001): 57–83. On Fez, see Susan Gilson Miller, Attilio Petruccioli, and Mauro Bertagnin, "The *Mallah*, the Third City of Fez," in *The Architecture and Memory of the Minority Quarter in the Muslim Mediterranean City*, eds. Mauro Bertagnin and Susan G. Miller (Cambridge, MA: Harvard Univ. Press, Harvard University Graduate School of Design, 2010), 80–109. For Marrakech, see Emily Gottreich, *The Mellah of Marrakech: Muslim and Jewish Space in Morocco's Red City* (Bloomington: Indiana University Press, 2007).

15 Jessica Marglin, *Across Legal Lines: Jews and Muslims in Modern Morocco* (New Haven: Yale University Press, 2016).

16 Aomar Boum, *Memories of Absence: How Muslims Remember Jews in Morocco* (Stanford: Stanford University Press, 2013).
17 Oren Kosansky, "The Real Morocco Itself: Jewish Saint Pilgrimage, Hybridity, and the Idea of the Moroccan Nation," in *Jewish Culture and Society in North Africa*, eds. Emily Gottreich and Daniel J. Schroeter (Bloomington: Indiana University Press, 2011), 341–360.
18 Moshe Rosman, *How Jewish Is Jewish History?* (Oxford: Littman Library of Jewish Civilization, 2009).
19 The term is adapted from Marshall Hodgson's idea of an "Islamicate civilization," which constructively acknowledges the participation and contributions of non-Muslims to the history and cultures of the Islamic world. As the term's critics point out, however, it does so by positing a secular sphere, which did not exist as such in the Islamic world historically. Marshall Hodgson, *The Venture of Islam. Conscience and History in a World Civilization* (Chicago: The University of Chicago Press, 1974).
20 Bernard Lewis, *Semites and Anti-Semites: An Inquiry into Conflict and Prejudice* (London: W. W. Norton, 1999), 121–122. Lewis goes on to say that there is also nothing in the history of the Jews under Islam "to compare with the progressive emancipation and acceptance accorded to the Jews in the democratic West during the last three centuries."
21 Bernard Lewis, *Jews of Islam* (Princeton: Princeton University Press, 1987).
22 See, for example, the polemical literature around the concept of "dhimmitude." Although this is mostly an internet phenomenon, which in the post 9/11 context has shifted the debate away from Jews as a minority toward Christians, it still borrows heavily from pseudo-scholarly works such as Bat Ye'or (pseudonym of Gisele Littman), *Understanding Dhimmitude* (2013); Irshad Manji, *The Trouble with Islam* (2007); and Phyllis Chesler, *The New Antisemitism* (2003).
23 See Emily Gottreich, "Rethinking the Islamic City from the Perspective of Jewish Space," *Jewish Social Studies* 11, no. 1 (2004): 118–146.
24 See Benjamin Ravid, "All Ghettos Were Jewish Quarters, but Not All Jewish Quarters Were Ghettos," *Jewish Culture and History* 10, nos. 2–3 (2008): 5–24.
25 Naomi Seidman, *Faithful Renderings: Jewish-Christian Difference and the Politics of Translation* (Chicago: University of Chicago Press, 2006), 3.
26 Chris Silver, "Tickling the Ivory in Tunisia: Messaoud Habib and the 1928 Columbia Recording Sessions," *Jewish Maghrib Jukebox Blogspot*, May 12, 2016.
27 For this reason, the cultural proximity of Jews and Muslims posed a real problem for Islamic jurisprudence, which worked hard to mark non-Muslims and distinguish them from believers. An area of particular debate was the bathhouse (*hammam*), where the shared practice of circumcision made Jewish men indistinguishable from Muslim men when unclothed. See Mohammed Hocine Benkheira, "Hammam, nudité et ordre moral dans l'islam médiéval," *Revue de l'histoire des religion* 224, no. 3 (2007): 319–371 and 225, no. 1 (2008): 75–128.

28 Indeed, all forms of nationalism challenged the imperial idea of cosmopolitanism. For the exclusionary nature of Algerian nationalism, see James McDougall, "Myth and Counter Myth: 'The Berber' as National Signifier in Algerian Historiographies," *Radical History Review* 86 (2003): 66–88. Based on his reading of the Dreyfus affair, Shlomo Avineri adduces that the "inclusivism of the universalistic principles of the French Revolution was tempered everywhere by the historicist exclusivism of much of modern nationalism." *The Making of Modern Zionism* (New York: Basic Books, 1981), 11.

29 For original Arabic version, see http://www.ism.ma/basic/web/ARABE/Textesdeloiarabe/DocConst.pdf. Accessed September 11, 2017.

30 The term and related concept was coined by S.D. Goitein, *A Mediterranean Society: The Jewish Communities of the Arab World as Portrayed in the Documents of the Cairo Geniza* (Berkeley: University of California Press, 1967); though it has been reformulated by others, including Norman Stillman ("commensality"), "The Commensality of Islamic and Jewish Civilizations," *Middle Eastern Lectures* 2 (1997): 81–94; Michael Laskier ("convergence"), with Yaacov Lev. *The Convergence of Judaism and Islam: Religious, Scientific, and Cultural Dimensions* (Gainesville: University Press of Florida, 2011); and Youssef Meri ("intertwinement"). http://intertwinedworlds.wordpress.com/. Accessed September 17, 2019. For a recent critique of "Jewish-Muslim relations" as a paradigm that automatically reduces Jews and Muslims to their linkages with "transnational webs of ethnoreligious solidarity and conflict," see Ethan Katz, *The Burdens of Brotherhood: Jews and Muslims from North Africa to France* (Cambridge, MA: Harvard University Press, 2015), 4–5.

31 Note that the six-pointed star is not exclusive to Jews in the numismatic and other representational traditions of the Middle East and North Africa.

32 Most Islamic legal traditions do not require non-Muslim women to convert to Islam in order to marry Muslim men, though they consider the offspring of such marriages to be Muslim. According to rumor, the mother of Sultan Ahmad al-Mansur (r. 1578–1603), buried nearby her son in the Sa'di tombs in Marrakech, was Jewish.

33 Daniel Schroeter has put this matter to rest once and for all in academic circles, but popular attitudes have been more resistant. "La Découverte des Juifs Berbéres," in *Relations Judéo-Musulmanes au Maroc: Perceptions et Réalités*, ed. Michel Abitbol (Paris: Editions Stavit, 1997), 169–187.

34 For some Moroccans, Jewish roots are the object of considerable pride. Interview with Professor 'Abd al-Majid al-Kohen, Marrakech, March 10, 2011. See also Oren Kosansky, "Reading Jewish Fez: On the Cultural Identity of a Moroccan City," *Journal of the International Institute* 8, no. 3 (2001).

35 The club is also active in humanitarian and charity work.

36 The term was coined by Ismar Schorsch to describe the image conveyed by the Orientalist scholar Moritz Steinschneider of Jews in the era of Islam's

ascendancy but can be extended more broadly to later periods as well: Ismar Schorsch, "Converging Cognates: The Intersection of Jewish and Islamic Studies in Nineteenth Century Germany," *Leo Baeck Institute Year Book* 55, nos. 3–36 (2010): 16.

37 Originally a radio station in Sweden, *Radio Islam* has more recently functioned as a website and podcast. Ahmed Rami is originally from Tafraoute in southern Morocco but gained political asylum in Sweden in 1973 following his involvement in a coup against Hassan II.

38 Jessica M. Marglin, "In the Courts of the Nations: Jews, Muslims, and Legal Pluralism in Nineteenth-century Morocco," PhD dissertation, 2013, Department of Near Eastern Studies, Princeton University. 17.

39 "Le Maroc ne compte déjà plus assez de juifs, alors s'il se met à perdre les plus illustres parmi eux." Karim Boukhari, "Terre d'Abraham," *Tel Quel*, no. 449, 27 Novembre au 3 Décembre 2010, 16.

40 Often commanded by the sultan himself, or by a prominent member of the court, *mahalla*-s were the primary means for the makhzan to impose and collect taxes in outlying regions. See Jocelyn Dakhliya, "Dans la mouvance de prince: La Symbolique du pouvoir itinérant au Maghreb," *Annales ESC* 3 (May–June 1988): 735–760.

41 See the discussion in Shaye Cohen, *The Beginnings of Jewishness: Boundaries, Varieties, Uncertainties* (Berkeley and Los Angeles, University of California Press, 2001).

42 Note in this context Jessica Marglin's persuasive conceptualization of a Mediterranean identity for Moroccan Jews in the modern period, which also applies to earlier periods: Jessica M. Marglin, "Mediterranean Modernity through Jewish Eyes: The Transimperial Life of Abraham Ankawa," *Journal of North African Studies* 20, no. 2 (2015): 34–68.

43 Here I am referring to isolated communities in late antiquity who may not have had access to the Talmud, as opposed to those who consciously rejected it in later periods, like the Karaites.

44 According to the findings of Daniel Schroeter, most Tamazight-speaking Jews were bilingual and tended to speak Arabic at home. Daniel Schroeter, "The Shifting Boundaries of Moroccan Jewish Identities," *Jewish Social Studies: History, Culture, Society* 15, no. 1 (2008): 148–149.

45 See the classic work by Antoine Fattal, *Le statut légal des non-musulmans en pays d'Islam* (Beirut: l'imprimerie catholique, 1958), and by the same author, "How Dhimmis Were Judged in the Islamic World," in *Muslims and Others in Early Islamic Society*, ed. Robert Hoyland (Aldershot: Ashgate, 2004), 83–102. A more recent and equally thorough treatment of *dhimma* in English is Anver M. Emon, *Religious Pluralism and Islamic Law: Dhimmis and Others in the Empire of Law* (Oxford, UK: Oxford University Press, 2012).

46 David Menashri, "The Jews of Iran," in *Antisemitism in Times of Crisis*, eds. Sander L. Gilman and Steven T. Katz (New York: New York University, 1991), 356. Note that there are differences of opinion within Shi'i thought as to whether *ahl al-kitab* are subject to *najas* or not.

47 The terms "sharif" and "sayid" have been used interchangeably during many periods of Islamic history, though the latter term has stronger associations with Shi'ism and in the modern period especially connotes descent from Ali's son Hussein, rather than from his brother Hassan.

48 Albert Memmi, *The Colonizer and the Colonized* (Boston: Beacon Press, 1967).

49 Some examples include Daniel J. Schroeter and Joseph Chetrit, " Emancipation and Its Discontents: Jews at the Formative Period of Colonial Rule in Morocco," *Jewish Social Studies* 13, no. 1 (2006): 170; Susan Gilson Miller, "The Mellah without Walls: Jewish Space in a Moroccan City: Tangier, 1860–1912," in *Revisiting the Colonial Past in Morocco*, ed. Driss Maghraoui (Abingdon, Oxon: Routledge, 2013), 80–109.

Chapter 1

1 This figure does not include conversions to Christianity, which are not recognized by the state. The note of an American diplomat made public by WikiLeaks suggests that there were 3000–4000 converts to Christianity in Morocco in 2009: Cable 09RABAT221_a, "Mixed Reviews of Morocco's Level of Religious Freedom," March 19, 2009.

2 A 2005 ruling by the King allows Moroccan mothers to pass citizenship onto their children, even if the fathers are not Moroccan, while the Moroccan citizenship law of 2013 allows for foreign female spouses of Moroccan men to apply for naturalization. The application of these laws has been inconsistent.

3 Prior to this, his title was "Mawlay," often rendered in European works as "Sultan."

4 Abu Ubayd al-Aziz al-Bakri, "The Book of Routes and Realms," in *Corpus of Early Arabic Sources for West Africa*, ed. Levtzion et al. (Princeton: Markus Wiener publishers, 2000), 62–87; For more on al-Bakri see *Encyclopaedia of Islam*, 2nd ed., s.v. 'Abū 'Ubayd al-Bakrī'.

5 Amjad Hemidach, "Moroccan Jews and Muslims: A Model of Tolerance for the World," *Morocco World News*, February 3, 2015.

6 The classic colonial source for Malikism in Morocco is Georges Drague, *Esquisse d'histoire religieuse au maroc* (Paris: Peyronnet, 1951). For more recent scholarly treatments, see David Powers, *Law, Society, and Culture in the Maghrib, 1300–1500* (Cambridge: Cambridge University Press, 2002) and Etty Terem, *Old Texts, New Practices: Islamic Reform in Modern Morocco* (Stanford: Stanford University Press, 2014), both of which make great strides in historicizing Maliki law. For a study of

Malikism during the period of its institutionalization, see Camilo Gomez-Rivas, *Law and the Islamization of Morocco under the Almoravids: The Fatwas of Ibn Rushd al-Jadd to the Far Maghrib* (Leiden: Brill, 2014). For a rare discussion of Jews in select Maliki rulings, see Meir Bar Asher, "Le Statut des Juifs chez les Malikites du Maroc," in *Perception et Réalités au Maroc: Relations Judéo-Musulmans*, ed. Michel Abitbol (Paris: CRJM, 1998), 259–274; more general remarks can be found in Matthias Lehmann, "Islamic Legal Consultation and the Jewish-Muslim 'Convivencia': Al-Wansharîsî's Fatwâ Collection as a Source for Jewish Social History in Al-Andalus and the Maghrib," *Jewish Studies Quarterly* 6, no. 1 (1999): 25–54.

7   See H. Z. Hirschberg,. "The Problem of the Judaized Berbers." *The Journal of African History* 4, no. 3 (1963): 313–339, and the more recent intervention by Daniel Schroeter, "On the Origins and Identity of Indigenous North African Jews," in *North African Mosaic: A Cultural Reappraisal of Ethnic and Religious Minorities*, eds. Nabil Boudraa and Joseph Krause (Newcastle: Cambridge Scholars Press, 2007), 164–177.

8   Daniel Schroeter, "Ifrane (of the Anti-Atlas; also Ifran, Oufrane)," *Encyclopedia of Jews in the Islamic World Online*. Accessed September 25, 2017.

9   Daniel Schroeter, "Ifrane (of the Anti-Atlas; also Ifran, Oufrane)." *Encyclopedia of Jews in the Islamic World Online*. Accessed September 25, 2017. Schroeter underlines the mythic origins of this story, noting that the historical record for the Jewish community of Ifrane dates only from the seventeenth century.

10 International Association of Jewish Genealogical Societies, *"Ifrane d'Anti-Atlas (Oufrane)" International Jewish Cemetery Project*, February 16, 2010, http://www.iajgsjewishcemeteryproject.org/morocco/oufrane-ifrane-anti-atlas.html. Accessed October 2, 2018. See also Vincent Monteil, "Les juifs d'Ifran (Anti-Atlas marocain). - Cimetières - Ancêtres - Tombe de Youssef ben Mimoun," *Hespéris* 35 (1948): 151–162. Other accounts suggest that the Jewish martyrs of Oufrane were burned at the stake, see Issachar Ben-Ami Ben Ami, *Saint Veneration among Jews of Morocco* (Detroit: Wayne State Press, 1998), 251.

11 Descendants of the Jews of Oufrane commemorate the event by refraining from lighting fire on the anniversary of the martyrdom, which falls on the 17th of Tishri in the Hebrew calendar.

12 Daniel Schroeter, "Ifrane (of the Anti-Atlas; also Ifran, Oufrane)." *Encyclopedia of Jews in the Islamic World Online*. Accessed September 25, 2017.

13 Some early Islamic sources assert that the Imazighen apostatized between 8 and 12 times before finally accepting Islam. See the discussion in Michael Brett, "The Islamisation of Morocco from the Arabs to the Almoravids," in *Ibn Khaldun and the Medieval Maghrib*, ed. Michael Brett (London: Ashgate, 1999), 58.

14 Abdelmajid Hannoum, *Colonial Histories, Post-colonial Memories: The Legend of the Kahina, a North African Heroine* (Portsmouth, NH: Heinemann, 2001), xviii (18).

15 "Arab" and "Muslim" are purposely being used interchangeably in this discussion of the conquests. It should be noted that scholars debate the merits of each term, since the conquerors were neither all Arab nor all Muslim at any given time, though sources from the period of the conquests tended to refer to them in ethnic rather than religious terms. See Robert Hoyland, *In God's Path: The Arab Conquests and the Creation of an Islamic Empire* (Oxford: Oxford University Press, 2015), 5–6.

16 For more on the Kahina, see, in addition to Hannoum's work, H.Z. Hirschberg, *A History of the Jews in North Africa*, vol. 1, *From Antiquity to the Sixteenth Century* (Leiden: Brill, 1974), 91–96.

17 Qur'an, 2:256.

18 Michael Brett, "The Islamisation of Morocco from the Arabs to the Almoravids," *Journal of Moroccan Studies* 2 (1992): 57–71.

19 Michael Brett, quoted in Samir Ben-Layashi and Bruce Maddy-Weitzman, "Myth, History, and Realpolitik: Morocco and Its Jewish Community," *Journal of Modern Jewish Studies* 9, no. 1 (2010): 89.

20 Ibid.

21 Fred Astren, "Rereading the Muslim Sources: Jewish History in the Early Islamic Period," in *Jerusalem Studies in Arabic and Islam* 35, ed. Yohanan Friedmann (2009): 83–130.

22 There were still other methods for assimilating new Muslims who were not Arabs. The early conflation of the two identities eventually gave way to a separation of terms as Persians, Greeks, and Imazighen, and others adopted Islam without necessarily giving up their respective ethnic or linguistic identities. The system for acculturating these new non-Arab Muslims was known as *muwala*, a sort of fostering that attached recent converts as clients to Arab tribes. It was controversial because all Muslims are considered equal in Islamic tradition, yet the cultural dominance of Arabness was difficult to dispense with in the early Islamic period.

23 For a historiographical discussion of the Jews of Medina and a methodologically groundbreaking treatment of their religious beliefs and practices, see Haggai Mazuz, *The Religious and Spiritual Life of the Jews of Medina* (Leiden: Brill, 2014).

24 Note that the Islamic sources were all written well after the events they describe and that no contemporaneous Jewish sources exist for this encounter. Astren, "Re-reading," 83.

25 Qur'an, 109:6.

26 Malik b. Anas, *al-Muwatta; Muwatta al-Imam Malik wa-sharhu hu tanwir al-hawalik* (Cairo: Maktabat al-akhira, 1951), 363.

27 There is disagreement about whether the document should be associated with 'Umar b. al-Khattab, the second caliph (r. 634–644) or whether the title may refer to a later Umayyad caliph, 'Umar b. 'Abd al-'Aziz (r. 717–720).

28 "Zunnar" is a later term. The Pact uses the term "*mintaqa*," but the principle of requiring *dhimmi*-s to wear a belt is the same. Milka Levy-Rubin, *Non-Muslims in*

29. For a translation of the document, see Abu Bakr al-Turtushi, *Siraj al-Muluk* (Cairo, 1872), 229–230. *Internet Modern History Sourcebook*, ed. Paul Halsall. Accessed August 10, 2016.
30. Matthias Lehmann, "Islamic Legal Consultation and the Jewish-Muslim 'Convivencia': Al-Wansharisi's Fatwa Collection as a Source for Jewish Social History in Al-Andalus and the Maghrib," *Jewish Studies Quarterly* 6, no. 1 (1999): 31.
31. Leo Africanus, *Description de l'Afrique*, ed. and trans. A. Epaulard, 2 vols. (Paris: Librairie d'Amérique et d'Orient, 1956), 85–86.
32. Mercedes García-Arenal, "Jewish Converts to Islam in the Muslim West," *Israel Oriental Studies* 17 (1997): 230.
33. The ban on building new synagogues or restoring existing ones has roots in the 423 Byzantine law of Honorius and Theodosius. Antoine Fattal, *Le statut légal des non-musulmans en pays d'islam* (Beirut: Imprimerie Catholique, 1958), 178.
34. For the development of the individual schools of Islamic jurisprudence, see Wael Hallaq, *The Origins and Evolution of Islamic Law* (Cambridge: Cambridge University Press, 2005).
35. Ibadism, a school that splits off from the mainstream early in Islamic history and remains theologically isolated from both Sunnism and Shiism, is also well represented in North Africa.
36. Terem, *Old Texts, New Practices*, 11.
37. For further discussion of what "Moroccan Islam" entails, see Dale Eickelman, *Moroccan Islam Tradition and Society in a Pilgrimage Center* (Austin: University of Texas Press, 1981).
38. In addition to support by private funders, King Mohammed VI is believed to have donated significant sums from his personal fortune to ensure the maintenance of Jewish sites and the restoration of Jewish cemeteries.
39. For a discussion of the Maliki school's particular attractiveness to Imazighen, see Mohamed El-Mansour, "Moroccan Islam Observed," *The Maghreb Review* 29, nos. 1–4 (2004): 208–218.
40. Brett, "The Islamisation of Morocco from the Arabs to the Almoravids," 63.
41. Muhammad al-Tawil, *The Special Characteristics of the Maliki madhhab*. Lamp Post Productions, October 21, 2004. Accessed July 8, 2016.
42. Lawrence Rosen, *Two Arabs, a Berber, and a Jew: Entangled Lives in Morocco* (Chicago: University of Chicago Press, 2015), 164.
43. Powers, *Law, Society, and Culture in the Maghrib,* 1–9. For a detailed discussion of al-Wansharisi and especially his influence on al-Wazzani, see Terem, *Old Texts, New Practices,* 2.
44. One of al-Wansharisi's best-known rulings is that Muslims living under non-Muslim rule are obligated to emigrate to Muslim-ruled lands, which became the

predominant Maliki position. For the development of Maliki thought on this issue, beginning with Malik b. Anas, see Khaled Abou Fadl, "Islamic Law and Muslim Minorities: The Juristic Discourse on Muslim Minorities from 8th to 17th Century CE/2nd to 11th Hijrah," *Islamic Law and Society* 1, no. 2 (1994): 141–187.

45 The movement of Islamic reform led by Muhammad 'Abduh and others in the *mashriq* was slow to enter Morocco, although figures like the nineteenth-century scholars Abdallah al-Sanusi and Abu Sha'ib al-Dukkali succeeded in importing some of its ideas. See R. Marston Speight, "Islamic Reform in Morocco," *The Muslim World* 53, no. 1 (1963): 41–49.

46 The Zahiri jurist Ibn Hazm was the author of one such critique; no doubt the social interaction involved when Muslims bought meat from Jews was also at issue in this context. See Camilla Adang, "Ibn Hazm's Criticism of some 'Judaizing' Tendencies among the Malikites," in *Medieval and Modern Perspectives on Muslim-Jewish Relations*, ed. Ronald L. Netter (Luxembourg: Harwood Academic Publishers, 1995), 3.

47 See Janina M. Safran, "Rules of Purity and Confessional Boundaries: Maliki Debates about the Pollution of the Christian," *History of Religions* 42, no. 3 (2003): 197–212. Note that this is an area where Sunni and Shi'i Islam diverge, with Shi'i jurisprudence holding a much stricter view of *dhimmi* impurity, in practice often leading to harsher treatment of Jews.

48 Bathing is likewise an area where some of the differences between Shi'ite and Sunni attitudes are manifest. In early twentieth-century Yemen, for example, Jews were not allowed to bathe together with Muslims and had to remain downstream from them if bathing in rivers or streams. Mark Wagner, *Jews and Islamic Law in Early Twentieth-century Yemen* (Bloomington: Indiana University Press, 2015), 56.

49 John Hunwick, *Jews of a Saharan Oasis: The Elimination of the Tamantit Community* (Princeton, NJ: Markus Wiener Publishers, 2006), 9.

50 Aomar Boum, *Memories of Absence: How Muslims Remember Jews in Morocco* (Stanford: Stanford University Press, 2013), 49.

51 For Jewish gold and silversmithing traditions, which date back to the biblical era, see Ester Muchawsky-Schnapper, "Jewelry Smithing." *Encyclopedia of Jews in the Islamic World*. Accessed March 30, 2018. For Muslims' negative view of metalsmithing, see Muhammad b. 'Abdullah Al-Kharashi, *Commentary of Al-Kharashi on the Mukhtasar of Khalil b. Ishaq*, vol. 2 (Cairo, 1900–01), 43.

52 Jacob Oliel, "Tamentit." *Encyclopedia of Jews in the Islamic World Online*. Accessed March 30, 2018.

53 For a thorough treatment of the trans-Saharan caravan trade in Morocco, Mauritania, Senegal, and Mali, including information on Jews' involvement, see Ghislaine Lydon, *On Trans-Saharan Trails: Islamic Law, Trade Networks, and Cross-*

cultural Exchange in Nineteenth-century Western Africa (Cambridge: Cambridge University Press, 2009).

54 According to Geniza documents, Sijilmasi Jews traveled all the way to Baghdad to conduct business. Phillip Ackerman-Lieberman, "Sijilmasa." *Encyclopedia of Jews in the Islamic World Online*. Accessed March 30, 2018. For a recent historical geography of Sijilmasa based on decades of research, see James Miller and Ronald Messier, *The Last Civilized Place: Sijilmasa and Its Saharan Destiny* (Austin: University of Texas Press, 2015).

55 My retelling of the story of the Jews of Touat is based on Hunwick's *Jews of a Saharan Oasis*, which contains a partial translation of al-Maghili's writings as well as related sources. For further analysis of the legal implications of the case, see Lehmann, "Islamic Legal Consultation and the Jewish-Muslim 'Convivencia,'" 25–54.

56 Hunwick, *Jews of a Saharan Oasis*, 3.

57 Islamic law dictates different terms for towns that surrender peacefully to Muslim rule than for those where it had to be imposed by force. Anver M. Emon, *Religious Pluralism and Islamic Law: Dhimmis and Others in the Empire of Law* (Oxford, UK: Oxford University Press, 2012), 89.

58 Hunwick, *Jews of a Saharan Oasis*, 7.

59 Ibid., 33.

60 Ahmad b. Ahmad Baba al-Tunbukti, *Nayl al-Ibtihaj* (Tarablus: Manshurat Kulliyyat al-daʿwa al-Islamiyya, 1989), quoted in Hunwick, *Jews of a Saharan Oasis*, 62.

61 Al-Maghili took part in a similar event in nearby Gourara in 1492, and an attack on the Jews of Tlemcen in 1518 was perhaps inspired by him, though he had died some years before. Hunwick, *Jews of a Saharan Oasis*, 64.

62 Some nineteenth-century observers believed that the Saharan nomads known as the Daggatoun, a shunned people who lived under the protection of the Tuareg, were originally Touati Jewish refugees. See, for example, Mordechai Abisrur, *Les Daggatoun: Tribu d'origine juive demeurant dans le désert du Sahara* (Paris: Bulletin AIU, 1880).

63 Hunwick, *Jews of a Saharan Oasis*, 63.

64 Ousman Murzik Kobo, *Unveiling Modernity in Twentieth-century West African Islamic Reforms* (Leiden: Brill, 2012), 39–40.

65 For detailed explanation of the tax responsibilities of *dhimmi*-s, see Fattal, *Le statut légal des non-musulmans*, 286–287.

66 Qur'an, 9:29.

67 *Jewish Missionary Intelligence* 8 (September 1894), 120.

68 Germain Mouette, "The Travels of the Sieur Mouette in the Kingdoms of Fez and Morocco," in *A New Collection of Voyages and Travels*, ed. John Stevens (London: British Library, 1711), 102.

69 Susan Gilson Miller, "Dhimma Reconsidered: Jews, Taxes, and Royal Authority in Nineteenth-century Tangier," in *In the Shadow of the Sultan: Culture, Power, and Politics in Morocco*, ed. Susan Gilson Miller and Rahma Bourqia (Cambridge: Harvard University Press, 1999), 103–126.

70 Shlomo Deshen, *Mellah Society: Jewish Community Life in Sherifian Morocco* (Chicago: University of Chicago Press, 1989), 60–61.

71 Nahum Slouschz, *Travels in North Africa* (Philadelphia: Jewish Publication Society of America, 1927), 455.

72 William Lemprière, *A Tour through the Dominions of the Emperor of Morocco*, 3rd ed. (London, 1813), 180.

73 Ibn Dani, 13 Jumada II 1283/October 23, 1866, Marrakesh 2, Direction des Archives Royales, Rabat, Morocco.

74 *Times of Morocco*, May 26, 1887, and June 30, 1887.

75 *Jewish Chronicle*, March 14, 1894.

76 Eugene Aubin, *Morocco of Today* (London: J. M. Dent & Co., 1906); José Bénech, *Marrakech: Explication d'un mellah* (Paris: H. Rohr, 1949).

77 In an 1810 French report discussing the makhzan's finances, Napoleon's envoy captain Burel counted the *jizya* as one of the four main sources of government revenue. Antoine Burel, *La Mission du Capitaine Burel au Maroc en 1808* (Paris: Arts et métiers graphiques, 1953).

78 The author goes on to wax about the "fresh bloom of her cheek," her "beautiful glossy hair," and her "silken eyelashes." Joseph Benjamin, *Eight Years in Asia and Africa, from 1846–1855* (Hanover: self-published, 1863), 321.

79 Mme. Abbou, "En Pélérinage," December 19, 1933, Maroc: II.B.9-13: 1348, Archives of the AIU, Paris, France.

80 On the difference between "*walaya*" and "*waliya*," see Vincent Cornell, *Realm of the Saint: Power and Authority in Moroccan Sufism* (Austin: University of Texas Press, 1999), xvii–xxi. In Tamazight, the term used is "Agurram." In Hebrew, such a figure might be referred to as *tsaddiq* [sage] or *qodesh* [holy one].

81 Ben-Ami, *Saint Veneration*, 131. Note that the overall number of saints is much larger, close to 700. The lower figure cited here only includes those venerated by Muslims, whether alone or jointly.

82 A qualitatively important exception is Mohammad V, whose mausoleum in Rabat is visited by Moroccan Jews on pilgrimage.

83 The classical work on Moroccan sainthood is Ernest Gellner, *Saints of the Atlas* (Ann Arbor: University of Michigan, 1969). The topic was taken up again by Vincent Cornell, whose work on the *Jazuliya* is considered definitive: Vincent Cornell, *The Realm of the Saint*. See also: Sahar Bazzaz, *Forgotten Saints: History, Power, and Politics in the Making of Modern Morocco* (Cambridge: Center for Middle Eastern Studies, Harvard University, 2010).

84 Ahmad b. Muhammad b. Ajibah al-Hasani, *Iqaz al-himam fi sharh al-hikam* (Cairo: Mustafa al-Babi al-Halabi wa Awladuhu, 1961), 5.
85 Ben-Ami, *Saint Veneration*, 141.
86 Ibid., 140.
87 Ibid., 158.
88 The Moroccan term for pilgrimages by Muslims is *moussem*.
89 This was the view of Maimonides, for example, which put him at odds with some of the more rigid Ashkenazi scholars of his day who were quicker to endorse Jewish martyrdom in these circumstances.
90 On the subject of Jews and legal plurality in Morocco, see the groundbreaking work of Jessica Marglin, *Across Legal Lines: Jews and Muslims in Modern Morocco* (New Haven: Yale University Press, 2016).
91 The contemporary polemical term "dhimmitude" ignores historical context altogether.

Chapter 2

1 The two phrases come together in an interview conducted by Bruce Maddy-Weitzman: "In a conversation with a Moroccan Berber activist, I referred to David M. Hart's article, 'Scratch a Moroccan, Find a Berber.' My interlocutor quickly suggested that the author should have added an addendum: 'Scratch a Berber Find a Jew!'" *The Berber Identity Movement and the Challenge to North African States* (Austin: University of Texas Press, 2011), 242 fn44. A quip along similar lines is attributed to Gertrude Stein: "Scratch a Spaniard and You Find a Saracen."
2 Arièle Nahmias, "Moroccan Educators at Yad Vashem," *Yad Vashem*, January 2010, http://www.yadvashem.org/yv/en/education/news/2010/european_department_01_10.asp. Accessed October 27, 2016.
3 See Gilbert Achcar, *The Arabs and the Holocaust: The Arab-Israeli War of Narratives* (New York: Holt and Co., 2009).
4 With regard to the risks involved, Kamal Hachkar's film *Tinghrir-Jerusalem: Echos from the Mellah*, 2013, met with protests, harassment, and calls for boycott when it opened in Morocco in 2013. Filmed partially in Israel and exploring Amazigh-Jewish memory, it was perceived by critics as promoting "normalization" of relations between Israel and the Arab world.
5 Samir Ben Layashi, "Secularism in the Moroccan Amazigh Discourse," *Journal of North African Studies* 12, no. 2 (2007): 153–171.
6 The term "Arab spring" originated in the Western media and only came into wide usage with the revolts in Egypt. In Tunisia, where the protests first began with the self-immolation of Muhammad Bouazizi in December of 2010, the

original phrase "jasmine revolution" has since given way to "dignity revolution." In Morocco, the protests that began 2 months later are known as the February 20 movement.

7   In Ben Ali's Tunisia, Arabization was achieved by force. The "Child Protection Code," enacted in 1995, stipulated that "Arab and Islamic values" be inculcated from a young age. It was forbidden to give babies Amazigh first names; Amazigh language, culture, and history were entirely absent from school curricula as well as from cultural life and the media. In Libya, conformity to Qaddhafi's peculiar brand of Arab nationalism led not only to the negation of Amazigh language and culture as purportedly colonial creations, but to the torture and imprisonment of anyone who might try to assert an Amazigh identity. See Aisha al-Rumi (pseudonym), "Libyan Berbers Struggle to Assert Their Identity Online," *Arab Media and Society*, no. 8 (2019): https://www.arabmediasociety.com/post_issue/winter-spring-2019/. Accessed September 17, 2019.

8   For an examination of the political salience of different identity markers in modern Morocco, including Jewishness, see Jonathan Wyrtzen, *Making Morocco: Colonial Intervention and the Politics of Identity* (Ithaca: Cornell University Press, 2015).

9   For a taxonomy of Moroccan religious practices and their origins, see the classic work by the Finnish social anthropologist Edward Westermarck, *Ritual and Belief in Morocco* (London: Macmillan, 1926).

10 George Joffe, "Maghribi Islam and Islam in the Maghrib," in *African Islam and Islam in Africa: Encounters between Sufis and Islamists*, eds. Eva Evers Rosander and David Westerlund (Athens (Ohio): Ohio University Press; London: Hurst, 1997), 60.

11 "Tamazight" is used as a general term for all Moroccan Amazigh languages, though technically it refers to that spoken in the Middle Atlas specifically. The others include Tashelhit/Shilha ("Chleuh" in French and Jewish usage) spoken in the southwestern High Atlas and northern Anti Atlas, and Tarifit/Riffian in the Rif Mountain region. "Judeo-Berber" is sometimes used to indicate Jewish variations of these languages. For a thorough treatment of language and ethnicity in Tashelhit-speaking areas especially, see Katherine Hoffman, *We Share Walls: Language, Land, and Gender in Berber Morocco* (Malden, MA: Blackwell Pub., 2008).

12 The Greek term *barbarous* (Eng. "barbarian") was adopted by Romans to describe the inhabitants of North Africa, whence the later term "Barbary." For the etymology and historical trajectory of "Berber," see Ramai Rouighi, "The Berbers of the Arabs," *Studia Islamica* 106, no. 1 (2011): 49–76.

13 Maddy-Weitzman, *The Berber Identity Movement*, 32. The claim is found in Jewish sources as well, including the Andalusian Jewish vizier and poet Shmuel Hanagid: Maya Shatzmiller, *The Berbers and the Islamic State: The Marinid Experience in Pre-Protectorate Morocco* (Princeton, NJ: Markus Wiener Publishers, 2000), 23.

14 Another myth proposes that the original community of the Talmud was located not in Babylon or Jerusalem, but in the Sous. Joseph R. Rosenbloom, "A Note on the Size of the Jewish Communities in the South of Morocco," *Jewish Journal of Sociology* 8, no. 2 (1966): 209.

15 With regard to the slow evolution of Judaism over time, see Shaye Cohen, *The Beginnings of Jewishness* (Berkeley and Los Angeles: University of California Press, 1999). With regard to the same issue in the Islamic context, see Fred Donner, *Muhammad and the Believers* (Cambridge, MA: Harvard University Press, 2012). Donner's somewhat controversial work makes an argument for a slow development of Islam that begins as a community of monotheistic "believers" and only in time emerges as a separate religion.

16 See Layashi and Maddy-Weitzman, "Myth, History, and Realpolitik," 89–106. The authors also make the important observation that "the number of Judaized Berbers, and the percentage of North African Jews who are descendants of Berber converts, cannot be ascertained, and, like so much else regarding the subject, is a subject of disagreement." Page 90.

17 Hirschberg, "The Problem of the Judaized Berbers," 315.

18 Ibn Khaldun, *Al-Muqaddimah*, vol. 1, *Kitab al-Ibar*, trans. F. Rosenthal (Bulaq, 1284 A.H.), 45, quoted in Hirschberg, "The Problem," 317. Support for Ibn Khaldun's theories regarding the Canaanite origins of the Imazighen can be found in Shatzmiller, *The Berbers and the Islamic State*, 18–19.

19 Genetic studies to date support the idea of Moroccan Jewish endogamy more than they do a shared Arab, Amazigh, and/or sub-Saharan African origin for Moroccan Jews. See Doron Behar et al., "Counting the Founders: The Matrilineal Genetic Ancestry of the Jewish Diaspora," *PLoS one* 3, no. 4 (2008): e2062. https://doi.org/10.1371/journal.pone.0002062 (consulted October 3, 2017).

20 Schroeter, "On the Origins and Identity of Indigenous North African Jews," 164–177. There exist three Passover *haggadot* in Judeo-Tamazight, but they were specially commissioned. See Lily Kahn and Aaron D. Rubin eds., *Handbook of Jewish Languages* (Leiden, Boston: Brill, 2016), 121.

21 Michael Willis, *Politics and Power in the Maghreb: Algeria, Tunisia and Morocco from Independence to the Arab Spring* (London: Hurst & Co., 2012), 204–205.

22 Paul A. Silverstein, "The Kabyle Myth: Colonization and the Production of Ethnicity," in *From the Margins: Historical Anthropology and Its Futures*, ed. Brian Keith Axel (Durham: Duke University Press, 2003), 122–135.

23 Mohamed Benhlal, *Le collège d'Azrou: Une élite berbère civile et militaire au Maroc (1927–1959)* (Paris: Éditions Karthala, 2005).

24 For a discussion of the 1930 *dahir* and its resurgence in the 1990s with the Amazigh activist movement, see David M. Hart, "The Berber Dahir of 1930 in Colonial Morocco: Then and Now (1930–1996)," *The Journal of North African Studies* 2, no. 2 (1997): 11–33.

25 Despite its emancipatory language, the 1918 *dahir* actually restricted Jews' traditional judicial autonomy. See Schroeter and Chetrit, "Emancipation and Its Discontents," 170–206.
26 Katherine Hoffman and Susan Gilson and Miller eds., *Berbers and Others: Beyond Tribe and Nation in the Maghrib* (Bloomington and Indianapolis: Indiana University Press, 2010), 4.
27 In a Jewish context, the most basic binary (after Jew and non-Jew) is that between Ashkenazim and Sephardim. Yet both groups were internally more diverse than is usually acknowledged, and they did not divide as neatly along geographic lines (Europe vs. MENA) as is also often presumed. Sephardic Jews settled throughout southern Europe even after the expulsion, and Ashkenazi Jews fleeing European anti-Semitism often sought refuge in the Islamic world. The Ottoman Empire, as we will see in the next chapter, welcomed both the Sephardic exiles from Spain and also Ashkenazi Jews fleeing Eastern European pogroms. In the twentieth century, Morocco similarly harbored Ashkenazi Jews fleeing the Nazis.
28 I mention these types of cases in particular since rulings by Moroccan rabbis in these two areas had a major impact on Jewish life worldwide. For the latter issue, see Elimelech Westreich, "Historical Landmarks in the Tradition of Moroccan Jewish Family Law: The Case of Levirate Marriages," in *Studies in Medieval Halakhah in Honor of Stephen M. Passamaneck*, eds. Alyssa Gray and Bernard Jackson (England: D. Charles Publications, 2007), 279–322.
29 Haïm Zafrani describes a kabbalistic amulet from Marrakech, which consists of a cryptograph of the four Hebrew letters *aleph*, *mem*, *nun*, and *tet* and is placed in a woman's mouth to hasten labor. Haïm Zafrani, *Two Thousand Years of Jewish Life in Morocco* (Jersey City: Ktav Publishing House/American Sephardi Federation, 2005), 46.
30 There are reports that *genizot* have been found in Morocco in Oufrane, Rabat, Tamegrout, and Agadir.
31 Deshen, *The Mellah Society*, 9.
32 Cairo Genizah (T-S 12.3), Letter; poetry. Cambridge: Cambridge University Library, Cairo Genizah (T-S 12.3), Cambridge University Digital Library. Accessed October 31, 2017.
33 Cairo Genizah, T-S 16.335, Legal document. Cambridge: Cambridge University Library, Cairo Genizah, T-S 16.335, Cambridge University Digital Library. Accessed October 31, 2017.
34 In addition to the selective inclusion of Hebrew and Aramaic terms, the main difference between Judeo-Arabic, Judeo-Berber, and the "Muslim" versions of these languages lies in the pronunciation of certain letters. For example, Jews will often transpose the letters *sin* and *shin*. Simon Levy, "The Arabic Dialects of Morocco's Jews," *Langage et société*, no. 143 (2013): 41–51.

35 For a thorough discussion of the use of Tamazight and Arabic by Jews in Amazigh regions, see the recent doctoral dissertation by Sarah Frances Levin, "Narrative Remembrance: Close Encounters between Muslims and Jews in Morocco's Atlas Mountains" (PhD dissertation, University of California, Berkeley, 2017).
36 Jews in the Middle East tended to have greater proficiency in classical Arabic than did Jews in the Maghrib. See Lisa Lital Levy, "Jewish Writers in the Arab East: Literature, History, and the Politics of Enlightenment, 1863–1914" (PhD dissertation, University of California, Berkeley, 2017), 7.
37 Oren Kosansky, "When Jews Speak Arabic: Dialectology and Difference in Colonial Morocco," *Comparative Studies in Society & History* 58, no. 1 (2016): 10.
38 Yosef Tobi, "The Flowering of Judeo-Arabic Literature in North Africa, 1850–1950," in *Sephardi and Middle Eastern Jewries: History and Culture in the Modern Era*, ed. Harvey E. Goldberg (Bloomington: Indiana University Press, 1996), 213–225.
39 Yossef Chetrit, "Tifnout (Valley)." *Encyclopedia of Jews in the Islamic World Online*. Accessed September 25, 2017. See also Alexander Beider, "Jews of Berber Origin: Myth or Reality?" in *Hamsa. Journal of Judaic and Islamic Studies* 3 (2017): 38–61. For a more in-depth treatment, see by the same author, "Judeo-Arabic and Judeo-Spanish in Morocco and Their Sociolinguistic Interaction," in *Readings in the Sociology of Jewish Languages*, ed. Joshua A. Fishman (Leiden: E.J. Brill, 1985), 261–279. A survey taken in 1936 suggests that three-fourths of Morocco's 161,000 Jews at the time were bilingual in Arabic and Tamazight and that 25,000 were mono-speakers of Tamazight. Maddy-Weitzman, *The Berber Identity*, 147. Given later findings by scholars including Chetrit and Schroeter, the 1936 estimates were probably an exaggeration.
40 It is classified by linguists as an Afro-Asiatic language with roots in southern Arabia.
41 Levin, "Narrative Remembrance," 61.
42 Regina Keil-Sagawe, "The Writer Edmond Amran El Maleh: A Moroccan Jew with Arabo-Berber Roots." *Qantara*, Lewis Gropp. Accessed March 31, 2011.
43 Claudia Roden, "Jewish Food in the Middle East," in *A Taste of Thyme: Culinary Cultures of the Middle East*, eds. Richard Tapper and Sami Zubaida (London: Tauris Parke, 2000), 156.
44 See Emily Gottreich, "Rethinking the 'Islamic City' from the Perspective of Jewish Space," *Jewish Social Studies* 11, no. 1 (2004): 118–146.
45 Silver's remark was based on his reading of work by Mustapha Chelbi and Nadya Bouzar-Kasbadji. Chris Silver, "Listening to the Past: Music as a Source for the Study of North African Jews," *Hespéris-Tamuda* 51, no. 2 (2016): 243–255.
46 Daniel Schroeter and Emily Gottreich, eds., "Rethinking Jewish Culture and Society in North Africa," in *Jewish Culture and Society* (Bloomington: Indiana University Press, 2011), 16.
47 The scholar and performer Vanessa Paloma has gone to great lengths to reconstruct the Sephardic musical repertoire of Morocco. See most recently her article, "*Kol*

b'Isha Erva: The Silencing of Jewish Women's Oral Traditions in Morocco," in *Gender and Law in the Maghreb*, eds. Doris Gray and Nadia Sonneveld (Cambridge: Cambridge University Press, 2017), 263–288.
48. Levin, "Narrative Remembrance."
49. Joseph Chetrit, "Music and Poetry as a Shared Cultural Space for Muslims and Jews in Morocco," in *Studies in the History and Culture of North African Judaism*, eds. Moshe Bar-Asher and Steven D. Fraade (New Haven: Yale Program in Judaic Studies, 2011), 65–103.
50. Philip D. Schyuler, "Rwais and Ahwash: Opposing Tendencies in Moroccan Berber Music and Society," *The World of Music* 21, no. 1 (1979): 65–80.
51. Mohamed Elmedlaoui, "'Ahwash' (of the Anti-Atlas; also Ifran, Oufrane)," *Encyclopedia of Jews in the Islamic World Online*. Accessed September 25, 2017.
52. Levin, "Narrative Remembrance," 98.
53. "Berber Influences in Moroccan Jewish Music," *Mosaic*, April 13, 2016.
54. Daniel Schroeter, "Views from the Edge: Jews in Moroccan Rural Society (Ighil n'Ogho, 1917–1998)," in *Hikrei Ma'arav u-Mizrah: Studies in Language, Literature and History Presented to Joseph Chetrit*, vol. 2, eds. Yosef Tobi and Dennis Kurzon (Jerusalem: Carmel Publishing, 2011), 171–192.
55. Hirschberg, *A History of the Jews in North Africa*, vol. 1, 265–267. According the French colonial scholar Roger le Tourneau, Moroccan Muslims also associated metalwork with black magic: Roger Le Tourneau, *Fez in the Age of the Marinides*, trans. Besse Alberta Clement (Norman: University of Oklahoma Press, 1961), 94–105.
56. Shelomo Dov Goitein, *Mediterranean Society: The Jewish Communities of the Arab World as Portrayed in the Documents of the Cairo Geniza*, vol. 1, *Economic Foundations* (Berkeley: University of California Press, 2000), 100.
57. Hirschberg, *A History of the Jews in North Africa*, vol. 1, 268.
58. As Daniel Schroeter suggests, "While the ethnic origins of the Jews who lived among the Berbers may never be known, the interpenetration of influence is such that it is analytically useful to refer to a Judeo-Berber language and culture." Daniel Schroeter, "Berber Jews," *Encyclopedia of Jews in the Islamic World Online*. Accessed September 25, 2017. Similarly, Susan Slyomovics notes that many Moroccans' origins are obscured by the fact that Jews and Muslims often had the same last names, though with different spellings: Susan Slyomovics, "Self-determination as Self-definition: The Case of Morocco," in *Negotiating Self-determination*, eds., Hurst Hannum and Eileen F. Babbit (Lanham: Lexington Books, 2006), 140.
59. Note that a similar practice attended to Islam's eastern expansion, which led to the Shu'ubi rebellions among Persian *muwali*-s. For extensive treatment of this topic, see Sarah Bowen Savant, *The New Muslims of Post-conquest Iran* (Cambridge, UK: Cambridge University Press, 2015).
60. John Iskander, "Devout Heretics: The Barghawata in Maghribi Historiography," *The Journal of North African Studies* 12, no. 1 (2007): 37–53. The Tunisian historian Mabrouk

Mansouri argues that it was entirely plausible for a Jew to adopt a position of leadership in the tenth-century Maghrib. See his "Image of the Jews among the Ibadi Imazighen," in *Jewish Culture and Society in North Africa*, eds. Gottreich and Schroeter, 56.

61 For a detailed historical geography of Sijilmasa, see Messier and Miller, *The Last Civilized Place*.

62 Ibid., 119–120.

63 M.J. Viguera, "Sijilmasa." *Encyclopedia of Jews in the Islamic World Online*. Accessed September 25, 2017.

64 Abraham Ibn Ezra, "Aha Yarad 'al Sfarad Ra'min ha-Shamayim" [From the Heavens Troubles Descended upon Spain], in *Twilight of a Golden Age: Selected Poems of Abraham Ibn Ezra*, ed. Leon J. Weinberger, 2nd ed. (Tuscaloosa: University of Alabama Press, 2011), 96. Messier and Miller, *The Last Civilized Place: Sijilmasa*.

65 For a detailed account of the Almoravid founding of Marrakech, see Camilo Gómez-Rivas, *Law and the Islamization of Morocco under the Almoravids: The Fatwas of Ibn Rushd al-Jadd to the Far Maghrib* (Leiden; Boston: Brill, 2015), 49–59.

66 Abou Mohammed Salah b. Abdel-Halim, *Roudh el-kartas: histoire des souverains du Maghreb (Espagne et Maroc) et annales de la ville de Fès*, trans. Auguste Beaumier (Paris: Imprimerie impériale, 1860), 213. Note that the Almoravids also did not hesitate to use Christian mercenaries: Hasan Ahmad Mahmud, *Qiyamdawlat al-murabitin: Safhah mushriqa min tarikh al-maghrib fi-l-'usur al-wusta* (Cairo: al-Nahdahal-Misriyah, 1957).

67 Hirschberg, *A History of the Jews in North Africa*, vol. 1, 123.

68 Michael Brett and Elizabeth Fentress, *The Berbers* (Oxford: Blackwell, 1996), 107.

69 It should immediately be noted that the Almohads were equally if not more hostile toward Muslims who fell short of their strictures than they were toward *dhimmi*-s, though historians have emphasized the Almohads' anti-*dhimma* stance to such an extent that the overall picture of this period has been distorted. The focus on Jews is warranted here given the subject matter, but for an important corrective to Almohad historiography, see Amira K. Bennison, "Almohad *tawhid* and its Implications for Religious Difference," *Journal of Medieval Iberian Studies* 2, no. 2 (2010): 195–216.

70 The persecution of Jews by the Almohads is confirmed by materials from the Cairo geniza, among other sources. See M.J. Viguera, "Almohads." *Encyclopedia of Jews in the Islamic World Online*. Accessed September 25, 2017.

71 Muhyi al-Din Abi Muhammad al-Marrakushi, *Kitab al-mu'jib fi talkhis akhbar al-Maghrib*, ed. and trans. Reinhart Pieter Anne Dozy (Leiden: E.J. Brill, 1881), 223.

72 Delfina Serrano Ruano, "Explicit Cruelty, Implicit Compassion: Judaism, Forced Conversions and the Genealogy of the Banū Rushd," *Journal of Medieval Iberian Studies* 2, no. 2 (2010): 218.

73 Ibn Ezra, "Aha Yarad 'al Sfarad Ra'min ha-Shamayim" [From the Heavens Troubles Descended upon Spain], in Weinberger, *Twilight of a Golden Age*, 96.

74 Messier and Miller, *The Last Civilized Place: Sijilmasa*, 119.

75 Montgomery Watt, *The Decline of the Almohads: Reflections on the Viability of Religious Movements, History of Religions* 4, no. 1 (1964): 28.
76 Sarah Stroumsa, ed., "An Almohad Fundamentalist?" in her *Maimonides in His World, Portrait of a Mediterranean Thinker* (Princeton, NJ: Princeton University Press, 2009), 53–83.
77 David Corcos, "The Jews of Morocco under the Marinides," *The Jewish Quarterly Review* 54, no. 4 (1964): 273.
78 The Italian term "Getto/Ghetto" translates to "foundry" in English. It is believed to refer to the area of a munitions factory in Venice to which that city's Jews were transferred in 1516.
79 For more on the process of the founding and peopling of the *mellah*, see Susan Gilson Miller, "The Mallah: The Third City of Fez," in *The Architecture and Memory of the Minority Quarter in the Muslim Mediterranean City*, eds. Susan Gilson Miller and Mauro Bertagnin (Cambridge: Aga Khan Program, Harvard University, 2010), 81–109.
80 Up to 250,000 people lived in Fez during the second half of the twelfth century, making it the most populated city in the world according to some accounts: Tertius Chandler and Gerald Fox, *3000 Years of Urban Growth* (New York, NY: Academic Press, 1974).
81 Daniel Schroeter points out that Jews were the only segment of the Moroccan population whose status was exclusively based on the sultan's personal protection, a situation partly attributable to their shared circumstance of isolation. Daniel Schroeter, *The Sultan's Jew: Morocco and the Sephardi World* (Stanford: Stanford University Press, 2002), 12.
82 Susan Gilson Miller, citing the sixteenth-century Spanish visitor to Morocco Luis de Marmol. Miller, "The Mallah," 87. Marmol is talking about a later period, but the pattern extends to earlier centuries as well.
83 Maya Schatzmiller, "Ibn Baṭash, Aaron (Hārūn)." *Encyclopedia of Jews in the Islamic World Online*. Accessed October 16, 2018.
84 Shatzmiller, *The Berbers and the Islamic State*, 64.
85 David Corcos's explanation for the Marinid's benevolent attitude toward Jews, namely that the Zanata Berber tribal federation to which the Marinids belonged also included a large group of Judaized Berbers, is not supported by the historical evidence.
86 The anthropologist Paul Silverstein has done extensive analysis of the Goulmima carnival. See in particular his "Masquerade Politics: Race, Islam, and the Scales of Amazigh Activism in Southeastern Morocco," *Nations and Nationalism* 17, no. 1 (2011): 65–84; and also "A New Morocco? Amazigh Activism, Political Pluralism, and Anti-Anti-Semitism in the Wake of Tahrir," *Brown Journal of World Affairs* 18, no. 2 (2012): 129–140.
87 Sarah Levin, "Wit, Ruse, Rivalry and Other Keys to Coexistence: Reflections of Jewish-Muslim Relations in Berber Oral Traditions," in *North African Mosaic*, ed. Boudraa, 191–192.

88 In 2009, some Moroccan Amazigh activists made headlines by refusing to show their solidarity with Palestinian victims of the Israeli assault on Gaza. See the compilation of articles in "Berbers, Where Do You Stand on Palestine?" *MEMRI Special Dispatch*, no. 2262 (2009): https://www.memri.org/reports/berbers-where-do-you-stand-palestine. Accessed September 17, 2019.

89 See Aomar Boum, *Memories of Absence: How Muslims Remember Jews in Morocco* (Stanford: Stanford University Press, 2013).

Chapter 3

1 An earlier version of some portions of this chapter appeared in Emily Gottreich, "Of Messiahs and Sultans: Shabbatai Zevi and Early Modernity in Morocco," *The Journal of Modern Jewish Studies* 12, no. 2 (2013): 1–26.

2 A Moroccan embassy sent to England in the summer of 1600 proposed a Moroccan-English alliance against their mutual enemy, Spain, that included a detailed proposal for establishing colonies in the New World. Queen Elizabeth ultimately rejected Sultan Ahmad al-Mansur's memorandum. See Mercedes García-Arenal, *Ahmad al-Mansur: The Beginnings of Modern Morocco* (Oxford: One World, 2009), 87–96.

3 According to Ibn Khaldun, dynasties of nomadic origin never last more than a few generations in power, since they lose the group feeling that drove them to success once they become accustomed to the luxuries of city life. Ibn Khaldun based his cyclical theory of history on his observations of North African dynastic rule. See Stephen Cory, "Breaking the Khaldunian Cycle?: The Rise of Sharifianism and the Basis for Legitimacy in Early Modern Morocco," *Journal of North African Studies* 13, no. 3 (2008): 371–387.

4 Muhammed as-Saghir b. al-Hajj b. 'Abd Allah al-Ifrani, *Nuzhat al-Hadi bi-Akhbar li Muluk al Qarn al-Hadi* (Fez, n.p.,—c. 1890), quoted in Jacques Caille, *La ville de Rabat jusqu'au Protectorat français: histoire et archéologie*, vol. 1 (Paris: Vanoest, 1949), 209.

5 Qur'an 33:33.

6 Ibn Khaldun disputes the Idrisids' credentials; see Cory, "Breaking the Khaldunian Cycle?" 373.

7 For the bases of the critique against Sa'di legitimacy, see Mercedes García-Arenal, "Sainteté et Pouvoir Dynastique au Maroc: La Résistance de Fès aux Sa'diens," *Annales. Histoire, Sciences Sociales* 45, no. 4 (1990): 1019–1042.

8 Alt. *Sabbatai Zevi, Sevi*.

9 The damage done to traditional Jewish authority never completely healed, even as the weakening of the bonds of Jewish law by the Sabbateans cleared the way for some of the most significant innovations in Judaism in the following centuries,

including Hasidism, the Reform movement, and Zionism. Gershom Scholem, *Sabbatai Sevi: The Mystical Messiah*, trans. R.J. Zwi Werblowsky (Princeton: Princeton University Press, 1973), 1626–1676.

10 The only contemporary account of Shabbatai's conversion is by the Ottoman historian and official Abdi Pasha. For a translation, see Marc Baer, *Honored by the Glory of Islam* (Oxford: Oxford University Press, 2008), 127. Baer also notes that Ottoman narratives of Shabbatai's conversion emphasize the power of the sultan's gaze.

11 Scholem, *Sabbatai Ṣevi*, 570.

12 Francesca Trivellato, *The Familiarity of Strangers: The Sephardic Diaspora, Livorno, and Cross-cultural Trade in the Early Modern Period* (New Haven: Yale University Press, 2009).

13 Guadalajara, where the Zohar's author Moses de Leon lived, was not part of the Morocco-based Almohad Empire, nor was it brought into the Muslim *taifas* that followed its demise during Moses' lifetime. But even with Guadalajara in the hands of the Castilian Christians, ideas spread quickly between Christian- and Muslim-ruled areas, and from throughout the Iberian Peninsula to Morocco.

14 *Wikisource, The Free Library*, s.v. "Moses b. Maimonides," "Epistle to Yemen/Complete." Accessed August 3, 2017.

15 Mercedes García-Arenal, "Attentes messianiques au Maghreb et dans la péninsule Ibérique: du nouveau sur Sabbatai Zevi," in *Lucette Valensi à l'oeuvre: une histoire anthropologique de l'Islam méditerranéen*, eds. François Pouillon and and Lucette Valensi (Paris: Editions Bouchene, 2002), 225–242. See also by the same author, "Imam et Mahdi: Ibn Abî Mahallî," *Revue des Mondes Musulmans et de la Méditerranée* 91–94 (2000): 157–180.

16 Rachel Elior, "The Kabbalists of Draa" [Hebrew]. *Pe'amim* 24 (1985): 36–73.

17 Ya'akov Moshe Toledano, *Ner Hama'arav* (Jerusalem: A.M. Lunz printing press, 1911), 150.

18 Scholem, *Sabbatai Sevi*, 644.

19 See Benson Akutse Mojuetan, "Myth and Legend as Functional Instruments in Politics: The Establishment of the Alawi Dynasty in Morocco," *Journal of African History* 16, no. 1 (1975): 17.

20 The coincidence of Shabbatai's emergence with sightings of the ten tribes was striking to Christian millenarians, who embellished and helped further disseminate the rumors in Europe and the Ottoman Empire. Scholem, *Sabbatai Sevi*, 332–333. This did not happen in Morocco given the limited Christian presence there.

21 A.Z. Aescoly, "A Flandrian Newsletter Concerning the Sabbatean Movement," in *Dinaburg Jubilee Volume* [Hebrew], eds. Yitzhak Baer, Y. Guttman, and M. Shovah (Jerusalem: Hotsa'at Bet-hamidrash lemorim ha'ivri bi-yerushalayim, 1949): 215–236.

22 Note that this term is also used to refer to Muslim families of Fez considered to be of Jewish origin. See Mercedes García-Arenal, "Les Bildiyyin de Fès, un Groupe de Néo-musulmans d'origine Juive," *Studia Islamica*, no. 66 (1987): 113–143.
23 See the account of R. Judah reprinted in Hirschberg, *A History of the Jews in North Africa*, vol. 1, 405–446.
24 An oral tradition among Jews in Marrakech has it that no less a personality than Joseph Karo, author of the *Shulhan Arukh*, came to Morocco to help decide the issue of *shkhita* once and for all.
25 Although the converso phenomenon was even more common among Portuguese Jews, relatively few of them immigrated to Morocco.
26 Robert Assaraf, *Eléments de l'histoire des juifs du Meknès* (Rabat: Centre de recherche sur les Juifs du Maroc, 2010), 39.
27 Scholem, *Sabbatai Sevi*, 649–650. According to Moyal, when Elisha Ashkenazi was in Salé in 1650 he stayed in Sasportas's home. Elie Moyal, *The Shabbatean Movement in Morocco: Its History and Sources* [Hebrew] (Tel Aviv: Am 'Oved, 1984), 18.
28 Assaraf, *Eléments*, 40–41.
29 Jacob Sasportas, *Sisat Novel Tsvi*, letter from Sasportas to the Maghrib (Jerusalem: Mosad Bialik, 1954), 328.
30 Jacob Sasportas, *Sitat Novel Tsvi*, letter from Aaron Sibony to Sasportas (Jerusalem: Mosad Bialik, 1954), 333.
31 Germain Moüette, *Relations de captivité dans les royaumes de Fez et de Maroc*, ed. Xavier Girard (Paris: Mercure de France, 2002), 47–49.
32 Scholem, *Shabbatai Sevi*, 4.
33 Ibid., 648.
34 Benson Akutse Mojuetan, "Legitimacy in a Power State: Moroccan Politics in the Seventeenth Century during the Interregnum," *International Journal of Middle Eastern Studies* 13, no. 3 (1981): 351.
35 Henri de Castries and Pierre de Cenival, eds., *Les sources inédtites de l'histoire du Maroc: archives et Bibliothèques des Pays-Bas*, vol. 2 (Paris: P. Geunthner, 1934–53), 399. For a full-length study on Samuel Pallache, see Mercedes García-Arenal and Gerard Wiegers, *A Man of Three Worlds: Samuel Pallache, A Moroccan Jew in Catholic and Protestant Europe* (Baltimore: Johns Hopkins University Press, 2003).
36 Ait Ishaq is the name of the sub-tribe of the Sanhaja from which the Dila'iya *zawiya* drew its members. For the history of the Dila'iya *zawiya*, see Mohamed Hajji, *Al-zawiya al-dila'iya* (Rabat: s.n., 1988). Unfortunately, Hajji's work does not contain any discussion of the Jewish population of the *zawiya*.
37 Ahmad al-Nasiri, *Kitab al-istiqsa' li-akhbar duwal al-maghrib al-aqsa*, vol. 7 (Casablanca: Dar al-kitab: 1956), 17.
38 Mojuetan, "Legitimacy in a Power State," 351.
39 Ibid., 351.

40 Judah b. Obed Attar, "Divre ha-yamim shel Fez," in *Un Recueil de Textes Historiques Judéo-Marocains,* eds. Georges Vajda and Samuel ben Saul Danon (Paris, Larose: 1951), 51.
41 Vajda, *Un Recueil de Textes Historiques Judéo-Marocains,* 51.
42 Muhammad al-Qadiri, *Nashr al-mathani,* ed. and trans. Norman Cigar (London: Oxford University Press, 1981), 111. Al-Zayyani rather confusingly refers to Mawlay Rashid entering Fez through "The Mellah of the Muslims." Ahmad Al-Zayyani, *al-Turjuman al-mu'rib 'an duwal al-mashriq wa-l-maghrib,* ed. and trans. O Houdas (Paris: Ernest Leroux, 1886), 17.
43 That is, they gave him the *bay'a* [oath of allegiance]. Note that the use of the term "Sultan" is a convention in writing about Moroccan history but in practice the title "Mawlay" was favored.
44 A generic term applied to Imazighen in Jewish texts. *Kisse ha-Melakhim* by Raphael Moses Elbaz, MSS 1007, Sassoon Library, Letchworth, England, quoted in Moyal, *Shabbatean Movement in Morocco,* 39.
45 *Encyclopedia of Islamic Philosophy,* s.v., "Judaism and Sufism."
46 Attar, *Divre ha-yamim shel Fez,* 53.
47 It is worth mentioning that the chronicle also ignores the Ibn Mish'al legend, whereby Mawlay Rashid is believed to have proven himself worthy of being sultan by defeating a rich Jewish tyrant in Taza. See H. Z. Hirschberg, *History of the Jews in North Africa,* vol. 2, *From the Ottoman Conquests to the Present Time* (Leiden: Brill, 1974), 247. The silence of the Moroccan rabbis and community leaders on the topic of Shabbatai Tsvi is indeed deafening and may be indicative of a wish to cover up shameful events. Moyal devotes an entire chapter to the phenomenon. Moyal, *Shabbatean Movement in Morocco,* 185–193.
48 Sasportas, *Sisat Novel Tsvi,* letter from Aaron Sibony to Sasportas, 324.
49 Moshe Rafael Elbaz, *Kisse Melahkim,* as excerpted in Hirschberg, *History of the Jews in North Africa,* vol. 2, 246.
50 Sasportas, *Sisat Novel Tsvi,* letter from Jacob b. Sa'adon to Sasportas, 335. Note that "Morocco" was also used to refer to the city of Marrakech specifically during this period.
51 Sasportas, *Sisat Novel Tsvi,* letter from Aaron Sibony to Sasportas, 326.
52 Scholem, *Sabbatai Sevi,* 468.
53 Sasportas, *Sisat Novel Sevi,* 31.
54 Ibid., 341.
55 Ibid., 163.
56 "Zawiya" is often treated as the name of the town in the Jewish sources but refers to the area around the Dila *zawiya* (also called *dar zawiya,* the house of the zawiya.)
57 He is referring here to the "remnant" Jews who stayed behind clandestinely in the area of the *zawiya* after the community was ordered to leave. Sasportas, *Sisat Novel Tsvi,* 354.

58 Jacob Sasportas, *Ohel Ya'akov* (Amsterdam: Hertz Levi Rofe, 1737), 319.

59 In his own analysis, Hirschberg is much less equivocal than Sasportas, for whom the possibility of official retribution for Sabbateanism is mostly implied. Hirschberg asserts that Mawlay Rashid's persecution of Jews in certain Moroccan towns (Marrakech, Tadla, and the Dila *zawiya*) and not in others is an indication of a specifically anti-Sabbatean (as opposed to generally anti-Jewish) policy. Hirschberg, *History of the Jews in North Africa*, vol. 2, 248.

60 Letter from Avraham Sibony reproduced in Sasportas, *Sisat Novel Tsvi*, 324–326.

61 Scholem, *Sabbatai Sevi*, 815–820.

62 Louis de Chénier, *The Present State of the Empire of Morocco*, vol. 1 (London: G.G.J. and J. Robinson, 1788), 354–355.

63 Baruch of Arezzo, "The Story of Joseph Ibn Tsur," in *Sabbatai Zevi: Testimonies to a Fallen Messiah*, ed. and trans. David Halperin (Oxford: Litman Library of Jewish Civilization, 2007), 92.

64 Jane Hathaway, "The Mawza' Exile at the Juncture of Zaydi and Ottoman Messianism," *Association for Jewish Studies Review* 29, no. 1 (2005): 111–128. See also P.S. van Koningsveld, J. Sadan, and Q. al-Samarrai, *Yemenite Authorities and Jewish Messian-ism. Ahmad b. Nasir al-Zaydi's Account of the Sabbathian Movement in Seventeenth Century Yemen and Its Aftermath* (Leiden: Leiden University, Faculty of Theology 1990).

65 The proprietary attitude of the *makhzan* over its coterie of court Jews is indicated by a letter from 1606, in which the Moroccan ambassador to the Hague expresses his outrage over the injury done to "his" Jew when a Dutch agent shaved off his beard. April 24, 1606, *Les sources inédites de l'histoire du Maroc, pays bas*, vol. 1, 144–145.

66 See Emily Gottreich, "On the Origins of the Mellah of Marrakech," *International Journal of Middle East Studies* 35, no. 2 (2003): 287–305.

67 As late as 1669 traditional Jewish fast days were boycotted by Sabbateans in Morocco. The movement began to wane after that, though the emergence of Jacob b. Sur in Meknes in the 1670s temporarily reenergized it.

68 Gottreich, "On the Origins," 361.

69 Baer, *Honored by the Glory of Islam*, 123.

70 See Haim Zafrani, *Kabbale, vie mystique et magie* (Paris: Maisonneuve et Larose, 1986): 487.

71 Baruch of Arezzo, "The Story of Joseph Ibn Tsur," 90.

72 Ibid., 91.

73 Moyal, *The Shabbatean Movement in Morocco*, 131.

74 Baruch of Arezzo, "The Story of Joseph Ben Sur," in *Inyeney Shabbatai Sevi* [Hebew] ed. Aron Freimann (Berlin: H. Itzkowski, 1912), 40–78, quoted in Scholem, *Sabbatai Sevi*, 896.

75 He had been forced to return to Morocco when en route home to Palestine; he "lost all the money he had collected, because his companion, the scholar and

kabbalist Solomon Navarro, fell in love with a gentile woman when he came to Reggio in Italy, married her, and apostatized from his religion." Sasportas, *Sisat Novel Sevi*, 136.

76 Clifford Geertz, *Islam Observed: Religious Development in Morocco and Indonesia* (Chicago: University of Chicago Press, 1971), 45.

77 Note that Daniel Toledano of Meknes, one of Mawlay Isma'il's advisors, was an anti-Sabbatean activist. Moyal, *The Shabbatean Movement in Morocco*, 83.

78 See discussion in Matt Goldish, *The Sabbatean Prophets* (Cambridge MA: Harvard University Press, 2009), 163.

79 Schroeter, "The Shifting Boundaries of Moroccan Jewish Identities," 150. In the case of Sharifism, however, the Islamic science of genealogies insures relatively accurate lineages. In Morocco, a special office was introduced in the fourteenth century to register and certify sharifian births, deaths, and marriages.

80 A British traveler by the name of G.R. Beauclerk describes an annual event in which a young Jewish virgin would be selected and enclosed in a crate. The community would then watch and wait for her to become pregnant by the "Holy Ghost," which would lead to her giving birth to the messiah. G.R. Beauclerk, *A Journey to Morocco in 1826* (London: Poole and Edwards, 1828).

81 Joffe, "Maghribi Islam," 63.

Chapter 4

1 His voyage is recounted in *Reconnaissance au Maroc, 1883–1884*, 4 vols. (Paris: Challamel, 1888).

2 The curator did not suggest that the local Jews would be any more gullible than the Muslims, but rather that "with centuries of abuse and persecution behind them, [the Jews] would instinctively protect de Foucauld from Muslims, even though they saw through his masquerade." Marion Mill Preminger, *The Sands of Tamanrasset; The Story of Charles de Foucauld* (New York: Hawthorn Books, 1961), 61, quoted in Aomar Boum, *Memories of Absence: How Muslims Remember Jews in Morocco* (Stanford, California: Stanford University Press, 2013), 50. Boum notes that there were other colonial ethnographers better versed in Arabic than Foucauld who knew something about Islam and local customs and who did successfully pass as Muslims while traveling and living in Morocco. Boum, *Memories of Absence*, 49. To Boum's list I would add Ali Bey Al-Abbassi, a.ka. Domènec Badia Leblich, the Spanish explorer and author of *Travels of Ali Bey in Morocco, Tripoli, Cyprus, Egypt, Arabia, Syria, and Turkey, between the Years 1803 and 1807* (London: Longman et al., 1816).

3 Foucauld, *Reconnaissance au Maroc*, Avant-Propos, 25.

4   Most famously, the English physician John Davidson was killed in Morocco by members of the Harib tribe while on his way to Timbuktu in 1836. John Davidson, *Notes Taken during Travels in Africa* (London: J.L. Cox and Sons, 1839).

5   There are several important exceptions to this rule, including the visit to Paris by the Moroccan scholar Muhammad al-Saffar as part of a diplomatic mission in 1845. See Muhammad Saffar, *Disorienting Encounters: Travels of a Moroccan Scholar in France in 1845–1846, The Voyage of Muhammad As-Saffar*, ed. and trans. Susan Gilson Miller (Berkeley: University of California Press, 1992).

6   Pierre de Cenival, "L'église chrétienne de Marrakech au XIIIe siècle," *Hespéris-Tamuda: Archives Berbères et Bulletin de l'Institut des Hautes- Études Morocaines* 7 (1927): 69–83.

7   Several women straddled this line: Edith Wharton, for example, wrote about her trip to Morocco in the fall of 1917 in an overtly Orientalist mode. A more intimate perspective can be found in the writings of the English governess Emily Keene (1849–1944), who married and had two sons with the sharif of the al-Wazzani *zawiya*. Keane learned Arabic and considered herself "a hybrid." Emily, Shareefa of Wazzan, *My Life Story* (London: Edward Arnold, 1912). Another interesting figure is the English writer Nina Epton, a close ally of the Moroccan nationalist movement during the post–Second World War period who became the bête noire of the French colonial authorities because of her political activities in support of Moroccan independence.

8   Interviews done by Aomar Boum in the Sous region suggest that contemporary Moroccans make no distinction between Foucauld's visit and the larger project of French imperialism that followed: Boum, *Memories of Absence*, 24. For the definitive work on European travel writing on the MENA and its connection to European imperialism, see Edward Said, *Orientalism* (New York: Vintage Books, 1979).

9   Aomar Boum, "Abisrur, Mordechai." *Encyclopedia of Jews in the Islamic World Online*. Accessed October 16, 2018. For a fuller biography of Mordechai, see Jacob Oliel, *De Jerusalem à Tombouctou: L'odyssée saharienne du rabbin Mardochée, 1826–1886* (Paris: Éditions Olbia, 1998).

10 Ismael Diadie Haidara, *Les Juifs à Tombouctou: Recueil Des Sources Écrites Relatives Au Commerce Juif À Tombouctou Au XIXe Siècle* (Bamako: Editions Donniya, 1999), 31.

11 Auguste Beaumier, "Premier établissement des Israélites à Tombouctou," *Bulletin de la Société de Géographie* 5, no. 19 (1870): 345–370.

12 Foucauld, *Reconnaissances au Maroc*, 9.

13 Ibid., 52.

14 Ibid., 53–54.

15 For a discussion of colonialism's claims to liberal progress, see Frederick Cooper, *Colonialism in Question: Theory, Knowledge, History* (Berkeley: University of California Press, 2005), especially the introduction: "Colonial Questions, Historical Trajectories," 3–32.

16 Walter Harris, *The Land of an African Sultan: Travels in Morocco, 1887, 1888, and 1889* (London: S. Low, Marston & Co., 1889), 219.
17 The Alawi dynasty, which came to power in the seventeenth century, ruled Morocco during the period Foucauld describes and remains in power today. The reigning sultan traditionally divided his time between the royal capitals at Fez, Marrakech, and Meknes, making regular forays (Ar. *mahalla*-s) into the rural areas to collect taxes and reaffirm his authority. Given the decentralized nature of the Moroccan state, longer absences from the countryside could lead to looser loyalties and sometimes open rebellion.
18 Foucauld, *Reconnaissances au Maroc*, 395.
19 Letter from Nissim Falcon, Headmaster of Alliance Israélite Universelle (AIU) School in Marrakech, to President of the AIU. September 2, 1907, Maroc: Comités Locaux et Communautés, VII.B, Archives of the AIU, Paris, France.
20 The term "colonial" is meant loosely in this chapter. France did not establish a settler colony in Morocco like it did in Algeria, but via the institutions of the Protectorate France still held the reins of political power.
21 For a similar rethinking of Moroccan colonial history on a broader scale, see the introduction by Driss Maghraoui, "Locating New Layers of Moroccan Colonial History," in his edited volume, *Revisiting the Colonial Past in Morocco* (London: Routledge, 2013), 220–230.
22 Mohammed Kenbib, "Changing Aspects of State and Society in Nineteenth-century Morocco," in *The Moroccan State in Historical Perspective 1850–1985*, ed. Abdelali Doumou, trans. Aye Kwei Armah (Dakar, Senegal: Codesria, 1990), 19.
23 Susan Gilson Miller, *A History of Modern Morocco* (Cambridge, UK: Cambridge University Press, 2013), 59.
24 Walter Harris, *Morocco That Was* (Westernport: Negro Universities Press, 1970), 80.
25 His subjects complained that the car obscured their view of him. "Faits Divers," *Le Réveil du Maroc*, January 12, 1899.
26 Harris, *Morocco That Was*, 81.
27 In the Middle East, indigenous Christians, especially Armenians, often held these positions.
28 See Sarah Abrevaya Stein, "Dividing South from North: French Colonialism, Jews, and the Algerian Sahara," *Journal of North African Studies* 17, no. 4 (2012): 773–792.
29 See Jessica Marglin, "The Two Lives of Mas'ud Amoyal: Pseudo-Algerians in Morocco, 1830–1912," *International Journal of Middle East Studies* 44, no. 4 (2012): 651–670.
30 In 1931, 162,000 Europeans were living in Morocco, the majority (60 percent) of them of French origin. As cited in Miller, *A History of Modern Morocco*, 112. By contrast, the *pieds noirs* (European settlers) in Algeria numbered close to a million.

31 In 1879, the British Ambassador to Morocco, Sir John Drummond Hay, reported that out of a total of 200,000 Jews in Morocco, the 1500 "wealthiest" were under European protection. John Drummond Hay to Löwy, President of the Anglo-Jewish Association, November 24, 1879, ADP:5, Archives du Ministère des Affaires Étrangères (AAE), France.

32 For Morocco specifically, see Daniel Schroeter and Joseph Chetrit, "Emancipation and Its Discontents: Jews at the Formative Period of Colonial Rule in Morocco," *Jewish Social Studies: History, Culture, Society* 13, no. 1 (2006): 170–206. It is important to recognize that such trends were never all-encompassing. Many individual Jews refused European protection or justice when offered, and communal resistance to the AIU schools was common, particularly from the religious leaders who deeply resented its secularizing program (see below).

33 Mark Cohen, *Under Crescent and Cross: The Jews in the Middle Ages* (Princeton, NJ: Princeton University Press, 1994).

34 Letter from Jewish representatives in Britain (Anglo-Jewish Association) to Ambassador al-Haj Muhammad al-Zibdi, July 25, 1876, quoted in *Al-Watha'iq, Mudiriya al-Watha'iq al-Malikiya*, no. 5 (Rabat: al-Matba'at al-Malikiya, 1981), 19.

35 For a study of *tujjar al-Sultan*, see Michel Abitbol, *Temoins et acteurs: les Corcos et l'histoire du Maroc contemporain* (Jerusalem: Institut Ben Zvi, 1977), and Daniel Schroeter, *The Sultan's Jew* (Stanford: Stanford University Press, 2002).

36 For some of the other ways the protégé system weakened Morocco, see Leland Louis Bowie, "The Protégé System in Morocco: 1880–1904" (PhD dissertation, Ohio State University, 1970).

37 Benchimol's special status is noted in Article 6 of the Madrid Convention.

38 Jessica Marglin, "In the Courts of the Nations: Jews, Muslims and Legal Pluralism in Nineteenth-century Morocco" (PhD dissertation, Princeton University, 2013), 275.

39 Légation de la République Française au Maroc, April 1891, II.B.9-13: 5864, 22, Archives of the Alliance Israélite Universelle (AIU), Morocco.

40 This process accelerated in the wake of the *dahirs* of 1913 and 1915. Promulgated under the French Protectorate, these two edicts gave preferential treatment to Europeans in buying land. See Jonathan Wyrtzen, *Making Morocco: Colonial Intervention and the Politics of Identity* (Ithaca: Cornell University Press, 2015), 88–89.

41 See Mohammed Kenbib, "Structures traditionnelles et protections étrangères au Maroc au XIXe siècle," *Hespéris-Tamuda* 22, no. 1 (1984): 69–83 and idem., *Les protégés*.

42 Aomar Boum, "Schooling in the Bled: Jewish Education and the Alliance Israélite Universelle in Southern Rural Morocco, 1830–1962," *Journal of Jewish Identities* 3, no. 1 (2010): 4.

43 Daniel J. Schroeter, "Slave Markets and Slavery in Moroccan Urban Society," *Slavery & Abolition* 13, no. 1 (1992): 204.

44 Kenbib, "Changing Aspects," 22.
45 In that instance, Montefiore had traveled to Alexandria and Istanbul to meet with Ottoman officials in the wake of a blood libel made against a group of Syrian Jews following the disappearance of a Franciscan monk. A group of Damascene Jews was accused of ritual murder and their synagogue was looted; three of the accused died in prison and one converted to Islam. Montefiore succeeded in winning the release of the rest of the imprisoned Jews and went on to secure a *firman* [Turk., edict] from the Ottoman sultan against the spread of blood libels in the empire.
46 Kenbib further points out that Montefiore's visit to Marrakech was directly preceded by a terrible explosion the previous day, in which two hundred Moroccans were killed. He notes that the nineteenth-century Moroccan historian Ahmad al-Nasiri linked the "subversive intentions" of Montefiore's visit and the explosion together as part of the same catastrophe. Mohamed Kenbib, *Juifs et Musulmans au Maroc, 1859–1948* (Rabat: University Mohammed V, Faculté des lettres et des sciences humaines, 1994), 150 fn78.
47 Despite Jewish Morocco's undeniable poverty in the nineteenth century, "distressed" is still a relative term, particularly insofar as European observers tended to view *dhimma* status as part and parcel of Jewish suffering. Jews in Morocco could easily be seen as downtrodden in the sense that the majority were poor and illiterate, but not necessarily any more so than their Muslim neighbors, and sometimes less so. But the Muslim masses had no European allies to advocate on their behalf.
48 It is worth noting that certain western and central European Jews felt much the same way about "Ostjuden," Eastern European Jews whose migrations westward were causing them similar embarrassment.
49 Joseph Halévy. Rapport à l'Alliance Israélite Universelle sur l'état des écoles françaises dans les communautés juives du Maroc, August 8, 1876, IX.A.67-73, Archives of the Alliance Israélite Universelle (AIU), France.
50 See the articles in the volume edited by Ivan Kalmar and Derek Penslar, *Orientalism and the Jews* (Waltham, MA: Brandeis University Press; Hanover: University Press of New England, 2005).
51 Emily Gottreich and Daniel Schroeter, "Rethinking Jewish Culture and Society in North Africa," in *Jewish Culture and Society*, eds. Gottreich and Schroeter, 10.
52 See title of the 1984 memoir by Alfred Goldenberg, former director of AIU school in Marrakech. Alfred Goldenberg, "Quand J'Étais Un 'Missionaire' de l'Alliance," *Les Cahiers de l'Alliance Israélite Universelle*, no. 208 (1984): 43–48.
53 AIU schools were established south of Marrakech in and beyond the Atlas Mountains in the twentieth century, under the French Protectorate.
54 Aron Rodrigue, "Alliance Israélite Universelle Network," *Encyclopedia of Jews in the Islamic World Online*. Accessed October 16, 2018.

55 Prior to the intervention of the AIU, a small group of Moroccan Jews involved in trade and diplomacy had long been proficient in European languages, and even in Hebrew, which they sometimes used to conduct trade with Jews from other countries. The AIU broadened that base of multilingualism, particularly by educating girls.

56 Coriat, September 16, 1901, Maroc: XXVII.E.414-442, Archives of the AIU Paris, France.

57 Louis Brunot and Elie Malka, *Textes Judéo-Arabes de Fès: Textes, Transcription, Traduction, Annotée* (Rabat: Ecole du Livre, 1939), v.

58 Susan Gilson Miller, "Gender and the Poetics of Emancipation: The Alliance Israélite Universelle in Northern Morocco, 1890–1912," in *Franco-Arab Encounters*, eds. L. Carl Brown and Matthew Gordon (Beirut: AUB Press, 1996), 237.

59 Aron Rodrigue, "Alliance Israélite Universelle Network." *Encyclopedia of Jews in the Islamic World Online*. Accessed October 18, 2016.

60 Moise Levy, September 16, 1901, Écoles, Maroc: XXVII.E.417-442, Archives of the AIU Paris, France.

61 Miller, "Gender and the Poetics of Emancipation," 6.

62 See Michael Laskier, "The Alliance Israélite Universelle and the Struggle for Recognition within Moroccan Jewish Society, 1862–1912," in *The Sephardi and Oriental Jewish Heritage: Studies*, ed. Issachar Ben Ami, vol. 1 (Jerusalem: Magnes Press, Hebrew University, 1982).

63 Letter from students to Lyautey, October 1912, Maroc: II.B.9-13: 4280, Archives of the AIU Paris, France.

64 The clash between French and Maghribi Judaism is beautifully captured in Joann Sfar's graphic novel and film, *The Rabbi's Cat*.

65 Michael Laskier, *The Alliance Israélite Universelle and the Jewish Communities of Morocco, 1862–1962* (Albany: State University of New York Press, 1983), 81–82.

66 Maimonides, who fled with his family from Cordoba to Fez in the mid-twelfth century, is the best-known such figure, but Moroccan Judaism has a rich intellectual tradition that includes many luminaries. See Haim Zafran, *Two Thousand Years of Jewish Life in Morocco*, especially chapter five, "Intellectual Life: Culture and Religion."

67 Jonathan Katz, "'Les Temps Héroïques': The Alliance Israélite Universelle in Marrakech on the Eve of the Protectorate," in *Jewish Culture and Society*, eds. Gottreich and Schroeter, 283.

68 Miller, "Gender and the Poetics of Emancipation," 233.

69 Lawrence Rosen, *Two Arabs, a Berber, and a Jew: Entangled Lives in Morocco* (Chicago: University of Chicago Press, 2015), 284.

70 Emily Gottreich, *The Mellah of Marrakesh: Jewish and Muslim Space in Morocco's Red City* (Bloomington: Indiana University Press, 2007), 79.

71 The AIU survived Moroccan independence and, in the post-1956 era, reemerged in a nationalized and Arabized form under the name *al-Ittihad*, serving what quickly became a majority Muslim population of students.

72 The broader Europeanization and Westernization trends in Middle Eastern and North African societies were more complex and went well beyond state-centered reforms and were motivated by any number of factors, including emulation in its own right as opposed to mere defensive posturing.

73 For a discussion of Moroccan reform program of the nineteenth century, see Miller, *A History of Modern Morocco*, 28–55. For more on Morocco's environmental history specifically, see Rosenberger, Bernard, and Hamid Triki, "Famines et épidémies au Maroc aux XVIe et XVIIe siècles," *Hespéris-Tamuda* 15, no. 1 (1973): 5–104. The impact of drought on food supply in the nineteenth century is treated in Stacy Holden, *The Politics of Food in Modern Morocco* (Gainesville: University of Florida Press, 2009).

74 An Arabic transcription of the Marrakech census can be found in Khalid Ben. Srhir, "Wathiqa ghayr munshura 'an millah Murrakush fi-l-qarn al-tasi' 'ashr," *Hespéris-Tamuda* 35, no. 2 (1997): 25–71. For a discussion of the impact of the census on spatial and social arrangements in the Marrakech *mellah*, see Gottreich, *Mellah of Marrakesh*, 29–70.

75 Schroeter, *The Sultan's Jew*, 90–93.

76 For the spatial history of Jewish Tangier, see Susan Gilson Miller, "The Mellah without Walls: Jewish Space in a Moroccan City, Tangier 1860–1912," in *Revisiting the Colonial Past in Morocco*, ed. Driss Maghraoui (New York: Routledge, 2013), 19–37.

77 Kenbib, "Structures Traditionnelles et Protections Etrangeres au Maroc au XIXe Siecle," 79–101. In extending this argument more broadly, we find that the Jewish experience in general also doesn't fit well into postcolonial theoretical paradigms, which are highly critical of the very forces that helped Jews emerge from "out of the ghetto" in Europe: enlightenment, modernity, liberalism, etc. insofar as they were forcibly imposed by Europe on the colonized world. See Ethan Katz, Lisa Moses Leff, and Maud Mandel, eds., "Introduction: Engaging Colonial History and Jewish History," in *Colonialism and the Jews* (Bloomington: Indiana University Press, 2017), 1–25.

78 Hesitant to affirm the French fantasy of continuing Moroccan sovereignty during the Protectorate, Moroccan historians of a nationalist bent have been reluctant to integrate this interlude into the broader sweep of Moroccan history. See Miller, *A History of Modern Morocco*, 2–3.

79 See Daniel Schroeter, "Nahum Slouschz." *Encyclopedia of Jews in the Islamic World Online*. Accessed October 16, 2018.

80 For a thorough discussion of the mechanisms of Jewish "emancipation" in Algeria, see Joshua Schreier, *Arabs of the Jewish Faith: The Civilizing Mission in Colonial Algeria* (New Brunswick, NJ: Rutgers University Press, 2010).

81 In 1913 AIU president Narcisse Leven wrote to Lyautey requesting that Moroccan Jews be placed under the extraterritorial jurisdiction of French courts. Lyautey rejected the idea. Similarly, a French law promulgated in 1920 allowed foreigners in Morocco to apply for French citizenship, but it did not apply to Moroccan Jews.

82 Schroeter and Chetrit, "Emancipation and its Discontents," 170–171.

83 In addition to ethnic and linguistic variation, Moroccan Jews were also divided by class, especially in urban settings, where there was often a distinct oligarchy and proletariat in the *mellah*. It was usually the wealthiest Jewish merchant as opposed to a rabbi or other religious leader who represented individual communities as *shaykh al-yahud*. See Mohammed Kenbib, "Les Relations entre Musulmans et Juifs au Maroc 1859–1945: Essai Bibliographique," *Hespéris-Tamuda* 23 (1985): 84.

84 See Daniel Schroeter, *Merchants of Essaouira: Urban Society and Imperialism in Southwestern Morocco, 1844–1886* (Cambridge; New York: Cambridge University Press, 1988).

85 Susan Gilson Miller, "Making Tangier Modern: Ethnicity and Urban Development, 1880–1930," in *Jewish Culture and Society*, eds. Gottreich and Schroeter, 128–149.

86 Jamaâ Baïda, *La presse marocaine d'expression francaise, des origines à 1956* (Rabat: Publications de la Faculté des Lettres et des Sciences Humaines, 1996). For more on the Moroccan Jewish press, see Pierre Cohen, *La Presse Juive editée a Maroc, 1870–1963* (Rabat: Éditions et Impressions Bouregreg Communication, 2007).

87 Daniel Rivet, *Lyautey et l'institution du protectorat français au Maroc, 1912–1925* (Paris, L'Harmattan: 1988), as quoted in Miller, *A History of Modern Morocco*, 93–94.

88 Gottreich, *Mellah of Marrakech*, 133.

89 Kenbib, *Juifs et Musulmans*, 431–433. For a first-hand account of the economic situation of Jewish craftsmen and artisans in Marrakech, see 9 Shawwal 1 1298/14 September 1881, Marrakesh 4, Archives of the Direction des Archives Royales, Rabat.

90 Edmund Burke III, *Prelude to Protectorate in Morocco* (Chicago: University of Chicago Press, 1976), 180.

91 Letter from White to Grey, March 9, 1912, FO413: 56, Archives of the Public Record Office (PRO), London.

92 Yaron Tsur, "Morocco (1912–1956)," *Encyclopedia of Jews in the Islamic World Online*. Accessed October 16, 2018.

93 Schroeter and Chetrit, "Emancipation and Its Discontents," 179.

94 Danielle Lévy-Mongelli, ed., "Un Cas particulier d'alienation culturelle: les juifs d'Afrique du nord dans l'aventure colonial française," in *Juifs du Maroc: identité et dialogue. Actes du colloque international sur la communauté juive marocaine: vie culturelle, histoire sociale et évolution* (Paris, December 18–21, 1978) 252.

95 Yaron Tsur, "Morocco (1912–1956)," *Encyclopedia of Jews in the Islamic World Online*. Accessed October 16, 2018.

Chapter 5

1. The two ideologies overlapped considerably with the exception of the role played by non-Muslims, which in theory was more prominent in pan-Arabism. For a detailed analysis of the spread of pan-Islamism from the Ottoman Empire to Morocco, see Edmund Burke, "Pan-Islam and Moroccan Resistance to French Colonial Penetration, 1900–1912," *The Journal of African History* 13, no. 1 (1972): 97–118; also Jamil Abun-Nasr, "The Salafiyya Movement in Morocco: The Religious Bases of the Moroccan Nationalist Movement," in *Social Change: The Colonial Situation*, ed. Immanuel Wallerstein (New York, London and Sydney: John Wiley & Sons, 1966), 489–502.
2. Bassam Tibi, *Arab Nationalism: A Critical Inquiry* (New York: St. Martin's Press, 1971), 111.
3. For a historical exploration of the Arab Jew, see Emily Gottreich, "Historicizing the Concept of Arab Jews in the Maghrib," *The Jewish Quarterly Review* 98, no. 4 (2008): 433–451, and the partner piece, Lital Levy "Historicizing the Concept of Arab Jews in the *Mashriq*," *The Jewish Quarterly Review* 98, no. 4 (2008): 452–469. More recently, Levy has published an overview of these debates: "The Arab Jew Debates: Media, Culture, Politics, History," *Journal of Levantine Studies* 7, no. 1 (Summer 2017): 79–103.
4. The publication *The Arab Nation* first began appearing in Morocco during this time.
5. Burke, "Pan-Islam," 103. Jerusalem also was home to a sizeable Moroccan community including both Jews and Muslims.
6. The communists and the nationalists were not categorically opposed to one another, which allowed for overlapping allegiances among some Jews. As Alma Heckman explains, "The mainstream Moroccan nationalist movement Istiqlal and the PCM had a waxing and waning of rapprochement and disavowal, acceptance of common cause and revulsion." Alma Heckman, "Radical Nationalists: Moroccan Jewish Communists 1925–1975" (PhD dissertation, University of California, Los Angeles, 2015), 42.
7. The formulation of primary and secondary resistances is loosely borrowed from Terence Ranger, "Connexions between 'Primary Resistance' Movements and Modern Mass Nationalism in East and Central Africa," Part I, *The Journal of African History* 9, no. 3 (1968): 437–453. I thank David Stenner for guiding me toward this analytic framework and source. Edmund Burke defines primary resistance as "the attempt to forge new ways of uniting the local population by cutting across tribal, linguistic, and religious affiliations," which he then uses to analyze pan-Islamic movements in Morocco. Burke, "Pan-Islam," 99.
8. Michael Laskier, "The Instability of Moroccan Jewry and the Moroccan Press in the First Decade after Independence," *Jewish History* 1, no. 1 (1986): 40.

9   The claim that Moroccan independence was achieved without violence has been shown to be an overstatement. See Susan Gilson Miller, *A History of Modern Morocco* (Cambridge: Cambridge University Press, 2013), 151–152.
10 See, for instance, Laskier, "The Instability of Moroccan Jewry," 39–54.
11 This discussion of the Mauchamp affair relies heavily on Jonathan G. Katz, *Murder in Marrakech: Emile Mauchamp and the French Colonial Adventure* (Bloomington: Indiana University Press, 2006) and the earlier article on which it is based, "The 1907 Mauchamp Affair and the French Civilising Mission in Morocco," *The Journal of North African Studies* 6, no. 1 (2006): 143–166. See also Ellen Amster, "The Many Deaths of Dr. Emile Mauchamp: Medicine, Technology, and Popular Politics in Pre-Protectorate Morocco, 1877–1912," *International Journal of Middle East Studies* 36, no. 3 (2004): 409–428. A hagiographic biography of Mauchamp was written shortly after his death, Henri Guillemin, *Biographie du docteur Émile Mauchamp* (Châlon-sur-Saône: E. Bertrand, 1910). Mauchamp's own study of Moroccan medicine, which he characterized as witchcraft, was published posthumously as *La Sorcellerie au Maroc* (Paris: Dorbon-Aîné, 1911).
12 Katz, "The 1907 Mauchamp Affair," 151.
13 Ibid., 152.
14 *British Medical Journal*, s.v. "Obituaries," March 30, 1907, 785.
15 Most of these doctors were indeed men, but there were some exceptions, like Dr. Francoise Legey who came to Morocco in 1910 and had a tremendous impact on women's healthcare. Ellen Amster, "Medicine and the Saints: Science, Islam, and the Colonial Encounter in Morocco," *Social History of Medicine: The Journal of the Society for the Social History of Medicine* 27, no. 3 (2014): 159.
16 Katz, "The 1907 Mauchamp Affair," 156.
17 Amster, "Many Deaths," 409.
18 Katz, *Murder in Marrakech*, 2.
19 Ibid., 13.
20 Patricia Goldsworthy, "Images, Ideologies, and Commodities: The French Colonial Postcard Industry in Morocco," *Early Popular Visual Culture* 8, no. 2 (2010): 147–167.
21 William Lemprière, *A Tour from Gibraltar to Tangier* (London: J. Walter; J. Johnson; and J. Sewell, 1791), 185. Thomas Hodgkin and John Davidson are other European doctors who also left detailed accounts of Moroccan Jewry.
22 For a discussion of the different gender norms among Muslims and Jews in Morocco, see Susan Gilson Miller, "Gender and the Poetics of Emancipation: The Alliance Israélite Universelle in Northern Morocco, 1890–1912," in *Franco-Arab Encounters*, eds. Leon Carl Brown and Matthew Gordon (Beirut: The American University of Beirut Press, 1996), 229–258; also Emily Gottreich, "Rethinking the 'Islamic City' from the Perspective of Jewish Space," *Jewish Social Studies*, New Series, 11, no. 1 (2004): 118–146.

23 Further contributing to the stigmatization of Jewish space in Morocco were the prevalence of alcohol and prostitution. See Gottreich, "Rethinking the 'Islamic City,'" 118–146.
24 Amster, "Many Deaths," 417; Katz, *Murder in Marrakech*, 50.
25 September 3, 1900, Maroc: II.B.9-13: 4844, Archives of the AIU, Paris, France.
26 "Sur la Fréquence du trachome dans la population Israélite de Marrakech et sur les moyens d'y remédier," April 1, 1926. Maroc: II.B.9-13: 1718, Archives of the AIU, Paris, France.
27 Amster, "Medicine and the Saints Science,"159.
28 Al-Mukhtar, Muhammad b. al-'Arabi to the amin al-'umana (chief inspector) of Marrakech, Marrakech 7, July 6, 1885, Direction des Archives Royales, Rabat, Morocco.
29 Katz, *Murder in Marrakech*, 92.
30 January 23, 1906 (date received). Maroc: XXVI.E.398-416: 2278/8, Archives of the AIU, Paris, France.
31 Nissim Falcon, June 21, 1906, Maroc: XXVI.E.398-416:4380/4, Archives of the AIU, Paris, France.
32 The European (French and English) community of Marrakech at the time consisted of just nine adults and their children. A portrait of the group can be found in Katz, *Murder in Marrakech*, 77.
33 Ibid., 78.
34 Lennox to Madden, March 19, 1907, FO413/45. Archives of the PRO, London, England.
35 Nissim Falcon, May 14, 1907, Maroc: XXVI.E.398-416: 398a: 3719, Archives of the AIU, Paris, France.
36 Edmund Burke, *Prelude to Protectorate in Morocco* (Chicago: University of Chicago Press, 1976), 180. The author draws a distinction between the tribal impetus for resistance in the Maghrib and the *mashriq*, where resistance came largely from the urban classes.
37 John P. Halstead, *Rebirth of a Nation: The Origins and Rise of Moroccan Nationalism, 1912–1944* (Cambridge: Harvard University Press, 1967), 6.
38 Emily Gottreich, *The Mellah of Marrakesh: Jewish and Muslim Space in Morocco's Red City* (Bloomington: Indiana University Press, 2007), 12.
39 In the colonial literature, the term "Kabyle" usually connotes the Amazigh tribes in northern Algeria whose complex political organization and aspirations both thwarted their colonial masters and attracted considerable attention by theorists. See Hugh Roberts, *Berber Government: The Kabyle Polity in Pre-colonial Algeria* (London: I.B. Tauris, 2018). The term "Kabyle" was sometimes loosely applied to Moroccan Amazigh tribes as well, though in this case inaccurately, as the Rehamna are Arab.

40 Nissim Falcon, May 5, 1907, Maroc: VII.B.: déclassé, Archives of the AIU, Paris, France.

41 Bubeker to Lowther, June 5, 1907, FO413/45, Archives of the Public Record Office (hereafter PRO), London, England.

42 Lennox to Madden, May 6, 1907, FO413/45, Archives of the PRO, London, England.

43 Katz, *Murder in Marrakech*, 114.

44 Mohammed Kenbib, "Fez Riots (1912)." *Encyclopedia of Jews in the Islamic World Online*. Accessed October 16, 2018.

45 Ibid.

46 Mohammed Kenbib, "Fez Riots (1912)." *Encyclopedia of Jews in the Islamic World Online*. Accessed October 16, 2018.

47 Ibid., for a detailed account of the events by an eyewitness, see Vidal Serfaty, "Le 'Tritl' (saccage) de Fès en 1912," *Etsi, Revue de Genealogie et d'Histoire Sefarades* 8, no. 28 (2004).

48 Joseph Tedghi, "Fez," *Encyclopedia of Jews in the Islamic World Online*. Accessed October 16, 2018.

49 Jessica Marglin, "Tetouan." *Encyclopedia of Jews in the Islamic World Online*. Accessed October 16, 2018.

50 Abdelaziz Chehbar, "Jawanib min tarikh jama'at yahud Titwan. Basamat sifaradia fi fada maghribi," *Hespéris-Tamuda Special Edition: Jews of Morocco and the Maghreb: History and Historiography* 2 (2016): 316.

51 A.B. Yehoshua, "Beyond Folklore: The Identity of the Sephardic Jew," *Quaderns de la Mediterrània* 14 (2010): 151–152.

52 Chehbar, "Jawanib min tarikh jama'at yahud Titwan," 324.

53 In the words of the nineteenth-century Moroccan historian al-Nasiri: "A tumult broke out in the town, ... the hand of the mob stretched out to plunder, and even [normal] people took off the cloak of decency ... People of the jabal [Rif], and the Arabs, and the riffraff began to pillage and steal; they broke down the doors of the houses and the shops ... keeping at it the whole night until the morning." Al-Nasiri, *Kitab al-istiqsa* (Casablanca: Manshurat wizarat al-thaqafah wa-l-ittisal, 2001), quoted in Miller, *History of Modern Morocco*, 25, 40 fn25.

54 Chehbar, "Jawanib min tarikh jama'at yahud Titwan," 334. Note that this is a common trope in about Jews in the Islamic world and elsewhere, more typically utilized by the invaded rather than the invader in order to reveal Jews' supposed treachery.

55 An earlier *Purim de los Cristianos* dating from the sixteenth-century "Battle of the Three Kings" reflected an earlier attitude toward Spain. It was made by the Jews of Ksar al-Kabir in commemoration of the Moroccan victory that saved them from having to return to Spanish suzerainty and the Inquisition.

56 Jessica Marglin, "Tetouan." *Encyclopedia of Jews in the Islamic World Online.* Accessed October 16, 2018.
57 Juan Bautista Vilar, *Tetuán en el resurgimiento judio contemporaneo, 1850–1870* (Caracas: Asociación Israelita de Venezuela & Centro de Estudios Sefardíes de Caracas, 1985).
58 Susan Gilson Miller, "Kippur on the Amazon: Jewish Emigration from Northern Morocco in the Late Nineteenth Century," in *Sephardi and Middle Eastern Jewries. History and Culture in the Modern Era*, ed. Harvey E. Goldberg (Bloomington: Indiana University Press, 1996), 196.
59 Mevliyar Er, "Abd-el-Krim al-Khattabi: The Unknown Mentor of Che Guevara," *Terrorism and Political Violence* 29, no. 1 (2017): 144.
60 Jamaâ Baïda, "The Emigration of Moroccan Jews 1948–1956," in *Jewish Culture and Society in North Africa*, 323.
61 Abdelkrim admonished: "Above all, do not do anything. This war cannot be lost, for there are two possibilities: we are defeated by the tiny Jewish state, and we will be the laughing stock of the world; or we win, and we will have the whole world against us. So what to do? Let the Jews colonize the Palestinians. We will be dealing with a classic colonial situation, and the Palestinians will liberate themselves, as Moroccans, Tunisians and Algerians will one day free themselves." "Historical Figures: Morocco," Amazigh World, North America, 2002. Accessed March 26, 2018.
62 Similar naming patterns can be seen in Morocco's other *mellah*-s. Street names in Moroccan cities were commonly known but not marked prior to the colonial period. Under the Protectorate, many streets (and whole towns) were given European names and signage. With Moroccan independence, the nationalists removed the colonial street signs and replaced them with their own. In recent years, many of the earlier Jewish names have been restored and indicated with signage.
63 For a discussion of French colonial policy, see Raymond F. Betts, *Assimilation and Association in French Colonial Theory, 1890–1914* (Lincoln: University of Nebraska Press, 2005).
64 Given the lack of checks on a rural *qa'id-*'s power, an abusive one could be disastrous for Jews, who would have to flee to the nearest capital for help. Such was the case in Demnat and N'tifa in the mid-1890s and Taroudant in 1909. In Asni in 1914, it was the Jews' own *shaykh al-yahud* who was the source of the abuse and whom the local Jews implored the makhzan to remove: Raphael Danon, n/d 1914, Maroc: VII.B:1852/2, Archives of the AIU, Paris, France.
65 Ranger, "Connexions between 'Primary Resistance' Movements and Modern Mass Nationalism in East and Central Africa: II," 631.
66 For further explanation of this phenomenon, see Halstead, *Rebirth of a Nation*, 172–174.

67 The document mentions "Israélites" five times, once in the context of secondary education and the special role of the AIU, the other four twinned with "Muslims" in the context of Jewish representation on proposed councils and chambers of commerce, etc. The word "Arab" appears thirty-nine times. Plan de réformes marocaines. Élaboré et présenté à S.M. le Sultan, au Gouvernement de la République française et à la Résidence Générale au Maroc par le Comité d'Action Marocaine, December 1934, Archives of Centre Mohamed Hassan Ouazzani pour la démocratie et le développement humain. http://mohamedhassanouazzani.org/plan-de-reformes-marocaines/. Accessed March 28, 2018.

68 Allal al-Fassi, *The Independence Movements in Arab North Africa*, trans. Hazem Zaki Nuseibeh (Washington, DC: American Council of Learned Societies, 1954), 218.

69 Yaron Tsur, "Morocco 1912–1956," *Encyclopedia of Jews in the Islamic World Online*. Accessed October 16, 2018.

70 Michael Laskier, *North African Jewry in the Twentieth Century: The Jews of Morocco, Tunisia, and Algeria* (New York: New York University Press, 1994), 170.

71 I have taken that question up elsewhere. See Gottreich, "Historicizing the Concept of the Arab Jew."

72 "Divinity School Members Protest Verdict on Baha'i," *The Harvard Crimson*, January 18, 1963. The Moroccan Supreme Court overturned their verdict in November that year under international (particularly American) pressure.

73 David Hart argues that nationalists' revolt against Berber *dahir* was primarily intended as a defense of Islam and not a gesture of inclusion toward the Imazighen, whom the nationalists still viewed as "illiterate and boorish tribal rustics." David M. Hart, "The Berber Dahir of 1930 in Colonial Morocco: Then and Now (1930–1996)," *The Journal of North African Studies* 2, no. 2 (1997): 18.

74 Mohammed Kenbib, "Wifaq, al-," *Encyclopedia of Jews in the Islamic World Online*. Accessed October 16, 2018.

75 Marc Sabbah, "La responsabilité des notables," *al-istiqlal*, July 13, 1956, quoted in Laskier, *North African Jewry in the Twentieth Century*, 189–190.

76 Translation by Alma Heckman. I am grateful to Daniel Schroeter for sharing this document with me.

77 Marc Sabbah and David Azoulay, "Regarding the World Jewish Congress Reunion," *a-'Alam*, September 15, 1961 [Arabic].

78 Laskier, *North African Jewry in the Twentieth Century*, 215–216.

79 "Communique by Patriotic Jews," *al-Tahrir*, February 17, 1961.

80 *Le Monde*, September 8, 1955, quoted in Laskier, *North African Jewry in the Twentieth Century*, 171.

81 Laskier, *North African Jewry in the Twentieth Century*, 171.

82 Baïda, "Emigration of Moroccan Jews," 326.

83 Laskier, *North African Jewry in the Twentieth Century*, 99.

84 Baïda, "Emigration of Moroccan Jews," 328.
85 "Jewish Leaders in Morocco Protest Minister's Statement on Jews," *Jewish Telegraphic Agency*, August 31, 1962.
86 *Jewish Telegraphic Agency*, January 20, 1960.
87 The sinking of the Pisces is a pivotal event in the 2008 Moroccan film *Goodbye Mothers*, directed by Mohamed Ismail. Casablanca: Maya Films, 2007. The film depicts the difficult decision of a Jewish family from Casablanca to emigrate to Israel in the early 1960s. The father leaves in advance of his wife and children but dies in the shipwreck, after which the mother quickly succumbs to illness. The orphaned brother and sister are then adopted by the father's Muslim associates, symbolically depicting the embrace of Jews by the Moroccan nation. For a discussion of how Jews are depicted in Moroccan cinema, see Aomar Boum and Oren Kosansky, "The 'Jewish Question' in Post-colonial Moroccan Cinema," *International Journal of Middle East Studies* 44, no. 3 (2012): 421–442.
88 Marechal Hubert Lyautey, "Le Sionisme au Maroc," August 8, 1924, MA17-40: 778, Archives du Ministère des Affaires Étrangères, Paris, France.
89 Zvi Yehuda, "Zionist Activity in Southern Morocco: 1919–1923," *Revue des études juives* 119, no. 4 (1985): 365–366.
90 Ibid., 365.
91 Yaron Tsur, "Morocco 1912–1956," *Encyclopedia of Jews in the Islamic World Online*. Accessed October 16, 2018.
92 The AIU opened an agricultural school in Marrakech in 1936, but they expected its graduates to manage farms owned by colonial settlers in Morocco, not work on *kibbutzim* in Israel.
93 Yaron Tsur, "l'Avenir Illustré (Casablanca)." *Encyclopedia of Jews in the Islamic World Online*. Accessed October 16, 2018. For a fuller treatment of the Jewish press in Morocco, see Pierre Cohen, *la Presse Juive Editee au Maroc, 1870–1963* (Rabat: Editions Bouregreg, 2007).
94 *Jewish Telegraphic Agency*, September 21, 1961.
95 Mohammed Kenbib, "Moroccan Jews and the Vichy Regime, 1940–1942," *The Journal of North African Studies* 19, no. 4 (2014): 545.
96 Mohammed Hatimi and Aomar Boum, "Blessing of the Bled: Rural Moroccan Jewry during World War II," in Aomar Boum and Sarah Abraveya Stein, *The Holocaust and North Africa*, Stanford: Stanford University Press, 2019, 113–131.
97 Kenbib, "Moroccan Jews and the Vichy Regime," 540–553.
98 Daniel Schroeter, "Between Metropole and French North Africa: Vichy's Anti-Semitic Legislation and Colonialism's Racial Hierarchies," in Boum and Stein, *The Holocaust and North Africa*, pp. 19–49.
99 Kenbib, "Moroccan Jews and the Vichy Regime," 547.

100 Ethan Katz, "Mediterranean Resisters: José Aboulker and the Jewish Uprising That Helped Win the War" (paper presented at the conference: On the Margins of the Holocaust: Jews, Muslims, and Colonialism in North Africa during the Second World War, Convened by the United States Holocaust Memorial Museum, Center for Jewish Studies, and Center for Near Eastern Studies, University of California, Los Angeles (UCLA), Los Angeles, California. November 15–16, 2015)

101 Alma Rachel Heckman, "Multivariable Casablanca: Vichy Law, Jewish Diversity, and the Moroccan Communist Party," *Hespéris-Tamuda Special Issue, Jews of Morocco and the Maghreb: History and Historiography* LI, no. 3 (2016): 16.

102 Orit Bashkin, *New Babylonians: A History of Jews in Modern Iraq* (Stanford: Stanford University Press, 2012), 141–182. See also Joel Beinin, *The Dispersion of Egyptian Jewry: Culture, Politics, and the Formation of a Modern Diaspora* (Berkeley: University of California Press, 1998), 142.

103 Heckman, "Radical Nationalists," 249.

104 Michael Laskier, "Jewish Emigration from Morocco to Israel: Government Policies and the Position of International Jewish Organizations, 1949–1956," *Middle Eastern Studies* 25, no. 3 (1989): 323.

105 Ibid., 331.

106 Ibid., 324.

107 Mohammed Hatimi, "Jewish Moroccan Organizations and the Difficult Choice between the Zionist Call and the Challenge of an Independent Morocco 1947–1961" (PhD dissertation, Mohammed V University of Rabat, 2007) [Arabic]. Frédéric Abécassis, "Questions about Jewish Migrations from Morocco: 'Operation Mural' (Summer 1961): Return from Diaspora or Formation of a New Diaspora?" (paper presented at Questions about Jewish Migrations from Morocco, Jerusalem, Israel, 2013), 73–82.

108 Baïda "Emigration of Moroccan Jews," 330.

109 Mark A. Tessler and Linda L. Hawkins, "The Political Culture of Jews in Tunisia and Morocco," *International Journal of Middle East Studies* 11, no. 1 (1980): 62.

110 Michael Laskier, *The Alliance Israélite Universelle and the Jewish Communities of Morocco, 1862–1962* (Albany: State University of New York Press, 1984), 340–342.

111 For a discussion of the Moroccan Jewish diaspora and its relationship to Morocco, see Oren Kosansky, "The Real Morocco Itself: Jewish Saint Pilgrimage, Hybridity, and the Idea of the Moroccan Nation," in *Jewish Culture and Society*, eds. Gottreich and Schroeter, 341.

112 According to a 1923 report from the AIU, "the underlying reasons for these departures appear to be above all economic." See "An Alliance Report on a Wave of 'Aliya from Fez to Palestine with Suggestions on How to Stem the Tide," in Norman Stillman, *Jews of Arab Lands in Modern Times* (Philadelphia: Jewish Publication Society of America, 1991), 316.

113 Aomar Boum, "From 'Little Jerusalems' to the Promised Land: Zionism, Moroccan Nationalism, and Rural Jewish Emigration," *The Journal of North African Studies* 15, no. 1 (2010): 51–69.
114 Emanuela Trevisan Semi, "Double Trauma and Manifold Narratives: Jews' and Muslims' Representations of the Departure of Moroccan Jews in the 1950s and 1960s," *Journal of Modern Jewish Studies* 9, no. 1 (2010): 107–125. Abécassis, "Questions about Jewish Migrations from Morocco," 73–82.
115 Miller, *A History of Modern Morocco*, 159.
116 Baïda, "The Emigration of Moroccan Jews," 321.
117 Aomar Boum, *Memories of Absence : How Muslims Remember Jews in Morocco* (Redwood City, CA: Stanford University Press, 2014), 140–142.
118 This is the narrative thrust of most depictions of the Moroccan Jewish exodus in popular culture, as in the above-mentioned 2007 film *Goodbye Mothers*, as well as the 2007 drama-comedy *Where Are You Going, Moshe?* directed by Hassan Benjelloun. Morocco: Filmoption International, 2007.
119 Chehbar, "Jawanib min tarikh jamaat yahud Titwan," 334–336. The original author of the story is given as Ishaq b. Shamwil (Isaac son of Samuel).
120 Ella Shohat, *Taboo Memories, Diasporic Voices* (Durham: Duke University Press, 2006), 337.
121 Robert Watson, "Between Liberation(s) and Occupation(s): Reconsidering the Emergence of Maghreb Jewish Communism, 1942–1945," *Journal of Modern Jewish Studies* 13, no. 3 (2014): 382.
122 Heckman, "Radical Nationalists," 102.
123 Zreik, Raef, "When Does the Settler Become a Native? (with Apologies to Mamdani)," *Constellations* 23, no. 3 (2016).
124 Its academic theorists include Ammiel Alcalay, Yehouda Shenhav, Lital Levy, and Ella Shohat; among Moroccan Jews specifically, both Gil Anidjar and Sami Shalom Chetrit have written extensively on the topic.
125 Nationalists in the cultural sense rather than the political/national sense, that is.

Conclusion

1 For example, in 2013 the *makhzan* revoked a pardon that it had given to a Spanish man serving time in prison for abusing Moroccan children when his early release sparked mass protests.
2 GDP growth in Morocco during the last quarter of 2017 was just below 4 percent: "Morocco GDP Growth Rate," *Trading Economics*, 2018, https://tradingeconomics.com/morocco/gdp-growth. Accessed September 17, 2018.
3 Ella Shohat, *On the Arab-Jew, Palestine, and Other Displacements* (London: Pluto Press, 2017), 56–59.

4 Aomar Boum, "From '*Little Jerusalems*' to the Promised Land: Zionism, Moroccan Nationalism and Rural Jewish Emigration," *The Journal of North African Studies* 15, no. 1 (2010): 51–69.

5 Further aggravating the situation was the fact that a big wave of immigrants from the Soviet Union arrived in Israel soon thereafter and were given exactly the opposite reception that Moroccan Jews had received. Israeli Prime Minister Golda Meir, who had once referred to Moroccan Jews as "black animals" [Yid., *chaye shvartze*], continued to fan the flames of *mizrahi* frustration: she applauded these "real Jews" from Russia who would "provide us with heroes" and ordered her government to give them special benefits.

6 Gabbay was born in Israel but his parents are from Casablanca. He is preceded in this position by another Moroccan Jew, Amir Peretz, who is originally from Boujad. Despite these gains, anti-Moroccan racism is nonetheless still apparent in the ranks of the Labor party, as seen in the remarks of artist and commentator Yair Garbuz at a left-wing rally in 2015, when he claimed that Israel was being controlled by "amulet-kissers, idol-worshippers and people who prostrate themselves at the graves of saints." Jonathan Lis, "Artist's 'Idol-worshippers' Remarks at anti-Netanyahu Rally Draw Ire," *Haaretz*, March 9, 2015.

7 France is also home to Europe's largest Muslim population, numbering 5.7 million people.

8 Michel Abitbol, "The Integration of North African Jews in France," *Yale French Studies*, no. 85, Discourses of Jewish Identity in Twentieth-century France (1994): 248–261.

9 Fear of anti-Semitism and Israel's expanding economy have inspired a wave of emigration from France to Israel by Jews of Maghribi origin in recent years. See Peter Beaumont, "Why Are French Jews Heading to Israel in Such Numbers?" *The Guardian*, January 16, 2015. For a detailed discussion of Jewish immigration to France from North Africa and the resulting reformulation of Muslim-Jewish relations in this new context, see two outstanding recent works on the subject: Ethan B. Katz, *The Burdens of Brotherhood: Jews and Muslims from North Africa to France* (Cambridge, MA: Harvard University Press, 2015), and Maud Mandel, *Muslims and Jews in France: History of a Conflict* (Princeton, NJ: Princeton University Press, 2014).

10 Susan Gilson Miller, "Kippur on the Amazon: Jewish Emigration from Northern Morocco in the Late Nineteenth," in Goldberg, ed., *Sephardi and Middle Eastern Jewries*, 190–209.

11 "Moroccan Jews," *Wikipedia*. Accessed March 7, 2019.

12 *United States Census*, April 1, 2010.

13 Aomar Boum, "The Mellahs of Los Angeles: A Moroccan Jewish Community in an American Urban Space," *AJS Perspectives* (Fall 2017).

14 N/A, *Rehabilitation of the Jewish Cemeteries of Morocco: The Houses of Life* (Casablanca, 2015). Published under the High Patronage of His Majesty Mohammed VI, King of Morocco.
15 A less official museum with a significant Jewish ethnographic collection exists in the village of Akka. See Aomar Boum, "The Plastic Eye: The Politics of Jewish Representation in Moroccan Museums," *Ethnos* 75, no. 1 (2010): 49–77.
16 "Phosphate: Morocco's White Gold—Businessweek" *Bloomberg Businessweek*, November 4, 2010.
17 The claim was recently reiterated on Aljazeera in an interview with Maria Carrion, the director of the fi-Sahara film festival: Hannah McNeish, "Western Sahara's Struggle for Freedom Cut Off by a Wall," *Aljazeera*, June 4, 2015.
18 See Cnaan Liphshiz, "Moroccan Jews Protest UN Stand on 'Occupied' Western Sahara," *The Forward*, May 9, 2016. The World Jewish Congress sent an official delegation to Morocco just a month before Ban Ki-Moon made his comments. They met with officials including the prime minister and made a public pronouncement of their support for the Moroccan position on the Western Sahara: "American Jewish Committee Slams Ban Ki-moon's Ignorance of Moroccan History," *Morocco World News*, March 17, 2016.
19 "Moroccan Jews Reportedly Protest UN View on 'Occupied' Sahara," *Jewish Telegraphic Agency*, May 9, 2016.
20 Ibid. "Moroccan Jews Protest UN Stand on 'Occupied' Western Sahara," *The Forward*, April 3, 2018.
21 Mois Benarroch, *Gates to Tangier*, trans. Sara Maria Hasbun (Babelcube Inc., 2017).
22 The law was applied in 2010 when a group of Christian charity workers were deported from Morocco after being accused of proselytizing among the children in an orphanage they ran in the Middle Atlas town of Ain Leuh.
23 The full text of the Marrakech Declaration is available in English here: "Marrakesh Declaration" Religions for Peace, January 25–27, 2019, http://www.marrakeshdeclaration.org/files/Bismilah-2-ENG.pdf. Accessed September 17, 2019.
24 Emanuela Trevisan Semi, "Double Trauma and Manifold Narratives: Jews' and Muslims' Representations of the Departure of Moroccan Jews in the 1950s and 1960s," *Journal of Modern Jewish Studies* 9, no. 1 (2010): 107–125.
25 Aomar Boum, *Memories of Absence: How Muslims Remember Jews in Morocco* (Stanford: Stanford University Press, 2014), 13–14.
26 Ibid., 158.
27 The novels in Arabic are: Mohamed Ezz el-Din el-Tazi, *Ana al-mansi* (Casablanca: The Moroccan Cultural Center, 2015); Hassan Aourid, *Cintra]* (Rabat: Matba'at al-ma'arif al-jadida, 2016); Idris al-Malayani, *Cazanfa* (Tangier: Dar al-ayn, 2016); Hassan Riyad, *Zawiyat al-imyan* (Casablanca: Ministry of Culture Publications, 2009); Ahmed al-Sabki, *Bab al-sha'aba* (Rabat: Top Press Publications, 2011). The

novel in French is El Hassane Aït Moh, *Le Captif de Mabrouka* (Paris: Editions L'Harmattan, 2010).

28 Morocco is not the only setting in which Muslim filmmakers are tackling this knotty theme. Nadia Kamel's *Salata Baladi* [*An Egyptian Salad*] recounts the story of her mother's rediscovered Jewish roots in Egypt and her decision to visit her cousin in Tel Aviv (Women Make Movies, 2008). *Forget Baghdad* by "Samir" is inspired by the experiences of the Shi'i filmmaker's father in the Iraqi communist party with his many Jewish comrades (Germany/Switzerland, 2003). Jewish-themed films by Muslim filmmakers have also appeared in Tunisia: *A Summer in La Goulette: Un été à La Goulette* (directed by Férid Boughedir. Tunisia: Marsa Films, 1996); and in Iran *The Jews of Iran* (directed by Ramin Farahani. Netherlands: NIK Media, 2005).

29 "Morocco's little idyll of Jewish-Muslim coexistence," *The Economist*, November 2, 2017. For an astute study of Israeli tourism in Morocco, see André Lévy, *Return to Casablanca: Jews, Muslims, and an Israeli Anthropologist* (Chicago: University of Chicago Press, 2015).

30 They include filmmakers like Kathy Wazana, Simone Bitton, and Meital Abicasis. The same can be said of the Sami Shalom Chetrit film *Come, Mother* in which Chetrit and his aging mother search for her classmates from her rural Moroccan AIU class of 60 years earlier. *Come Mother: Azi Ayima*. Directed by Sami Shalom Chetrit. Israel, 2010.

31 To give credit where it is due, Egyptian television did an about-face during in 2015, when it screened "The Jewish Quarter," a Ramadan series that featured respectful portrayals of Jews engaged in religious rituals and normal life. See "For Egypt, TV Show's Shocking Twist Is Its Sympathetic Jews," *The New York Times*, June 23, 2015.

32 Rothberg applies a postcolonial framework to the memory of the Holocaust, bringing to bear histories other than the Jewish or European ones. See Michael Rothberg, *Multidirectional Memory: Remembering the Holocaust in the Age of Decolonization* (Stanford: Stanford University Press, 2009).

33 Daniel Schroeter and Yossi Chetrit, "Emancipation and Its Discontents," *Jewish Social Studies* 13, no. 1 (2006): 198.

Bibliography

Abdel-Halim, Abou Mohammed Salah b. *Roudh el-kartas: Histoire des souverains du Maghreb (Espagne et Maroc) et annales de la ville de Fès*. Translated by Auguste Beaumier. Paris: Imprimerie Impériale, 1860.

Abisrur, Mordechai. *Les Daggatoun: Tribu d'origine juive demeurant dans le désert du Sahara*. Paris: Bulletin AIU, 1880.

Abitbol, Michel. *Témoins et acteurs: les Corcos et l'Histoire du Maroc contemporain*. Jerusalem: Institut Ben Zvi, 1977.

Abou Fadl, Khaled. "Islamic Law and Muslim Minorities: The Juristic Discourse on Muslim Minorities from 8th to 17th Century CE/2nd to 11th Hijrah." *Islamic Law and Society* 1, no. 2 (1994): 141–187.

Abun-Nasr, Jamil. "The Salafiyya Movement in Morocco: The Religious Bases of the Moroccan Nationalist Movement." In *Social Change: The Colonial Situation*, edited by Immanuel Wallerstein, 489–502. New York, London and Sydney: John Wiley & Sons, 1966.

Achcar, Gilbert. *The Arabs and the Holocaust: The Arab-Israeli War of Narratives*. New York: Holt and Co., 2009.

Adang, Camilla. "Ibn Hazm's Criticism of Some 'Judaizing' Tendencies." In *Medieval and Modern Perspectives on Muslim-Jewish Relations*, edited by Ronald L. Netter, 1–15. Luxembourg: Harwood Academic Publishers, 1995.

Aescoly, A. Z. "A Flandrian Newsletter Concerning the Sabbatean Movement." In *Dinaburg Jubilee Volume* [Hebrew], edited by Yitzhak Baer, Y. Guttman, and M. Shovah, 215–236. Jerusalem: Hotsa'at Bet-hamidrash lemorim ha'ivri biyrushalayim, 1949.

Africanus, Leo. *Description de l'Afrique*. Translated and edited by A. Epaulard, 2 vols. Paris: Librairie d'Amérique et d'Orient, 1956.

Al-Abbassi, Ali Bey, a.k.a. Domènec Badia y Leblich. *Travels of Ali Bey in Morocco, Tripoli, Cyprus, Egypt, Arabia, Syria, and Turkey, between the Years 1803 and 1807*. London: Longman, Hurst, Rees, Orme, and Brown, 1816.

Al-Bakri, Abu Ubayd. "The Book of Routes and Realms." In *Corpus of Early Arabic Sources for West Africa*, edited by Nehemia Levtzion and J. F. P. Hopkins, 62–87. Princeton: Marcus Weiner publishers, 2000.

Alcalay, Ammiel. *After Jews and Arabs: Remaking Levantine Culture*. Minneapolis: University of Minnesota Press, 1992.

al-Hasani, Ahmad Ibn Muhammad ibn Ajibah. *Iqaz al-himam fi sharh al-hikam*. Cairo: Mustafa al-Babi al-Halabi wa-Awladuhu, 1961.

Al-Hasani, Ahmad. *Iqaz al-himam fi sharh al-hikam*. Cairo: Mustafa al-Babi al-Halabi wa-Awladuhu, 1961.

Al-Ifrani, Muhammed al-Saghir. *Nuzhat al-hadi bi-akhbar li-muluk al-qarn al-hadi*. Fez, n.p., c. 1890.

Al-Kharashi, Muhammad b. 'Abdullah. *Commentary of Al-Kharashi on the Mukhtasar of Khalil b. Ishaq*, vol. 2. Cairo, 1900–01.

Al-Marrakushi, Muhyi al-Din. *Kitab al-mu'jib fi talkhis akhbar al-maghrib*. Translated and edited by Reinhart Pieter Anne Dozy. Leiden: E.J. Brill, 1881.

Al-Nasiri, Ahmad b. Khaled. *Kitab al-istiqsa*. Casablanca: Manshurat wizarat al-thaqafa wa-l-ittisal, 2001.

Al-Qadiri, Muhammad. *Nashr al-mathani*. Edited and translated by Norman Cigar. London: Oxford University Press, 1981.

Al-Turtushi, Abu Bakr. *Siraj al-muluk*. Cairo, Egypt: *Matba'at al-khayriya*, 1872, 229–230.

Al-Zayyani, Ahmad. *al-Turjuman al-mu'rib 'an duwal al-mashriq wa-l-maghrib*. Edited and translated by O. Houdas. Paris: n.p., 1886.

Amster, Ellen. "The Many Deaths of Dr. Emile Mauchamp: Medicine, Technology, and Popular Politics in Pre-Protectorate Morocco, 1877–1912." *International Journal of Middle East Studies* 36, no. 3 (2004): 409–428.

Amster, Ellen. "Medicine and the Saints: Science, Islam, and the Colonial Encounter in Morocco." *Social History of Medicine: The Journal of the Society for the Social History of Medicine* 27, no. 3 (2014): 604–606.

Anidjar, Gil. *The Jew, the Arab: A History of the Enemy*. Stanford: Stanford University Press, 2003.

Assaraf, Robert. *Eléments de l'histoire des juifs du Meknès*. Rabat: Centre de recherche sur les Juifs du Maroc, 2010.

Astren, Fred. "Rereading the Muslim Sources: Jewish History in the Early Islamic Period." *Jerusalem Studies in Arabic and Islam* 35 (2009): 83–130.

Aubin, Eugene. *Morocco of Today*. London: J.M. Dent & Co., 1906.

Avineri, Shlomo. *The Making of Modern Zionism*. New York: Basic Books, 1981.

Baer, Marc. *Honored by the Glory of Islam*. Oxford: Oxford University Press, 2008.

Baïda, Jamaâ. "The Emigration of Moroccan Jews 1948–1956." In *Rethinking Jewish Culture and Society in North Africa*, edited by Emily Benichou Gottreich and Daniel J. Schroeter, 321–333. Bloomington: Indiana University Press, 2011.

Baïda, Jamaâ. *La presse marocaine d'expression francaise, des origines à 1956*. Rabat: Publications de la Faculté des Lettres et des Sciences Humaines, 1996.

Bar-Asher, Meir. "Le Statut des Juifs chez les Malikites du Maroc." In *Perception et Réalités au Maroc: Relations Judéo-Musulmans*, edited by Michel Abitbol, 259–274. Paris: CRJM, 1998.

Barber, Benjamin. *Jihad vs. McWorld*. New York: Ballantine Books, 1996.

Bashkin, Orit. *New Babylonians: A History of Jews in Modern Iraq*. Stanford: Stanford University Press, 2012.

Bazzaz, Sahar. *Forgotten Saints: History, Power, and Politics in the Making of Modern Morocco.* Cambridge: Center for Middle Eastern Studies, Harvard University, 2010.

Beauclerk, G. R. *A Journey to Morocco in 1826.* London: n.p., 1828.

Beaumier, Auguste. "Premier établissement des Israélites à Tombouctou." *Bulletin de la Société de Géographie* 5, no. 19 (1870): 345–370.

Beinin, Joel. *The Dispersion of Egyptian Jewry: Culture, Politics, and the Formation of a Modern Diaspora.* Berkeley: University of California Press, 1998.

Ben Srhir, Khalid. "Wathiqa ghayr munshura 'an millah Murrakush fi-l-qarn al-tasi' 'ashr." *Hespéris-Tamuda* 35, no. 2 (1997): 25–71.

Ben-Ami, Issachar. *Saint Veneration among the Jews of Morocco.* Detroit: Wayne State University Press, 1998.

Bénech, José. *Marrakech: Explication d'un mellah.* Paris: H. Rohr, 1940.

Benhlal, Mohamed. *Le college d'Azrou: Une elite berbère civile et militaire au Maroc (1927–1959).* Paris: Éditions Karthala, 2005.

Benjamin, Joseph. *Eight Years in Asia and Africa, from 1846–1855.* Hanover: self-published, 1863.

Benkheira, Mohammed Hocine. "Hammam, nudité et ordre moral dans l'islam médiéval." *Revue de l'histoire des religion* 224, no. 3 (2007): 319–371.

Bennison, Amira K. "Almohad Tawhid and Its Implications for Religious Difference." *Journal of Medieval Iberian Studies* 2, no. 2 (2010): 195–216.

Boum, Aomar. "From 'Little Jerusalems' to the Promised Land: Zionism, Moroccan Nationalism, and Rural Jewish Emigration." *The Journal of North African Studies* 15, no. 1 (2010): 51–69.

Boum, Aomar. "The Mellahs of Los Angeles: A Moroccan Jewish Community in an American Urban Space." *AJS Perspectives* (Fall 2017), 42–43.

Boum, Aomar. *Memories of Absence: How Muslims Remember Jews in Morocco.* Stanford: Stanford University Press, 2013.

Boum, Aomar. "Schooling in the Bled: Jewish Education and the Alliance Israélite Universelle in Southern Rural Morocco, 1830–1962." *Journal of Jewish Identities* 3, no. 1 (2010), 1–24.

Boum, Aomar and Oren Kosansky. "The 'Jewish Question' in Post-colonial Moroccan Cinema." *International Journal of Middle East Studies* 44, no. 3 (2012): 421–442.

Bowie, Leland Louis. "The Protégé System in Morocco: 1880—1904," PhD dissertation, Ohio State University, 1970.

Boyarin, Jonathan and Daniel Boyarin. *Powers of Diaspora: Two Essays on the Importance of Jewish Culture.* Minneapolis: University of Minnesota Press, 2002.

Brett, Michael. "The Islamisation of Morocco from the Arabs to the Almoravids." In *Ibn Khaldun and the Medieval Maghrib*, edited by Michael Brett, 57–71. London: Ashgate, 1999.

Brett, Michael and Elizabeth Fentress. *The Berbers.* Oxford: Blackwell, 1996.

Brown, L. Carl and Matthew Gordon, eds. *Franco-Arab Encounters.* Beirut: AUB Press, 1996.

Brunot, Louis and Elie Malka. *Textes Judéo-Arabes de Fès: Textes, Transcription, Traduction, Annotée*. Rabat: Ecole du Livre, 1939.

Burel, Antoine. *La Mission du Capitaine Burel au Maroc en 1808* (Paris: Arts et métiers graphiques, 1953).

Burke, Edmund. "Pan-Islam and Moroccan Resistance to French Colonial Penetration, 1900–1912." *The Journal of African History* 13, no. 1 (1972): 97–118.

Burke, Edmund. *Prelude to Protectorate in Morocco*. Chicago: University of Chicago Press, 1976.

Campos, Michelle. *Ottoman Brothers: Muslims, Christians, and Jews in Early Twentieth-century Palestine*. Stanford: Stanford University Press, 2010.

Chahbar, Abdelaziz. "Jawanib min tarikh jama'at yahud Titwan. Basamat sifaradia fi fada maghribi." *Hespéris-Tamuda Special Edition: Jews of Morocco and the Maghreb: History and Historiography* 2 (2016): 313–341.

Chénier, Louis de. *The Present State of the Empire of Morocco*. vol. 1. London: G.G.J. and J. Robinson, 1788.

Chetrit, Joseph. "Music and Poetry as a Shared Cultural Space for Muslims and Jews in Morocco." In *Studies in the History and Culture of North African Judaism*, edited by Moshe Bar-Asher and Steven D. Fraade, 65–103. New Haven: Yale Program in Judaic Studies, 2011.

Chetrit, Sami Shalom. *Intra-Jewish Conflict in Israel: White Jews, Black Jews*. Abingdon, UK: Routledge, 2013.

Cohen, Julia. *Becoming Ottomans: Sephardi Jews and Imperial Citizenship in the Modern Era*. New York: Oxford University Press, 2014.

Cohen, Mark. *Under Crescent and Cross*. Princeton, NJ: Princeton University Press, 1994.

Cohen, Pierre. *La Presse Juive éditée au Maroc, 1870–1963*. Rabat: Editions et Impressions Bouregreg Communication, 2007.

Cohen, Shaye. *The Beginnings of Jewishness: Boundaries, Varieties, Uncertainties*. Berkeley and Los Angeles: University of California Press, 1999.

Cooper, Frederick. *Colonialism in Question: Theory, Knowledge, History*. Berkeley: University of California Press, 2005.

Corcos, David. "The Jews of Morocco under the Marinides." *The Jewish Quarterly Review* 54, no. 4 (1964): 271–287.

Cornell, Vincent. *The Realm of the Saint: Power and Authority in Moroccan Sufism*. Austin: University of Texas Press, 1998.

Cory, Stephen. "Breaking the Khaldunian Cycle?: The Rise of Sharifianism and the Basis for Legitimacy in Early Modern Morocco." *Journal of North African Studies* 13, no. 3 (2008): 371–387.

Dakhliya, Jocelyn. "Dans la mouvance de prince: La Symbolique du pouvoir itinérant au Maghreb." *Annales ESC* 3 (May–June 1988): 735–760.

Davidson, John. *Notes Taken during Travels*. London: J. L. Cox and Sons, 1839.

De Castries, Henri and Pierre de Cenival, eds. *Les sources inédites de l'histoire du Maroc: archives et Bibliothèques des Pays-Bas*, vol. 2. Paris: P. Geunthner, 1934–1953.

De Cenival, Pierre. "L'église chrétienne de Marrakech au XIIIe siècle." *Hespéris: Archives berbères et bulletin de l'Institut des hautes-études Morocaines* 7 (1927): 69–83.

Deshen, Shlomo. *Mellah Society: Jewish Community Life in Sherifian Morocco*. Chicago: University of Chicago Press, 1989.

Donner, Fred M. *Muhammad and the Believers*. Cambridge: Harvard University Press, 2012.

Drague, Georges. *Esquisse d'histoire religieuse au maroc*. Paris: Peyronnet, 1951.

Eickelman, Dale. *Moroccan Islam Tradition and Society in a Pilgrimage Center*. Austin: University of Texas Press, 1981.

Elbaz, Vanessa Paloma. "*Kol b'Isha Erva*: The Silencing of Jewish Women's Oral Traditions in Morocco." In *Gender and Law in the Maghreb*, edited by Doris Gray and Nadia Sonneveld, 263–289. Cambridge: Cambridge University Press, 2017.

Elior, Rachel. "The Kabbalists of Dra" [Hebrew]. *Pèamim* 24 (1985): 36–73.

El-Mansour, Mohamed. "Moroccan Islam Observed." *The Maghreb Review* 29, nos. 1–4 (2004): 208–218.

Emon, Anver M. *Religious Pluralism and Islamic Law: Dhimmis and Others in the Empire of Law*. Oxford: Oxford University Press, 2012.

Er, Mevliyar. "Abd-el-Krim al-Khattabi: The Unknown Mentor of Che Guevara." *Terrorism and Political Violence* 29, no. 1 (2017): 137–159.

Fattal, Antoine. "How *Dhimmis* Were Judged in the Islamic World." In *Muslims and Others in Early Islamic Society*, edited by Robert Hoyland. Aldershot: Ashgate, 2004.

Fattal, Antoine. *Le statut légal des non-musulmans en pays d'islam*, 83–102. Beirut: L'imprimerie catholique, 1958.

Flamand, Pierre. *Diaspora en terre d'Islam: Les communautés israélites du sud marocain*. Casablanca: Imprimeries réunies, 1959.

Flemming, Katie. *Greece: A Jewish History*. Princeton, NJ: Princeton University Press, 2008.

Foucauld, Charles de. *Reconnaissance au Maroc, 1883–1884*. Paris: Challamel, 1888.

García-Arenal, Mercedes. *Ahmad al-Mansur: The Beginnings of Modern Morocco*. Oxford: One World, 2009.

García-Arenal, Mercedes. "Attentes messianiques au Maghreb et dans la péninsule Ibérique: du nouveau sur Sabbatai Zevi." In *Lucette Valensi à l'oeuvre: une histoire anthropologique de l'Islam méditerranéen*, edited by François Pouillon and Lucette Valensi. Paris: Editions Bouchene, 2002.

García-Arenal, Mercedes. "Imam et Mahdi: Ibn Abî Mahallî." *Revue des Mondes Musulmans et de la Méditerranée* 91–94 (2000): 157–180.

García-Arenal, Mercedes. "Jewish Converts to Islam in the Muslim West." *Israel Oriental Studies* 17 (1997): 227–248.

García-Arenal, Mercedes. "Les Bildiyyin de Fès, un Groupe de Néo-musulmans D'origine Juive." *Studia Islamica*, no. 66 (1987): 113–143.

García-Arenal, Mercedes. "Sainteté Et Pouvoir Dynastique Au Maroc: La Résistance De Fès Aux Sa'diens." *Annales. Histoire, Sciences Sociales* 45, no. 4 (1990): 1019–1042.

García-Arenal, Mercedes and Gerard Wiegers. *A Man of Three Worlds: Samuel Pallache, A Moroccan Jew in Catholic and Protestant Europe*, 225–242. Baltimore: Johns Hopkins University Press, 2003.

Geertz, Clifford. *Islam Observed: Religious Development in Morocco and Indonesia*. Chicago: University of Chicago Press, 1968.

Geertz, Clifford, Hildred Geertz, and Lawrence Rosen. *Meaning and Order in Moroccan Society: Three Essays in Cultural Analysis*. Cambridge: Cambridge University Press, 1979.

Gellner, Ernest. *Saints of the Atlas*. Ann Arbor: University of Michigan, 1969.

Goitein, Shelomo Dov. *Mediterranean Society: The Jewish Communities of the Arab World as Portrayed in the Documents of the Cairo Geniza*. Berkeley, California: University of California Press, 1967–1999.

Goldberg, Harvey E., ed. *Sephardi and Middle Eastern Jewries: History and Culture in the Modern Era*. Bloomington: Indiana University Press, 1996.

Goldenberg, Alfred. "Quand J'Étais Un 'Missionaire' de l'Alliance." *Les Cahiers de l'Alliance Israélite Universelle*, no. 208 (1984): 43–48.

Goldish, Matt. *The Sabbatean Prophets*. Cambridge, MA: Harvard University Press, 2009.

Goldsworthy, Patricia. "Images, Ideologies, and Commodities: The French Colonial Postcard Industry in Morocco." *Early Popular Visual Culture* 8, no. 2 (2010): 147–167.

Gómez-Rivas, Camilo. *Law and the Islamization of Morocco under the Almoravids: The Fatwas of Ibn Rushd al-Jadd to the Far Maghrib*. Leiden; Boston: Brill, 2015.

Gottreich, Emily. "Historicizing the Concept of Arab Jews in the Maghrib." *The Jewish Quarterly Review* 98, no. 4 (2008): 433–451.

Gottreich, Emily. *The Mellah of Marrakech: Muslim and Jewish Space in Morocco's Red City*. Bloomington: Indiana University Press, 2007.

Gottreich, Emily. "Of Messiahs and Sultans: Shabbatai Zevi and Early Modernity in Morocco." *The Journal of Modern Jewish Studies* 12, no. 2 (2013): 1–26.

Gottreich, Emily. "On the Origins of the Mellah of Marrakech." *International Journal of Middle East Studies* 35, no. 2 (2003): 287–305.

Gottreich, Emily. "Rethinking the Islamic City from the Perspective of Jewish Space." *Jewish Social Studies* 11, no. 1 (2004): 118–146.

Guillemin, Henri. *Biographie du docteur Émile Mauchamp*. Châlon-sur-Saône: E. Bertrand, 1910.

Haidara, Ismael Diadie. *Les Juifs à Tombouctou: Recueil Des Sources Écrites Relatives Au Commerce Juif À Tombouctou Au XIXe Siècle*. Bamako: Editions Donniya, 1999.

Hajji, Mohamed. *Al-zawiya al-dila'iya*. Rabat: n.p., 1988.

Hallaq, Wael. *The Origins and Evolution of Islamic Law*. Cambridge, UK: Cambridge University Press, 2005.

Halperin, David, ed. and trans., *Sabbatai Zevi: Testimonies to a Fallen Messiah*. Oxford: Litman Library of Jewish Civilization, 2007.

Halstead, John P. *Rebirth of a Nation: The Origins and Rise of Moroccan Nationalism, 1912-1944*. Cambridge: Harvard University Press, 1967.

Hannoum, Abdelmajid. *Colonial Histories, Post-colonial Memories: The Legend of the Kahina, a North African Heroine*. Portsmouth, NH: Heinemann, 2001.

Harris, Walter. *The Land of an African Sultan: Travels in Morocco, 1887, 1888, and 1889*. London: S. Low, Marston & Co., 1889.

Harris, Walter. *Morocco That Was*. Westerport: Negro Universities Press, 1970.

Hart, David M. "The Berber Dahir of 1930 in Colonial Morocco: Then and Now (1930-1996)." *The Journal of North African Studies* 2, no. 2 (1997): 11-33.

Hathaway, Jane. "The Mawza' Exile at the Juncture of Zaydi and Ottoman Messianism." *Association for Jewish Studies Review* 29, no. 1 (2005): 111-128.

Hatimi, Mohammed. "Blessing of the Bled: Rural Jewries during the World War II," in Aomar Boum and Sarah Abraveya Stein, *The Holocaust and North Africa*, Stanford: Stanford University Press, 2019, 113-131.

Hatimi, Mohammed. "al-Jama'at al-yahudiyya al-maghribiya wa-l-khiyar al-sa'b bayna nida' al-sahyuniya wa-rihan al-maghrib al-mustaqil, 1947-1961." PhD dissertation, Faculty of Letters of Sais-Fès, 2007.

Heckman, Alma Rachel. "Multivariable Casablanca: Vichy Law, Jewish Diversity, and the Moroccan Communist Party." *Hespéris-Tamuda Special Issue Jews of Morocco and the Maghreb: History and Historiography*, no. 3 (2016): 13-34.

Heckman, Alma Rachel. "Radical Nationalists: Moroccan Jewish Communists 1925-1975." PhD dissertation, University of California, Los Angeles, 2015.

Hirschberg, Zeev Haim. *A History of the Jews in North Africa*, 2 vols. Leiden: Brill, 1981.

Hirschberg, Zeev Haim. "The Problem of the Judaized Berbers." *The Journal of African History* 4, no. 3 (1963): 313-339.

Hodgson, Marshall. *The Venture of Islam. Conscience and History in a World Civilization*. Chicago: The University of Chicago Press, 1974.

Hoffman, Katherine. *We Share Walls: Language, Land, and Gender in Berber Morocco*. Malden, MA: Blackwell Pub., 2008.

Hoffman, Katherine and Susan Gilson Miller, eds. *Berbers and Others: Beyond Tribe and Nation in the Maghrib*. Bloomington and Indianapolis: Indiana University Press, 2010.

Holden, Stacy. *The Politics of Food in Modern Morocco*. Gainesville: University of Florida Press, 2009.

Hoyland, Robert. *In God's Path: The Arab Conquests and the Creation of an Islamic Empire*. Oxford: Oxford University Press, 2015.

Hunwick, John. *Jews of a Saharan Oasis: The Elimination of the Tamantit Community*. Princeton, NJ: Markus Wiener Publishers, 2006.

Iskander, John. "Devout Heretics: The Barghawata in Maghribi Historiography." *The Journal of North African Studies* 12, no. 1 (2007): 37-53.

Joffe, George. "Maghribi Islam and Islam in the Maghrib." In *African Islam and Islam in Africa: Encounters between Sufis and Islamists*, edited by Eva Evers Rosander and David Westerlund. Athens, Ohio: Ohio University Press, 1997, 55–78.

Kahn, Lily and Aaron D. Rubin, eds. *Handbook of Jewish Languages*. Leiden, Boston: Brill, 2016.

Kalmar, Ivan and Derek Penslar, eds. *Orientalism and the Jews*. Waltham, MA: Brandeis University Press, 2005.

Karo, Joseph. *Shulhan Arukh*. Venice: n.p., 1565.

Katz, Ethan. *The Burdens of Brotherhood: Jews and Muslims from North Africa to France*. Cambridge, MA: Harvard University Press, 2015.

Katz, Ethan, Lisa Moses Leff, and Maud Mandel, eds. *Colonialism and the Jews*. Bloomington: Indiana University Press, 2017.

Katz, Jonathan G. "The 1907 Mauchamp Affair and the French Civilising Mission in Morocco." *The Journal of North African Studies* 6, no. 1 (2006): 143–166.

Katz, Jonathan G. *Murder in Marrakesh: Émile Mauchamp and the French Colonial Adventure*. Bloomington and Indianapolis: Indiana University Press, 2006.

Katz, Jonathan G. "Les Temps Héroïques: The Alliance Israélite Universelle in Marrakech on the Eve of the Protectorate." In *Rethinking Jewish Society and Culture in North Africa*, edited by Emily Gottreich and Daniel Schroeter. Bloomington: Indiana University Press, 2011, 282–301.

Keane, Emily, Shareef of Wazan. *My Life Story*. London: Edward Arnold, 1912.

Kenbib, Mohammed. "Changing Aspects of State and Society in Nineteenth-Century Morocco." In *The Moroccan State in Historical Perspective 1850–1985*, edited by Abdelali Doumou and translated by Aye Kwei Armah. Dakar, 11–28. Sengal: Codesria, 1990.

Kenbib, Mohammed. *Juifs et Musulmans au Maroc, 1859–1948*. Rabat: University Mohammed V, 1994.

Kenbib, Mohammed. "Moroccan Jews and the Vichy Regime, 1940–1942." *The Journal of North African Studies* 19, no. 4 (2014): 540–553.

Kenbib, Mohammed. "Structures Traditionnelles et Protections Etrangeres au Maroc au XIXe Siecle." *Hespéris Tamuda* 22, no. 1 (1984): 79–101.

Kenbib, Mohammed. "Les Relations entre Musulmans et Juifs au Maroc 1859–1945: Essai Bibliographique." *Hespéris-Tamuda* 23 (1985): 83–104.

Kobo, Ousman Murzik. *Unveiling Modernity in Twentieth-century West African Islamic Reforms*. Leiden: Brill, 2012.

Kosansky, Oren. "All Dear unto God: Saints, Pilgrimage and Textual Practice in Jewish Morocco." PhD dissertation, University of Michigan, 2013.

Kosansky, Oren. "Reading Jewish Fez: On the Cultural Identity of a Moroccan City." *Journal of the International Institute* 8, no. 3 (2001): https://quod.lib.umich.edu/j/jii/4750978.0008.305?view=text;rgn=main.

Kosansky, Oren. "The Real Morocco Itself: Jewish Saint Pilgrimage, Hybridity, and the Idea of the Moroccan Nation." In *Jewish Culture and Society in North Africa*, edited by Emily Gottreich and Daniel J. Schroeter, 341–360. Bloomington: Indiana University Press, 2011.

Kosansky, Oren. "When Jews Speak Arabic: Dialectology and Difference in Colonial Morocco." *Comparative Studies in Society & History* 58, no. 1 (2016): 10.

Laroui, Abdallah. *The History of the Maghrib: An Interpretive Essay*. Princeton, NJ: Princeton University Press, 1977.

Laskier, Michael. *The Alliance Israélite Universelle and the Jewish Communities of Morocco, 1862–1962*. Albany: State University of New York Press, 1984.

Laskier, Michael. "The Alliance Israélite Universelle and the Struggle for Recognition within Moroccan Jewish Society, 1862–1912." In *The Sephardi and Oriental Jewish Heritage: Studies*, edited by Issachar Ben Ami, vol. 1, 191–202. Jerusalem: Magnes Press, Hebrew University, 1982.

Laskier, Michael. "Jewish Emigration from Morocco to Israel: Government Policies and the Position of International Jewish Organizations, 1949–1956." *Middle Eastern Studies* 25, no. 3 (July 1989): 323–362.

Laskier, Michael. "The Instability of Moroccan Jewry and the Moroccan Press in the First Decade after Independence." *Jewish History* 1, no. 1 (1986): 39–54.

Laskier, Michael. *North African Jewry in the Twentieth Century: The Jews of Morocco, Tunisia, and Algeria*. New York: New York University Press, 1994.

Laskier, Michael and Yaacov Lev. *The Convergence of Judaism and Islam: Religious, Scientific, and Cultural Dimensions*, 191–212. Gainesville: University Press of Florida, 2011.

Layashi, Samir Ben and Bruce Maddy-Weitzman. "Myth, History, and Realpolitik: Morocco and Its Jewish Community." *Journal of Modern Jewish Studies* 9, no. 1 (2010): 89–106.

Layashi, Samir Ben. "Secularism in the Moroccan Amazigh Discourse." *Journal of North African Studies* 12, no. 2 (2007): 153–171.

Le Tourneau, Roger. *Fez in the Age of the Marinides*. Translated by Besse Alberta Clement. Norman: University of Oklahoma Press, 1961.

Lehmann, Matthias. "Islamic Legal Consultation and the Jewish-Muslim 'Convivencia': Al-Wansharîsî's Fatwâ Collection as a Source for Jewish Social History in Al-Andalus and the Maghrib." *Jewish Studies Quarterly* 6, no. 1 (1999): 31.

Lemprière, William. *A Tour from Gibraltar to Tangier*. London: Lemprière, 1791.

Lemprière, William. *A Tour through the Dominions of the Emperor of Morocco*, 3rd ed. London: Tayler and co., 1813.

Levin, Sarah. "Narrative Remembrance: Close Encounters between Muslims and Jews in Morocco's Atlas Mountains," PhD dissertation, University of California, Berkeley, 2017.

Levin, Sarah. "Wit, Ruse, Rivalry and Other Keys to Coexistence: Reflections of Jewish-Muslim Relations in Berber Oral Traditions." In *North African Mosaic: A Cultural Reappraisal of Ethnic and Religious Minorities*, edited by Nabil Boudraa, 191–192. Newcastle, UK: Cambridge Scholars Publishing, 2007.

Lévy-Mongelli, Danielle, ed. "Un Cas particulier d'alienation culturelle: les juifs d'Afrique du nord dans l'aventure colonial française." In *Juifs du Maroc: identité et dialogue. Actes du colloque international sur la communauté juive marocaine: vie culturelle, histoire sociale et évolution,* 247–255. Paris, December 18–21, 1978.

Levy-Rubin, Milka. *Non-Muslims in the Early Islamic Empire: From Surrender to Coexistence.* Cambridge, UK: Cambridge University Press, 2011.

Levy, Lital. "The Arab Jew Debates: Media, Culture, Politics, History." *Journal of Levantine Studies* 7, no. 1 (Summer 2017): 79–103.

Levy, Lital. "Historicizing the Concept of Arab Jews in the *Mashriq.*" *The Jewish Quarterly Review* 98, no. 4 (2008): 452–469.

Levy, Lital. "Jewish Writers in the Arab East: Literature, History, and the Politics of Enlightenment, 1863–1914," PhD dissertation, University of California, Berkeley, 2017.

Levy, Simon. "The Arabic Dialects of Morocco's Jews." *Langage et société* 143 (2013): 41–51.

Lewis, Bernard. *Jews of Islam.* Princeton: Princeton University Press, 1987.

Lewis, Bernard. *Semites and Anti-Semites: An Inquiry into Conflict and Prejudice.* London: W. W. Norton, 1999.

Lydon, Ghislaine. *On Trans-Saharan Trails: Islamic Law, Trade Networks, and Cross-cultural Exchange in Nineteenth-century Western Africa.* Cambridge: Cambridge University Press, 2009.

Maddy-Weitzman, Bruce. *The Berber Identity Movement and the Challenge to North African States.* Austin: University of Texas Press, 2011.

Maghraoui, Driss. *Revisiting the Colonial Past in Morocco.* London: Routledge, 2013.

Mahmud, Hasan Ahmad. *Qiyam dawlat al-murabitin; Safhah mushriqah min tarikh al-maghrib fi-l-'usur al-wusta.* Cairo: al-Nahdahal-Misriyah, 1957.

Malik b. Anas. *Al-Muwatta' al-imām malik wa- sharhu hu tanwir al-hawalik.* Cairo: Maktabat al-akhira, 1951.

Mansouri, Mabrouk. "Image of the Jews among the Ibadi Imazighen." In *Jewish Culture and Society in North Africa*, edited by Emily Benichou Gottreich and Daniel J. Schroeter, 45–58. Bloomington: Indiana University Press, 2011.

Marglin, Jessica. *Across Legal Lines: Jews and Muslims in Modern Morocco.* New Haven: Yale University Press, 2016.

Marglin, Jessica. "In the Courts of the Nations: Jews, Muslims and Legal Pluralism in Nineteenth-century Morocco," PhD dissertation, Princeton University, 2013.

Marglin, Jessica. "Mediterranean Modernity through Jewish Eyes: The Transimperial Life of Abraham Ankawa." *Journal of North African Studies* 20, no. 2 (2015): 34–68.

Marglin, Jessica. "The Two Lives of Mas'ud Amoyal: Pseudo-Algerians in Morocco, 1830–1912." *International Journal of Middle East Studies* 44, no. 4 (2012): 651–670.

Marston Speight, Robert. "Islamic Reform in Morocco." *The Muslim World* 53, no. 1 (1963): 41–49.

Mauchamp, Émile. *La Sorcellerie au Maroc.* Paris: Dorbon-Ainé, 1911.

Mazower, Mark. *Salonica, City of Ghosts: Christians, Muslims and Jews 1430–1950.* New York: Vintage Books, 2006.

Mazuz, Haggai. *The Religious and Spiritual Life of the Jews of Medina*. Leiden: Brill, 2014.

McDougall, James. "Myth and Counter Myth: 'The Berber' as National Signifier in Algerian Historiographies." *Radical History Review* 86 (2003): 66–88.

Memmi, Albert. *The Colonizer and the Colonized*. Boston: Beacon Press, 1967.

Menashri, David. "The Jews of Iran." In *Antisemitism in Times of Crisis*, edited by Sander L. Gilman and Steven T. Katz, 353–371. New York: New York University, 1991.

Mill Preminger, Marion. *The Sands of Tamanrasset; The Story of Charles de Foucauld*. New York: Hawthorn Books, 1961.

Miller, James and Ronald Messier. *Sijilmassa: The Last Civilized Place*. Austin: University of Texas Press, 2015.

Miller, Susan Gilson. "Apportioning Sacred Space in a Moroccan City: The Case of Tangier, 1860–1912." *City & Society* 13, no. 1 (2001): 57–83.

Miller, Susan Gilson. "The Beni Ider Quarter of Tangier in 1900: Hybridity as a Social Practice." In *The Architecture and Memory of the Minority Quarter in the Muslim Mediterranean City*, edited by Mauro Bertagnin and Susan G. Miller, 138–173. Cambridge, MA: Harvard University Press, Harvard University Graduate School of Design, 2010.

Miller, Susan Gilson. "Colonialism, Spatial Configurations and Science. The Mellah without Walls. Jewish Space in a Moroccan City: Tangier, 1860–1912." In *Revisiting the Colonial Past in Morocco*, edited by Driss Maghraoui. Abingdon, 19–37. Oxon: Routledge, 2013.

Miller, Susan Gilson. "Dhimma Reconsidered: Jews, Taxes, and Royal Authority in Nineteenth-century Tangier." In *In the Shadow of the Sultan: Culture, Power, and Politics in Morocco*, edited by Susan Gilson Miller and Rahma Bourqia, 103–126. Cambridge: Harvard University Press, 1999.

Miller, Susan Gilson, ed. and trans. *Disorienting Encounters: Travels of a Moroccan Scholar in France in 1845–1846, The Voyage of Muhammad As-Saffar*. Berkeley: University of California Press, 1992.

Miller, Susan Gilson. "Gender and the Poetics of Emancipation: The Alliance Israélite Universelle in Northern Morocco, 1890–1912." In *Franco-Arab Encounters*, edited by L. Carl Brown and Mathew Gordon, 229–252. Beirut: AUB Press, 1996.

Miller, Susan Gilson. "Kippur on the Amazon: Jewish Emigration from Northern Morocco in the Late Nineteenth Century." In *Sephardi and Middle Eastern Jewries. History and Culture in the Modern Era*, edited by Harvey E. Goldberg, 190–209. Bloomington: Indiana University Press, 1996.

Miller, Susan Gilson. "Making Tangier Modern: Ethnicity and Urban Development, 1880–1930." In *Jewish Culture and Society*, edited by Emily Gottreich and Daniel J. Schroeter, 128–149. Bloomington: Indiana University Press, 2011.

Miller, Susan Gilson. "The Mallah: The Third City of Fez." In *The Architecture and Memory of the Minority Quarter in the Muslim Mediterranean City*, edited by Susan Gilson Miller and Mauro Bertagnin, 81–109. Cambridge: Aga Khan Program, Harvard University, 2010.

Miller, Susan Gilson. "The Mellah without Walls: Jewish Space in a Moroccan City, Tangier 1860–1912." In *Revisiting the Colonial Past in Morocco*, edited by Driss Maghraoui, 19–37. New York: Routledge, 2013.

Mojuetan, Benson. "Legitimacy in a Power State: Moroccan Politics in the Seventeenth Century during the Interregnum." *International Journal of Middle Eastern Studies* 13, no. 3 (1981): 347–360.

Mojuetan, Benson. "Myth and Legend as Functional Instruments in Politics: The Establishment of the Alawi Dynasty in Morocco." *Journal of African History* 16, no. 1 (1975): 17–27.

Monteil, Vincent. "Les juifs d'Ifran (Anti-Atlas marocain) - Cimetières - Ancêtres - Tombe de Yousef ben Mimoun." *Hespéris: Archives Berbères et Bulletin de l'Institut des Hautes-Études Marocaines*, no. 35 (1948): 151–163.

Moüette, Germain. *Relations de captivité dans les royaumes de Fez et de Maroc*, ed. Xavier Girard. Paris: Mercure de France, 2002.

Moyal, Elie. *The Shabbatean Movement in Morocco: Its History and Sources* [in Hebrew]. Tel Aviv: Am 'Oved, 1984.

Naar, Devin. *Jewish Salonica: Between the Ottoman Empire and Modern Greece*. Stanford: Stanford University Press, 2016.

Oliel, Jacob. *De Jerusalem à Tombouctou: L'odyssée saharienne du rabbin Mardochée, 1826–1886*. Paris: Éditions Olbia, 1998.

Pennell., C.R. "How and Why to Remember the Rif War, 1921–2021." *The Journal of North African Studies* 22, no. 5 (2017): 798–820.

Powers, David. *Law, Society, and Culture in the Maghrib, 1300–1500*. Cambridge: Cambridge University Press, 2002.

Ranger, T.O. "Connexions between 'Primary Resistance' Movements and Modern Mass Nationalism in East and Central Africa (Part I)." *The Journal of African History* 9, no. 3 (1968): 437–453.

Ravid, Benjamin. "All Ghettos Were Jewish Quarters, but Not All Jewish Quarters Were Ghettos." *Jewish Culture and History* 10, nos. 2–3 (2008): 5–24.

Rivet, Daniel. *Lyautey et l'institution du protectorat francais au Maroc, 1912–1925*. Paris: L'Harmattan, 1988.

Roberts, Hugh. *Berber Government: The Kabyle Polity in Pre-colonial Algeria*. London: I.B. Tauris, 2018.

Roden, Claudia. "Jewish Food in the Middle East." In *A Taste of Thyme: Culinary Cultures of the Middle East*, edited by Richard Tapper and Sami Zubaida, 153–158. London: Tauris Parke, 2000.

Rogers, Amanda. "Warding Off Terrorism and Revolution: Moroccan Religious Pluralism, National Identity and the Politics of Visual Culture." *Journal of North African Studies* 17, no. 3 (2012): 458.

Rosen, Lawrence. *Two Arabs, a Berber, and a Jew: Entangled Lives in Morocco*. Chicago: University of Chicago Press, 2015.

Rosenberger, Bernard and Hamid Triki. "Famines et épidémies au Maroc aux XVIe et XVIIe siècles." *Hespéris Tamuda* 15, no. 1 (1973): 5–104.

Rosenbloom, Joseph R. "A Note on the Size of the Jewish Communities in the South of Morocco." *Jewish Journal of Sociology* 8, no. 2 (1966): 204–213.

Rosman, Moshe. *How Jewish Is Jewish History*. Oxford: Littman Library of Jewish Civilization, 2009.

Rouighi, Ramai. "The Berbers of the Arabs." *Studia Islamica* 106, no. 1 (2011): 49–76.

Safran, Janina M. "Rules of Purity and Confessional Boundaries: Maliki Debates about the Pollution of the Christian." *History of Religions* 42, no. 3 (2003): 197–212.

Said, Edward. *Orientalism*. New York: Vintage Books, 1979.

Sasportas, Jacob. *Ohel Ya'akov*. Amsterdam: n/p, 1737.

Sasportas, Jacob. *Sisat Novel Sevi*, edited by I. Tishby. Jerusalem: Mosad Bialik, 1954.

Satloff, Robert. *Among the Righteous: Lost Stories from the Holocaust in Arab Lands*. New york: Public Affairs/Hachette, 2006.

Savant, Sarah Bowen. *The New Muslims of Post-conquest Iran*. Cambridge: Cambridge University Press, 2015.

Scholem, Gershom. *Sabbatai Sevi: The Mystical Messiah*. Translated by R.J. Swi Werblosky. Princeton: Princeton University Press, 1973.

Schorsch, Ismar. "Converging Cognates: The Intersection of Jewish and Islamic Studies in Nineteenth Century Germany." *Leo Baeck Institute Year Book* 55 (2010): 3–36.

Schreir, Joshua. *The Merchants of Oran: A Jewish Port at the Dawn of Empire* (Stanford: Stanford University Press, 2017).

Schroeter, Daniel. "La Découverte des Juifs Berbéres." In *Relations Judéo-Musulmanes au Maroc: Perceptions et Réalités*, edited by Michel Abitbol, 169–187. Paris: Editions Stavit, 1997.

Schroeter, Daniel. *Essaouira: Urban Society and Imperialism in Southwestern Morocco, 1844–1886*. Cambridge: Cambridge University Press, 2010.

Schroeter, Daniel. "On the Origins and Identity of Indigenous North African Jews." In *North African Mosaic: A Cultural Reappraisal of Ethnic and Religious Minorities*, edited by Nabil Boudraa and Joseph Krause, 164–177. Newcastle: Cambridge Scholars Pub, 2007.

Schroeter, Daniel. "The Shifting Boundaries of Moroccan Jewish Identities." *Jewish Social Studies: History, Culture, Society* 15, no. 1 (2008): 145–164.

Schroeter, Daniel. *The Sultan's Jew: Morocco and the Sephardi World*. Stanford, Calif.: Stanford University Press, 2002.

Schroeter, Daniel. "Slave Markets and Slavery in Moroccan Urban Society." *Slavery & Abolition* 13, no. 1 (1992): 204.

Schroeter, Daniel. "Views from the Edge: Jews in Moroccan Rural Society (Ighil n'Ogho, 1917–1998)." In *Hikrei Ma'arav u-Mizrah: Studies in Language, Literature and History Presented to Joseph Chetrit*, edited by Yosef Tobi and Dennis Kurzon, vol. 2, 171–192. Jerusalem: Carmel Publishing, 2011.

Schroeter, Daniel and Emily Gottreich, ed. *Jewish Culture and Society in North Africa*. Bloomington: Indiana University Press, 2011.

Schroeter, Daniel and Joseph Chetrit. "Emancipation and Its Discontents: Jews at the Formative Period of Colonial Rule in Morocco." *Jewish Social Studies: History, Culture, Society* 13, no. 1 (2006): 170–206.

Schyuler, Philip D. "Rwais and Ahwash: Opposing Tendencies in Moroccan Berber Music and Society." *The World of Music* 21, no. 1 (1979): 65–80.

Seidman, Naomi. *Faithful Renderings: Jewish-Christian Difference and the Politics of Translation*. Chicago: University of Chicago Press, 2006.

Serfaty, Vidal. "Le 'Tritl' (saccage) de Fès en 1912." *Etsi, Revue de Genealogie et d'Histoire Sefarades* 8, no. 28 (2005): 10–13.

Serrano Ruano, Delfina. "Explicit Cruelty, Implicit Compassion: Judaism, Forced Conversions and the Genealogy of the Banū Rushd." *Journal of Medieval Iberian Studies* 2, no. 2 (2010): 217–223.

Sfar, Joann. *The Rabbi's Cat*. New York: Pantheon Books, 2005.

Shatzmiller, Maya. *The Berbers and the Islamic State: The Marinid Experience in Pre-Protectorate Morocco*. Princeton: Markus Wiener Publishers, 2000.

Shenhav, Yehouda. *The Arab Jews: A Postcolonial Reading of Nationalism, Religion, and Ethnicity*. Stanford: Stanford University Press, 2006.

Shohat, Ella. *On the Arab Jew, Palestine, and Other Displacements: Selected Writings of Ella Shohat*. London: Pluto Press, 2017.

Shohat, Ella. *Taboo Memories, Diasporic Voices*. Durham, NC: Duke University Press, 2006.

Silver, Chris. "Listening to the Past: Music as a Source for the Study of North African Jews." *Hespéris-Tamuda* 51, no. 2 (2016): 243–255.

Silverstein, Paul. "The Kabyle Myth: Colonization and the Production of Ethnicity." In *From the Margins: Historical Anthropology and Its Futures*, edited by Brian Keith Axel, 122–155. Durham: Duke University Press, 2003.

Silverstein, Paul. "Masquerade Politics: Race, Islam, and the Scales of Amazigh Activism in Southeastern Morocco." *Nations and Nationalism* 17, no. 1 (2011): 65–84.

Silverstein, Paul. "A New Morocco? Amazigh Activism, Political Pluralism, and Anti-Anti-Semitism in the Wake of Tahrir." *Brown Journal of World Affairs* 18, no. 2 (2012): 129–140.

Slouschz, Nahum. *Travels in North Africa*. Philadelphia: Jewish Publication Society of America, 1927.

Slyomovics, Susan. "Self-determination as Self-definition: The Case of Morocco." In *Negotiating Self-determination*, edited by Hurst Hannum and Eileen F. Babbit, 135–157. Lanham: Lexington Books, 2006.

Stein, Sarah Abraveya. "Dividing South from North: French Colonialism, Jews, and the Algerian Sahara." *Journal of North African Studies* 17, no. 4 (2012): 773–792.

Stillman, Norman A. "The Commensality of Islamic and Jewish Civilizations." *Middle Eastern Lectures* 2 (1997): 81–94.

Stillman, Norman A. *The Jews of Arab Lands: A History and Source Book*. Philadelphia: Jewish Publication Society, 1979.

Stillman, Norman A. *The Jews of Arab Lands in Modern Times*. Philadelphia: Jewish Publication Society, 1991.

Stroumsa, Sarah. *Maimonides in His World, Portrait of a Mediterranean Thinker.* Princeton: Princeton University Press, 2009.

Terem, Etty. *Old Texts, New Practices: Islamic Reform in Modern Morocco.* Stanford: Stanford University Press, 2014.

Tessler, Mark A. and Linda L. Hawkins. "The Political Culture of Jews in Tunisia and Morocco." *International Journal of Middle East Studies* (February 1980): 59–86.

Tibi, Bassam. *Arab Nationalism: A Critical Inquiry.* New York: St. Martin's Press, 1971.

Tobi, Yosef. "The Flowering of Judeo-Arabic Literature in North Africa, 1850–1950." In Toledano, Ya'akov Moshe. *Ner Hama'arav,* edited by A.M. Lunz, 213–226. Jerusalem: n.p., 1911.

Trevisan Semi, Emanuela. "Double Trauma and Manifold Narratives: Jews' and Muslims' Representations of the Departure of Moroccan Jews in the 1950s and 1960s." *Journal of Modern Jewish Studies* 9, no. 1 (2010): 107–125.

Trivellato, Francesca. *The Familiarity of Strangers: The Sephardic Diaspora, Livorno, and Cross-cultural Trade in the Early Modern Period.* New Haven: Yale University Press, 2009.

al-Tunbukti, Baba Ahmad b. Ahmad. *Nayl al-Ibtihaj.* Tarablus: Manshurat Kulliyyat al-da'wa 'l-Islamiyya, 1989.

Tsur, Yaron. *A Torn Community; The Jews of Morocco and Nationalism, 1943–1954.* Tel Aviv: Am Oved, 2001 (Hebrew).

Van Koningsveld, P.S., J. Sadan, and Q. al-Samarrai. *Yemenite Authorities and Jewish Messian-ism. Ahmad b. Nasir al-Zaydi's Account of the Sabbathian Movement in Seventeenth Century Yemen and Its Aftermath.* Leiden: Leiden University, Faculty of Theology, 1990.

Vilar, Juan Bautista. *Tetuán en el resurgimiento judio contemporaneo, 1850–1870.* Caracas: Asociación Israelita de Venezuela & Centro de Estudios Sefardíes de Caracas, 1985.

Wagenhofer, Sophie. "'We Have Our Own History': Voices from the Jewish Museum of Casablanca." In *Memory and Ethnicity: Ethnic Museums in Israel and the Diaspora,* edited by Emanuela Trevisan Semi, Dario Miccoli, and Tudor Parfitt, 169–194. Cambridge: Cambridge Scholars Publishing, 2013.

Wagner, Mark. *Jews and Islamic Law in Early Twentieth-century Yemen.* Bloomington: Indiana University Press, 2015.

Watson, Robert. "Between Liberation(s) and Occupation(s): Reconsidering the Emergence of Maghreb Jewish Communism, 1942–1945." *Journal of Modern Jewish Studies* 13, no. 3 (2014): 381–398.

Watt, Montgomery. "The Decline of the Almohads: Reflections on the Viability of Religious Movements." *History of Religions* 4, no. 1 (1964): 23–29.

Weinberger, Leon J. *Twilight of a Golden Age: Selected Poems of Abraham Ibn Ezra,* 2nd ed. Tuscaloosa: University of Alabama Press, 2011.

Westermarck, Edward. *Ritual and Belief in Morocco.* 2 vols. London: Macmillan, 1926.

Westreich, Elimelech. "Historical Landmarks in the Tradition of Moroccan Jewish Family Law: The Case of Levirate Marriages." In *Studies in Medieval Halakhah in Honor of Stephen M. Passamaneck*, edited by Alyssa Gray and Bernard Jackson, 279–322. Liverpool: D. Charles Publications, 2007.

Willis, Michael. *Politics and Power in the Maghreb: Algeria, Tunisia and Morocco from Independence to the Arab Spring*. London: Hurst & Co., 2012.

Wyrtzen, Jonathan. *Making Morocco: Colonial Intervention and the Politics of Identity*. Ithaca: Cornell University Press, 2015.

Yehoshua, A. B. "Beyond Folklore: The Identity of the Sephardic Jew." *Quaderns de la Mediterrània* 14 (2010): 151–152.

Zafrani, Haim. *Études et recherches sur la vie intellectuelle juive au Maroc de la fin du 15e au début du 20e siècle*. Paris: Geuthner, 1972.

Zafrani, Haim. *Kabbale, vie mystique et magie: judaïsme d'Occident musulman*. Paris: Maisonneuve et Larose, 1986.

Zafrani, Haim. *Two Thousand Years of Jewish Life in Morocco*. Jersey City: Ktav Publishing House/American Sephardi Federation, 2005.

Zreik, Raef. "When Does the Settler Become a Native? (with Apologies to Mamdani)." *Constellations* 23, no. 3 (2016), 351–364.

Archives

Archives de l'Alliance Israélite Universelle (AIU), Paris
Archives du Ministère des Affaires Étrangères (AAE), Paris
Direction des Archives Royales (DAR), Rabat
Archives of the Public Record Office (PRO), London

Historical Newspapers

Jewish Chronicle, London
Jewish Missionary Intelligence, London
Jewish Telegraphic Agency, New York City
Al-Moghreb al-Aksa, Tangier
Le Réveil du Maroc, Tangier
Times of Morocco, Tangier
l'Univers israélite, Paris

Index

'Abd al-Hafidh (Sultan) 123, 137, 142
Abdelkrim 146, 221 n.61
Abduh, Muhammad 193 n.45
Abi Mahalli, Shaykh Ibn 81
Abisrur, Mordechai 102–5
Academie des Belles Lettres 124
Adelson Family Foundation 51
Aflalo, Albert 154
Aflaq, Michel 131
Africanus, Leo 29
ahl al-kitab 132, 183
Ahwash 63
Ait Ishaq 88, 206 n.36
Alarcón, Pedro Antonio de 144
Alawi dynasty 10, 16, 23, 39, 79, 87–90, 95, 97, 109, 123, 150, 211 n.17
Algeria 12, 25, 33, 35, 65, 69, 79, 102, 105, 108, 111, 114, 115, 123–4, 135, 137, 151, 156, 158–61, 168, 178
aliyah 154, 163, 164, 167, 174
Alliance Israélite Universelle (AIU) 57, 115–21, 122–5, 133, 134, 138–41, 143, 146, 151, 156, 174, 175, 213 n.53, 214 n.55, 215 n.71, 223 n.92
alliancism 120, 121, 133, 148, 156, 160, 167
Almohads (al-muwahhidun) 10, 15, 29, 45, 54, 59, 67–9, 71, 103, 183, 202 n.69, 202 n.70
Almoravids *(al-murabitun)* 10, 20, 30, 36, 54, 65–7
Amazighity 13–16, 22, 25, 51–65, 72, 79, 151
    Almohads 67–9
    Almoravids 65–7
    Marinids 69–71
    philosemitism 72
amir al-mu'minin (commander of the faithful) 12, 20, 142, 154, 159, 171
Amster, Ellen 137
anti-Semitism 11, 52, 107, 117, 134, 140, 176, 226 n.9
Arabic language 7, 36, 58–61, 73, 131, 151–3, 168, 172, 200 n.35

Arabism 131, 177
Arab-Israeli war 10, 147, 155, 163
"*al-'arabiyya diyalna*" 59
Arabization 14, 54, 197 n.7
Arab Nationalist Conference (1913) 131
Arabness 16, 17, 130–3, 150, 151, 166, 168
Arabs 14, 17, 25, 132, 150, 151
    arrival of 4, 11, 20
    and non-Arabs 132
Arab spring 52–3, 72, 171, 172, 182, 196–7 n.6
artisanry 63
Ashkenazim 68, 70, 82, 85, 95, 157, 159, 173–4, 176, 199 n.27
Assidon, Sion 154, 162
Assouline, Pierre 176
autochthonous Jews *(toshavim)* 16, 53, 58, 64, 73, 83–5, 95, 97, 144
l'avenir illustre 157
Averroes (Ibn Rushd) 68
Ayache, Germaine 162
'Abd al-'Aziz (Sultan) 40, 109, 121, 137
Azoulay, Audrey 176, 177
Azoulay, David 158

Baïda, Jamaâ 165
al-Bakri, Abu Ubayd 20, 65, 79
Ban-Ki Moon 178
Banque Pariente 144
Barghawata 65
Battle of the Three Kings 134, 220 n.55
Beauclerk, G. R. 209 n.80
Ben Ali, Zine El Abidine 53, 197 n.7
Benarroch, Mois 179
Benatar, Hélene Cazès 167
Benkirane, Abdelilah 30
Bensur, Joseph 95–7
Bentolila, Salvador 1
Berberism 51–58, 64, 69, 77, 134
Berdugo, Serge 184 n.6
bilad al-sudan 34, 65, 104
bildiyin 83
Black Panther movement (Israel) 154, 174

246   *Index*

Boum, Aomar 72, 180, 209 n.2, 210 n.8
British Medical Journal 136
Bu Ihlas 23
Burke, Edmund 217 n.7

Canada 10, 176
Cardoso, Abraham Miguel 93, 97
Casablanca 1, 9, 107, 109, 125, 137, 142, 152, 155–64, 171, 173, 177, 180–82, 184 n.5
Casanegra (film) 182
Chetrit, Sami b. 178
Chetrit, Yossi 183
Child Protection Code (1995) 197 n.7
Christianity 6, 10, 22, 25, 27, 29, 67–70, 78, 84, 103, 111, 112, 116, 131, 179, 180, 189 n.1
College of Azrou (1927) 57
colonialism 8, 17, 21, 122, 130, 132, 134, 147, 168, 210 n.15, 211 n.20
Comité d'Action Marocain (CAM) 149
le Comité du Maroc 137
communism 148, 161–3
Constitution (2011) 171, 172
constitutional reforms 171
Constitution of Medina 27, 177, 179
convivencia 68
Corcos, David 203 n.85
Corcos, Yeshoua 40, 125, 140
cosmopolitanism 8, 187 n.28
countermyths 54–7
Crémieux, Adolphe 111, 117
Crémieux decree 111, 114, 124, 156, 161, 168
cross-pollination 68, 90

dafina 62, 181
Daggatoun 194 n.62
dahir 2, 57, 116, 121, 126, 148, 149, 159, 212 n.40, 222 n.73
Danan, Ibn 88, 90
dar al-Islam 38, 37
darija 59, 152
Davidson, John 210 n.4
"Declaration of Marrakech" 179
Dehodencq, Alfred 41
"development towns" 173
dhimma/dhimmis 6, 15, 20, 26–30, 32–6, 38, 40, 42, 43, 45, 66–9, 70, 110–15, 122, 130, 134, 141, 150, 159, 180, 183, 199 n.25, 213 n.47
"dhimmitude" 186 n.22, 196 n.91
diarna 181
diasporism 4
dignity revolution 196–7 n.6
Dila'iya zawiya 88–91
discrimination 64, 149, 159, 174, 179
dissimulation 68, 84
diversity 2, 8, 13, 55, 57, 60, 71, 177
"double trauma" 180
Draa, Rabbi David Halevi 42
al-durus al-hasaniyya 31

Elbaz, Vanessa Paloma 200–1 n.47
El Maleh, Edmond Amran 11, 60, 143, 163
Elmaleh, Gad 176
emigration 22, 29, 135, 154–8, 163–6, 179, 180, 226 n.9
English language 24, 32, 87, 106, 172
Ephraim 23, 58
Ephrati, King 23
Epistle on Forced Conversion (Maimonides) 68
Epton, Nina 210 n.7
ethnicity 57–8
    artisanry 63–4
    foodways 61–2
    language 58–61
    music 62
Europe 98, 108, 112, 116, 175
    colonialism 8, 17, 110, 115, 131, 134, 143, 147
    and French encroachment 108–10
    Jewish intervention and AIU 115–20
    mission civilisatrice 105–8
Europeanization 117, 118, 122, 130, 134, 172, 215 n.72
Ezra, Abraham Ibn 66, 68

Falcon, Nissim 140, 141
Fanon, Franz 136
al-Fassi, Allal 149, 151, 155
fatwa 32, 36, 37
February 20 movement 53, 171, 196–7 n.6
Fez 9–10, 13, 30–2, 37, 41, 56, 68–71, 81, 88–91, 142–3, 147, 148, 161
fitna 78, 90, 96
foodways 61–2
Foucauld, Charles de 102–8, 110, 209 n.2, 211 n.17

France 105, 123, 142, 154, 158–63, 175
    Declaration of the Rights of Man 112
    historic protection 111
    politique berbere 56
French 58, 60, 64, 111, 159
    citizenship 106, 111, 124, 134, 156, 159, 160, 168, 216 n.81
    colonialism 21, 109, 143
    encroachment 108–10
    imperialism 120, 159, 210 n.8
    language 35, 118, 119, 125, 152, 172, 175
    military 147
    naturalization 114, 156
    occupation of Oujda 138, 140
    Protectorates 12, 16, 104, 113, 119, 123, 126, 134, 142, 156, 157, 159, 212 n.40
French Revolution 112, 187 n.28
Front de libération nationale (FLN) 151

Gabbay, Avi 175, 226 n.6
García-Arenal, Mercedes 29
gender equality 172
Geniza
    collection 58
    documents 194 n.54
"Getto/Ghetto" 203 n.78
globalization 3, 172
Goitein, S. D. 8, 187 n.30
Goodbye Mothers (film) 223 n.87
Goulmima carnival 71–2
Grand Caids/Great Lords 115
"Great Berber Revolt" 64
Guadalajara 205 n.13
Guide of the Perplexed 59–60

Hachkar, Kamal 181, 196 n.4
hadith 27, 30
Hagiz, Jacob 82–3
al-Haj, Muhammad 88
Hakétia 13, 57, 84
halakha 5, 97
halakhic culture 44, 183
halal 33, 61
Halevy, Joseph 117
harb titwan (war of Tetouan) 109
Haroche, Serge 176
Harris, Walter 106, 107
Hart, David M. 222 n.73

Hassan II 172, 188 n.37
Hay, John Drummond 212 n.31
Hazm, Ibn 193 n.46
Hebrew 5, 6, 8, 21, 23, 25, 35, 44, 55, 58–61, 65, 72, 82–6, 119, 152, 177
Hebrew Immigrant Aid Society (HIAS) 165
Hemdat Yamim 93
henotheists 23
hillula (pl. *hillulot*) 44
Hirschberg, Zeev Haim 208 n.59
Hodgson, Marshall 186 n.19
Hoffman, Katherine 57
hofjuden 70
Hunwick, John 37, 194 n.55

Ibadis 192 n.35
Ila al-Amam 162
illiteracy 172
Imazighen 8, 9, 15, 16, 30, 31, 53–7, 63–5, 69, 73, 134, 148–51, 168, 179, 190 n.13
immigration 37, 157, 175–6, 226 n.9
imperialism 11, 16, 116, 120, 159, 161
independence 1, 10, 12, 17, 20, 32, 64, 116, 120, 127, 130–5, 138, 148–56, 161–4, 167, 173, 174, 175, 178
integration 3, 5, 8, 10, 11
international zone 123, 144
intifada 143
Iran 15
Iraq 6–8
Islam 1–2, 5, 6, 19–22, 25, 26, 33, 45, 46, 54, 55, 64–5, 68, 87
    arrival of 4, 11, 14, 150
    civilization 6, 186 n.19
    continual relevance 168
    conversion 9, 41, 80, 84, 117, 136
    and Judaism 5, 42
    Pact of 'Umar 30
Islamicate Jews 5, 6
Islamic law 10, 15, 30, 34, 38, 61, 78, 148, 159, 194 n.57
Islamism 7, 131, 177, 217 n.1
Islamization 14, 24–6, 54
Isma'il, Ibn Sharif (Sultan) 21, 94–6
Ismail, Mohamed 181, 223 n.87
Israel 51–3, 153, 155, 163, 164, 167, 173–4, 226 n.9
istiqlal 149–53, 154, 158, 160, 166
al-ittihad 215 n.71

jasmine revolution 196–7 n.6
Jerusalem 21–4, 67, 82, 104, 132, 135, 136, 144, 150, 165, 174, 181
Jewish Ashura 72
"Jewish dahir" 57
Jewish Joint Distribution Committee 167
Jewishness 3, 4, 21, 92, 130–3, 162, 182, 183
The Jewish Quarter 6, 13, 23, 41, 61, 69, 89, 94, 106, 122, 125, 140–2, 228 n.31
Jewish Wedding in Morocco 138
jihad 69, 87, 134, 137, 147
jizya (tax) 28, 35, 38–41, 44, 45, 66, 67
joint saint veneration 7, 41–4
Judaism 3, 5, 7, 9, 13–14, 16, 22, 25, 27, 30, 33, 35, 38, 41, 42, 53, 55, 68, 69, 79, 84, 91, 95–8, 119, 178, 181, 183
Judeo-Arabic 6, 59–60, 143
Judeo-Berber 60, 197 n.11
juntas 13
Justice and Development Party (PJD) 52

Kabbalah 80, 82, 95
Kabyle 141, 219 n.39
Kadima 163
Kahina 25, 52, 56, 69, 185 n.11
kashrut 6, 61
Katz, Jonathan 120, 137, 140
Kenbib, Mohammed 115, 143, 213 n.46, 215 n.77
kettubot 84
Khaldun, Ibn 22, 25, 56, 69, 77, 204 n.3
khamsa 2
Khmelnitsky 86
Kohanim 25, 85
Kosansky, Oren 59
Küçük Kaynarca peace treaty 111
Kurdish separatism 172
Kuzari 68

Lakhmari, Noureddine 182
languages 6, 7, 35, 53–4, 58–61, 72, 73, 84, 110, 118–20, 124, 125, 131, 144, 150, 152, 168, 172, 197 n.7, 197 n.11
Laroui, Abdallah 185 n.11
latif prayer 149, 151
Law of Perpetual Allegiance 19
leadership 77, 79, 117, 149, 152, 155, 156
legitimacy 11, 16, 20, 42, 79, 96–8, 154, 159
Lempriere, William 40, 138, 139

Le Tourneau, Roger 201 n.55
Leven, Narcisse 216 n.81
Levy, Lital 217 n.3
Lévy, Simon 162, 165
Livorno 82
Luria, Isaac 80–2
Lyautey, Louis Hubert 119, 123–6, 137, 156, 216 n.81

Maddy-Weitzman, Bruce 196 n.1
madrasa 5
al-Maghili, Muhammad 'Abd al-Karim 36, 37, 46, 104, 194 n.61
Maghrib 8, 13, 14, 19, 25, 33, 54–6, 71, 82, 87, 103, 121, 130, 132, 134, 171, 175, 182
al-maghrib al-aqsa 12, 24
mahalla 12, 188 n.40
Mahdism 69, 81, 96
mahiya 62
Maimonides, Moses 7, 10, 14, 59, 68, 69, 81, 97, 196 n.89, 214 n.66
makhzan (Moroccan government and administration) 2, 12, 16, 38, 40, 44, 52, 70, 72, 87, 93–6, 108–10, 113, 114, 121, 122, 127, 134, 136, 140–3, 145, 159, 160, 162, 171, 177, 178, 188 n.40, 195 n.77, 208 n.65, 225 n.1
Malik b.Anas, Abu 'Abdullah 30, 34
Malikism 10, 15, 20, 29–38, 43–5, 67, 189 n.6, 192–3 n.44
Mansouri, Mabrouk 201–2 n.60
al-Mansur, Ahmad (Sultan) 77
maraboutic crisis 77, 87
"marabouts" 77
Marglin, Jessica 11, 188 n.42
mariages précoces 118
Marinids *(Banu Marin)* 69–71
Marrakech 10, 30, 40, 63, 66–70, 77, 81, 82–5, 87, 91, 92, 94, 103–4, 107, 114, 116, 117, 118, 121, 122, 125, 126, 135–42, 157, 175, 177, 179, 180, 206 n.24, 213 n.46
al-Marrakushi, 'Abd al-Wahid 67
mashriq 8, 25, 82, 132, 182, 193 n.45
maskilim 58, 97
Mauchamp, Émile 135–42, 147, 167, 218 n.11
Medina (Arabia) 27, 30–2
madina 69, 136

megorashim 14, 16, 58, 83, 84, 97, 144
Meknes 13, 22, 55, 68, 70, 85, 90, 91, 94–6, 139
mellah 3, 6, 13, 23, 41, 69–72, 89, 94, 106, 122, 125, 127, 130, 138–43, 145, 147, 158, 164, 166, 177, 216 n.83, 221 n.62
Memmi, Albert 17, 127
messiah 77–81, 85, 92–5
messianism 69, 79–83, 95
Middle East 6, 7, 11, 12, 15, 21, 24, 26, 30, 33, 46, 54–6, 58, 111, 112, 118, 121, 126–7, 131, 146, 150, 172, 178, 182
migration 21, 23, 82, 103, 162, 167, 175, 176
Miller, Susan Gilson 57, 118, 165
millet system 98, 116
Mimouna 7, 9, 62, 178, 180
mintaqa 191–2 n.28
mission civilisatrice 105–7
Mission Scientifique du Maroc 124
mitnagdim 97
Al-mi'yar al-mu'rib 32
mizmor l'david 58
Mizrahi identity 173
mizrahim 157, 173, 181
mizrahi vote 180
modernization 121–2, 126, 174
Mohammed IV 121
Mohammed V, King 151–2, 154, 156
Mohammed V University 9
Mohammed VI Institute for the Training of Imams 2
Mohammed VI, King 1, 179, 192 n.38
monolatrists 23
Montefiore, Moses 115, 116, 121, 213 n.45, 213 n.46
moriscos 78, 87
Moroccan Islam 2–4, 7, 15, 19–24, 30, 35, 43
Moroccan Refugee Aid Committee 167
moshavim 173
Mouette, Germain 85
moussem 196 n.88
mudawana 172
Muhammadiya Association of Scholars (*al-rabita al-muhammadiya li-l-'ulama*) 2
multiculturalism 8, 176
multidirectional memory 183

music 6, 62, 166
Muslim-Jewish relations 8, 27, 30, 36, 43, 55, 115, 177
Muslims
  Amazigh 51–3
  attitudes 27–8
  authority 15, 39, 92, 141
  and *dhimmis* 34
  and Jews 2, 5, 6, 11, 16, 20, 34, 40, 41, 56, 60, 61, 63, 69, 71, 72, 82, 126, 131, 133, 147, 150–5, 160, 161, 182
  jurists 29, 33
  majority 15, 112, 179
  and non-Muslims 3, 8, 15, 20, 26, 28, 30, 32, 33, 36, 38, 44, 45, 131, 217 n.1
  population 117, 138, 156, 168, 183
  rule 6, 20, 25–8
muwala 191 n.22

nahda 60, 125, 132
najas 15, 33
Naqqash, Samir 7
al-Nasiri, Ahmad b. Khaled 213 n.46, 220 n.53
al-Nasser, Gamal 'Abd 155
national identity 3, 21, 150, 180
nationalism 3, 124, 131–3, 148–51, 154, 156–8, 168, 187 n.28
nizam 121–2
North Africa 6, 7, 12, 13, 15, 16, 20–3, 24–6, 29, 30, 33, 36, 37, 46, 52–6, 78, 93, 104, 110–13, 118, 121, 126, 127, 131, 145, 158, 163, 168, 183

"Operation Yachin" 165
origin myths 54–7, 82
Ottoman Empire 4, 16, 70, 80–6, 90, 95–9, 103, 110–12, 116
Ouaknine, Marc Alain 176
Oufran, Jews of 23, 24

"pacification" 105, 137
Pact of 'Umar 27, 30, 35, 38, 68, 70
Palestine National Congress 132
Pallache, Jacob 82
Pallache, Samuel 14, 87
pan-Arabism 131–2, 146, 148, 150, 167, 168
pan-Islamism 8, 131, 217 n.1

Pariente, Moses 144
Parti Communiste Marocain (PCM) 161–3
Parti de Libération et Socialisme (PLS) 162
Parti democratique de l'independence (PDI) 152
Parti du Progres et Socialisme (PPS) 163
People of the Book 6, 38, 183
perpetual allegiance principle 114–15
pied noire 168
pilgrims, Jewish 44
piyyutim 7, 42
pluralism 179
Polisario 178
political crisis 77, 123
politique berbère 56
Popular Front for the Liberation of Palestine 167
poverty 126, 163, 172, 174, 213 n.47
promised land 22
Protectorate 12, 16, 45, 64, 104, 119, 120–7, 133, 134, 137, 139, 141, 142, 143, 146, 148, 156–63
protégé system 39, 110–15, 122, 126, 133
Purim de los Cristianos 145, 220 n.55

Qaddafi, Muammar 53
qadi 28, 36, 37, 147
al-Qadir, 'Abd 108
qalansuwa 28, 68
Qayrawan 30
Qur'an 7, 25, 27, 28, 30, 33, 38, 65, 68, 108, 149

"The Rabbi's Hotel" 177
Radio Islam 11, 188 n.37
al-Rahman, Mawlay Muhammad b.'Abd 109, 116
Rami, Ahmed 11, 188 n.37
Rashid, b. 'Ali al-Sharif (Mawlay) 89, 207 n.42, 207 n.47, 208 n.59
rawd al-qirtas 56
Reconnaissance au Maroc (Foucauld) 102, 105
reforms 40, 121–3, 148, 171
Regulation of Tangier (1863) 113
religious authorities 13, 40, 42, 96
resistance 133–5, 147–8
    communism and socialism 161–2
    Fez, treaty of 142–3
    independence movement 148–56
    and recidivism 25
    Spanish zone and Rif war 144–7
    Vichy interlude 158–61
Rif war 135, 144–7, 167
"righteous gentiles" 52
Roden, Claudia 62
Rosen, Lawrence 31–2
Rothberg, Michael 183, 228 n.32
Royal Institute of Amazigh Culture in Rabat (IRCAM) 53
rumiyin 83

Sabbah, Marc 152–5, 158
Sabbateanism 80–7, 91–9, 208 n.59
Sabbath 1, 61–3, 66, 119
Sa'dis 16, 23, 65, 69, 77, 86, 87, 94
Said, Edward 136
saint veneration 7, 41–4
salafi 148, 149
salafiya jihadiya movement 1
Salem, Nagwa 7
Sallah Shabati (1964) 174
Sarfaty, Abraham 11, 21, 154, 162
Sasportas, Jacob 85, 91–3, 97
sayyid-s 78, 189 n.47
Schorsch, Ismar 187 n.36
Schroeter, Daniel 159, 183, 187 n.33, 188 n.44, 201 n.58, 203 n.81
secularism 52, 72, 150, 161
seffa 61
"Semite" 21
Semitic languages 6, 59, 124
Sephardic Jews 14, 58, 68, 71, 73, 78, 79, 81, 83–6, 90, 97, 98, 125, 144, 173, 199 n.27
sexuality 71, 118
Shabbatai Tsvi 79–83, 84, 86, 91–4, 95–8, 205 n.10, 205 n.20, 207 n.47
shari'a (Islamic law) 5
Sharifism 16, 73, 78–9, 87–9, 96, 97, 209 n.79
Shawiya 137, 142
shaykh al-yahud 39, 140, 216 n.83, 221 n.64
al-Shaykh, Muhammad (Sultan) 83
Shi'ism 15
shkhita 84, 206 n.24
Shohat, Ella 167
shurafa 78
Sijilmasa 36, 65–6, 68, 70, 81
Silver, Chris 62, 200 n.45

Silverstein, Paul 203 n.86
sira 27
Sisat Novel Tsvi 85
Slat al-Fassiyin 30
Slimane, Mawlay 24
Slouschz, Nahum 124–5
Slyomovics, Susan 201 n.58
socialism 161–3
    Arab 131
    communism and 160–3
    Israel 173–4
Spanish
    exiles 5, 85
    Inquisition and subsequent expulsion 14, 68
    Protectorate 16, 64, 123, 146
    zone 144–7
spirituality 14, 16, 20, 30, 80–3, 84, 165
Star of David 9, 72, 177
Sufi lodges (*zawiya*-s) 13, 16, 79, 81, 87–92, 96, 207 n.56
Sufism 16, 43, 77, 78, 79, 81, 87, 87–90, 96, 98, 134, 149
Sultan, Leon René 159–63

Tafilalt 57, 71, 81, 89, 120
Talmud 13, 23, 58
"Tamazgha" 54
Tamazight 14, 23, 25, 53–4, 57, 60–1, 65, 131, 168, 172–3, 195 n.80, 197 n.11, 200 n.35
Tanzimat 98, 121
tawhid 15, 67
Taymiyya, Ibn 38
Tetouan 109, 144, 145–8, 156, 164–6, 179
Thomas, Samuel Torjman 63
Tinghrir-Jerusalem: Echos from the Mellah (film) 196 n.4
Tisha b'Av 85, 90, 93
Tlemcen 35–8, 89
Toledano, Meir 154
tolerance 2, 6, 20, 35–8, 45, 55, 69, 103, 177
toshavim 14, 16, 53, 58, 64, 73, 83–5, 95, 97, 144
Touat 35–8
Toynbee, Arnold 6
Treaty of Madrid 114
Trevisan Semi, Emanuela 180

tribal nationalism 141
tribalism 3
al-tritl 143
Tufayl, Ibn 68
tujjar al-sultan (royal merchants) 14, 94, 108, 212 n.35
Tumart, Ibn 15
Tunisia 12, 33, 52, 55, 69, 123, 156, 158, 171, 196–7 n.6, 197 n.7

umma 27, 69, 186 n.26
United States 10, 51, 112, 114, 164, 165, 173, 176, 177, 181

Vichy 148, 158–61, 167
ville nouvelle 142
violence 1, 2, 10, 11, 71, 134, 137, 143, 147, 151, 155, 172
La Voix des communautés 152

Wadi Salib protests 154
Wa'ish, Abraham 87
wali allah 42
al-Wansharisi, Ahmad 32–4, 36, 192–3 n.44
Wattasids 71, 83
al-Wazzani, Muhammad al-Mahdi 16, 21, 27, 33, 44, 78
Westernization 121–2, 215 n.72
al-wifaq 152–4
World Federation of Moroccan Jews 178

Yad Vashem 51
Yathrib 27
Yazid, Mawlay 10, 24, 145
Years of Lead 171
Yehoshua, A. B. 144
yeshiva 5, 68, 82, 92, 104

Zafrani, Haïm 199 n.29
zawiya-s (Sufi lodges) 13, 16, 79, 81, 87–92, 96, 207 n.56
Zaydan, Mawlay 77, 87
Zionism 11, 17, 72, 117, 132, 133, 148, 151–7, 161, 163, 166–9, 174
Zohar 80
zunnar 28, 68, 191–2 n.28

www.ingramcontent.com/pod-product-compliance
Lightning Source LLC
Chambersburg PA
CBHW070028010526
44117CB00011B/1748